The Living Economy

The Living Economy

A NEW ECONOMICS IN THE MAKING

Edited by Paul Ekins

Routledge & Kegan Paul
London and New York

First published in 1986 by
Routledge & Kegan Paul plc
11 New Fetter Lane, London EC4P 4EE

Published in the USA by
Routledge & Kegan Paul Inc.
in association with Methuen Inc.
29 West 35th Street, New York, NY 1001

Set in Bembo 10 on 11 pt
by Columns of Reading
and printed in Great Britain
by Billing & Sons Ltd
Worcester

Library of Congress Cataloging in Publication Data

The Living economy.
    Collection of papers from The Other Economic Summit (TOES).
    Bibliography: p.
    Includes index.
    1. Economics.   2. Economic development.
I. Ekins, Paul.   II. The Other Economic Summit (Organization)

British Library CIP Data also available

ISBN 0-7102-0946-0 (paper)
       0-7102-0758-1 (cloth)

Dedicated to the memory of E.F. Schumacher, author of *Small is Beautiful* and father of 'economics as if people mattered'

Contents

FIGURES AND TABLES

FOREWORD

It is appropriate that this seminal book has been dedicated to my late father, Dr E. F. Schumacher. He would have been delighted to have been associated with the array of outstanding thinkers and practitioners whose ideas have been so succinctly presented in this volume, Had he been alive he would have no doubt wished to have been a contributor himself.

The Living Economy covers a variety of topics from agricultural methods and policy to health and world trade reform. Contributors come from a wide diversity of countries and continents including the USA, Europe, Africa, and the Far East. Each section is worth reading in its own right, for itself and, indeed, by itself. It is a book to be browsed through, reflected upon and enjoyed at one's leisure. Together the contributions form a rich tapestry of insights and inspirations. They are in no way a simple repetition of Schumacher's thoughts. Rather, they form an authentic part of a wider intellectual tradition of which he was also a part, albeit an early and important one.

Fritz, as he was known to his friends, was the younger son of Hermann Schumacher, who was Professor of Economics at Berlin University. Even as a young boy he was both academically brilliant and politically outspoken, with a strong sense of social responsibility and care for the poor. These attributes led him first to study in Oxford, England, and Columbia University, New York. Subsequently, when Hitler came to power, he emigrated to England where he spent the remainder of his life.

Fritz Schumacher's contribution to the intellectual heritage of his time was unique. Even while a German refugee in England, working as a farm labourer during the Second World War, and still only thirty years old, he was instrumental in laying down with Lord Beveridge the foundations of the modern welfare state in the United Kingdom. The great economist John Maynard Keynes regarded him as his true intellectual successor and was greatly stimulated by his insights into international currency and world trading reform.

As the post-war economy in western Europe recovered, Schumacher's interests extended further afield, particularly with regard to the growing plight of the less developed countries. During his travels to India and Burma during the mid 1950s, he witnessed the growing polarity between the rich and poor, the town and country, and the industrial and rural aspects of life, as well as the distressing gulf which separated the western nations from those in the east. At this time, too, he began to appreciate the power and importance of a religious faith in the lives of ordinary people. The convergence of these influences, coupled with his own very active intellect, led him to seek a synthesis of economic laws and spiritual values which he hoped would move the hearts and minds of rich and poor alike. From Buddhism he took the concepts of 'the Middle Way' and the values of non-violence, reverence for nature, and a loving care for the least advantaged. From western economics he inherited an understanding of the power of science and technology and of the analytical methods of the western intellectual tradition. From his own observations, he saw that the latter could not easily be transplanted into the former unless both were raised to a higher level of integration. Thus was developed his then revolutionary idea of intermediate technology and later appropriate technology.

From this initial breakthrough in thinking, Schumacher's fertile mind began to formulate an entirely new set of economic values and principles based on a 'human scale' which added up to a new life-style both for the developing and industrialised world. These ideas were first encapsulated in his book *Small is Beautiful*, published in 1973, some twenty years after his first visit to India and Burma. The book coincided with the oil crisis of 1973, and came a year after the publication of the Club of Rome's widely-read predictions about the inherent contradictions in contemporary industrial economic and social patterns (Meadows *et al.*, 1972). In *Small is Beautiful* Schumacher re-presented the Club of Rome's computer-based predictions in the form of a devastatingly simple, popularly-presented economic philosophy, and proposed some positive solutions to the current global crisis. By this time, his early ideas about technology had broadened into theories of industrial development generally, of alternative forms of ownership, of alternative resource and environmental futures and even of different approaches to education.

The contributors to this book share the same spirit and vision as Fritz did in his day. Every one is, in his or her own right, a pioneer, a thinker and a person concerned for others. Nearly all cover subjects on which Fritz did not develop his thinking thoroughly. What he and they have in common is a vision of economics in which every man, woman and child and their Earth are of prime importance. The New Economics does not falsely seek affluence for the few at the expense of the many, nor the destruction of the environment which underpins all human activity.

Like *Small is Beautiful*, this book follows a 'middle way', a way of concern and moderation which unites people, truly articulating an economics 'as if people mattered'.

Christian Schumacher
Surrey, January 1986

PREFACE AND ACKNOWLEDGMENTS

This book derives from two years' work of The Other Economic Summit (TOES).[1] TOES is an independent, international initiative, seeking to develop and promote a New Economics, based on personal development and social justice, the satisfaction of the whole range of human needs, sustainable use of resources and conservation of the environment. In 1984 and 1985 TOES organised two conferences focused on the London and Bonn Economic Summits respectively. These conferences drew some of the leading thinkers and practitioners of the New Economics from all over the world.

The conferences were based on nearly fifty expert papers, spanning the whole range of economic activity and concerns, and it is these papers that form the heart of this book. Large sections of the papers have been reproduced more or less in their entirety. Some papers have been heavily cut, the contents of others have been distributed between more than one chapter.

A full list of the TOES papers for 1984 and 1985 appears in Appendix 1, with their original titles and brief biographical details of their authors. The edited papers in the book sometimes have a different title, depending on their contents after editing and on their position in the book's structure. Some papers have not been included as papers at all, but have made their contribution through extended quotations or through a summary of their contents. Where, within a paper, reference to another part of the book seems appropriate, that reference has been made as part of the paper, without editorial intrusion. I have generally tried to keep editorial notes to a minimum.

The edited titles and various contributions of the paper-writers are listed in the Contents pages. Numbered notes within each chapter are placed at the end of the chapter to which they refer. Where the reference in the text is simply to a book, the note gives the name of the author and the date of publication. The full title and publication details of all books so listed are given in the

Bibliography. Relevant addresses for each part of the book are given in Appendix 2.

As editor, my first debt of gratitude is to the paper-writers, both for the immensely stimulating quality of their work and for their sympathetic understanding over the cuts and alterations that were an inevitable part of the editing process. A wealth of detail has, of course, been sacrificed in that process, or this book would have been more than twice its present length. For those who regret this as much as I, I can only suggest that they refer to the original papers and assure them that they will not be disappointed. The papers in Part I have been especially savagely cut. That part was originally the same length as the others, but in the interests of producing a book of manageable size and because I felt the book's main purpose to be describing the New Economics rather than analysing the old, it was cut right back, a painful and difficult process. I hope, though, that the shortened text still conveys in some part the authentic quality of those thinkers, whose wisdom and insights have made such an invaluable contribution to the process of rethinking economic theory.

There were some important areas that were not covered adequately by the TOES conferences, and I am extremely grateful to have had advice in these areas from a number of specialists: on banking, Shann Turnbull, an investment banker from Sydney; on co-operating, Paul Derrick, for many years a researcher with the International Co-operative Alliance; and on taxation, David Chapman, convenor of the UK Green Party's Economics Working Group. Michael Linton, of Landsman Community Services in Canada, was also most enlightening about community currencies. I drew heavily on papers by all these people, which are referenced as appropriate.

In addition to this specific advice, I was most fortunate to receive detailed comments on the manuscript as a whole from James Robertson and Harford Thomas, who somehow squeezed out of their busy schedules the time to read and make immensely helpful suggestions about the first draft. Thanks are also due to Avril Fox, who saved me many hours at a time when I was busiest, by preparing the book's Index. Grateful acknowledgment must also be made here for permission to reprint two of the pieces in this book: to Third World Affairs, for Robert Chambers' paper in Chapter 13, and to Select Books, Singapore, for Shann Turnbull's paper in Chapter 7.

In the last analysis, of course, the responsibility for the final version of this book rests with me. In particular, the contributors to it should only be assumed to agree with the sections that are directly attributed to them. While much that is good in *The Living Economy* has come from others, any shortcomings in the editorial comment, emphasis or conclusions should be laid at my door alone.

It goes without saying that this book would not have been written at all had it not been for the inspiration and energy which brought The Other Economic Summit (TOES) into being. In this connection, special mention must be made of Sally Willington, who had the original idea for TOES; of the members of the TOES Steering Committee, listed in Appendix 3, who gave freely of their time and expertise to carry TOES through; of the charitable trusts and other organisations, listed in Appendix 4, which provided the financial support that enabled TOES to take place; and of the TOES Secretariat, David Kemball-Cook and Rita Purvis, and the dedicated band of volunteers, too numerous to mention individually here, who worked way past the call of duty, so that these two important international conferences could be staged on the shortest of proverbial shoe-strings.

I think the book also calls for a word of explanation about the readers for whom it is intended. Firstly, it is not meant solely for those with a technical economic background. There is therefore a certain amount of fairly basic explanation of economic concepts, where this is essential to the material that follows. On the other hand, it is my keen hope that economists will find much in this book to intrigue and stimulate them, so that, in some places, there is some quite sophisticated economic argument. If the economists are prepared on occasion to check their impatience, and the non-economists do not mind labouring a bit or reaching for their dictionary now and then, the book will have succeeded in straddling two stools without falling between them.

I hope too that *The Living Economy* will appeal to people from many different countries, as the TOES conferences have done. The papers, of course, come from all over the world, and I have tried to internationalise the editorial sections as far as possible. Inevitably, however, I have drawn heavily on UK evidence and experience, with which I am obviously best acquainted. This was out of necessity rather than Anglocentrism, and I hope that this material will be of some relevance to others in, perhaps, very different circumstances.

There may be some economists who will object to the use in the book's title of the phrase 'new economics', feeling that, in fact, many of the ideas between these covers have been mooted by economists at some time or another, and that the 'old economics' is quite capable of absorbing or adapting to them, if need be. The veteran Paul Samuelson would probably take this line – early on in the twelfth edition of his legendary textbook (now co-authored with William Nordhaus), he writes: 'Economics is inherently an evolutionary science, changing to reflect shifting trends in society and the economy' (Samuelson and Nordhaus, 1985).

This may be true enough, but the question then arises: how much evolution do you need to throw up a new species? In using the phrase 'new economics' it is my perception that the discipline under discussion is actually so different from 'old economics' as to necessitate the adjective 'new'. And this newness is not just in a normative sense, in the application of new attitudes and value judgments, important though these are. It also applies to positive economics, the study and measurement of economic 'reality'. Without getting involved prematurely in the argument, I think it will become apparent that the New Economics is actually based on a different perception of reality itself, it embodies a change in outlook as fundamental as, say, the Copernican revolution in astronomy. That is not to say that old economic tools and concepts will not continue to be most useful. But they will be used in a disciplinary context that is, at least, 'new' and, some might say, is no longer really even 'economics' at all.

TOES is an ongoing initiative and will continue to develop and campaign for a 'sane, humane and ecological' New Economics. But the publication of this book marks the end of the first phase of its work. One of its objectives during this time has been to bring together the new economic ideas which were surfacing throughout the 1970s and, sporadically, before, and place them within a coherent, consistent theoretical framework, which would facilitate their comprehension, promotion and further development. This book embodies a first attempt at such a framework, a fusion of new economic theory, policy and practice, which contains hope for those millions whose lives are blighted by the waste, hopelessness and destructiveness of the present economic system, and which provides a basis for the future health, wealth and well-being of us all.

Paul Ekins
London, October 1985

NOTE

TOES' address is 42 Warriner Gardens, London SW11 4DU.

INTRODUCTION

Economics is at an impasse. Its instruments are blunted. Its direction is confused. The broad post-war consensus has evaporated, the experts resort to increasingly desperate remedies and public opinion is both sceptical and bewildered.

Nothing seems to work as it used to. Investment doesn't bring down unemployment. Neither does growth. Inflation has become endemic, worrying even in the most tightly managed economies and always threatening to become more so. Third World indebtedness aborts world development and threatens to topple the international financial system. New technologies dominate people rather than liberating them. The natural environment is deteriorating rapidly world-wide and its resources are under unprecedented pressure. Most paradoxical, perhaps, is the continued existence, even in the richest societies, of poverty with progress. Even as technological change promises virtually unlimited production, the most basic material human needs still go unmet. Old people die of hypothermia while the shops overflow with videos and computer games.

A crisis of such dimensions indicates a fundamental failure of method. The very assumptions which form the basis of conventional economics are now unsound. Having ceased to describe the real world in its theories, economics has become incapable of acting coherently on the real world in practice. A new start is needed, an economic approach that is consistent with the science, technology, values and attitudes of the late twentieth century.

Part I of this book probes conventional economic disarray, focusing first on its obsession with economic growth and assessing the prospects for growth-led economic recovery. This leads on to an analysis of unemployment. The focus then shifts to the international arena, surveying briefly the whole range of North-South issues and giving special consideration to international debt, the arms trade and the health implications of conventional patterns of economic development. Finally, this part of the book questions current indicators of economic progress, being especially critical of the use of Gross National Product (GNP) in this sense.

Part II elaborates the theory of the New Economics as it has so far been developed through the work of TOES. It is concerned with human needs, with the nature of work, with economic self-reliance and with health as wealth. Like Part I, it ends with a consideration of indicators of economic progress, but this time the notion of such progress has been redefined in the light of the theoretical discussion that has gone before. Thus the new basket of indicators described in the long chapter at the end of Part II comprises a comprehensive measure of wealth and human welfare in the broadest, most realistic sense.

Part III moves on from theory to policy and action. It describes mechanisms for increasing public access to land. Community currencies and decentralised banking are explored as means of keeping the creation of wealth under local control, and the concepts of saver sovereignty and social investment are introduced to take account of the social objectives of economic activity. The shift to more flexible working patterns is noted and applauded, and reforms in the taxation and benefit systems are put forward to take this into account, notably the introduction of a basic income guarantee. A new order of industrial priorities is defined, and the growth industries within that order are identified, together with criteria of technological assessment and choice, so that technology may serve people rather than the reverse. Co-operatives and common-ownership enterprises have an important part to play in this framework of new industry, and the economic recovery that they bring about will be locally based and oriented towards the communities in which they operate. Such economic development, rooted in its local context, is equally appropriate for developed and developing countries, and two outstanding examples from the Third World are described in some detail, as is the shift in development priorities, which the encouragement of such initiatives necessitates. Transnational corporations have a major contribution to make to this development process, given the necessary international regulation to guarantee the ethics of their conduct and a willingness to decentralise and become more flexible, so that their activity can more easily serve the development priorities of their host country. Finally the shift in values and attitudes which underlies this new economic thinking is summarised.

Such a theme cannot be developed without the most wide-ranging criticism of conventional economics, and this will be couched in uncompromising terms. It should be clear from the outset that it is economic orthodoxy that is being challenged in this way. There are, and always have been, economic dissidents who have investigated some of the topics to be raised here. One can note in this connection the work of Boulding, Hirsch, Kapp, Mishan, the Club of Rome, and, of course, E.F. Schumacher, some of which is listed in the Bibliography. But these contributions, despite their merits, have remained on the margins of economic practice. Orthodoxy continues to hold sway in virtually all countries, spanning the political spectrum.

One key phrase of this orthodoxy is 'economic growth'. Another is 'full employment'. A third, in the market countries at least, is 'free trade', based on comparative advantage. These are the objectives that underpin conventional economic thinking. The Final Communiqué of the Bonn Economic Summit, issued on behalf of governments of the democratic left, right and centre, was a classic expression of this orthodoxy. It resounded with commitments to full employment, with exhortations to roll back the creeping frontiers of protectionism and, no less than twelve times in the first five pages, with unqualified, indiscriminate endorsement of the desirability and necessity of economic growth. This is, overwhelmingly, the economics of our time. It is this economics that is overripe for reform.

PART ONE

The need for a new economics

Before embarking on critique, it is perhaps as well to start with a definition of terms, in this case with the meaning of the word 'economics'. The Concise Oxford Dictionary describes it as the 'practical science of the production and distribution of wealth'. It is also sometimes thought of as the science which gives guidance as to the optimum allocation of scarce resources between competing uses for the maximisation of human welfare. Both these definitions throw useful light on the overall approach to economics to be taken here.

First, economics is about the production and *distribution* of wealth. Thus, since the distribution of wealth is an inherently political matter, any attempt to present or interpret economics as somehow apolitical or merely pragmatic is either misguided or worse. All systems of distribution have a political basis, of which economics, as the study of those systems, must at the very least be aware. Second, the raw material of economics is *resources* – land, labour, capital, in particular. It is not primarily about money. Money is useful to economics when money values accurately reflect the real values with which economics is concerned. When money does not give an accurate account of such values – and we will come across many situations in which this is the case – then economics must go behind the money values, directly to the resources or activities themselves. Third, the purpose of economics is to find out how to increase human welfare. Human welfare is a complex condition, the increase of which involves far more than the mere maximisation of production and consumption. Welfare has to do with health and human needs, with mental, emotional and spiritual matters, as well as with physical well-being and with social and environmental issues. Thus economics needs to be informed by psychology, sociology and ecology, if it is avoid a narrow, materialistic reductionism that may be counter-productive of welfare as a whole.

Thus it is with a perception of economics as a politically-aware, interdisciplinary science of resources and their best use that the following critique of conventional economic thinking is conducted.

ECONOMIC GROWTH: MEDICINE OR DISEASE?

Most current economic policy, indeed the very orientation of economic theory, boils down to the pursuit of economic growth, as indicated by an increasing Gross National Product (GNP). An economy that is growing at 3 per cent per annum is thought to be performing adequately, more growth is splendid, less growth is worrying, no growth or negative growth indicates widespread economic failure. The assumption is that growth is good and more is better. It is as if economists had never heard of cancer. It is extraordinary that an entire social science, and the dominant discipline in today's world at that, can effectively have come to be based on such a simplistic assumption. It is in the rejection of this assumption that the New Economics parts company most decisively from conventional economic theory.

The assumption is rejected on three main grounds. The first is that it confuses means with ends. The end purpose of economic activity is to increase human welfare. One way of doing this *may be* through some form of economic growth. But a *growth equals welfare* equation has no logical validity at all, for it begs three vital questions: growth of what? growth for whom? growth with what side-effects?

The answers to these questions have far more to do with the growth/welfare relation than the mere fact of economic growth itself. It is only by:

- showing that the growth has taken place through the production of goods and services that are inherently valuable and beneficial;
- demonstrating that these goods and services have been distributed widely throughout society;
- and proving that these benefits outweigh any detrimental effects of the growth process on other parts of society

that one can arrive at any sort of assessment as to whether a particular instance of economic growth is in fact a good or bad thing. Such an evaluation will vary, depending on personal attitudes and on the political perspective, and will still say nothing about economic growth in general. In time, perhaps, certain patterns of economic growth might come to be recognised as benign and life-enhancing, while others are perceived as wasteful, polluting or inequitable, as the case may be. Conventional economic thinking makes little or no attempt to make this assessment, nor has it developed the conceptual or political tools for such a task. For the New Economics, their development and implementation is of the most fundamental importance.

The second flaw in the growth assumption, explored later in more detail, lies in its failure to appreciate the reality of a finite planet. A 3% growth rate implies a doubling of production and consumption every twenty-five years. In the last twenty years, the decline in the resource base and global environmental degradation that are the result of growth economics have been impeccably documented, as will be seen. But growth economists and the politicians they advise still assume that economic growth on an indefinite basis is both possible and desirable, and hasten on towards environmental bankruptcy. The New Economics, in contrast, is rooted in the recognition that human life and economic activity are an interdependent part of the wider ecological processes that sustain life on earth and will either operate sustainably within those processes or bring about their own demise.

The third main ground for rejecting economic growth as the overriding policy objective is that its pursuit is actually likely to intensify the very economic problems which it is meant to solve, chief among them inflation and unemployment. This is because of the pattern of resource allocation to which the pursuit of economic growth inevitably seems to give rise, as will be explained.

The claim of economics to pre-eminence among social sciences is largely based on its supposed ability to inform political choice about the allocation of land, labour, capital and other resources in order to maximise human welfare. Its concept of opportunity costs is based on the recognition that a certain pattern of allocation, intended to achieve certain goals, always involves the loss of other benefits, which might have been yielded by a different allocation. Growthists, believing that growth equals increased welfare, allocate resources in such a way as to maximise growth. The argument will now be made that this allocation involves an extremely specific and limited pattern of resource use, a pattern which has a high opportunity cost, negative implications for both employment and inflation, and which is inherently self-defeating, i.e. the very process of pursuing indiscriminate growth makes that growth unsustainable.

ECONOMIC GROWTH: THE POLITICAL ECONOMY OF RESOURCE MISALLOCATION

Barbier (TOES, 1984) points out that economic growth depends on two factors: an increasingly efficient, in cost terms, combination of inputs in order to increase output, and an increase in the national income in order to be able to purchase that output. In the so-called advanced industrial economies, the increasingly efficient combination of inputs has, in practice, meant the substitution of capital and raw materials for human labour in the production process. Thus the growth pattern of resource allocation in these countries has involved:

- a decrease in the labour/output ratio (less labour per unit of output);
- an increase in the capital/output ratio (more physical capital per unit of output);[1]
- an increase in the long-term use of energy and raw materials per unit of output;
- an increase in environmental stress.

In the era of mechanisation, the labour/output ratio fell so that the same number of people were able to produce greatly increased output. In the current era of automation, with the labour/output ratio still falling, the trend is for the same aggregate output to be produced by even fewer people, and the displaced labour is not being fully redeployed. The faster the labour/output ratio falls, the more growth is necessary just to maintain employment. If it falls and growth is constrained, unemployment is the inevitable result. Thus the pursuit of indiscriminate economic growth, by tending to reduce the labour/output ratio in an environment that cannot generate the necessary growth to absorb the extra labour, creates unemployment rather than reducing it. The question now arises: why cannot the economic environment generate the necessary growth, as it did in the past? The answer lies in the other three elements of the resource allocation pattern.

The increasing capital/output ratio means, as Barbier says, that 'the future capital needs of advanced industrial economies may be so pressing that there is serious concern as to whether these economies can generate sufficient savings to meet these needs'; he quotes Brown 1978, Giarini 1980 and Madden 1976, in support of this view. Unprecedented levels of indebtedness and high interest rates indicate both that there is a shortage of capital available for investment and that savings are not being generated fast enough to create it. Both these factors act as a brake on growth and with increasing capital-intensity there may well not be enough capital to increase aggregate output fast enough to compensate for a falling labour/output ratio. Unemployment is the result.

Capital-intensity has traditionally been associated with resource- and energy-intensity. Given the past wasteful use of natural resources, there is undoubtedly now scope for using them more efficiently, especially in the case of energy. But in the long term the law of entropy is inviolable: increasing production and consumption must entail increasing natural resource use. The law of entropy can be economically interpreted to mean that the transformation of energy and materials must always involve a process of qualitative dissipation from a more useful (low entropy) to a less useful (high entropy) state, i.e. resources become wastes.[2]

Whether increasing capital-intensity will continue to result in increasing resource-intensity is debatable. What is certain is that economic growth in advanced economies was made possible by the more intensive use of natural resources in the past and will result in greater resource use in the future, especially if the same pattern of growth is emulated by the economies of the South. Increasing natural resource use can only result in increasing vulnerability of the global economy to price shocks such as the oil price rises in the 1970s. Unless the pattern of natural resource use changes, and as real depletion starts to be felt across a wide range of resources, future price shocks and long-term upward pressure on prices will stifle any growth that is dependent on intensive use of natural resources.

As with increasing resource use, increasing environmental stress has also been an inevitable result of economic growth in the past. The law of entropy again decrees that growth must result in the increasing emission of wastes into an environment that is already overburdened with them. More investment in pollution abatement is certain to be necessary. The capital requirements of this will put further pressure on capital financing and further constrain expansion and economic productivity. Moreover, environmental 'goods' (e.g. clean air, pure water), which at a lower level of economic activity were effectively 'free', will come to have an economic cost, resulting in further inflationary pressure.

In short, economies that are subjected to policies that seek indiscriminately to increase economic growth can expect to suffer from high and increasing unemployment because they will not have the capital to generate growth fast enough to absorb shed labour. They will become increasingly indebted and suffer high interest rates in their attempt to satisfy their capital needs. The growth they generate will be inherently inflationary and vulnerable to price shocks of increasing severity, and more and more of such growth will be devoted to mitigating the effects of the growth itself in such areas as human health and the environment. Barbier concludes: 'Economic policy-makers should concentrate on tackling these problems directly and abandon the emphasis on growth as the primary objective of economic activity.'

THE REALITY OF A FINITE PLANET

Harford Thomas (TOES, 1984) surveyed the related themes of population, resources and the environment. The message is of the utmost simplicity and has been confirmed by reports from a wide range of sources of unquestionable eminence and authority: the *World Conservation Strategy*, prepared by the International Union For the Conservation of Nature and Natural Resources, in collaboration with the United Nations Environment Programme and the World Wildlife Fund (IUCN, 1980); the Brandt Report (Brandt, 1980); the *Global 2000 Report to the President*, commissioned by President Carter (*Global 2000*, 1981); the Global Possible Conference in 1984 of international scientists, policy-makers and corporate planners (World Resources Institute, 1984); and the Worldwatch Institute's *State of the World* annual publication (Brown et al., 1984 and 1985). All these confirm the unsurprising fact that exponential population growth, combined with increasing per capita consumption of resources, combined with increasing destruction and exploitation of the natural environment, is unsustainable, is already resulting in calamity and will result in catastrophe sooner rather than later if current trends are not reversed.

As far as population is concerned, it clearly needs to stabilise as soon as possible, with as little increase as possible over present levels. In the Third World there has been a significant change in governmental attitudes in recent years, and countries totalling 90% of the population in the developing world have introduced or are now introducing family planning programmes (World Bank, 1984).[3] But the root cause of population growth and of much environmental destruction remains poverty. As Thomas says:

Economic and social development is a precondition for slowing down and eventually halting population growth. Therefore . . .

it is in the common interests of humankind to ensure that the developing countries are enabled to make sustainable economic and social progress as rapidly as possible . . . . jobs and better wages, health care and better nutrition, better education, emancipation of women, access to family planning, these are the conditions in which family sizes fall, as has happened in the developed countries.

The major impact on the world's resources does not, however, come from the developing countries. The high-income countries, with about one-fifth of the world's population, actually consume about two-thirds of the world's resources, an 8:1 per capita consumption ratio. Much of the global environmental depletion and degradation is, of course, the result of this consumption of resources and the disposal of related wastes. So the rich countries, in addition to enabling sustainable and environmentally-sound development in poor countries, have an absolute obligation to use less resources with less environmental impact themselves. Unfortunately conventional economics is quite unable to recognise, formulate or give effect to this obligation. Economic policy currently makes no distinction between renewable and non-renewable resources, nor does it take future scarcity into account, nor does it routinely evaluate the costs of environmental degradation with a view to preventing that degradation from taking place (environmental impact assessments are still very much the exception rather than the rule, and apply not at all to such global phenomena as soil erosion, acid rain, deforestation, desertification and the greenhouse effect). The development of concepts and mechanisms that will take account of such considerations is of prime importance if we are to move from an economics of growth to, as Herman Daly calls it (TOES, 1984), a steady-state economy.

A steady-state economy (SSE) is an economy with constant stocks of artifacts and people. These two populations (artifacts and people) are constant but not static. People die and artifacts depreciate. Births must replace deaths and production must replace depreciation. These 'input' and 'output' rates are to be equal at low levels, so that the life-expectancy of people and durability of artifacts will be high. The two flows may be merged into the concept of 'throughput'. The throughput flow begins with depletion, followed by production, depreciation, and finally pollution as the wastes are returned to the environment. The economy maintains itself by this throughput in the same way that an organism maintains itself by its metabolic flow. Both economies and organisms must live by sucking raw materials (low entropy) from the environment and expelling wastes (high entropy) back to the environment. In an SSE this throughput must be limited in scale, so as to be within the regenerative and assimilative capacities of the eco-system.

It is important to be clear about what is *not* constant in an SSE. Knowledge and technology are not held constant. Neither is the distribution of income nor the allocation of resources constant. The SSE can develop qualitatively, but does not grow in quantitative scale, just as the planet earth, of which the economy is a sub-system, develops without growing.

Daly does not identify only physical constraints to growth. There are also ethical and social constraints. Ethically, there are the needs of future generations of people for resources and environmental goods, and the needs of other species for habitats undisturbed by human activity. Socially, the growth ethic fosters a glorification of self-interest, greed and competition, in which, as J.S. Mill put it, 'Men do not desire to be rich, but to be richer than other men.' Quite apart from the unlikelihood of such an attitude leading to social justice and cohesion, it is also self-defeating. Everyone cannot be richer than everyone else. Relative improvement is a zero-sum game in the aggregate, in which one person's gain is another's loss. This makes the growth ethic a recipe for disillusion and dissatisfaction.

Thus, in terms of both physical resources and social insight, the economics of the steady state is very different from growth economics, and the policies it generates form much of the substance of this book. As far as resources and the environment are concerned, all that needs to be said now is that steady-state economics 'treats the money-values of profit and loss balance sheets and income and expenditure budgets as secondary to resource accounting, which makes a sustainability assessment of use, conservation and future availability' (Thomas, TOES, 1984).

The economics of the steady state is a highly practicable economics. The Global Possible Conference already mentioned stressed that the knowledge, expertise and resources for the economic transformation to sustainability are amply available. What is lacking is the political will to deploy them.

We must mobilise now to achieve the global possible . . . . . If we remain inactive, whether through pessimism or complacency, we shall only make certain the darkness that many fear
(World Resources Institute, 1984).

THE SCOURGE OF UNEMPLOYMENT

If there were no other evidence of economic malfunction, current levels of unemployment alone would call conventional economics into question. Its combination of the factors of production is so skewed that, at the same time as capital is becoming increasingly scarce and costly, and resource depletion is also becoming of major concern, millions of pairs of willing hands are condemned to enforced idleness. New technologies, which should be providing a relief from drudgery and enriched working opportunities, are in fact becoming a nightmare of impoverishment for millions.

Paul Sparrow has pointed out (TOES, 1985) that if by unemployment we mean the number of people who would like paid work but cannot find it, then there are far more unemployed in the UK than the official figures suggest. Government statistics have been repeatedly massaged downwards for political reasons, and Sparrow estimates that at March 1985 there were 4.3 million unemployed in the UK (one million more than officially indicated) plus nearly 900,000 unregistered women who would like part-time work. Sparrow notes evidence that even the United States, which has generated more new 'jobs' than the UK, has experienced a pauperisation of work, so that poverty there has increased in both relative and absolute terms.

If the extent of unemployment is under-reported, its true social and economic costs are also grossly under-estimated. Sparrow calculates the direct annual financial cost of unemployment to the UK Exchequer, in terms of lost taxation and increased benefits, as over £20 billion. As for social costs, Sparrow's Table I.1 indicates those to be taken into account. On top of this there is then the loss of output caused by running the economy below full employment, which Sparrow puts at over £21 billion. Finally, there is the cost of the wasted human investment, the education and training which individuals are unable to put to productive use.

Apart from the cost of lost production, wasted education and training are realised as lost investment in two other main ways:

1 charged in proportion to the amount of each individual's working life spent unemployed;

2 charged in proportion to the degree to which unemployed individuals downgrade their skills to re-enter the labour market (Sparrow, TOES, 1985).

Table 1.1 Community running costs of unemployment to be accounted for

Increased amount of *retirement pensions* due to fall in economic activity of old age pensioners

Increased *demand on health service* due to psychological and physical effects on health of unemployed and poor

Costs of increased *crime* resulting from high unemployment including:
– policing costs
– increased prison population
– vandalism repair
– insurance claims

Cost of controlling *social and industrial unrest* such as Summer Riots of 1981 and Miners Strike of 1984/85, again including policing costs, prison costs, vandalism repair, insurance claims.

Given wastage of resources of this magnitude, it is hardly surprising that confidence in economics, the supposed science of resource allocation, is at such a low ebb.

We have already seen in general terms how the pursuit of economic growth will intensify unemployment rather than alleviate it. Fleming, in a detailed sectoral analysis of the UK economy (TOES, 1984), shows why the economy cannot absorb the labour shed by technological innovation. The only sector that seems to have any large-scale potential for new employment is that of low-technology goods and services, but that potential is constrained by the problem of income distribution. This analysis fits well with the growing evidence from both the US and the UK economies that it is, in fact, the low-paid service sector that is providing the bulk of new jobs.[4]

Fleming goes on to question the ability of the economy to maintain the level of transfer payments at high permanent levels of unemployment.

Every newly-unemployed person means lower revenue for the government (in the form of lower national insurance contributions, income tax, value added tax and – on average – corporation tax). Yet it also means increased demand for government payments. At low levels of unemployment this has a stabilising effect: government spending is increased automatically as unemployment rises. But at high levels of unemployment, the system breaks down. It follows that there exists an upper limit for unemployment above which there is no means of maintaining the real value of transfer payments. A government that attempted to do so would be forced to tax firms and individuals so heavily that prices would rise, leading to a fall in the exchange rate, a rise in the cost of imports, a fall in living standards, and eventually a complete failure to obtain the items, including agricultural raw materials, for which the economy relies on overseas supplies.

This course of events is a result of the fact that prices on the international market are set by the most efficient producers. Those who cannot produce close to those prices go out of business. Thus Fleming calls for ways to work within local rather than international price structures, a theme that is taken up and explored later in this book. This approach essentially comprises a new emphasis on economic self-reliance. As Fleming puts it:

> Up to now the goal of economic management has been economic growth. From now on it should be economic maturity – the ability to make economic choices without the unchallengeable, binding control of the exchange price vector . . . . We have a new emancipation issue on our hands. We need to make an economy in which people can participate in production, appropriate to their material needs, irrespective of whether their output can find a buyer on the wider market: an economic emancipation just as pressing as the political emancipation of the nineteenth and twentieth centuries, but much harder to achieve.

THE INTERNATIONAL ECONOMIC DISORDER

> When we describe the present situation as a 'crisis', we imply that things have happened abruptly or even unexpectedly. The fact of the matter is that they have taken a long time to build up. Developing countries have expressed their dissatisfaction with the world economic system for several decades now – and they mean the world trading system, the world's monetary system and the world's financial system. The so-called financial 'crisis' is in fact the most visible part of a relentless process in which problems have accumulated, in many aspects foreseeably, for years.
>
> Javier Perez de Cuellar[5]

TRICKLING DOWN AND OUT

The model of development through industrial growth, which is the dominant model everywhere, has been a mixed blessing for the industrialised countries. They have certainly experienced great resource depletion and environmental pollution and many of their economies are now extremely vulnerable to the international market. Moreover, it is now clear that the costs of continuing to follow this model, especially those of unemployment, far outweigh the benefits. Nevertheless, ordinary citizens did experience a general rise in living standards for a number of decades.

For much of the so-called developing world, however, this model, which has been the core of a whole set of inappropriate Western values, has had far worse effects. It has ravaged the resources and environments of many countries. Far from involving an emancipation from colonialism, it has all too often substituted for it an economic and technological dependence on the industrialised countries, wiping out in the process many traditional economic activities and disrupting the economies of whole regions. Rural areas have been depopulated and many cities turned into megalopolitan shanty-towns. Above all, this model of development, combined with population growth, has left hundreds of millions of people utterly destitute and raised an unprecedented spectre of perpetual famine, starvation and war.

Anila Graham (TOES, 1984) describes the 'trickle-down' process by which development was supposed to come about:

> The theory assumes that the prosperity of the poor countries is linked to that of the rich countries. Thus, as long as the latter continued to grow, economic expansion in the developed countries would be transmitted to the developing countries through the free-play of market forces. Third World deficiencies in technology and capital would be made good by developed countries, through this 'trickle-down' process, thus leading to the economic 'take-off' of developing countries. The stark facts, however, show that even in the post-war period of unprecedented economic expansion in developed countries up to 1973, the existing international order failed to meet the basic needs of the vast majority of the world's population and confined the benefits of economic growth very largely to privileged minorities.

Huge disparities remain between rich and poor nations. Moreover, the gap continues to widen; between 1950 and 1980 real per capita income in these low-income countries grew by a

mere $80; in industrial market-economy countries it rose by
$6,530. A large proportion of the population of developing
countries suffers from endemic poverty. About 800 million
people, nearly one in three of those living in low-income
countries and over one in six of the world's population, live in
absolute poverty – at the very margin of existence with grossly
inadequate food, shelter, health and education.
(Commonwealth Secretariat, 1982).

Even in the early 1970s, disillusion with growth and trickle-
down was setting in, as it became obvious to many poor countries
that they would not get richer simply by the rich countries getting
richer. Graham writes:

It is of fundamental importance that the persistent confusion of
growth with development should be avoided. The hope that
faster economic growth in developing countries by itself would
benefit the broad masses of poor people has not been fulfilled.
The problem of ideologies of growth is that they have had too
little concern for the quality of growth. The prime objective of
development is to lead to self-fulfilment and creative
partnership in the use of a nation's productive forces and its full
human potential.

The search for new ideas was reflected in some of the findings
of the Cocoyoc Declaration[6] and the Charter of Economic
Rights and Duties of States,[7] which include:

The need for developing countries to adopt their own
policies;
The recognition that the experience of the West was largely
irrelevant to the needs of developing countries;
The realization that the road to prosperity did not necessarily
lie in development on the Western model and integration into
the existing world economic system;
The belief that the goal of development was not to close the
gap or catch up with the developed world, but for developing
countries to make better use of their own resources and cater
more for the basic needs of their populations.

What was needed was a radical change in the whole structure
of world economic relations involving the abolition of the
existing system of dependency which constituted a vital element
in the persistence of the under-development of the Third
World.

THE DEBT CRISIS

Unfortunately this well-meaning declaration had not become fixed firmly enough in policy before the oil price rises of 1973 set the international financial system awash with petrodollars. Third World countries started to borrow. Susan George (TOES, 1985) charts the course of the debt crisis.

The 1970s were the palmy days when young loan officers from Argentina to Zaire were given lofty targets (along with the certain knowledge that they would be somewhere else when the loans came due); when governments succumbed to the temptations of apparently endless easy money. Ignoring the lessons of at least the past 150 years, during which numerous countries repudiated or defaulted on their debts, Walter Wriston (then President of Citibank) declared that 'countries do not fail to exist' and thus would necessarily pay back their loans. Western private bank lending to the Third World grew at an average 25% a year between 1973 and 1981; this was on top of the debt owed by LDCs to public sources (other than governments, the World Bank, etc.).

The second oil shock of 1979 plunged the world economy into four years of virtual stagnation. In the wake of global recession, the heedless nature of the banks' lending policies became evident to all. The borrowers confronted the reality that their private debt was short-term and at 'variable' (market-determined) interest rates that invariably fluctuated upward. These rates rose from just 6% in the mid 1970s to an average 16.5% in 1981. Each 1% rise added $6 billion to the LDC's annual debt service bill.[8]

Not only were interest payments devouring a larger, and more unpredictable, amount of their export earnings; these earnings were themselves doing a nosedive – the collapse of commodity prices between 1980 and 1982 caused developing countries an aggregate loss of export earnings that amounted to $21 billion (Graham, TOES, 1984). What is more, their debt had been drawn in dollars and in the years after 1980 the dollar more than doubled in value, jacking up not only the debt bill itself, but also the price of essential imports like oil and foodstuffs. By the end of 1983 the situation was as in Table I.2.

Thus by 1983 the trickle-down from rich to poor had become a 'stream-up' from poor to rich: the transfer of resources from the developing to the developed world amounted in that year to $21 billion.[9]

Table 1.2   The first figure indicates what each of the countries below owed as of late 1983; the second indicates their debt service ratio, i.e. the repayment of debt and interest as a percentage of exports of goods and services.

Country	Debt ($US billions)	Ratio (percentage)
Brazil	91	115
Mexico	83	128
Argentina	45	133
South Korea	40	23
Venezuela	32	78
Indonesia	28	17
Philippines	26	79
Turkey	18	20
Algeria	17	29
Chile	17	80
Peru	14	89
Morocco	12	67
Columbia	12	32
Nigeria	12	18

Source: American Express *International Debt, Banks and the LDCs* (American Express, London, 1984)

Eastern Europe is also heavily indebted and Yugoslavia, Romania, Poland and Hungary are under IMF tutelage; Israel owes $23 billion, or more than 100% of its GNP, but these countries are excluded here. Many countries, especially in Africa, owe less in absolute terms, but a great deal relative to their repayment capacity. None of them alone is a real threat to the banking system, but all are under IMF surveillance and subject to 'adjustment' programmes.

(These ratios include excess short-term debts. Since 1983 a substantial portion of these debts have been rescheduled, so that present debt-service ratios are now considerably lower. Ed.)

It is worth noting at this point that the words 'debt crisis' mean different things to different interest groups. To creditor banks and governments in the North, they mean the possibility of the collapse of the international financial system through default on debt. To debtor countries they mean the immense economic problems caused by trying to service their debt with deteriorating international conditions over which they have no control. To the poor in debtor countries, they simply mean starvation.

The International Monetary Fund (IMF) is the Northern-dominated institution with the task of saving the international financial system and forcing debt repayment. Susan George has documented what the IMF 'adjustment' programmes have meant for the poorest peoples in Brazil, Mexico, the Philippines, the Dominican Republic and Peru. Western bankers have expressed themselves satisfied with such 'adjustment' to the extent that some now even consider the debt problem as good as solved. In a paper to the 1985 World Conference of the Society for International Development in Rome, Horst Schulman, Deputy Managing Director of the Washington-based Institute of International Finance, wound up by saying 'Economic historians writing about the debt problem of the 1980s may well wonder what all the fuss was about.' The Peruvians whose health has been permanently damaged by eating chicken-feed would assuredly be able to explain this to such historians – if they were asked and if they were still alive, neither of which is very likely.

Susan George emphasises the injustice of forcing the poor in debtor countries to fund the debt repayments:

> We know for certain that it was the elites in the less developed countries, and more often than not the military, who were responsible for incurring the heavy debts to begin with. It was they who borrowed in order to buy Phantom jets or large 'development' schemes benefitting only themselves, they who sent the suitcases full of money north to private accounts, they again who maintained internal security forces to keep their own people 'in their place'. If one principle of any 'ethical economics' should be 'Those who reap the benefits should also pay the costs', then IMF adjustment programmes aimed at insuring debt repayment take us farther than ever from that goal.

George also exposes the ideological and political basis of the IMF:

> To understand the philosophy and practice of the Fund, one must understand *why* it lends, or, in its own parlance, *to what end* it provides 'balance of payments supports' to heavily indebted countries. The answer lies in the IMF's Charter, whose first article prescribes six objectives for the organisation. Among these are 'To facilitate balanced *growth of international trade*' and, again, '[to] seek the elimination of exchange restrictions that hinder the *growth of world trade*' (my emphasis).
> The doctrines of free trade and comparative advantage are the Fund's foundations. Upon these rocks, dating from Adam

Smith and Ricardo, is founded the IMF secular religion. The term is accurate: these doctrines are articles of faith. The Fund takes for granted that the best economic relations among nations are those 'in which there is the highest degree of free trade in goods and services'.[10] As for comparative advantage, one need not alter a line in Ricardo's original formulation to capture the IMF's view: 'It is quite important to the happiness of mankind that our own enjoyment should be increased by the better distribution of labour, by each country producing those commodities for which by its situation, its climate and its natural or artificial advantages, it is adapted, and by their exchanging them for the commodities of other countries.'[11] These principles are the Fund's *sine qua non* and dictate its behaviour. For example, the principle of free trade requires that membership in the Fund 'automatically carries the pledge to dismantle exchange controls' because such controls 'are the most effective barriers to imports, far more effective than protective tariffs'.[12] Other obstacles to trade such as quotas, restrictions on foreign investment, etc., are also actively discouraged by the fund.

One doesn't have to look far to see in whose interest this emphasis on free trade operates. As US Treasury Secretary Donald Regan has said:

The IMF is essentially a non-political institution . . . but this does not mean that US political and security interests are not served by the IMF. On the contrary it serves us well by containing economic problems, which could otherwise spread through the international community . . . and supporting open, market-oriented economies consistent with Western political values. Judged on this criterion, US appropriations for the IMF can be an excellent investment.[13]

George adds:

Further evidence that the IMF is one of the several instruments used by the powerful countries for managing the world system in their interests is the Fund's exclusive concern for debtors and possible sources of financial destabilisation *in the Third World*. As of the end of 1984, Third World countries (about 2.6 billion population) owed an estimated $895 billion. As of the same date, the United States of America (220 million population) owed nearly twice as much for twelve times fewer people.[14] Neither a record budget deficit nor a record balance of trade deficit in the US appears to worry the IMF – although the US is sucking much-needed capital from the rest of the world to finance both. The US national debt amounted to 35% of its GNP in 1983 and is expected (by the Congressional Budget Office) to reach 50% of GNP in another four years.

The implications of borrowers' greater involvement in world trade are also not hard to fathom. George again:

> Investment of all kinds will go into export industries or export crops – not into basic necessities, including food, for local people. Higher prices to peasant producers (one of the Fund's stated policies), even if fully implemented, will not compensate city dwellers, those living on fixed incomes, the landless, the unemployed and underemployed (nor even the peasants themselves) that make up the overwhelming majority of the population, for the phenomenal cost-of-living increases that accompany 'adjustment': Kenya is reportedly exporting foodstuffs in spite of near-famine conditions in parts of the country. Brazil is the second largest agro-exporter in the world, whereas 60% of the Brazilian population is estimated to be suffering varying degrees of malnutrition with outright starvation in the North-east.

The devastating effect of this export-or-bust attitude on the debtor countries' environment can also easily be imagined. Those that have little export potential except for food will give their best land over to cash crops for export, while peasants have to find their subsistence on marginal, vulnerable land that is soon ecologically degraded. Not just soils, but waters and forests, as well as minerals, can be expected to be mercilessly mined in order to repay the Northern banks. And as more and more countries, producing similar goods, are forced into the export markets, the prices of their goods fall further, so that they have to produce more just to stand still as far as repayments go. George sums up the action priorities on the debt issue for those who feel that there must be an alternative to inhumane 'adjustment'.

> The Northern establishment will only act to change present Fund policy if it feels its own interests are at stake. The ultimate threat to those interests may be the political one, as discontent rises and people feel they have nothing left to lose. The 'IMF riot' is a new term in the international political vocabulary, and the spread of an anti-Fund mentality could ultmately become more destabilising for the West than the debt crisis itself.
>   At the theoretical level, we urgently need effective alternatives to the theories that underpin IMF actions – comparative

advantage, 'perfect' competition, 'free' trade and markets. Meanwhile, ecologists should be documenting the impact of 'export-or-perish' policies on the LDC environments – there is a dearth of such information on Africa, especially.

Concerned people in the North should also encourage measures, some of which have even been proposed by bankers, to relieve the debt burden. Among these are forgiveness of individual loans (Sweden and Holland have done this); fixed, lower interest rates; pegging loans to a basket of currencies or of commodity prices, not just to the dollar; rescheduling of debt with much longer maturities, perhaps under auspices of a new international institution like a world central bank or an 'international debt discount corporation'.[15]

To which need only be added the importance of tying future loans and aid to new, different development strategies, which are geared to the sustainable satisfaction of the basic needs of the poorest people in the Third World. One of the corner-stones of the New Economics is social justice. There is no area in which such a consideration is in more need of urgent promotion than in the field of international debt.

THE ARMS TRADE

According to Tony Humm (TOES, 1985), the accumulated military expenditure of the Third World amounts to $845 billion, of which at least $190 billion was spent on imported major weapons (all 1983 prices).[16] Over 80% of these weapons were supplied by four countries: USSR, USA, France, Britain, in that order of market share. Humm shows this market to be as competitive as one would expect from its size, and as complex as one would expect from its political and strategic importance. What it is not, however, is strictly economically profitable for the exporting countries:

The most common defence of arms exports cites the commercial advantages of the trade, and we have looked at levels of employment and apparent balance of payments advantages in the major exporting countries. However, these apparent advantages must be viewed as being conditional on the maintenance of a 'warm mobilisation base', not as independently positive attributes. The economies of scale provided through exports are asserted to reduce the domestic unit cost of equipment. But whether additional production contributes to historic costs depends on the price at which the product is exported. Because the market is so competitive, arms are exported at marginal, rather than full economic cost (sometimes at even lower prices). In Britain the Committee of Public Accounts 1976-7 found that the Royal Ordnance Factories priced at marginal cost for most exports.[17] France is often criticised for its predatory pricing, but even the French are undercut. India was in the process of buying Mirage 2000 aircraft (made by Dassault) when they decided to build the Soviet MiG 29 and 31 under licence. The Dassault executive complained, 'it was much cheaper . . . . Soviet aircraft have no price.'[18]

It is also argued that arms exports open gateways to further civil trade, establishing contacts which assist a country's general export drive. However, a British Treasury report (1983) found that the costs of 'winning' overseas orders for construction and engineering contractors was unjustifiable on economic grounds. Relatively few companies benefit (from the subsidies required) and it is an extremely expensive way of reducing domestic unemployment (between £50,000 and £200,000 to finance one job).

'Spinoff' from research into armaments is also asserted to be economically beneficial. But the diffusion of technology into the civil sector is rare, in fact the structure of defence industries is so idiosyncratic that large firms which produce civil and military goods keep the two divisions separate for fear of contamination from the inefficient practices of the arms division.[19] Historically, the military have guaranteed markets for some electronics equipment, but military R and D is a project-oriented activity to derive particular weapons systems, and as such even British ex-Defence Minister Geoffrey Pattie admits, the 'civilian spinoff is limited'.

Governments guarantee the existence of their own arms industries by subsidising profits (a typical contract will cover costs of production plus an agreed profit) and both formally and informally protecting domestic markets, although occasionally paying lip service to greater competition. They spend enormous sums of money developing equipment which has no civil value, employing from the best of scientifically-trained personnel (about 40,000 scientists and technologists are employed in defence work in Britain), and ensuring the adequacy of markets and subsidies, so that (usually) privately owned firms can risklessly pursue profit while society at large pays the bills. The advantages of exporting arms are then cited as unequivocal economic payoffs, while the tremendous opportunity costs, 'crowding out' of investment and skilled personnel from potentially dynamic sectors and the subsequent loss of growth, are conveniently ignored.

For the Third World countries which buy these weapons, the opportunity cost is immense, as Humm says:

> These arms kill indirectly, by diverting scarce economic resources from basic development needs (nutrition, medical care, housing and education) to often non-essential, conspicuous military consumption. The UN, attempting to quantify this process, found for an 'average' developing country, with a GNP per capita of almost $350 (in 1970 prices) and population of 8.5 million, the first $200 million of arms imported would:
> - add approximately 20 infant deaths per 1000 live births
> - decrease average life expectancy by three to four years
> - result in thirteen to fourteen fewer literate adults out of every one hundred.[20]

Third World countries are also setting up their own arms industries. Humm again:

> India now employs 250,000 armaments workers, while Brazil has 100,000. Israel will export arms worth $1.2 billion in 1984 (about 39% of Israeli industrial exports), sales which are almost all made to other Third World countries.[21] It would be a mistake, however, to imagine that the development of arms-manufacturing capacity in these countries contributes to their domestic economic health. The costs have been enormous. Brazil is one of the most indebted countries in the world; who knows what the creation of an arms industry cost her? The foreign affairs adviser to the Governor of Rio de Janeiro, Clovis Bragagao, is in no doubt: 'In Brazil, the government subsidises heavily the arms industry, giving them money, tax exemptions, and a lot of other privileges. Naturally this converts a lot of civil industry into the arms industry. It also converts institutes and research centres to produce technology for the future of weapons in Brazil. And of course it is draining resources from other areas, mainly our deficient social areas, to the arms industry.'[22]

The trade in arms is, of course, just a small fraction of global military expenditure, now running at $800 billion annually, and there are no easy answers to the tragedy of wasted resources that this represents. But from an economic point of view the evidence is clear: arms exports are not even clearly profitable for exporting countries, while arms imports have done little to prevent wars between importing countries and have ensured that, when these wars occur, they are much more costly than they would otherwise have been. For both exporting and importing countries, non-military expenditure is economically far more productive, in terms of jobs and utility, and more socially beneficial. There can be little doubt that no sort of economic progress is possible for the majority of the world's peoples as long as such a high proportion of the world's resources – human, physical, financial – is pumped into the means of destruction. To quote UN Secretary-General Perez de Cuellar again:

> The world can either continue to pursue the arms race with characteristic vigour, or move consciously and with deliberate speed towards a more stable and balanced social and economic development within a more sustainable international economic order worldwide. It cannot do both.[23]

HEALTH AND DEVELOPMENT

Just as economic growth in itself says nothing about economic progress until some light has been shed on the questions 'growth of what, for whom?', so the word 'development' is ambiguous until some clarification has been given as to what has been developed, to whose benefit and at what costs. Mira Shiva (TOES, 1985) shows that much 'development' in India has had a disastrous effect on the lives of the rural poor, the tribals and the nomads, in several different ways: sometimes their economies have been disrupted so that they have been left poorer by the development; sometimes their physical environment has been devastated by the development; sometimes their traditional social structures have been undermined in a destructive way. It is important to note that in each of these cases it is possible for the economy as a whole to have shown 'growth'. It is just that the benefits of growth have by-passed the communities that have been adversely affected, often accruing to distant urban proprietors or being reflected in the profits of companies that are based elsewhere. In these cases, a far better indicator of positive or negative development than monetary measures is the health of the people concerned.

Shiva first stresses that before Western influence in India, the sub-continent had a sophisticated and accessible system of primary health care, which gave importance to the physical, emotional, mental and spiritual dimensions of health. Under colonial rule this traditional system was marginalised and, as Shiva says, 'With the total disruption of indigenous peoples' way of life and denial of their life-support systems, impoverishment and ill-health grew', whereupon Western health-care practices were imported, of which a joint report by the Indian Council of Medical Research (ICMR) and Indian Council for Social Science Research (ICSSR) stated: 'The imported and inappropriate model of health services is top-heavy, over-centralised, heavily curative in its approach, costly and dependency-creating' (ICMR/ICSSR, 1980).

Despite huge investment in the whole Western-style medical industry complex, Shiva reports that in many crucial areas – goitre, leprosy, TB, child mortality, low birth weight, vitamin-deficiency induced blindness – health status is not only not improving, it is actually deteriorating. This is because, as she says,

> These diseases affect the vulnerable groups, like the women, children and the poor, most severely and are caused not so much by the *absence* of medical services as by the *existence* of deprivations of basic needs of food, water and healthy and safe environments . . . . We know conclusively that doctors, drugs, and medical care will fail to remedy health problems arising out of unmet needs of adequate food, safe and adequate water, healthy living and working conditions. The denial of these to an increasing number will be creating a very serious health and survival crisis. To the long list of health problems mentioned earlier, today is added death and disability due to misguided development.

Shiva gives many examples to back this assertion. Thus she quotes C. Gopalan's startling statistic that 'only less than 3 million of the 23 million (children) to be born (in India) in 1983 will be truly healthy, physically fit, productive and intellectually capable citizens of this country',[24] because of malnutrition. Yet she shows that 'there has been a definite shrinkage of the area of food-grain under cultivation, due to its replacement by more profitable cash and non-food crops'. Forestry schemes on rain-fed agricultural land with pulpwood species like eucalyptus are a 'prescription for desertification'[25] and drastically reduce food availability.[26] Yet the world's biggest development agency, the World Bank, is actively financing eucalyptus plantations. Shiva goes on:

> This crisis in the supply of food from the land is paralleled by a crisis in the supply of food from the sea . . . . Mechanisation and cold storage facilities that came with the 'Blue Revolution' have led to large-scale export of fish, the unpurchasability

and disappearance of fish even from the local markets on the coastline, and pushed 1.6 million traditional fishermen to the brink of starvation.

Just as important as the food crisis, and worsening even more worryingly, is the water crisis. Thus Shiva notes:

The pumping of underground water for the irrigation of cash crops, e.g. sugarcane, etc., is tending to be at the cost of water availability to the poor, who have no means of pumping out water, nor of repeatedly deepening their drying wells. 'In Uttar Pradesh's northern hill districts, out of 2,700 drinking water supply schemes provided by the State Government, 2,300 have failed as a result of the drying up of the sources of water.'[27]

Water scarcity as a threat to health was the basis of the recent historical judgment on 12 March 1984 by the Supreme Court in the Doon Valley case, which was a major success for the citizen groups and villagers of the Doon Valley, who have been fighting for their fundamental rights to water and a healthy life. Reckless deforestation and indiscriminate limestone mining for commercial purposes in the water catchment area in the geologically fragile Himalayan slopes had been the cause of a decrease in water flow of 60% and a drop in agricultural fertility of 50%[28] in a valley previously famous for its lychees and Basmati rice, showing yet again that patterns of resource utilisation are more critical to scarcity than mere multiplying numbers.

Until then the role of limestone as a storer and discharger of water had been totally overlooked, and economic value was put only on its role as an industrial raw material. It required a scientific eco-system study, a public litigation in the Supreme Court, a people's movement, spearheaded by 'Friends of the Doon' and the 'Save Missoorie Society', to remind the policymakers that *all* costs have to be calculated when talking of 'progress' and development.

Food and water are thus going down in supply. Chemicals are going up. Shiva again:

As in many other Third World countries, not only are our water resources drying up, but what remains is being shamelessly polluted with toxic industrial effluents and sewage. A staggering 70% of the available water in India is polluted, according to scientists at the National Environmental Engineering and Research Institute (Centre for Science and Environment, 1982).

Pesticides are also a major hazard.

At present only 7.2% of India's farmland is sprayed with pesticides and less than 20% of our food-grain production is derived from the high yielding variety. Yet we Indians have the highest levels of pesticide residues in the world, as shown by studies by the National Institute of Occupational Health . . . . DDT content in the body fat of Delhi residents has been found to be 26 ppm on average, while the maximum residue limit is 1.25 ppm. Babies ingest DDT-BHT residues in human milk in amounts that are 21 times the ADI (Acceptable Daily Intake).[29]

Some poisons are actually made to be ingested, and Shiva shows that the drug industry in India, far from promoting good health, is a major health hazard. Thus 46% of sales of 30,000 branded formulations are sold over the counter without prescription to people, many of whom cannot read the labels, by shopkeepers who may have been subject to deliberate drug misinformation by the manufacturers. At the same time, self-reliance in health and the role of families in health care are being slowly eroded.

Finally it must be stressed that these effects are by no means confined to India. In the first 1985 issue of the *Ecologist* such examples of misguided 'development' from Malaysia, Africa and South America, as well as India, are meticulously documented. In the magazine's editorial, Edward Goldsmith accuses the World Bank and the United Nations Food and Agriculture Organisation of 'creating the present escalation of human misery, malnutrition and famine in the Third World' and 'financing the destruction of the tropical world, the devastation of its remaining forests, the extermination of its wildlife [and] the impoverishment and starvation of its human inhabitants'.[30]

Perhaps even more significant than the accusation itself is the fact that, coming under pressure also from the US National Resource Defense Council, the World Bank was unable to shrug it off. A series of substantive congressional hearings in Washington followed, which led directly to the suspension of the loans for two of the most destructive projects. Whether this will actually lead to a change in World Bank policy and a much-needed redefinition of 'development' by that institution remains to be seen.

INDICATORS OF NO REAL MEANING

Given the erroneous assumptions underlying growth economics, it is not surprising that the indicators by which conventional economics measures 'progress' are, at best, limited, and, at worst, downright misleading. Most important among such indicators is the Gross National Product or GNP.

John Lintott (TOES, 1985) has pointed out that GNP was not, in fact, intended to be a measure of economic welfare. It was part of the national accounting system developed in the 1930s at a time when Keynesians were gaining the ascendant in economic management. 'For Keynesians', Lintott says, 'the object of the accounts was not to measure economic welfare but to measure aggregate demand', which is, of course, the key component in Keynesian economic thinking. However, whatever its genesis, growth economists soon came to regard GNP as an overall indicator of economic welfare, and it is almost universally so used today.

The error in using it thus can best be illustrated by asking various questions that should be put to any framework of indicators to elucidate the assumptions that underlie it:

What is measured? GNP measures all the goods and services which are provided through the market or through government expenditure.

- How is it measured? By aggregating all monetary expenditure.
- Who is it measured by? Information is collated from various sources and aggregated by the state.
- What for? Originally to measure aggregate demand, to provide a basis for Keynesian management of the economy.
- What significance is attached to it? While it is used as an aid to Keynesian management, its widest, most influential use, especially by politicians, is as an indicator of economic welfare, whereby growth in GNP is 'good', zero growth is 'bad' and negative growth is 'very bad'.
- What assumptions underlie such use?

    1 Any significant economic activity is monetary economic activity;
    2 the growthist assumptions discussed earlier: all GNP growth is good; the environment can sustain indefinite growth; growth is the panacea for most, if not all, economic problems.

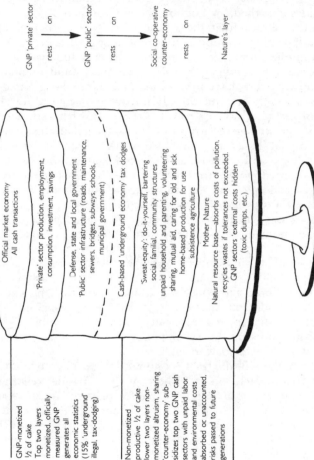

GNP 'private' sector

rests on →

GNP 'public' sector

rests on →

Social co-operative counter-economy

rests on →

Nature's layer

Official market economy
All cash transactions

'Private' sector production, employment, consumption, investment, savings

Defense, state and local government
'Public' sector infrastructure (roads, maintenance, sewers, bridges, subways, schools, municipal government)

Cash-based 'underground economy' tax dodges

'Sweat-equity': do-it-yourself, bartering social, familial, community structures unpaid household and parenting, volunteering sharing, mutual aid, caring for old and sick home-based production for use subsistence agriculture

Mother Nature
Natural resource base—absorbs costs of pollution, recycles wastes if tolerances not exceeded. GNP sectors 'external' costs hidden (toxic dumps, etc.)

GNP-monetized
½ of cake
Top two layers monetized, officially measured GNP generates all economic statistics (15% 'underground' illegal, tax-dodging)

Non-monetized productive ½ of cake lower two layers non-monetized altruism, sharing 'counter-economy' subsidizes top two GNP cash sectors with unpaid labor and environmental costs absorbed or unaccounted, risks passed to future generations

Figure 1.1 Total productive system of an industrial society (Three-layer cake with icing)
Copyright © 1982 Hazel Henderson

The growthist assumptions have already been challenged. With regard to assumption 1, Hazel Henderson (TOES, 1985) has given diagrammatic illustration of the true relation of the 'GNP-monetised' part of the national cake to the non-monetised part of it (Figure 1.1). GNP ignores or discounts everything in this diagram below the dotted line, including the 'underground' or 'black' economy, the 'social co-operative counter economy' and all the externalities absorbed, or not, by the environment.

We must be clear that these ignored sectors do not comprise some peripheral economic activity of marginal worth. As the diagram implies, together they provide the very foundation for all formal economic activity. Probably their very fundamentality is the reason why they have for so long been taken for granted, but it is clear that those who do so end up with a very unreliable picture of reality. Paul Sparrow (TOES, 1985) has estimated the worth of the human contribution to the part of the economy ignored by GNP: all the unvalued work which underpins the world of 'jobs' and employment. After Handy, 1984, he divides this unaccounted work into three sectors – the black economy, the voluntary economy, and the domestic or household economy – and adds a fourth, informal work exchange.

These sectors will be analysed in greater detail in Parts II and III. For the moment we need only note that Sparrow's calculations put the value of informal production at about 60% of GNP. The figure is quoted only for the broadest comparative purposes, because it is highly problematic to seek to give a cash value to informal economic activity, for reasons which will be explored later. But it is clear at the very least that the informal economy, compared to the formal economy, receives nothing like the attention in economic theory or policy that its size and extensive practice would seem to warrant.

These two parts of the total economy do not, of course, exist in isolation from each other. There is a dynamic relationship between them and it is quite possible for one part to grow at the expense of the other. In particular it is possible to take into the formal economic sector work that was previously unvalued, resulting in growth in GNP, although the goods and services actually produced may not have changed at all.

Consider in this light the great increase in the number of married women with jobs, who previously did domestic work in the non-monetary economy. GNP will rise both by the wages of the jobs they now do *and* by their extra expenditure on labour-saving devices, fast food, child care, and any other goods and services which they were wont to provide for themselves and their families free of charge. Yet the real increase in goods and services is measured by the difference between these quantities, rather than by their sum. The net change in welfare is even more difficult to compute. It will certainly not be reliably indicated by the sum of the extra wages and bought in goods and services. As far as the families are concerned, there may even be loss of welfare, if maternal care and home cooking are replaced by creches and take-aways. Clearly the interaction between GNP and the informal economy is crucial to consideration as to whether a society has actually benefited from growth.

Three points which have already been made about growth in general can briefly be recapitulated with regard to GNP. Firstly, increase in GNP by itself gives no indication of the sustainability of growth. If today's extra consumption is in fact undermining the natural resource base on which tomorrow's production depends, or storing up health problems through environmental degradation, then its contribution to welfare is dubious, to say the least.

Secondly, GNP only measures aggregate production, with no differentiation between who is doing the consuming or what is being consumed. Thus it is possible that, within or between nations, maldistribution of resources might result in a growth in GNP being predominantly caused by an increase in luxury consumption, while poor people actually become worse off. Within nations, GNP as a national aggregate statistic gives no idea of the health or otherwise of regional or local economies.

Thirdly, and very importantly, GNP takes no account of the costs of industrial production. If such costs are non-monetary, they are simply ignored; if they are monetary they are actually added in to GNP and accounted benefits. Thus it is quite possible that growth in GNP, far from representing greater human welfare, is actually an expression of greater social costs. As Hazel Henderson has put it:

> The social costs of a polluted environment, disrupted
> communities, disrupted family life, and eroded primary
> relationships may be the only part of GNP that is growing. We
> are so confused that we add these social costs (where monetary)
> into the GNP as if they were real, useful products. We have no
> idea whether we are going forward or backward, or how much
> of the GNP is social costs and how much of it is useful
> production that we intended (Henderson, 1981, p.12).

This dissatisfaction with GNP, though it may be coming to a head, is by no means a new phenomenon, as Hazel Henderson explains (TOES, 1985):

New indicators are proliferating to challenge GNP. Many of these new indicators were developed in the 1960s, and began deducting some of the social costs of urbanisation, congestion, crime, traffic delays, etc., from 'gross' GNP, thus arriving at slightly more sober assessments which drew attention to the 'bads' as well as the 'goods' of industrialisation. They included the Measure of Economic Welfare, proposed by William Nordhaus and James Tobin, 1971.[31] Japan's Net National Welfare (Japan Economic Council, 1973) also deducts some kinds of environmental damage and depletion of the Earth's natural 'capital'.

The debate was joined by such development economists as Irma Adelman and Cynthia Taft Morris (1973) and others, who focused on the propensity for income disparities to increase right along with GNP in developing countries, leading to the now familiar widening gap between rich and poor, both within and between nations. Such debates and new indicators were fostered by the more fundamental and encompassing works of Barbara Ward (1966) and her study of the economics of *Spaceship Earth* and similar paradigm-shifting efforts by Kenneth Boulding in *Beyond Economics* (1968) and the work of Sweden's Gunnar and Alva Myrdal[32] to name a few. David Morris of the Overseas Development Council (1980) joined in with the Physical Quality of Life Indicator (PQLI), which shifted attention to new measures of success in maintaining the quality of life in livable environments, housing, health care, education, as well as money-denominated income. During the same period the United Nations Environment Programme developed the Basic Human Needs (BHN) indicator (McHale, 1979), which shifted attention towards measuring how these broader indicators of quality of life affected all income groups, and particularly focused on measuring the success of a nation's economic policy by how well it met the basic human needs of its poorest citizens.

Further fundamental premises need to be addressed relating to the globalisation of economic patterns and whether the underlying logic of 'comparative advantage' can continue, based on global economic competition for markets, technology, capital, human and natural resources. Clearly it cannot, since it leads to unacceptable social and environmental costs and seems to be a war-prone system of winners and losers that becomes more horrifying with each day's news headlines. Obsolescent indicators still buttress this dying logic of national economic competition, even while covert protectionism is rampant everywhere. Understandably, politicians can no longer manage their domestic affairs in today's roller-coaster, global economy, since most of the variables are beyond their national boundaries, and the best-laid domestic investment and technological strategies can be upset each morning when the currency exchange markets open.

The last play of this globally-disordering system is currently facilitated by the hypnotic focus of economics on money. Today, as I have detailed elsewhere (Henderson, 1981, pp.40–2), money is fast losing all meaning as a measuring system for real-world production and value. Manipulated by politicians and central banks and now speeded up by electronic funds transfers in a multi-national banking system, and abstracted by global, 24-hour asset management, money bears little relationship to reality. Smart investors everywhere know that it is easier to 'make' money by speculating, arbitraging currency, playing interest-rate differentials and other forms of paper entrepreneurship, than to invest in a real factory employing real workers and producing real products anywhere in the real world.

Several of the alternative indicators to GNP have made inroads into purist GNP thinking. Indicators of health and other basic human needs, for example, are now widely used in development circles. But, overall, GNP still reigns supreme and, with hindsight, it is possible to see flaws in some earlier efforts, which have militated against their acceptance: excessive aggregation; the search for a single alternative to GNP; and conceptual confusion, both as to the purpose of the indicator and as to what was being measured. The approach taken in Part II, Chapter 6, seeks to build on earlier efforts and to avoid some of the pitfalls they revealed. As Henderson says (TOES, 1985):

> The acceptance of such indices could in itself be an indicator of the restoration of mental health to the human species as well as to the biosphere. We must never forget that, in the most scientific sense, *reality is what we pay attention to*. Indicators only reflect our innermost core values and goals, measuring the development of our own understanding.

That brings the first, shortest part of this book to a close. Clearly it is not a comprehensive review of the world economic scene, and much of the analysis is deepened and refined in Parts II and III. Part I will have served its purpose if it has highlighted some of the chief shortcomings of conventional economics and given a preliminary indication as to the approach that will be taken to remedy these. Before proceeding, it might be worth summarising the thrust of the argument so far.

At the root of the trouble in the advanced industrial economies is an obsession with economic growth. This has resulted in a serious misallocation of resoures, in the sense that labour is much underemployed, the natural environment is greatly over-stressed and there is some evidence of capital shortage. As far as unemployment is concerned, official figures seriously understate the problem, and there must be grave concern about the continuing ability to fund transfer payments at present levels if the numbers go on rising. Moreover, there is no sign of adequate job-creating potential in the formal economy as it is currently structured. Continuing pursuit of indiscriminate economic growth will only make these matters worse.

The pursuit of growth in industrialised countries has been linked to a model of Western industrial development, which has been applied in most countries and all continents. Even in its heyday, many of the poorest people in developing countries failed to benefit from the process. Now, after some years of recession, it is clear that only a handful of developing countries round the world have really taken off industrially, many of those that have tried are burdened with unserviceable levels of debt, the number of people in absolute poverty has risen and the global environment has taken a hammering that threatens the foundations of the biosphere.

With their money-based indicators and targets, oriented almost exclusively towards the formal economy, economists have consistently misread the situation and many of their prescriptions and remedies have actually caused it to deteriorate. Among other failings, these indicators are inclined to confuse costs and benefits, leave social and environmental factors out of account, and ignore the informal economy altogether as a source of work and wealth.

It is an awesome catalogue of failure and misconception, which the development of the new economic theory that follows seeks to remedy.

NOTES

1   Several recent studies have indicated that the capital/output ratio for some industrialised countries has been rising since the early 1970s, including Bailey, 1981, 1982; Bosworth, 1982; Cooper and Clark, 1982; Glyn, 1982; Rostow, 1980; Sargent, 1982. It is too early to tell, however, whether or not this is the beginning of a long-term trend. This uncertainty is compounded by the difficulty of aggregating physical capital.

2   For a brilliant analysis of the relevance of the entropy law to economics, see Georgescu-Roegen, 1971, and also Daly, 1977 and 1979.

3   The 'World Development Report, 1983' (World Bank, 1983) has an extensive statistical annex of world development indicators for 125 countries.

4   See Frances Williams, 'UK moves towards dual labour market', *Daily Telegraph*, 27 August 1985, and Morehouse and Dembo, 1984.

5   UN Secretary-General's address to the Council of the Americas, New York, 24 February 1983.

6   The Cocoyoc Declaration was adopted by the Joint UNCTAD/UN Environment Seminar on 'Patterns of resource use, environment and development strategies', Mexico, 1974.

7   Charter of Economic Rights and Duties of States, UN General Assembly Resolution 3281 (XXIX) of 12 December 1974.

8   Latin America Bureau, *The Poverty Brokers: the IMF and Latin America*, London, 1983. Other estimates published at different times put the additional burden for each interest rate point at $2 to $5 billion.

9   Figure given by Tom Clausen, President of the World Bank, at a European Management Forum, Switzerland, January 1984.

10   'The Bretton Woods World' in *Britannica Perspectives, II*, p.340, cited by Alejandor A. Lichauco in 'The international economic order and the Philippine experience', in Vivencio R. Jose (ed.), *Mortgaging the Future: the World Bank, the IMF and the Philippines*, Foundation for Nationalist Studies, Quezon City, Philippines, 1982.

11   David Ricardo, 'On the principles of political economy and taxation', in Piero Straffa (ed.), *Works and Correspondence of David Ricardo*, Cambridge, 1962, vol.1, p.132.

12   Lichauco, op. cit., p.15.

13   Hearings before the Sub-committee of the International Finance and Monetary Policy of the Committee on Banking, Housing and Urban Affairs, United States Senate, 98th Congress, 14 February 1983; cited in Richard Gerster, '40e Anniversaire de Bretton Woods: Le Fonds Monétaire International face à l'Evolution de l'Economic Mondiale' in I3M (Service d'Information Tiers Monde) *Le Fonds Monétaire International et le Tiers Monde*, Dossier no.15, Lausanne, 1984.

14   Claude Julien, 'L'empire du dollar', *Le Monde Diplomatique*, February 1985.

15   Some other solutions are listed in 'The US feels the backlash' in *South*, August 1984, p.19.

16   The figures are from *Technology*, 7 November 1983.

17   L. Freedman, *Arms Production in the United Kingdom: Problems and Perspectives*, RIIA, 1978.

18   *Business Week*, 22 October 1984.

19   I. Maddock, *Civil Exploitation of Defence Technology*, National

Economic Development Office, 1983.
20 B. Russet and D. Sylvan, 'The effects of arms transfers on developing countries'. Study for UN group of government experts on: 'Relations Between Disarmament and the Arms Trade' (A/36/356).
21 Stockholm International Peace Research Institute (SIPRI), *World Armaments and Disarmament*, 1980, p.87 and *Business Week*, op. cit.
22 Programme notes to Channel 4 TV documentary, *Arms Bizarre*, first shown 13 December 1983.
23 UN Secretary-General's Report on the relationship between disarmament and development, quoted in his Statement to the Opening Meeting of the UN Assembly's Special Session on Disarmament, 7 June 1982.
24 C. Gopalan, *Nutrition and Health Care Problems and Policies*, Nutrition Foundation of India, New Delhi, 1985, p.28.
25 J. Bandopadhyaya *et al.*, *Ecological Audit of Eucalyptus Cultivation*, The English Book Dept., Dehradun, 1985.
26 Vanaja Ramprasad and S.T.S. Reddy, 'Eucalyptus impact on nutrition project' in *Conflicts over Natural Resources*, United Nations University, 1985.
27 Nalini Jayal, 'Destruction of water resources – the most critical ecological crisis of East Asia'. Paper presented to IUCN (International Union for Conservation of Nature and Natural Resources) meeting, Madrid, 1984.
28 J. Bandopadhyaya, 'The Doon Valley eco-system'. A report for the Department of the Environment, 1983.
29 'Pesticides or biocides? Pesticides problems in India'. Paper compiled by the Pesticides Working Group, Kalpavriksha Environmental Action Group, New Delhi, 1985.
30 Goldsmith, E., 'Open letter to Mr. Clausen, President of the World Bank', *The Ecologist*, vol. 15, no.1/2, 1985.
31 See J. Lintott (TOES, 1985) for a critical analysis of Nordhaus and Tobin's Net National Welfare and other work in this area.
32 See, for example, Myrdal, 1973.

PART TWO

Putting people first

1 A FRAMEWORK FOR THE FUTURE

The purpose of this part of this book is to define the theoretical framework of the New Economics as it has so far been developed through the work of The Other Economic Summit. This framework is not yet a fully elaborated economic system, but its prime concepts and concerns are now quite clear and many of them have been defined in some detail. The paper in this chapter outlines many of the most important new ideas, some of which are then taken up and explored in more detail in later chapters. Some of the analysis from Part I is also further developed where appropriate.

The aim of the New Economics, as of conventional economics, is to facilitate economic development. The difference derives from its interpretation of the word 'development', which, to differentiate it from the present paradigm, is sometimes called 'Another Development'.

It is now a full decade since the Dag Hammarskjöld Foundation first coined the term 'Another Development' with the publication of its report *What Now: Another Development* (Dag Hammarskjöld Foundation, 1975), which asked fundamental questions about the viability of then prevailing models of world development and put forward a radically different approach. In particular, the report emphasised the difference between Another Development and primarily Western models of growth, industrialisation and the transfer of technology and culture from North to South.

Unfortunately the juggernaut of conventional development was at that time hurtling unstoppably down its preordained path, resulting in the intervening decade, as we have seen, in chronic unemployment and inflation in the North, mountainous international debt, unalleviated and absolute poverty for 800 million of the world's people, with half that number actually on the edge of starvation, and a whole continent, Africa, in the first stages of 'environmental bankruptcy' (Timberlake, 1985).

Much has been written about Another Development since 1975[1] and its basic principles are well understood. They were well expressed in *Another Development: Approaches and Strategies* (Dag Hammarskjöld Foundation, 1977):

Another Development would be:

- Need-oriented, that is, being geared to meeting human needs, both material and non-material. It begins with the satisfaction of the basic needs of those, dominated and exploited, who constitute the majority of the world's inhabitants, and ensures at the same time the humanisation of all human beings by the satisfaction of their needs for expression, creativity, equality, and conviviality and to understand and master their own destiny.
- Endogenous, that is, stemming from the heart of each society, which defines in sovereignty its values and the vision of its future. Since development is not a linear process, there could be no universal model, and only the plurality of development patterns can answer to the specificity of each situation.
- Self-reliant, that is, implying that each society relies primarily on its own strength and resources in terms of its members' energies and its natural and cultural environment. Self-reliance clearly needs to be exercised at national and international (collective self-reliance) levels, but it acquires its full meaning only if rooted at local level, in the praxis of each community.
- Ecologically sound, that is, utilising rationally the resources of the biosphere in full awareness of the potential of local ecosystems as well as the global and local outer limits imposed on the present and future generations. It implies the equitable access to resources by all as well as careful, socially relevant technologies.
- Based on structural transformations; they are required, more often than not, in social relations, in economic activities and in their spatial distribution, as well as in the power-structure, so as to recognise the conditions of self-management and participation in decision-making by all those affected by it, from the rural or urban community to the world as a whole, without which the above goals could not be achieved.

These five points are organically linked. Taken in isolation from each other, they would not bring about the desired result. For development is seen as a whole, as an integral, cultural process, as the development of every man and woman and the whole of man and woman. Another Development means liberation.

A remarkable fact underlying these basic principles of Another Development is that they are as valid for the industrial countries as for the Third World. The actual policies and technologies used to enact the principles will differ from country to country, to be sure, but the aims of the development process in each case are the same and will result in a convergence of development patterns, in terms of material living standards at least, rather than a divergence as at present. Whether North, South, East or West, the New Economics embodied in Another Development defines the way forward for us all.

'HUMAN-SCALE ECONOMICS: THE CHALLENGES AHEAD'
by Manfred Max-Neef

Three decades in which a technocratic, mechanistic and top-down development paradigm has been predominant have produced a kind of global crisis that has no precedent in history.

In almost any Third World country and, increasingly, in industrialized countries as well, we may grossly divide the population into two main groups. Firstly, there are those people who are directly or indirectly linked to a 'development strategy'. Secondly, there are those people – most often the majority – who are left to design their own 'survival strategy'. The fact that both groups still coexist the world over and that, furthermore, the increase of the latter group – both in absolute and relative terms – is indisputable, should be proof enough that the mechanistic possibilities of the so-called 'trickle-down effect' originally attributed to global development models, did not work.

The accumulated experience and frustrations have allowed for an alternative development paradigm to surface, which is generally identified as the 'bottom-up' approach. Although it is much older than the prevailing 'top-down' model, it has only in recent years gained sufficient 'respectability' to become the object of increasing attention among experts, policy-makers and the concerned public in general. The 1975 *What Now* Dag Hammarskjöld Report, while proclaiming the urgency as well as the philosophy for Another Development, was a decisive step in raising public and specialist consciousness with respect to the need to unleash new processes where the overriding goals of development and equity might truly converge.

Another Development as a process still needs much theoretical and practical consolidation. We know its principal components, but we still do not know how they should inter-relate for the whole to function harmoniously. A return to the human scale, active and creative public participation, satisfaction of fundamental human needs, ecological constraints, local self-reliance, are some of its basic goals. Size of systems (or critical systems size) and efficiency as a quality (not quantity) are two of its parameters. Bypassing of centralized power and authority, bureaucratic structures, mechanistic models and other technocratic instrumentalities are corner-stones of its philosophico-political foundations. All the pieces seem to be there. The grand question is how to put them all together.

Basic ideas, hypotheses and intuitions

A systematization related to the paradigm of Another Development should incorporate consideration of the following components:

    a) the question of macro–micro articulation;
    b) the invisible sector;
    c) the concept of human needs as a system;
    d) a reinterpretation of the concept of poverty;
    e) the problem of critical systems size;
    f) the aim of self-reliance;
    g) ecological constraints; and
    h) the question of indicators.

(a) Micro-macro articulation

The new paradigm is complex. Hence, no fixed rules or recipes can be applied universally. One should, however, start by keeping in mind the existence of the principle of contradiction. This principle may be stated in the following terms: *Any actions intended to improve something have at least one negative consequence.*[2]

Many examples can be given to show the validity of the principle. A trivial example may illustrate the idea. Let us consider a transportation system in terms of three parameters: size of the vehicles, comfort of the passengers and economy of the system. Given the size parameter, if we want to improve the comfort of the passengers, the economy of the system will deteriorate. If we want to improve the economy of the system, it will have to be at the expense of the passengers' comfort, since the vehicles will have to be more crowded. Both parameters cannot be improved simultaneously. Another example may be a housing project for marginal urban dwellers which, while locally solving a problem, will most probably accelerate the flux of rural-urban migration, thus worsening the housing problem as a whole.

Since Another Development starts at the base of society – that is, at the micro-level – the principle of contradiction will show its effects much more strongly to local development promoters than it would to national planners at the macro level. This is for the simple reason that negative effects can hardly be hidden at the local level, while they can be obscured or overlooked altogether at the macro level due to the use of abstract aggregated indicators.

The existence of the contradiction principle is determinant for the strategy of Another Development. In fact, as shall be shown later, it reinforces the idea of *collective self-reliance*, which is that actions cannot be locally isolated, but must necessarily complement each other. The effects of the principle of contradiction may be controlled (even if only partially) through the application, as a strategy, of the principle of complementarity, which may be stated thus: *Any actions intended to improve something somewhere, require at least one additional action somewhere else.*

The principle of complementarity must work both horizontally and vertically. A clear example of required horizontal complementarity is the example of the housing project mentioned earlier, where additional actions are required in that place where the migratory flux originates. The importance of vertical complementarity is contained in the arguments that follow.

One of the most important manifestations of the principle of contradiction may be found in the apparent micro-macro disarticulation brought about by the economistic development model. It is certainly astounding that, despite many cases of impressive GNP growth in Third World countries over the last decades (excluding the last few years of generalized crisis), poverty has increased dramatically, both in absolute and relative terms. In other words, while the macro processes seemed to improve, the conditions at the micro level constantly deteriorated, in most cases. The investigation and resolution of this paradox is of prime importance.

Despite the difficulties involved, since the experiences of many groups working at regional and local levels will have to be systematized, some description can be advanced with respect to how the problem may be tackled. Three scales (or three spaces) coexist in a form of dialectical struggle with one another: the local, the regional and the national scales. In most cases what we find is the national scale imposing its own development style, as well as its rhythm, upon the other scales, thus provoking disequilibriums and disarticulations. Hence, what is required is to design a system whereby what we call an 'Optimization of Scales' can be achieved.

The Optimization of Scales implies two basic principles. One is of a strategic nature, and has already been stressed in writings and documents about Another Development. It is the principle that whatever can potentially be solved at the local level, is what must be solved at the local level; the same holding for the other scales. The second principle has to do with synchronization of what we identify as the 'Socio-Rhythms'. That is, that the dynamics of each scale are determined by different rhythms. How these different rhythms can be brought to generate a harmonious whole must be investigated by confronting the observed experiences of groups and experts who have worked at the different scales. Sufficient information exists, although dispersed, so that a systematization of it may allow for what we consider to be a major breakthrough.

(b) The invisible sector

The sheer size of the so-called 'invisible' informal sector, especially in poor countries, makes it so important that excluding it from discussions about a nation's economy or living standards will give us a totally inadequate and misleading image of reality. We have little information about the size, variety and extension of the informal economy in Third World countries. In Sweden, time budget studies have shown that the working time in the formal economy, private and public sectors, amounts to 6 billion hours per year. The volume of work in the so-called 'white' economy, which only includes house-work (cooking, cleaning, washing), shopping, work with children, upkeeping, travel and a miscellaneous category, amounts to almost 7 billion hours per year. If such is the proportion in a country like Sweden, we should not be surprised if in many poor countries the size of the informal economy, which goes far beyond the 'white' economy, might be twice or three times that of the formal economy. Therefore, if we exclude such a voluminous sector from economic analysis, we shall only produce economic policies and development plans based on pure fiction.

Now, what is really disturbing is that the reason behind the exclusion of the informal sector from conventional economic analysis is not because it is considered to be unimportant, but because economists have not been able to agree on how to assign economic value to work carried out outside the formal market (or monetary) system. This is quite ludicrous. It confirms once again that we have become conditioned to accept economic theories which, instead of being capable of evaluating what is truly important and significant, grant only importance and significance to that which can be measured according to the existing rules of value.

(c) The concept of human needs
The concept of 'basic needs', as currently used, does not necessarily represent a way of breaking with the traditional paradigm of economic growth. Despite its widespread use, it still conceals vagueness and ambiguities. In fact, a prevalent short-coming in the existing literature and discussions about 'basic needs', or human needs in general, is that the fundamental difference between needs and satisfiers is either not made explicit or is overlooked altogether. As will be shown, this simple failure may be turning the entire venture of reorienting development efforts towards the satisfaction of human needs into no more than a cosmetic improvement of the economistic view of development.

It is here suggested that human needs must, first of all, be understood as a system: that is, all human needs are interrelated and interact. If we separate them into two broad categories of needs – needs of having and needs of being – we suggest the following system (similar to the one proposed by Mallman of the Bariloche Foundation, Argentina) composed of nine fundamental human needs: permanence (or subsistence), protection, affection, understanding, participation, leisure, creation, identity (or meaning) and freedom.

From such a classification (which can of course be further disaggregated) it follows, for example, that housing, food, income are not to be considered as needs, but as satisfiers of the fundamental need of permanence (or subsistence). By the same token, education is a satisfier of the need of understanding. Defense, cure and prevention are satisfiers of the need of protection, and so on.

This proposed differentiation is not arbitrary. On the contrary, it allows for relevant hypotheses, of which two basic ones may be pointed out. First: *fundamental human needs are finite, few and classifiable.* Second: *fundamental human needs are the same in all cultures and all historical periods. What changes, both over time and through cultures, is the form or the means by which these needs are satisfied.* Each economic, social and political system adopts different styles for the satisfaction of the same fundamental human needs. In every system they are satisfied, or not, through the generation, or non generation, of different types of satisfiers. We may go as far as to say that one of the aspects that defines a culture is its choice of satisfiers. Whether a person belongs to a consumerist or to an ascetic society, her fundamental human needs are the same. What changes is her choice of quantity and quality of satisfiers. Cultural change is – among other things – the consequence of dropping traditional satisfiers and adopting new or different ones.

Participation and freedom have a dual nature: in addition to being needs, *participation is a process and freedom is a condition* for the adequate satisfaction of the entire human needs system.

The concept of human needs described here represents a departure from the traditional strategy of 'basic needs' satisfaction. It is incompatible with the economic growth paradigm and coherent with the paradigm of Another Development. It must be stressed, however, that the proposed system must not be interpreted as a static approach to the question of human needs. In fact, each need can be satisfied at different and changing levels. Furthermore, each need can be satisfied intrahumanly, inter-humanly and extra-humanly; that is, in relation with oneself, in relation to others and in relation to the environment.

(d) The concept of poverty

The traditional concept of poverty is limited and restricted, since it exclusively refers to the predicaments of people who may be classified below a certain income threshold, again a strictly economistic concept. If, on the other hand, our system of fundamental human needs is taken as a reference, one should speak not of poverty, but of poverties. In fact, any fundamental human need that is not satisfied reveals a poverty: poverty of subsistence is due to insufficient income, food, shelter, etc.; poverty of protection is due to violence, the arms race, and so on; that of affection is due to authoritarianism, oppression and exploitative relations with the natural environment; of understanding, to bad quality of education; of participation, to marginalization and discrimination against women, children and minorities; of identity, to imposition of alien values upon local and regional cultures, forced migration, political exile, etc.; and so on. Through the widening of the concept it may be concluded that poverties affect both 'poor and 'rich' countries. This is important, because Another Development has been conceived as an alternative to fight all poverties and not just economic poverty.

Poverties interpreted in relation to human needs implies the opposite as well: the recognition of forms of wealth in relation to human needs. This is important because every human group is affected simultaneously by forms of poverty and of wealth. A methodology based on the proposed alternative interpretation of poverty can have applicability in programmes to improve the quality of life of marginal groups. It is the author's experience that a dynamic process of change can be brought about at the local level not only by designing from the start solutions for the problems of poverty, but often more effectively by stimulating first the elements of wealth. This will enhance people's self-confidence, which is a prerequisite for stimulating imagination and the will to tackle the existing poverties.

It can be observed that poverties affecting one or several human needs can generate what may be called a 'needs trade-off'. That is, when one need is clearly undersatisfied, the system as a whole tries to regain some form of balance by satisfying other needs at a different level. For example, in groups that are very poor in terms of subsistence, solidarity and mutual help may increase the sensation of protection, affection and participation. It is such trade-offs that must be detected since, in that manner, a process of change can be brought about in an organic and coherent way.

(e) Critical systems size

It is assumed that the size of systems within which people act and interact directly affects their possibilities of adequately satisfying certain of their fundamental human needs. Participation and identity are cases in point. Whenever a system (city, enterprise) grows beyond its critical size, the people involved may become (at best) 'efficient objects', at the expense of losing their possibilities of acting as 'creative subjects'. Another Development, being oriented on the satisfaction of human needs, requires a drastic revision of the concept of efficiency. The efficiency of a system should not be measured only in terms of its economic productivity (cost/benefit or capital/output ratios), but also, and more importantly, in terms of its ability to contribute to the satisfaction of the fundamental human needs of those who are, directly or indirectly, affected by that system.

Such an analysis may lead, for instance, to the conclusion that it may be both sensible and advisable to strive for the coexistence of several regional development styles within one country, instead of insisting on the prevalence of one national style, which has proven so far to be efficient for the enrichment of some regions at the expense of the depletion of others. 'National styles' are mostly conceived for the purpose of advancing or maintaining national unity. But unity does not mean uniformity. There may be a stronger basis for real unity when a multiformity of cultural potentials is allowed to flourish freely and creatively, having been given the opportunities, the technical support and the stimulus to do so.

(f) The aim of self-reliance

Self-reliance is a basic pillar of Another Development. However, the concept is often misunderstood. It does not mean autonomy or self-sufficiency, although either of these states may occasionally develop from it. It suggests a regeneration or revitalization through one's own efforts, capabilities and resources. Strategically it means that what can be produced (or what can be solved) at local levels should be produced (or should be solved) at local levels. The same principle holds for regional and national levels.

Self-reliance changes the way in which people are enabled to perceive their own potentials and capabilities, which have often been, or still are, self-depreciated as a consequence of the dominant center-periphery relations. The reduction of economic dependency, one of the aims of self-reliant development, is not intended to be a substitute for trade and exchange *per se*. There are always goods or services that cannot be generated or provided locally, regionally or nationally. Hence, self-reliance must necessarily achieve a collective nature. It must turn into a process of interdependence among equal partners as a means for solidarity to prevail over blind competition.

As opposed to the traditional paradigm, mainly concerned with the generation of material satisfiers (without much equity in ther distribution), self-reliant development allows for a more complete and harmonious satisfaction of the entire system of fundamental human needs. It does not generate satisfiers only for the needs of having, but for the needs of being as well. Through the reduction of economic dependency, subsistence is better protected, inasmuch as economic fluctuations (recessions, depressions, etc.) do more harm where a structure of center-periphery relations prevails. It enhances, furthermore, participation and creativity. It stimulates and reinforces cultural identity by increasing self-confidence. A better understanding of productive processes and technologies is also achieved when communities manage themselves.

(g) Ecological constraints

The behaviour generated by anthropocentrism, which sets the human species above nature, is an essential part of the traditional paradigm. The economistic vision of development, through its use of aggregated indicators such as the GNP, adds – without any discrimination – as positive all processes where market transactions are involved, regardless of whether they are productive, unproductive or destructive. Indiscriminate depletion of natural resources raises the GNP, as does a sick population which increases its consumption of pharmaceutical drugs and hospital services. Similarly, self-construction with local building materials is 'economically' less attractive than building with centrally mass-produced components and materials regardless of whether they are suited to climatic or other local characteristics.

Since Another Development is primarily concerned with the satisfaction of human needs of both present and future generations, it fosters an ecologically-sound concept of development. This implies, among other things, an effort to construct indicators capable of discriminating between what is positive and what is negative for a process of truly humanized development that can guarantee the availability of basic resources in the long run.

Traditional indicators are highly misleading. A dramatic example is that of the American farming system. Highly mechanized and dependent on petroleum, it is one of the least efficient systems in the world if measured in terms of the amounts of energy used for a given output of calories. On the other hand, if measured in monetary terms it generates huge profits and hence contributes to the growth of GNP. Such examples are valid also for Third World countries that have adapted to the conventional mode of 'development. In Mexico, according to information provided by the Xochically Foundation, it is estimated that about 19,000 k/cal are used up in order to put 2,200 k/cal of food on the table. The amount of energy spent in transportation of food products alone is in Mexico almost equal to the total energy required by the primary sector for the production of food products That such situations are accounted for as being positive is a conceptual aberration.

(h)   The question of indicators
The image we have of development is the image provided by its indicators. If these are inadequate, not only will our perception be distorted, but policies and actions will be counterproductive. As a reaction to the many distortions and poor results that have become evident during recent decades, the United Nations University set up the GPID Project (see note 2). Its contributions have been valuable and important and have allowed us to clarify many questions that remained elusive. However, certain aspects, especially those related to the micro level and to the lack of micro-macro articulation, have not yet been investigated.

The reality and problems of the micro level indicators cannot be interpreted merely as those of the macro level on a smaller scale. Therefore indicators for the local scale cannot be adapted from the macro indicators. They must be of an entirely different nature, capable of indicating degrees of human satisfaction and of human poverties; contradictions and complementarities; degrees of attainable and achieved self-reliance; processes that may work or break down given the size and structures of the local spaces and systems. In addition, the required indicators must serve to evaluate and assign value even to those human activities where no market transactions and monetary fluxes are involved. In short, we require indicators that tell us what happens in those sectors that are 'invisible' because they are excluded by orthodox indicators.

It is important to overcome some fads concerning development indicators. One is what might be called the 'scientific respectability' of the indicator. In this respect the economistic tradition – especially through the influence of econometrics – has imposed the convention that only cardinal indicators can be taken seriously, ordinal indicators or scales being regarded with suspicion. An increase of 12% in the yields of an agricultural product, or an improvement of the capital/output ratio of a certain productive activity, are accepted indicators of positive development. Whether the people who are an active part of the process are better or worse off after the cardinal goals have been achieved is seen as irrelevant. Such an attitude is very strange indeed, once we accept that development is about people and not about objects.

It is not suggested that cardinal indicators should be replaced by ordinal indicators. What is required is complementarity. Cardinal indicators are valid so long as they relate to human development or if they are complemented with other relevant indicators. Development at the human scale is development where human beings are. No abstraction is possible at the human scale. Indicators must, therefore, respond to this constraint. To produce such indicators – which may in addition be understood and handled by the communities themselves – is another fundamental purpose of an alternative paradigm, while bearing in mind that the aim is not simply a proliferation of indicators, because a large number of indicators can add up to a bad indicator.

NOTES

1 Among others, the Dag Hammarskjöld Foundation publishes a regular *Development Dialogue*, while the International Foundation for Development Alternatives publishes a bi-monthly *IFDA Dossier*.
2 This principle was well described and developed by the Rumanian team of the 'Goals, Processes and Indicators of Development' (GPID) Project of the United Nations University.

2 A QUESTION OF NEEDS

The question of human needs is of absolutely central significance to the New Economics. Indeed, the satisfaction of the whole range of human needs is often given as its chief priority. Certainly one of the starkest and most obvious paradoxes inherent in our present economic system is the co-existence of great affluence and great deprivation, both within the societies of the industrial nations and in the world economy as a whole. In many ways it seems that the problem of production has been solved. There is widespread agreement that the capacity adequately to feed, clothe and house everybody world-wide now exists, yet absolute material poverty still exists on a large scale even in the wealthiest countries. The economic system seems to be incapable of deploying its technical, human and financial resources to meet these deprivations. Human needs are overruled in favour of the economists' 'effective demand': those who have can buy more; those who have not get charity or nothing.

Consideration of this problem takes us into the deepest regions of the human psyche, for the question of human needs is an immensely complex one, far more complicated than the mere enumeration of the needs of subsistence, as Manfred Max-Neef made clear in the previous chapter. Here the approach is to examine the issue in three different, though complementary ways, which can broadly be characterised as the psychology of human needs, the politics of human needs and the relationship between human needs and the needs of the present economic system.

Taking the last point first, it can be seen that growth economics allied to effective demand depends for success (that is, for economic growth) on the production and sale of new goods to new markets. By definition, those with effective demand, the rich of the world, are already satisfying their needs of material subsistence. If they are to spend their surplus, which they must if the economy is to grow, new goods must be produced which they must be induced to want, or, preferably, as far as economic growth is concerned, to 'need'. Thus the creation of 'need', or, using the distinction between needs and satisfiers introduced earlier by Max-Neef, the endless production of *new satisfiers* for fundamental needs, and the complementary process of creating dissatisfaction with existing satisfiers, is a vitally important motor of the growth economy.

Just as satisfiers change, so do definitions and perceptions of poverty. In this light, poverty cannot be expressed solely in terms of the lack of hard and fast physical necessities, such as so many calories of food per day. It also depends on people's ability or otherwise to participate fully in the normal life of the society in which they are living, where norms are continually changing.

A simple example illustrates these points. In 1983 London Weekend Television and the MORI market research organisation conducted a survey into the nature of poverty in Britain.[1] Their results showed that more than two-thirds of people classed as 'necessities' items which only a half-century ago would certainly have counted as luxuries, including a refrigerator and a washing-machine. More than half put television in the same category – less than fifty years after the BBC established the first regular television service in the world. Thus, in a very real sense, the 'need' for a television has been created in the years since 1936. Other such 'needs' are doubtless being created now.

It is a process that merits close scrutiny, for while there can be no dispute that the creation of such 'needs' is necessary for the economic system, it is by no means certain whether this process contributes to the overall well-being even of the consumer seeking to satisfy these new 'needs', while it certainly diverts resources from those in greatest need as far as their most basic material subsistence is concerned.

'NEEDS AND COMMODITIES'
by Jeremy Seabrook

Those who propose economic alternatives often refer to them as though the problems were mainly technical. If these can be solved, it is felt, people will see the logic and necessity for change, and everything will fall naturally into place. The truth is that this takes no account of the real relationship between the majority of the people and the existing structures; and that, far from being a technical or intellectual problem, the habits of attachment to, and the fear of loss of, what already exists are deeply emotional and irrational.

If the status quo survives relatively unscathed, it is not because of apathy, as is sometimes asserted, but because of the creation of *dependency*, which is an essential part of its project.

Fear of change and loss is not necessarily a response that gives proof of people's 'natural' conservatism. For in spite of the recession, many people have found within consumer capitalism real relief from an older poverty. This predisposes them to look upon the system as progressive; and they are the more inclined to accept its version of common sense, its logic in pursuit of ends which – unlike, perhaps, at earlier times – now look benign. The system has not been slow to take advantage of this more general public acceptance of the exigencies of capital; and it has been swift to present all its products, services and commodities, through the cleansing power of advertising and promotion, as examples of shining innocence and benevolence. This means that all the violence that occurs in their production has been suppressed. For example, the clearance of subsistence farmers for the sake of beef-ranches in Central America is scarcely of concern to those whose function it has become to buy the results of this process, when they appear in the form of succulent hamburgers, dispensed through the transparent cleanliness and honesty of some Western hamburger bar. We have been led to live a divorce between what we buy in the West and its provenance. The appearance of such a vast range of goods and services has still a quasi-miraculous quality to people lately haunted by insufficiency; it retains something of the insubstantial aspect of a mirage. And we have permitted ourselves to be persuaded that the exchange of our money for these things represents freedom: 'What the People Want' sounds like a clarion call to liberation. Indeed, it has become sacrosanct: In other words, a taboo has been created.

We have to confront this prohibition. Our much-vaunted freedom of choice does not occur in a void. If freedom of choice has any meaning, it must surely imply choosing in the full knowledge of the foreseeable consequences, implications and effects of our choices. But we have given ourselves, or have been given, permission to live them only at the point of consumption, dissociated from any of the disagreeable consequences, like children carefully shielded by those who know best from any awareness that death and disease exist in the world. And these consequences which have been severed from our choices take their toll, not only in the lives of the poorest on earth, but equally within the rich societies of the West. The most urgent purpose of any real alternative must be to demonstrate the necessity of disengagement from these processes; and in such a way that it can be shown to be not impoverishment or loss, but liberation. For we are dealing with what Rudolf Bahro has called 'the occupied regions of our consciousness' (Bahro, 1982).

In order to suggest ways in which these occluded debates may be opened, we must not flinch from examining the daily reality of our subordinate and dependent status. I'd like to look at one commodity that has recently appeared on a large scale in many metropolitan countries. It is a prohibited commodity, and its effects are the more shocking, not because it is officially banned, but because it throws an oblique, if lurid, light on the more normal processes of buying and selling, and suggests something of the uncontrollable power of 'free' markets. In recent times, there has been much concern in the poor areas of the cities, especially in London and Merseyside, about the manner in which many young people, some of them little more than children, have gained access to heroin. The passage of this forbidden substance causes such agitation because it is a metaphor, or perhaps a caricature, of the ways in which permitted commodities pass on to the market. It has been said that heroin is the perfect capitalist commodity: it illuminates the circuits of the system so starkly. First of all, it is a cash-crop which distorts the economies of the poor countries in which it is grown. It requires great entrepreneurial skills to harvest, refine and transport by smuggling. It calls forth all the powers of ingenuity and risk-taking that are so much part of the ethos by which we live. Above all, it creates its own demand because it is addictive. In other words, *it creates its own need* in a spectacular way, it is true, but one which is uncomfortably close to the fabrication of needs which underlies the dynamic of the mainstream economy. And those who are hooked on it will do anything to get the money to fulfil the need. It is outlawed because of its destructive influence; yet how akin it is to other substances, commodities, sensations that are regarded as normal and acceptable objects of selling. Not only the obvious things – those products and cash-crops that have overlaid and wrecked patterns of survival and self-sufficiency in poor countries; not only the older colonial products of tea, sugar, coffee, cocoa and the industries that depend on them; but more recent patterns of farming and ranching and implanted agriculture that turns whole countries into 'offshore production units' of Western companies, whether for strawberries, beef, cucumbers or cattle-food; also junk-food which has more to do with chemicals than nourishment, and cosmetics which have more to do with nourishment than beauty, as well as the older stimulants and pacifiers: alcohol, tobacco. There are the more recent agents too, that have been introduced to modify human mood or consciousness, to make us accept the aberrant as normal: all the tranquillisers and somnifers, which also readily spill over into the forbidden territory of solvent abuse and glue. And this is before we even begin to look at the sensations that emanate from the entertainment industry, the crazes and fashions, the addiction to TV programmes which make people rush home each night for a rendezvous with shadows; the pop culture with its fantasies and images which become a substitute for real flesh and blood, the marketing of sexuality, the talent and youth of human beings harvested like corn.

The fear of loss, the anxiety of withdrawal – these must be the objects of attention for any alternative formulation. In the metropolitan Western countries, we, the people, have allowed ourselves to become markets – we have become capitalism's own need for growth and self-expansion. Our needs have become indistinguishable from those of the system. This is what gives it such strength and tenacity. For it means that we have internalised what was forced upon us at an earlier epoch, when we were essentially machines, labour for producing wealth; we have been transformed into the machines for consuming what we once produced: we have become like the very thing which oppressed us. This is the origin of our 'dependency', and it has its equivalent in the 'dependent' economies of the poor world. Indeed, both are an aspect of the same thing. And this is where we can identify our true interests with those of the poor. It is only through this recognition that a language of liberation will be forged. Our experience, as well as the experience of those who languish in poverty and disease, is a common one. What rich and poor alike have seen is the bypassing of human need, in order to perpetuate an autonomous and self-sustaining economy that knows nothing of human things. And the famished of the earth – brandished like a spectre to cow the rich into conformity – are our true allies and not our enemies.

What we need to say is that human needs are more complex and more intractable than the apparatus that purports to answer them through money. Money and human need belong to different realms of experience. And the dynamic of advanced capitalism depends upon exploiting this eternal mismatch, this shadowy approximation which, far from answering needs, merely distorts, evades and yet, because it cannot satisfy them, merely goads them on.

At Christmas 1983, there was a dramatic example of this cruel and bizarre process. The children of the United States were seized, spontaneously, it seems, by a rage for possession of what were called Cabbage Patch dolls. (These were dolls of cloth, each one slightly different, and were sold as foundlings; each child was expected to adopt his or her doll, and to sign papers promising to cherish it; the orphaned condition of the doll is a subtle symbol of a different kind of dispossession, with which American children can no doubt readily identify.) These dolls were soon sold out; and there were images of half-crazed mothers on TV, demanding tragically before the cameras to be told what they should say to their children, now that these artefacts had ceased to be available; were they expected to tell their children that Santa Claus had run out? Now there is no doubt that these dolls reponded to real needs of children: frightening, aching absences. But that these needs were for the items in question is another matter. And so it is with so many needs; yearnings and longings and desires that occur in a dimension inaccessible to those ubiquitous and intrusive markets.

We must look at the social production of need, and the mechanisms set in place to answer it. The definition of need has passed from human beings themselves, and has become vested in a limitless capacity to produce, which belongs, not to us, but to the vast and abstract productive power of capital. Confronted by a limitless range of marketed possibilities, we shall always remain dwarfed, diminished, inadequate. The familiar division of labour has its correspondence in a less recognisable fragmentation of need; so that the very abundance which the West has achieved becomes the raw material for strange new products, dissatisfactions and discontents, the manufacture of new forms of poverty and felt insufficiency. This is the mechanism whereby we clamour for a growth and expansion which has nothing to do with the human, but everything to do with capitalism.

The formulation of need requires to be reclaimed by human beings and disentangled from the confusion of commodities, symbols and images in which it has been caught up. The situation recalls those accounts of Engels, in *The Condition of the Working Class in England* in 1844, where he describes a sequence of industrial accidents, in which the bodies of the operatives had been caught up in pulleys, belts and engines, whirled round until they were mangled by the machinery. We have lived through a similar analogue of inextricable mixing of humanity and the machine. We are taunted and tormented by the fanfares and the enclosed self-worship of the markets. They contain, locked up in their invisible machinery, so many of our expropriated real powers and possibilities. Need has been turned against life.

This means that we are in the same business of liberation as those who have been pressed into the service of the same markets of the West, by exporting food they cannot afford to buy to nourish their children, those dispossessed of the means of subsistence and driven into the slums of Manila or Sao Paolo. For we are the other side of that oppression – we ARE the markets. We acknowledge this when we refer to human beings in terms of this abstraction – people talk of the teenage market, the youth market, the porn market, the luxury market. This process, which we are always encouraged to believe is a privilege, also involves a distortion and warping of our humanity; just as the absolute privations of the poorest of the earth do. But the difference is that the toll this takes on us has been effectively separated from all the marketed wonders and delights; and we have, in the West, lived in a collusive dissociation of all the ugly visitations of our own society from their social origins: not only the stress-related diseases, the sicknesses of over-indulgence and self-poisoning, but the loneliness, the pursuit of sterile fantasies, mental illness, violence, epidemics of crime or drug-abuse, alcoholism, the breakdown of human associations – these are some of the consequences of what we are asked to accept as a form of privilege. The sundering of all these ills from the social and economic processes which produce them has been the object of capitalism in our time. Above all, the connection has been concealed between the wasting of the flesh and muscle of the poor through undernourishment and overwork and the waste of the powers and energies of young people in the richest societies in the world, who are disabled by idleness and lack of skill and a sense of futility, when so much needs to be done in the world.

Our project must be to make connections that have been allowed to lapse, or have remained in shadow. Perhaps we have been afraid of bringing into the open an examination of those dependencies because we don't want to alienate those whose support we seek. But we must not permit alternative formulations to fall into pietistic generalities about the poor on the one hand, or into an avoidance of upsetting deep-rooted dependency on the other. We must illuminate the way we live and the plight of the poor for the common oppression they are. When these come together, they will make an explosive sense, and we shall see that our interests truly coincide with the interests of those whose lives are a daily witness to spoliation and loss.

●　●　●

The question of human needs is clearly related to perceptions of value and to human motivation. People will be likely to value most whatever they consider they need. Similarly they will be more motivated to satisfy needs than to achieve other goals. To illustrate the psychological complexity of the ground now being covered, four preliminary points can be made, taken from Robertson (TOES, 1985) but, again, differentiating between needs and satisfiers.

1 One human need is to be useful and valued. We have a need to develop and to use our capacity to contribute to the satisfaction of our own and other people's needs.
2 Satisfiers of needs are subjective and to that extent they cannot be objectively defined by experts. One human need is the freedom to define our own satisfiers.
3 Satisfiers of needs are culturally and socially determined. One human need is to live in a society whose dominant ethos does not impose satisfiers that conflict with the satisfaction of other needs for oneself or for others.
4 Satisfiers of needs are relative, in the sense that we are dissatisfied if we are much worse off than others. To that extent, one human need is to live in a society of equals.

Conventional economics takes an extraordinarily limited and simplified view of human motivation, as reflected in its concept of Financial Man, a quintessentially competitive human archetype, who orders his entire world to conform to the conditions of maximum monetary gain. Now probably no economist would try to equate Financial Man with real people. It is too obvious that the motivations of real people spring from far more complex sources than mere financial advantage: family, friends, neighbour-hood, country, the capacities for love, loyalty and worship, to name only a few. But, and this is the crucial point, our economic institutions, the businesses, banks and corporations which exert such a strong influence on every aspect of our lives and society, are almost invariably run *as if* maximum monetary gain was and should be their sole valid criterion of operation. The vast majority of executives who ruthlessly enforce the dictatorship of the bottom line accept no such tyranny in their personal lives. The workers, including the executives, who submit their skills and employed hours to the gods of profit and productivity, will often devote those same skills in the rest of their working lives to quite different, yet just as productive ends, whether of personal development or social service or both.

This inconsistency in our economics is not an inevitable nor an immutable state of affairs. There is no imperative for the economic system to be geared to profit rather than people. This is a political question which could and should be determined according to the needs, values and motivations of the people whom the system is supposed to serve. Modern psychology and market research show these to be infinitely more complex than the Pavlovian responses of Financial Man.

VALUES, GOALS' AND MOTIVATIONS

Christine MacNulty (TOES, 1985) describes a classification of values and attitudes based on Social Value Groups, as a means of understanding social change.

This approach to social change starts from the assumption that one of the main determinants of a society's structure and dynamics is the individual's values, beliefs, attitudes and concerns. In other words, any change in individual values and attitudes will manifest as changes in all aspects of society – the home, the workplace and the community – which will, in turn, affect all existing organisations and institutions.

Social change can be measured and analysed in a variety of ways. In the work of my company, Taylor Nelson Monitor, in the UK and Europe, we have taken a three-pronged approach. We have developed, tested and validated a psychological model, based on theories of motivation; we have taken a long-term historical, socio-cultural perspective, looking at the transitions from agricultural to industrial to post-industrial societies; we have collected data on social change from more than 20,000 respondents in twelve years and have factor-analysed and then clustered the trends. All three approaches have shown remarkable internal consistency, and have converged on the same conclusions.

At present the UK population can be divided between those with Sustenance values, Outer-Directed values and Inner-Directed values:

- Sustenance values relate to the basic necessity of survival and security. People holding such values live just to get by, and heed the rule 'safety first'.
- Outer-Directed values relate to the desire for prosperity and status. The Outer-Directed person is motivated by a desire to get on and get ahead.
- Inner-Directed values relate to the need for personal

growth and self-fulfilment. Inner-Directed people are concerned about developing themselves, yet identify sympathetically with others.

Within these broad value-categories, different groups have been identified, called Social Value Groups. In the UK there are two Inner-Directed groups (Self-Explorers, Social Resisters), two Outer-Directed groups (Conspicuous Consumers, Belongers), one group mid-way between Inner- and Outer-Directed (Experimentalists) and two Sustenance groups (Survivors, Aimless).

In her paper (TOES, 1985), MacNulty describes in detail the characteristics of these seven groups, which are summarised below.

Self-Explorers

They tend to be relatively well off, but tend also to be less materialistic than other groups, an attitude that is shown even amongst Self-Explorers with low incomes. They do not want to 'keep up with the Joneses' and do not succumb to advertising pressure. The most important personal aspect of their lives is their need to express themselves creatively. They value work – paid or unpaid – for its intrinsic interest, and work as hard at their leisure as they do at their jobs. They read more than other groups and are avid for information of all kinds.

Self-Explorers are politically and socially aware. Liberal and flexible in their attitudes towards their families and other people generally, they are more tolerant, understanding, empathetic and intuitive than other groups. They believe in women's rights and are active in support of single-issue groups and other 'causes'. They are innovative and can be influential, as the ideas they pioneer, for example holistic health and physical fitness, tend to be picked up by Conspicuous Consumers, with a time lag of five to ten years, with the Belongers following on after that.

Social Resisters

They tend to be more traditional, conservative and conventional in their views than the Self-Explorers. Their personal stance is highly moral, with a strong emphasis on personal integrity and responsibility. They are concerned with business ethics and are cautious and sceptical consumers. Industrious at work, and liking to 'improve' themselves with leisure, they are less innovative in both than Self-Explorers. Their main focus tends to be their families. They are politically and socially very aware, especially at the local level, where they are often to be found in community groups with a view to preserving aspects of life which they deem to be worthwhile and beneficial.

Experimentalists

Experimentalists are predominantly male, young and single – 60% of this group is below thirty-four years old. Their social class profile shows a bias towards the ABC1 social classes,[2] and a high proportion of them live in London and the South-East. Their personal needs, as their name suggests, are for new experiences. They want stimulation in their work and have an active leisure, though they will sacrifice the former to gain money for the latter, for they are materialistic and like to live fast. Their pleasure is in the 'doing' rather than in the end product. They live in the present rather than looking to the future. In the family they are the keenest of all groups to live their own lives and believe in equality of the sexes, but otherwise they are not particularly aware socially or politically. Compared to the Self-Explorers, they are more traditional in views and less innovative, rarely going out on a limb, but they are only slightly less liberal, happy to accord to others the freedom they seek for themselves.

Conspicuous Consumers

In their personal lives their main driving forces are a desire to acquire material possessions and a desire to increase their status. Keen to keep up with or exceed the Joneses, the appearance of a product is of greater importance to them than its function. Although they tend to be middle-income earners, they would like to earn more and are the most materialistic group. At work, although personal satisfaction is important, money is more so. At leisure they are no more active than the population as a whole and tend to engage in leisure pursuits for social reasons. They are not innovative, but like to be modern and up to date and so will follow trends quickly once they become fashionable. Their attitude to their families is fairly conventional. They will plan for the future, unlike the Experimentalists, and are concerned about self-improvement, but as the means to a more successful and wealthy life and not, like the Self-Explorers, as an end in itself. They are not particularly aware, socially or politically, unless they are directly affected by some issue, when they become vociferous.

Belongers

Belongers are Mr and Mrs Average. The only differences between their profile and that of the population as a whole are in age (fewer under twenty-four) and in a bias away from the DE social classes. Their lives are circumscribed by their devotion to family, home and work, towards which they exhibit traditional, conservative views. Their work satisfaction comes from good working conditions and good relations with their superiors. Their leisure is oriented towards their families and home and is less active than the previous groups. Financially in middle-income brackets, they are fairly materialistic, but like tried and tested products and are wary of change. Uninterested in, for example, the honesty and integrity of business, they are not at all aware socially or politically, and are unconcerned about self-development, which makes them the antithesis of the Self-Explorers.

Survivors

The most striking feature of the profile of the Survivor group is its strong working-class emphasis — 76% of Survivors are C2DE, compared with 54% of the total sample. Survivors are predominantly male and a significant proportion live in Scotland and the North. They tend to have less education and there is a higher proportion of unemployed, retired and widow(er)s than in other groups. At work money is more important to them than personal satisfaction. Their leisure activities, when they can afford them, tend to be passive (e.g. television) or traditional (e.g. pubs, football, bingo). They are often disillusioned with society, feeling hard done by and impotent. Politically and socially their views are very traditional, they are self-centred and they mistrust change. They have been disastrously affected by the recession.

Aimless

This group has a very marked demographic profile. It contains significantly more women than men. The age profile shows a polarisation of respondents into those below the age of twenty-four and those over sixty-five. The young Aimless are likely to be unemployed, while the elderly Aimless include retired people and 'solitary survivors'. It is in this last category that the majority of the Aimless women fall. The Aimless are heavily concentrated in the lower social classes. Regionally they are under-represented in London and the South-East and over-represented in the Midlands and North. The high unemployment in the North is obviously an important factor here. Work is of minimum importance to them and, when they can get it, is primarily a means of earning a living. Their leisure is constrained by lack of money and lack of enthusiasm to do anything. They are demoralised and alienated. Socially and politically they tend to be both reactionary and chauvinistic. They too have been hard hit by the recession.

It must be stressed that the purpose of Social Value Groups is not to put people into hard and fast categories. While individual human nature may have something to do with the groups in which people find themselves, a far greater influence is likely to be exerted by their education and social and financial status, and it is quite possible for people to move from one group to another. The classification is above all a tool for the understanding of social *change*, and its most interesting aspect is the way in which it shows up trends in the motivational 'map' of society. Thus the recession has driven people into the Sustenance groups, and the different profiles for the North and South of the UK are clearly indicative of the discrepancies of wealth and opportunity between them.

In overall figures in the UK, the Self-Explorers comprise 17% of the population and have grown slowly but consistently as a group over the past decade. The Conspicuous Consumers are also increasing and are currently about 20%. The Experimentalists are 12% and until 1985 were the fastest growing group. The Social Resisters and Belongers are declining slowly, the former now standing at 13%, the latter, which used to be the largest group, at 19%. There are 14% of Survivors, with rapid growth in the past two years, probably because of the recession, and 5% Aimless. Although this group has declined in the past few years, a worrying trend is that the young are increasing their proportion of the total. Although these figures are for the UK, the trends are comparable in other industrial countries.

The pattern of Western development seems to have been from Sustenance-driven deprivation to Outer-Directed overconsumption and then, recently, to Inner-Directed personal and political awareness. From an environmental and resource point of view, it is simply inconceivable that this pattern can be repeated on a global scale. Fortunately, there is no imperative for this Western progression: once the financial and psychological necessities of living are met, people can become Outer- *or* Inner-Directed, responding both to external norms and to internal feelings. Many non-industrialised societies are rich in Inner-Directed values and traditions, and it is an absolute priority that these societies should be given all the encouragement and support they need to retain and develop these values, rejecting the strident materialism of Western consumerism in favour of ecologically-sound development appropriate to their culture and resources.

The only form of encouragement and support that is likely to be acceptable is for industrial countries to adopt such development strategies themselves, making personal development and satisfaction of human needs, and the discouragement of over-consumption, the corner-stone of their economic and social policy. For this, these countries will require an explicit theory of human needs and will need to have worked out and understood the political implications.

The absence of a consistent, coherent theory of human needs which commands a broad consensus in society has led to much confusion and loss of impetus among those who are seeking to develop economic theory and mechanisms for the 'satisfaction of human needs', or 'production to meet needs', as a counter-weight or supplement to the 'effective demand' of the market. As Doyal and Gough put it (TOES, 1985):

> There exists a curious ambivalence about the notion of needs, and the distinction between needs and wants. When confronted head-on, many commentators will express doubt about the philosophical validity of *any* concept of human needs. But in everyday activities, and implicitly in their writing, they continue to use something very much like it. In debates on social policy, for example, the welfare state is often defined as the collective recognition by society of certain human needs and the organisation of mechanisms to meet them. Yet whenever the meaning of the term 'need' is theoretically probed, it is almost always rejected as 'socially relative' or 'subjective' by writers across the political spectrum.

Doyal and Gough also discuss some of the political aspirations of the new social movements, including the women's, peace and environmental movements, concluding:

> Political develements concerned both with the welfare state and with the broader goals of a future society *implicitly* utilise a concept of universal human needs. In so doing, they have made a coherent, rigorous and, above all, explicit theory of need all the more urgent.

The paper that follows is their attempt to articulate such a theory and to explore some of its economic and political consequences. The theory is elaborated in three stages. First, basic individual and societal needs are determined; second, the optimisation of individual needs-satisfaction is discussed; third, the social and ecological prerequisites for such optimisation are considered.

• • •

'HUMAN NEED AND STRATEGIES FOR SOCIAL CHANGE'[3]
by Len Doyal and Ian Gough

Basic individual and societal needs

There can be no question that, on the face of it, relativists who believe in the essential subjectivity of human need have a case. People do have strong feelings about what they need and these feelings do vary enormously between cultures and over time. But if any distinction is coherently to be drawn between wants and needs, a non-subjective demarcation criterion must be found. Galtung and Plant,[4] among others, have recently suggested an alternative approach which we hope to elaborate and improve upon.

They argue that analyses of need are integrally related to ideas about what is necessary for persons to be capable of any successful action – irrespective of the aim of the action or the perceptions or culture of the actor. 'Action' here is more than 'behaviour' – it involves purpose, and understanding an action requires knowledge of the person's reason for doing it. It is this which distinguishes human beings from animals.

While it may be true that all human goals are specific to particular cultures, in order to achieve any of these goals people have to act. It follows that there are certain preconditions for such actions to be undertaken – people must have the mental ability to deliberate and to choose, and the physical capacity to follow through on their decisions. To put this another way, in order to act successfully, people need physically to survive and need enough sense of their own identity or autonomy to initiate actions on the basis of their deliberations. *Survival* and *autonomy* are therefore basic needs: they are both conceptual and empirical preconditions for the achievement of other goals.

Really, it is health rather than survival – both physical and mental health – which is the most basic human need and the one which it is in the interests of individuals to satisfy before any others. As far as physical health is concerned, it must be recognised that there is a point beyond which the capacity for successful action is so reduced that the actor will be regarded by others as abnormal – however the abnormality may be culturally regarded. This notion of a base is also applicable to mental ill-health, although here the deciding factor is the incapacity to perform some tasks culturally regarded as normal without the excuse of a physical handicap, old age or poor physical health. Since the capacity for successful action will be proportional to the satisfaction of health needs of both kinds, they can be ranked. Thus in all cultures, people will be regarded as more or less 'healthy' – whatever the culture under consideration and however 'health' is conceptualised.

The second set of basic needs which must be met for actions to be successful relates to individual identity or autonomy – the private and public sense of 'self'. In order for actions to be identified as such, they must be initiated by individual people. 'Initiate' is a crucial word here, because a person who initiates an action is presumed to do so in a fundamentally different way from that in which a machine (e.g. a robot) does. The machine is understood with reference to its mechanism. But people consist of more than the relationships between their bodily components. They acquire their autonomy as individuals by being able to formulate aims and beliefs and to put them into practice. Hence, all things being equal, we hold individuals practically and morally responsible for their actions but we do not do the same for machines.

For the need for autonomy to be met in practice, teachers will be required who already possess their own autonomous identities and the physical and mental skills which go with them. People do not teach themselves to act, they have to learn;[5] and this is a further individual need which goes hand in hand with autonomy. Which skills are learned will vary from culture to culture, but they are not totally variable; there is a universal empirical base line defining what individuals must do to meet their needs for health and autonomy. For example, children have to learn to interact socially in minimally acceptable ways, irrespective of the specific cultural rules they follow in the process. Persistently lying to, or punching, one's fellows will never be a recipe for successful social interaction. Similarly, in all cultures, language skills are necessary as the medium through which people learn conceptually to order their world and to deliberate about what to do in it. In this sense, consciousness is essentially social, a by-product of educational interaction with others. It is not, as the song goes, that 'people who need people are the luckiest people in the world'. Everyone needs people to be anyone.

Thus far in our consideration of individual needs, we have assumed that it was possible for health and autonomy through education to be achieved. However, since learning is a social process, it necessarily involves individuals interacting in social groups. This means that certain prerequisites must be met for any such groups or for a society as a whole to function with any degree of long-term success. Individuals therefore have basic *societal needs* – those social preconditions for the achievement of the individual needs we have just described. These can be analysed in four categories.

The first concerns *material production*. In all cultures, it is necessary somehow to create the food, drink, clothing and shelter required for a minimal level of health to be achieved. Such activities constitute the material base of the culture. Of course, they will vary between cultures, especially when these are radically different. Material production is essentially social. Humans are not genetically endowed with the physiology or mentality to enable them to survive, much less prosper, on their own. Group interaction in the form of a division of labour is thus required, with the character and complexity of the rules differing with specific cultures and types of production.

The second requirement for the survival of any culture is *successful reproduction* – the process 'which begins with ovulation and ends when the child is no longer dependent on others for necessities of survival'.[6] This includes two separate elements: biological reproduction, and infant care and socialisation. Historically, the mechanism for fulfilling both types of reproductive need has been some form of family structure, though with a wide variation of kinship patterns. To say this, is not, of course, to endorse any particular set of social relations. It is simply to underline the societal need for certain types of technical and educational practices, for example midwifery and the learning of basic principles of infant care.

The third requirement for the success of any social system concerns *communication*. People are not born with an understanding of theories and practices relevant to the modes of production and reproduction in their society. Nor will they necessarily be predisposed to accept the particular system of allocation and distribution which typifies it. As we have seen, such understanding and acceptance has to be learned. This will in turn be based on an already existing culture: a body of rules which partly defines the form of life of the society involved. Such rules enable social goals to be achieved because through their linguistic expression they constitute the medium by which aims and beliefs are individually and collectively acted upon. The resulting communication obviously takes many forms, including the sharing of practical skills and the legitimation of modes of exchange and distribution.

Finally, it is clear that the mere existence of sets of rules – of a culture in our sense – will not guarantee their perpetuation or implementation. There must be some system of *political authority*, ultimately backed up by sanctions, which will ensure that they will be taught, learned and correctly followed. The exact character of such authority will vary enormously, depending on the size, complexity and equity of different societies. Yet, however centralised or dispersed the authority may be, it must be effective in its own terms if the society in question is to survive, let alone flourish. One does not have to believe in Hobbes' 'war of all against all' to accept this. It is a consequence of the importance which, as we have shown, attaches to rules as the social cement which ensures the possibility of social, and therefore of individual, survival.

In general then, these four societal needs – production, reproduction, cultural communication and political authority – constitute the structural properties which any minimally successful mode of social organisation must embody. The degree to which individual needs are met will depend in principle on such success, which will in turn depend on individuals who are healthy, autonomous and educated enough to know what is expected of them, how to do it and the implications of not doing it. This interdependence between individual and societal needs should make it clear that we are not adopting the sort of abstract individualism which, for example, is so often attributed to utilitarian writers. Yet, it should be equally clear that we do not accept forms of functionalism which presuppose that individuals simply mirror the structural properties of their social environment. *The only criterion for evaluating social systems which we are advocating thus far is: how far do they enable individual basic needs to be met?* We are conceptualising basic individual needs in a way that is independent of any particular social environment.

Optimising basic need satisfaction and human liberation

It should now be clear that there are certain preconditions which are necessary for successful human actions to be intelligible and to occur in any culture. Through equating these preconditions with individual and societal needs, we have apparently found a way round the problems of ethnocentricity with which we began. Yet it could still be argued that while our analysis has succeeded in stipulating such needs in conceptual and empirically minimal terms, it does little or nothing to show how they should be specified in concrete social situations. For once we move beyond points about which even few relativists would disagree (e.g. the human need for oxygen), the cultural symbolism through which needs are expressed can vary so radically as to suggest little possibility of cross-cultural agreement or comparison.

In order to get beyond this impasse we have to move away from an abstract and static notion of need, which is geared simply to the conditions under which successful action can occur. Instead we require a dynamic conception of how to optimise basic need satisfaction given the best understanding but without engaging in cultural imperialism or the dogmatic imposition of expertise. Only in this way can the basic goal of human liberation – optimising individual and societal need-satisfaction for all – be coherently expressed. Such liberation depends on the ability to select options to meet individual and societal needs, options which have emerged as a by-product of mental and manual labour down the ages, and to put them into practice. To regard the capacity for such choice as a basic human need is simply to insist that those denied it are disadvantaged compared to those who are not, and that this is not an unalterable situation. Of course, what choices individuals or groups in different cultures will make if they develop the requisite intellectual and mental capacity must remain an open question.

So much for the principle. What about the practice? Here we run into difficulties for three reasons. The first is that what is scientifically and technologically correct or incorrect can be a matter of some dispute. Some technologies, of course, just do indisputably work, are useful in the pursuit of basic needs and are better than others. Other technologies, however, are more dubious in this respect. The debate as to which is which is bound to be muddy and contentious, for technologies are inevitably associated with power, control and vested interest.

Second, disputes also rage over the appropriate social arrangements or practices for optimising the satisfaction of basic needs. Again, over some practices there is little dispute; for example, that the ability to read and write enhances the autonomy of children, whilst exposure to arbitrary physical violence inhibits it. However, in many areas there is an important ongoing debate, for example over the merits of home versus hospital delivery of babies. It is worth noting, however, that, even where social practices are hotly contested, it is implicitly assumed by the disputants that it is possible in principle to distinguish between correct and incorrect solutions.

Third, even if ways of rationally resolving these issues are found, others will materialise concerning resource constraints. A technology or a social practice which is 'appropriate' in the best sense of the word may exist but there may not be enough resources for it to be distributed universally. Some technologies or social practices (e.g. effective medicines, more successful agricultural methods, suitable housing, environmental regulation) will influence the basic needs of everyone. Others will be relevant to specific groups, for example educational techniques for infants, or special housing facilities for the elderly. In both cases, however, political and economic issues will be raised. How are these issues to be resolved from a liberational perspective?

Social and ecological conditions for human liberation

The question of how to maximise need-oriented understanding must be answered through the articulation of two final sets of needs: *communicational* and *constitutional*. We have repeatedly seen that all need-satisfaction is social in character, including the need for the progressive optimisation of choice. It follows that an important necessary condition for such maximisation is a framework of negotiations within which the most rational solutions to problems of technique and scarcity can be debated and decided. In his theory of critical communication, Habermas has implicitly argued that there are three necessary conditions for an 'ideal speech situation' within which such negotiations can occur.[7]

First, participants should possess the best available understanding of the technical issues raised by the problems they are trying to solve. In many cases, such knowledge will not itself be in dispute and the focal point of this stage of negotiation will be primarily educational. Second, if there is such a dispute and participants are debating the correctness of a particular mode of understanding, they will require specific methodological skills. If the understanding is technical, then established procedures of experimental assessment will be crucial. Conversely, if the issue to be decided is itself communicational, a different set of interpretative methods will be appropriate in order correctly to understand the meaning of actions. The third condition for optimising the success of critical communication is to minimise the influence of vested interests, which place unwarranted constraints on the direction and content of relevant debate. In this sense, the normative structure of the debate itself is just as important as correct information and relevant methodology. All of those who have the capacity usefully to contribute must be encouraged to do so, and all of those who would attempt to distort the course of the debate for purely contingent reasons must similarly be discouraged.

Some critics have argued that such a view of rationality is hopelessly idealistic, since all known speech situations are dominated by the contingencies of power, and that it is difficult under existing modes of social organisation to see how this could be otherwise. Habermas' response, which we endorse, is that while departures from this ideal are commonplace, the ideal itself is none the less implicit in the methods and content of arguments which currently do take place. There would be little point in ever arguing if we did not believe that rational deliberation is better than brute force. To the extent that one can rationally trust any mode of understanding, it will be because it is the outcome of extensive argument according to rules one also trusts.

In short, for the optimisation of basic need-satisfaction to be meaningfully and democratically negotiated – for liberation to be a practical proposition – individuals must have the right and the capacity so to negotiate. That is to say, humans also have constitutional needs which stipulate the social rules by which these rights and capacities will be guaranteed, irrespective of whatever other social rules they may happen to follow.

It is still an open question how much private enterprise, how much central planning and how much decentralised collective planning are necessary for efficient production oriented towards need-satisfaction. Basic questions about individual constitutional needs – what individuals are entitled to as a matter of right – cannot be decided by any simple reference to existing or socialist modes of production and reproduction.

With this question in mind, there has recently been a resurgence of interest in Rawls' theory of justice (Rawls, 1972). This envisages a hypothetical negotiation, very like Habermas' ideal speech situation, about the provision of 'primary goods' – a concept similar to, though broader than, our preceding account of basic needs. Rawls claims that the constitutional results of such deliberations would have three key characteristics. First, *basic liberties* (e.g. freedom of speech, freedom of assembly) would be protected, ensuring a democratic mode of political organisation. Only in this way would putative violations of individual rights be publicly debated and the other communicational advantages of democracy be put into practice. Second, *social inequality* would only be tolerated to the extent that it benefited the least well off through expanded production. In other words, Rawls does not deny that inequality may foster improvements in productivity, but he leaves to those who would so argue the burden of proof and the task of formulating workable policies to ensure an equitable distribution. Third, *equality of opportunity* would be instituted. Since Rawls argues that inequality can be legitimised only if it results in increased productivity, the third principle ensures that the competition for places in the resulting social hierarchy would be efficient and fair.

Only if all three principles are met will primary goods be maximised in quantity and justly distributed. Since basic freedoms are guaranteed, opportunity for the rational expansion of creative choice on an individual or collective basis would be maximised. In practice, this would mean recognising the value of accumulated civil, political and social rights achieved in western countries, but at the same time recognising their limits and inadequacies, for example in the fields of official secrets and the right to privacy. Since inequality is tolerated only to the extent that it can be seen to serve the interests of the least advantaged, the society envisaged is as progressive as is socially and materially possible. In practice this would mean that income differentials themselves would have to be costed and justified. And since equality of opportunity is guaranteed, the development of self-perpetuating elites, who might attempt to control critical discourse, is suppressed. In practice again this would involve moving beyond current policies to provide every person with the optimum access to educational, health and other welfare resources, whilst at the same time denying others certain rights of inheritance. It would also justify certain policies of positive discrimination in favour of disadvantaged groups.

Thus, to the extent that they can be put into practice, Rawls' three principles presuppose that people can collectively understand what is materially required to guarantee equality of opportunity. They thus embody some conception of basic needs similar to our own. Without an understanding of health and educational needs, along with an acceptance that they should in principle be optimally satisfied, the formulation of a coherent strategy for distributive justice would be impossible.

For those who find diagrams helpful, a schematic illustration of our theory is given in Figure 1. We would emphasise the dynamic nature of the model, both in the horizontal and vertical planes, as drawn. The vertical interactions are between the individual and society, as informed by the social debate. Movement in a horizontal direction represents the society's progress or regress,

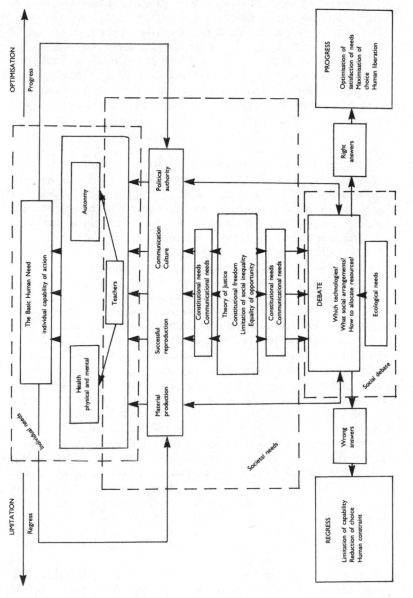

Figure 2.1 Schematic illustration of Doyal and Gough's theory of human needs

depending on whether the outcome of its social debate succeeds in increasing need-satisfaction or not.

We end up with an apparent paradox: that some type of central state responsibility, control and provision is a necessary prerequisite for the redistributive policies which are in turn preconditions for basic individual needs to be met in practice. However, in principle, the human need for liberation and the societal need for political authority are in no way incompatible. The question is not whether or not there should be a state. It is what sort of state it should be, and how it could meet the needs and rights of those it should serve rather than dominate.

Thus far, we have outlined in abstract terms some social conditions for fostering the optimisation of choice about the satisfaction of individual needs which were the starting point of our theory. It should be noted that all of these conditions concern various aspects of those societal needs which were shown to be so intimately related to such satisfaction. However, one final point remains to be made concerning the *ecological* constraints on the limits of economic production. It is not possible to improve the satisfaction of basic individual needs or the social preconditions for these unless sufficient material resources are available. The whole of our argument is based on this, yet there can be few who doubt that there are *some* natural limits to human production in a world of rapidly increasing population and industrialisation. Given that such limits exist, then the optimisation of individual need-satisfactions will not be constrained solely by the extent of human knowledge and the mode of its communication. Ultimately human needs have to be defined as those levels of health and autonomy which are available to all people in all societies, given present and probable future levels of resources. Thus it is important to stress that the logic of the politics of human need is irrepressibly global in scope: no group of humans can have their basic needs excluded from consideration. Moreover, nothing can justify the lack of equity with which these resources are at present consumed. It follows that, other things being equal, global redistribution should have priority over national redistribution. Finally, ecological considerations dictate that the need-satisfaction of future individuals needs to be taken into account in the present allocation of resources.

This being said – and we recognise its utopian ring – three last points are in order. First, ecological strategies for conserving and protecting the environment from needless waste and pollution may have such immediate and dramatic consequences for basic individual needs that they will quickly become incorporated into debates about wider political issues. This is beginning to happen, for example in the struggles concerning the toxic consequences of many industrial processes. Perhaps nothing more dramatically illustrates the distinction between needs and wants, and the ways in which this distinction can be moulded to serve arbitrary interests, than public demand for commodities which are known to be manufactured in ways which pollute the environment. Second, the conflicts of economic and other interests which plague attempts to protect the environment on a national level are exponentially compounded when one moves to the international arena. As a result most ecological struggles are at present restricted to those societies where the political process, at least in principle, gives them some chance of making an impact, and where a minimal level of basic need-satisfaction has already been achieved. Yet this situation runs the severe risk that the environmental needs of the developed countries could well be met at the expense of the basic needs of the rest of the world. The third point is that, if they are to be successful, international strategies for satisfying basic needs, such as those recently suggested by the ILO and the Brandt Report,[8] must conform to the same communicational and constitutional norms which we have argued are necessary for the success of national strategies. In particular, enormous constraints would have to be placed on the vested interests of the developed nations and of powerful groups within them. The political possibility of achieving such constraints and the circumstances under which it could be done is another open question. Indeed, at the moment, any effective answer seems almost inconceivable; but what is even more inconceivable is to stop trying to reach one – to relinquish the goal of human liberation on a global scale.

Many of the detailed implications for policy of these points still need to be elaborated. But it is clear that the Baconian vision of nature as an unending storehouse and unfillable cistern is over. The new reality is that awareness of the delicacy of the biosphere must now go hand in hand with democratically planned production for human need.

NOTES

1   S. Lansley and J. Mack, *Breadline Britain*, LWT/MORI, London, 1983.
2   The social classes are defined in *Social Trends* (Central Statistical Office, London, 1985) as follows:

A Higher management, administrative or professional workers
B Intermediate managerial, administrative, professional workers
C1 Supervisory, clerical, junior management, administrative and
   professional workers
C2 Skilled manual workers
D Semi-skilled manual workers
E State pensioners, widows (with no other earnings), casual or lowest
   grade workers, long-term unemployed.

3 This paper derives from an earlier article, 'A theory of human needs'
published in *Critical Social Policy*, Issue 10, Summer 1984. *CSP* is
available from 46 Elfort Road, London N5, UK.
4 J. Galtung, 'The basic needs approach' in Lederer, ed., 1980; Plant *et
al*, 1980.
5 When we refer to 'teachers' or 'education', we are using the terms in
their broadest sense, and not just referring to formal schooling.
6 M. O'Brien, *The Politics of Reproduction*, London, Routledge & Kegan
Paul, 1981.
7 Habermas' analysis of this issue is extremely complex. The best and
most detailed guide through his writings is T. McCarthy, 1978. For an
excellent introduction to Habermas' general theories, see R. Bernstein,
1979. For Habermas himself, see, for example, J. Habermas, 1976.
8 Cf. Conclusions of the 1976 World Employment Conference (ILO,
1977) and the Brandt Report (Brandt, 1980).

3 THE NATURE OF WORK

Economics shapes human lives in many different ways, but in no area is the economic/human interface so complicated and so in need of a conceptual overhaul than in the domain of work.

There are myriad views of work, many of them embedded in our deepest unconscious, having been transmitted over centuries, and often associated with religious teaching. There is the curse of work pronounced at the Fall; the concept of work as divine service, as in the monastic tradition; the idea of work as duty, as in the Puritan work ethic. There are the conflicting perceptions that work is a prime means of personal growth and self-fulfilment, or that it is something to do as little of as possible, to earn as much money as possible, to be spent on non-work, or leisure. Socially, work can be seen as an important means of self-definition in society, through which people gain a sense of usefulness, of status, of security, of where they fit into their community and into society at large.

E.F. Schumacher, in his three-part definition of human work, is characteristically visionary yet practical, blending work's individual and social aspects. The purpose of work is:

First, to provide necessary and useful goods and services.
Second, to enable every one of us to use and thereby perfect our gifts like good stewards. Third, to do so in service to and in co-operation with others, so as to liberate ourselves from our inborn egocentricity.

He then goes on to quote Albert Camus with approval: 'Without work all life goes rotten, but when work is soul-less, life stifles and dies' (Schumacher, 1979, pp.3–4).

Conventional economics, with its inexorable reductionist tendencies, has little use for the philosophical dimension of work, classifying it almost exclusively as 'disutility', the opposite of welfare. Leaving philosophy aside, it is in fact possible to identify at least four separate and largely distinct ways in which conventional economics deals with work.

The first way is to view work, or labour, as a cost of production, along with land, capital and other costs. This is, of course, the standard capitalist view. The terminology is important because, by calling work 'labour' and lumping it in with other economic variables, economists have found it easier to dissociate it from people, to forget that what they are actually referring to is people's skills and people's lives. Identifying it as a cost also gives it a pejorative connotation and indicates the direction of probable change, for economic management tends always to reduce costs, so that any system that identifies labour as a cost is bound always to seek to marginalise it or do away with it altogether.

The second way is to view labour as the source of all wealth, a view which was current well before the industrial age, but which, as the labour theory of value, was incorporated wholesale into economic thinking in the eighteenth and nineteenth centuries. It is this concept that then makes labour productivity such an important goal, for if labour is the source of all wealth, then enabling labour to work faster or more 'efficiently' is the only way of producing more, of getting 'richer'. It is also this view of labour that has given political power to the working classes, for their labour then becomes a force that can be pitted against the power of capital to employ. Marx was not slow to pick up the ethical implicaitons of this view with his analysis of 'surplus value', for if labour is the source of all wealth, and if, after paying the costs of production, there is a surplus, or profit, then by rights it should belong to the labourers that produced it. In this light, capital can be regarded as no more than a store of past labour, yet, under capitalism, it belongs to the owners or shareholders, rather than to labour. Therein lies at least one of the roots of class conflict.

These two views of labour, which we can loosely call the views of labour-cost and of labour-value, coexist uneasily in economic practice and the balance between them is always shifting. Currently two factors have dramatically emphasised the cost of labour and undermined its value. The first is the globalisation of production and the rise of the transnational corporation, the second is the shift in the thrust of new technology from mechanisation to automation. They will be discussed in turn.

While companies were nationally based, and while labour in all industrialised countries was organising simultaneously to achieve better pay and conditions, the costs of increased wages and other improvements could be added to the price of manufactures, and the benefits of improved productivity could be reflected in pay-packets, rather than lower prices or higher profits, across the international board. Prices remained more or less common to producing countries. However, the emergence of the newly industrialising countries, with their relative lack of organised labour and their workforces' expectations of far lower wages than in the rich countries, together with the new ability of companies, through transnationalisation, to relocate their operations in those areas with low labour costs and few environmental and other restrictions, has greatly increased the pressure on labour in the old industrialised countries. Higher wages or improved conditions there now definitely mean a loss of international competitiveness, an increase in imports and a decrease in the ability to export and, therefore, a loss of jobs. The need to export means that barriers to imports can be only sparingly used.

There are two main ways out of this unfavourable situation for labour: an increase in international labour solidarity, which is very difficult to achieve, or a delinking from the international market, through an increase in self-reliance.

This latter option will be explored more fully in Part III. Here it needs only to be stressed that delinking is very different from introducing protectionist measures in order to make the protected industries unfairly competitive in the international market. It is the gradual but systematic withdrawal from international trade in those areas where a country has the skills and resources to be self-reliant, so that it becomes able to satisfy its domestic market from its own production, and regains political control over its own course of development. In addition, it does not then contribute via its purchasing power to conditions that exploit people or the environment abroad.

The second factor, which can potentially reduce the value of labour almost to nothing, is the changing nature of new technology. In the early and middle years of industrialism, the technological thrust was towards mechanisation, toward the introduction of machines that worked with people to produce more than the people could by themselves. The machines may have destroyed traditional skills and communities, and required the migration of labour from country to town, but they kept labour very much in the picture and actually added to its economic value, what it could produce, and therefore to its bargaining power. The rise in the material living standards of the working classes in recent decades bears direct witness to the use of that bargaining power. Now, however, the thrust of technology is not towards mechanisation, a composite of labour and machines, but towards automation, which, far from enhancing the value of labour, does away with it almost altogether, except for a highly-skilled technocratic elite.

It is this twin pressure on labour in industrialised countries – international competition and automation – that has caused many analysts and, according to opinion polls, the public in the UK, at least, to conclude that full employment as traditionally conceived has gone forever. This has the most enormous implications for the third and fourth ways in which economics and work currently interact, namely the uses of employment as the main means of distribution of income, and as the main generator of taxation.

The taxation of employment to raise public funds stems from the second half of the last century, when labour really was the source of all wealth, and when, therefore, it was an obvious target when governments wanted to raise money. One inevitable result of such taxes has been to raise the cost of labour relative to other industrial costs, which has given added financial impetus to the whole move towards mechanisation and automation, in which labour is replaced by other resources and by untaxed, indeed tax-allowable capital goods. At a time when employment is very much in short supply, it seems absurd to go on financially discriminating against labour in this way. Taxation can surely be raised in other ways, and some of these are discussed in Chapter 10. This has been a blind spot in the labour movement, which has seemingly yet to realise that income tax costs jobs.

As for the use of employment as the main means of distributing income, with all its associated moral overtones of 'earning a living', this may have worked well enough in times of relatively full employment, but if widespread unemployment is here to stay, then it can be neither equitable nor efficient to distribute livelihoods through a mechanism that excludes *a priori* several million people and their families. Quite apart from the financial hardship involved, it is a recipe for social division and discontent. In this context, as in those considered previously, it is time that the interaction between work and economics is rethought.

• • •

'WHAT COMES AFTER FULL EMPLOYMENT?'
by James Robertson

Introduction

In Britain today several million people are unemployed. In the OECD countries the total number of people unemployed runs into several tens of millions. For Third World countries the situation is even worse. In 1982 the International Labour Organisation (ILO) estimated that a thousand million new jobs would have to be created by the year 2000 in order to achieve full employment worldwide. The Director-General of the ILO commented: 'It has to be fully understood that there will be no situation of full employment if we are speaking of conventional employment.'[1]

In fact, most conventional economists and politicians still seem to claim, though with diminishing assurance, that their particular policies will bring back full employment in the long run. But year by year these claims seem more and more like utopian wishful thinking, as the impact of labour-saving technology, the competitive pressures of international trade, and the reluctance of taxpayers to finance more public service jobs, point more and more clearly to the probability that much future economic growth, even if desirable on other counts, will be jobless growth.

The possibility cannot now be ignored that employment may be becoming an uneconomic way of getting much important work done, just as slavery became uneconomic in its time.[2] The realistic and responsible expectation must now be, not only that many years of high unemployment lie ahead, but that full employment may never return again. Realistic and responsible leadership must now take this contingency into account and act upon it.

The appropriate policies will be both practical and visionary. Practical action is urgently needed to ease the lot of the millions of people who face the prospect of continuing unemployment now. Societies which continue to propagate the job ethic and to link basic incomes with jobs, but which leave millions of people jobless, will continue to inflict great damage on those people and on themselves. But the practical action must also be visionary: the measures taken to alleviate the immediate problems of unemployment should also provide stepping stones to new ways of organising work which differ from conventional employment.

Three possible futures for work

There are three distinct views about the future of work.[3] The keyword for the first is employment. The keyword for the second is leisure. The keyword for the third is ownwork.

The 'Business As Usual' view assumes that employment will continue to be the normal form of work, and that most people's money incomes will be earned that way. This is how work has been organised and how incomes have been distributed in all industrialised countries since the industrial age began. This view is reflected in the debate that still continues between the conventional orthodoxies of Right, Left and Centre, not about whether but how full employment is to be restored. The assumption is that the industrialised countries will be able to bring about a reduction of working hours and a continuing shift out of employment in the manufacturing sector into employment in the information, knowledge and other service sectors of the economy, in such a way as will create jobs for all who want them. Not surprisingly, perhaps, academics such as Stonier (1983) are prominent among those who support this view, believing that education will be one of the main growth areas for jobs in the coming years. A further hope is that this revival of full employment and economic growth in the industrialised countries will create expanding markets for Third World products, and thereby lead to expanding employment opportunities for Third World countries too. The 'Business As Usual' view of the future of work as employment thus runs through the first Brandt Report (1980) and underlies its proposals for tackling the world's economic problems in the mutual interest of the North and the South.

The second view is based on a hyperexpansionist (HE) vision of a post-industrial society, in which the dominant trends of development during the industrial age are emphasised and accelerated. The growing gap between the more and the less highly skilled, and the growing distinction between core workers and peripheral workers,[4] will widen to the point where only a minority of citizens will be employed. These will be highly skilled, highly responsible, highly regarded, and highly paid members of a technocratic elite, employed to run the automated factories, put the space colonies into orbit, carry out research at the new frontiers of knowledge, and manage the largely automated financial, communication, education, health, and welfare services.

The rest of the population will have no useful work to do and will live lives of leisure (Jenkins and Sherman, 1979 and 1981).

Whether theirs is the leisure of affluence or that of poverty will depend on political decisions about the distribution of wealth. The past inability of those without direct economic power to live above subsistence, or even to achieve it, seems to suggest the latter, unless there is heightened moral awareness in this future society, or automated production is so abundant that goods can be ceded to the unemployed at no cost to the employed. Unless previously analysed ecological constraints can be bypassed whole-sale, such a level of production is simply not likely to be sustainable. In contrast to the typical industrial society, split between a˙ superior minority of employers and an inferior majority of employees, the so-called leisure society will be split between a superior minority of workers and an inferior majority of drones. This view has little to say about the future of work in Third World countries.

The third view of the future of work is part of a distinctly different vision of a post-industrialist society – based on a new direction of development, rather than on a continuation or acceleration of industrial-age trends. We may call this scenario sane, humane, and ecological (SHE), implying that higher priority than in the industrial age will be given to human growth, social justice, and ecological sustainability.

For today's industrialised countries, this view foresees a shift to a more decentralised society in which increasing numbers of people will organise useful and rewarding activity for themselves. Instead of a widening split between those who work and those who live lives of leisure, there will be a merging of work and leisure in many people's lives. Instead of a shift to a super-service society dominated by experts, there will be a shift to self-service and mutual aid; increasing numbers of people will take more control of their work and other aspects of their lives. Whereas technological developments in the earlier industrial age had a centralising effect which deprived people of the capacity to control their own work, and deprived many localities of economic autonomy, the technological developments of today already point in the other direction. In the fields of energy, food production, food preparation, information technology (including home com-puters), building, plumbing, decorating, electrical work, furnish-ing, clothing – even hardware manufacturing with small, inexpen-sive, versatile robots – advanced small-scale technologies will help to bring productive work back into the home and neighbourhood, and enable local work to meet a greater proportion of local needs than today. Instead of an employment society, or a leisure society, the post-industrial society will be an ownwork society.

For Third World countries, the SHE vision foresees a comparable shift away from centralised, 'trickle-down' development strategies, and from utopian hopes of one day achieving full employment in the formal economy, towards Another Development (see Part II, Chapter 1).

The SHE vision thus foresees, in industrialised and Third World countries alike, a growing tendency for development to aim at greater economic self-reliance, at every level: household, local and regional, as well as national. For the international economy this will mean a reversal of the past tendency towards an ever more specialised international division of labour and an ever greater degree of dependence by different nations on one another for economic essentials such as staple foods and energy supplies. Reversing these trends, supporters of the SHE scenario argue, could have the additional advantage of reducing causes of international tension and possible conflict.

A new policy approach

If we ask, not which of these three possible futures for work we like best, but which of them the actual future of work is most likely to resemble, the realistic answer must be that the actual future of work is almost certain to contain elements of all three. To some extent work will continue to be organised as jobs, and to some extent money incomes will continue to be linked with employment. To some extent there will continue to be a widening gap between the activities of the more highly and less highly skilled members of society, a general increase in leisure, and a weakening of the link between employment and income. And to some extent there will be a revival of local economies, a growth of self-organised work, and a blurring of work and leisure. A realistic approach to the future of work and the problems of unemployment must take all these elements into account.

However, if we ask which of the three possible futures for work contains most hope, a great deal of weight must be given to the third, the SHE scenario, centering around an increase in ownwork. Only by moving in that direction shall we be sure of avoiding the miseries of a Business As Usual society which continues to preach that everyone should have a job when jobs are no longer available, and the evils of a HE society in which an elite of superior workers dominates a mass of inferior drones. Moreover, it is a safe prediction that the actual future of work will tend quite strongly towards the SHE scenario. This is partly for negative reasons. The existing, centralised, employment-based ways of organising work, distributing income and providing welfare are beginning to break down; and it is difficult to see what remedies the Business As Usual and HE scenarios offer for this. But there are positive reasons too that support the SHE scenario. One of these, already mentioned, is that the new frontiers of technology face this way. Another is that changes in people's values are now moving this way too.[5]

That some shift towards economic revival at household and local levels is a likely prospect for the industrialised countries can be seen by reference to the four economic sectors shown in Table 3.1.[6]

Table 3.1 *Four-sector economy*

1 Capital-intensive large-scale production	2 Large-scale services
3 Local small-scale enterprises	
4 Household/neighbourhood sector	

Employment in sector 1, the capital-intensive, highly-automated, mass production sector, is bound to continue to decline. If businesses in this sector are to be internationally competitive, they must continue to improve their productivity – which means that employment in the sector must continue on a downward trend. If they are not internationally competitive, that in itself will bring a further decline in employment.

Employment in sector 2, the large-scale services sector, is also more likely to decline than to rise. Within the next five or ten years, office automation and structural changes in the financial service industry could very well bring a downturn in employment in banking, insurance and general commercial services, and limits on public expenditure are likely to preclude much expansion in employment in nationwide public services such as education and health.

This leaves sectors 3 and 4, the local and household sectors, as the main potential growth areas for work. New work in these sectors will include some expansion of conventional forms of employment in small local businesses and some expansion of home-based self-employment in professions and trades. But it will also include an expansion of work in a whole range of local activities and enterprises such as community businesses and community associations which, though they will have to be economically viable, will not be exclusively economic in the normal sense of the word. Similarly, it will include expanded household production of goods and services for direct consumption by household and family members and close neighbours – in other words, an expansion of the informal economy.

Expansion of useful work in the local and household sectors will reduce the dependency of localities and households on jobs provided by the large-scale organisations of sectors 1 and 2, as well as on goods and services purchased from them or provided by them at public expense. This reduction of dependency will be doubly significant. In the first place, it will contribute directly to the well-being of the localities and households concerned, many of whom today are suffering unemployment and hardship as a result of failed dependency on employing and social welfare organisations outside their own control. In the second place, by relieving the organisations of sector 1 and sector 2 of the obligation to provide routine work and routine services for localities and households which could provide such work and services for themselves, it will free those organisations to become more efficient in their own proper spheres. This will apply both to firms competing economically in international markets in ways in which local and household enterprises cannot be expected to compete, and to organisations providing sophisticated social services, such as hi-tech hospital services, which self-help and mutual aid at local and household levels cannot be expected to provide.

Some attributes of work: a review

During the age of employment, certain attributes of work have come to be taken for granted. These must now be reviewed.

Work as a dependent activity

Employment became the normal way of organising work when the common people were excluded from the land – for example, by the land enclosures of seventeenth- and eighteenth-century England. It was well understood at the time that, by depriving people of the chance of economic independence, the enclosures would make them dependent on paid labour and compel them to work for employers. It was hoped that 'the subordination of the lower ranks of society would be thereby considerably secured' (contemporary official report, quoted in Hill, 1969).

The introduction of the factory system brought a further loss of autonomy at work. For example, weavers in England in the early eighteenth century may often have been miserably poor, but at least they worked together in family groups in their cottages, in charge of their own work, fitting it in with other household activities, and talking, singing, and taking their meals as and when they themselves decided. Factory discipline put a stop to all that (Thompson, 1968).

Since then, so it is argued (Bravermann, 1974, Cooley, 1980), the development of scientific management has consistently aimed to limit the autonomy of employees at work. However that may be, there is no doubt that most people now take for granted their dependency on an employer to provide them with work. Whereas the common people of the eighteenth century protested and rioted against being turned into wage labourers, the trade unionists of the twentieth century protest and strike for their right to remain dependent on employment (Illich, 1981).

Work as activity under remote control
Just as individual people and households have lost control over their own work during the employment age, so towns and districts and localities have lost control over theirs. In industrialised and Third World countries alike, local work has come to be increasingly dependent on decisions taken elsewhere. Just as people and households have become increasingly dependent on earning money to spend on goods and services they no longer produce for themselves, localities likewise have become increasingly dependent on working for employers based elsewhere to earn money to spend on importing goods and services that they no longer produce locally for themselves. The vulnerability of many towns and districts all over the world today reflects this loss of local economic autonomy, just as the vulnerability of unemployed individuals reflects their lack of economic autonomy at the personal level.

Work as specialised activity
Ever since Adam Smith wrote *The Wealth of Nations* just over 200 years ago, specialisation has been regarded as synonymous with economic progress.

It has not just been individuals who have specialised in their work. Localities and regions have specialised in coal-mining, or steel-making, or ship-building, or fruit-growing, or coffee-growing, or fishing, or tourism, or glass-making, or whatever.

Whatever their speciality, specialist persons and specialist localities have become more and more vulnerable to economic changes outside their control. This vulnerability is now a key feature of the economic and social problems of the world today. It applies not only to the industrialised world. Precisely the same is true, often on an even more disastrous scale, for Third World countries.

For many people and in many places the desirable limit to economic specialisation has now been reached, if not passed. The relative costs and benefits of specialisation and self-reliance now tend to favour the latter.

Work as instrumental activity

As industrialised societies have developed, work has become more impersonal and the purposes of work have become more remote from people's own lives.

One early cause of this was that the technologies typical of the industrial age required increasing division of labour. They thus favoured large-scale organisation. Having pulled work out of the home into the factory, they led to the replacement of small factories by big ones. Then rail and, subsequently, road transport enabled people to commute longer and longer distances to work; until in due course, in late industrial societies, most people have come to accept that the energies which they channel into their working lives will be spent in places and on purposes unconnected with their home and family, their neighbours and their friends, and even the locality in which they live. The purposes of work have become instrumental, rather than intrinsic.

This instrumental character of most employment has disconnected people from a sense of personal responsibility for the outcome of their work in three particular respects: in terms of its contribution to their own self-development; in terms of its effect on the interests of other people; and in terms of its impact on the natural environment. Just as the dominant economic thinking of the industrial age has been blind to the needs of personal development, social justice and ecological sustainability, so employment, the dominant form of work during the industrial age, has largely excluded these from its objectives (Morris, 1885, and Schumacher, 1979).

Work as formal activity

Whereas our pre-industrial ancestors mostly worked to produce goods and provide services for themselves and one another on a person-to-person basis outside the market economy, we now work to produce goods and services as paid employees of organisations which provide them to customers, consumers and clients. In other words, work has migrated from the informal to the formal economy (for a fuller discussion of the formal/informal dual economy, see Robertson, 1983). So pervasive has been this process of formalisation, that politicians, economists, business people, trade unionists and many other people now assume that the formal economy, in which people's work takes the form of jobs and in which transactions have a money tag attached, is the only part of the economy that counts.

The shortcomings of GDP and GNP as measures of past economic progress and as targets for future economic achievement are now well-known and are detailed elsewhere in this book (see pp.32 ff. and Chapter 6). So far as work is concerned, the misconception is that paid work has positive value, but that unpaid work does not.

The assumption that people's economic and social activities don't really count unless the economists, accountants and statisticians can actually count them, is an example of the much more general 'Cartesian' approach that has been typical of every field of understanding during the industrial age. However, in the last few years the arbitrariness and irrationality of the assumption that the only important phenomena are those which can be measured and calculated has begun to be seriously challenged in such fields as medicine and science. Similarly, in the last few years an increasing number of people have begun to realise that we do actually live in a dual economy, part informal and part formal; that what we do for ourselves and one another outside the formal economy is significant; and that for the future the informal sector of activity may prove to be one of the most important growth areas for economic and social progress and for work.

Work as masculine activity
The spread of employment brought a deep split between men's work and women's work. As employment became the dominant form of work in the nineteenth and twentieth centuries, the father typically became the breadwinner going out to work, while the mother typically became the housewife staying at home. As money loomed larger in people's lives, the paid work of men achieved higher status than the unpaid work of women. Eventually this led women to insist that they should have employment rights equal with those of men, and women now have a somewhat fairer deal where paid work is concerned. But progress towards equality has been lop-sided; most men still

remain unwilling and unable to do their fair share of the unpaid work of running the household and raising the family. They still assume that the really important work is work done for employers for pay, and they give priority to that.

The paradox here is that many of the higher-status, typically masculine employments in factories, offices and other institutional places of work have served no directly necessary purpose, by contrast with typically feminine forms of unpaid activity in the household: bearing children, providing food, providing clothing, caring for the old and the sick, educating young children, and looking after the home. Men's work in the industrial age has typically been abstract, impersonal and instrumental. For example, men's work has been concerned with machines in factories, papers in offices, money in banks, and ideas in universities. Women's work, by contrast, has had its own intrinsic purposes; it has typically been concerned wth people; it has provided directly for basic human needs (Novarra, 1980).

Three factors are now reversing the conventional difference in status between men's work and women's work. First, attitude surveys in many industrialised countries show that a shift of values is taking place away from the masculine towards the feminine (Aspen Institute, 1983). It is widely believed that the present crisis of the industrialised way of life is a crisis of masculine values. Second, much of the physical work which men have hitherto done because of their physical strength can now be done by machines. Third, increasing numbers of people are beginning to think that the normal working life for the future will not be modelled on the pattern of continuing full-time employment that has been downgraded by the ever-growing dominance of part-time employment, family work at home, and voluntary work, together with spells of full-time employment, that has been typical of many women's working lives.[8]

Work as exclusive activity
Women are not the only members of society whose work status has been downgraded by the ever-growing dominance of employment over other forms of work. People reaching retirement age are made to feel their useful life is over. Teenagers not yet eligible to join the labour market are made to feel they can make no useful contribution. Unemployed people of working age are made to feel excluded and marginalised. Old, young and unemployed alike are discouraged from doing useful work of an informal kind. Work has become a stark question of either/or. Either you have a job or you don't work. Either your

contribution to the economy takes the form of a job, or you are excluded from work and perceived as a burden and a cost to be carried by those who do have jobs.

The implications for economics
These characteristic attributes of work in the form of employment – work as activity which is dependent, remotely controlled, specialised, instrumental, formal, masculine and exclusive – are likely to be sources of serious economic, social and personal vulnerability from now on. Many of the policy initiatives outlined in Part III of this book will help to encourage new forms of work as activity of which the main attributes will include independence, personal and local control, all-round capability, intrinsic goals, informality, a more equal balance between masculine and feminine values, and inclusiveness in the sense of giving everyone opportunities for useful work.

What will the spread of these new forms of work, with attributes quite different from those of employment, mean for economics as a system of thought?

The age of economics has, in fact, coincided with the age of employment. It is only over the last two hundred years that employment has developed as the dominant way of organising work, culminating in full employment (i.e. the provision of employment for all who want it) becoming a policy goal for governments. Similarly, it is only over the last two hundred years that economics has emerged as a dominant way of understanding and managing human affairs, culminating in economic policy becoming a central field of policy for governments. If the age of employment is now beginning to draw towards an end, what will this mean for economics? At the personal level, for example, will economics have anything helpful to say about the relative benefits and costs of different possible mixes of activity – including paid work, informal household and family work, voluntary local work, leisure activities, and so on – in one's own life? At the level of the local economy, will economics have anything helpful to say about the relative benefits and costs of varying degrees of local economic self-sufficiency (i.e. of using local work to produce goods and services to meet local needs), as contrasted with economic dependence on national and international factors outside local control?

Many other such issues will arise concerning the values to be placed on various kinds of work and related human activities, which conventional economics has ignored. The question is whether economics will turn out to have been a fairly short-lived structure of reasoning and speculation reflecting the values of the industrial age, during which time employment has been the dominant form of work; or whether economists will be able to extend their discipline to deal with choices that reflect the wider needs and activities of real people, as contrasted with those of *Homo economicus*, together with considerations relating to social justice and the sustainability of the ecosystem. Only time can give the answer.

NOTES

1 *Development Forum*, United Nations, New York, November 1982.
2 See the references to slavery in Adam Smith's *The Wealth of Nations* and Karl Marx's *Capital*.
3 See Robertson, 1983, for a fuller account of these scenarios.
4 See John Atkinson, 'Flexible firm takes shape', the *Guardian*, 18 April 1984.
5 In addition to Christine MacNulty's evidence, given earlier, see also Aspen Institute, 1983.
6 This four-sector model of the economy was termed 'plus-industrial' in *Management for the 21st Century*, Kluwer Nijhoff, London, 1982.
7 See Robertson, 1983, ch.3. Also Robertson's paper on 'The role of the formal sector in tomorrow's dual economy', given at a Swedish Government conference in June 1983.
8 I owe this point to Sheila Rothwell, who develops it in Part III (p.210).

4 IN SEARCH OF SELF-RELIANCE

Satisfaction of human needs and a reconceptualisation of the nature and value of work – these are two of the pillars of the new economic framework that must now replace our simplistic and increasingly counter-productive reliance on 'more output' as the means to greater welfare. A third pillar, which comprises a major break with conventional economic thinking, is a commitment to economic self-reliance.

The concept of self-reliance is the antithesis of much of the thinking behind the growth economy. Specialisation, the national and international division of labour, the theory of comparative advantage – these formed the intellectual, organisational backbone of the industrial revolution. Through these concepts, and others, such as the free market, thinkers like Smith and Ricardo explained the economic innovations of their time and provided a theoretical basis for the rationalisation, consolidation and extension of an economic practice which has developed into the global economy of today. This economy is now characterised by, among other things, over-specialisation, fragmentation, inequity, disadvantage, and a debilitating dependency: of peripheries on centres, of some countries on other countries, of people on 'the system'. These are the problems to which the New Economics' emphasis on self-reliance is addressed.

'TOWARDS A NEW ECONOMICS: ON THE THEORY AND PRACTICE OF SELF-RELIANCE'
by Johan Galtung

Much has already been said in criticism of classical/neo-classical economics. Here only two points have to be made about conventional theory, concerning the conditions under which that theory arose:

1   Conventional theory emerged at a time when a new form of power was growing in significance: contractual power based on *quid pro quo*, willing buyer meeting willing seller, as opposed to the normative power of the Church and the coercive power of King and law, police and military. Of course, neither normative nor coercive power disappeared from the scene, but contractual power, carried not only by economics but also by law (but not punitive law) had been growing steadily in importance, making rational calculation of advantages, and comparative advantages, not only possible but desirable to the point of becoming a basic way of approaching other human beings in general and all sorts of problems in particular. Cost-benefit analysis became the basic paradigm.

2   Conventional theory was carried into the limelight of academia by a new class, the merchants, the *tiers état*, fighting its way up against the two solid layers that were the carriers of normative and coercive powers respectively, the Church and the aristocracy. In other words, there were very concrete actors with very concrete interests behind conventional theory. They knew what they wanted and classical economics became their intellectual expression. Unfortunately, because of the accounting and book-keeping which they had been doing for many centuries, they had fallen into some bad habits: looking at the costs and benefits from a very limited angle, only considering their own firm and that which could be monetised, leaving out the rest of society and leaving out the 'externalities'. Later on, economics developed from business economics to national economics, treating the country like a firm, repeating the same mistake at the level of the world system, resulting in a fragmented world, a segmented vision. The externalities were never brought into the scheme. These externalities can be positive or negative: benefits of education, employment, an improved social structure, a sense of achievement or psychological challenge; or costs of depletion, pollution, dependency and deprivation.

Thus classical economics has been biased from the very beginning. It liberates human beings from the fear of punishment. As long as you play the game, you can enter the market; abide by the rules and you have a wide range of behaviour at your disposal, whether you are a willing buyer or a willing seller or both. This is by and large to be seen as positive: what it means is increased freedom, not only for individuals, but also for groups and countries. Human rationality and ingenuity are made use of, one is steered by the hope for positive rewards, rather than by the fear of negative punishment, whether in this world or the next.

But on the other hand, normative constraints are lost. Behaviour becomes rational, but also immoral. 'There is nothing so innocent as the man calculating his profit' becomes the adage of the system, which may be subjectively and individually true, but is objective and social nonsense. No man or woman in their right mind would behave within the family as they do in the market. Compassion and concern are key words here, but they also stand for an extended rationality: lack of compassion and lack of concern may bring short-term gains but long-term disaster, partly by eliminating my trade partner, partly by pitting us against each other in ways that may mark the end of both of us.

Of course, this is known and taken into account as part of market behaviour, but usually only within a narrow range of economic attentiveness, and usually only among equals. The damage done to the weak is less visible. The weak are often far away, in remote corners of the world where misery and pollutants may accumulate and soil be depleted. In a similar vein, non-economic consequences such as the lack of challenge and lack of training ensuing from being merely the carrier of wood and water, the provider of raw materials and commodities, will not be taken into account because they fall outside the *intellectual* horizon – just as the weak are outside the *social* horizon and the remote corners outside the *geographic* horizon.

In other words, we assume that people in general, and economists and businessmen in particular, have limited horizons, and are themselves unable to see clearly the consequences of the actions they engage in. This tendency is strengthened rather than weakened by an economic theory which tends to be both fragmented and segmented, reinforcing the fact that it is obviously in people's immediate, short-term interest to see the world that way, to focus on the benefits accumulating in their portion of the world economic system, rather than the costs accumulating beyond the horizon.

From this one can draw two conclusions when it comes to the reshaping of economic theory and practice. First, economic theory has to expand and become global and holistic. It has to reach into the remotest corners, the deepest recesses of geographical and social space, so as to take into account the impact everywhere. Thus it has to be transdisciplinary so as to encompass not only economic causes and consequences but also those in other fields. Obviously this is a programme for an enormous expansion of economic thought, to bring it into harmony with the expansionism of economic practice, to make the practice transparent. Second, there is the opposite possibility of contracting economic practice to this side of the social and geographical horizon, making the theory very holistic within that more limited scope, so that the costs and benefits in a broad sense can become visible to everybody.

My own view is that one should probably try to do both, globalising the theory while localising the effect of the practice. The former may be intellectually too ambitious by itself. The latter, which has very much to do with the theory and practice of self-reliance, may be more realistic. At the same time, the first perspective is always with us, calling for a new type of global interdependence. The conclusion is: self-reliance *and* global interdependence, the themes of the next two sections.

On the economics of self-reliance

The basic principles of self-reliance, in my view, are as follows.

First, some mechanism in addition to the market must be found for the satisfaction of basic human needs, while at the same time not limiting economic activity *a priori* to the basics. The satisfaction of people's basic needs is obviously the *sine qua non* of self-reliance. The present opposite tendency is still to equate a demand backed up with money with a human need, because at least one human being 'needs' it, or at least demands it.

Second, we have to ask how we can produce what is needed, relying on ourselves, on our own production factors, meaning nature (land, raw materials, energy); labour, skilled and unskilled; capital, liquid and fixed; research, basic and applied; and administration. All these factors, as well as the output, the goods and services, come in crude and refined versions. In conventional theory, protected by a misapplication of Ricardo's ideal comparative advantages, a division of labour takes place with the centre applying refined factors for the refined production of refined products and the periphery applying crude factors for the crude production of crude products, exchanging these with each other. Thus, the centre treats the periphery as an external sector of its own economy: as a place to fetch or use nature and dump pollutants; as a place to use cheap labour and dump excess labour from back home (a major function of colonialism); as a place to export excess, tied capital for specific investment purposes and from which to import profits, in a broad sense, as untied capital; as a place to carry out research projects that could not be done at home, while at the same time importing researchers trained at the expense of the periphery country; and as a place to administer, but not be administered by, issuing SOPs (standard operating procedures) from the centre. Self-reliance implies a total rejection of this 'division of labour', a rejection of the use of others as an external sector for dumping the negative externalities and of denying them the positive externalities in a production process. It means treating others like an *internal* sector.

Hence the basic rule of self-reliance is this: *produce what you need using your own resources, internalising the challenges this involves, growing with the challenges, neither giving the most challenging tasks (positive externalities) to somebody else on whom you become dependent, nor exporting negative externalities to somebody else to whom you do damage and who may become dependent on you.*

By producing what we consume and consuming what we produce, rather than doing either through exchange, by definition we keep the externalities, positive and negative, for ourselves. The justification for so doing is clear: we will enjoy the positive externalities, rather than giving them away, and at the same time will be responsible ourselves for the negative externalities (e.g. pollution, depletion, dirty, degrading, boring work, highly inegalitarian income distributions, top-heavy social formations). We can fight the negative consequences ourselves, the distance between cause and effect being a short one.

For instance, an obvious way of preventing pollution of rivers from riverside factories would be to force the management of the factory to drink downstream water; the rule would have an immediate impact. Moreover, there is another hidden moral behind this little example: it is not enough that the effects are localised in the sense of being this side of the horizon. They also have to hit high up where decisions are made or at least can be more easily made. Those who have made the beds have an obligation to lie on them.

Thus self-reliance cuts both ways: it preserves the positive externalities by trading much less upwards, and protects against the negative externalities by trading much less downwards. It is a measure of economic defence as well as a pact of non-aggressiveness. In self-reliance there is both an element of enlightened egoism (don't give away the positive externalities) and enlightened altruism (don't damage others by exporting negative externalities).

Yet the third consideration is that there may well be a discrepancy between the list of what is needed and the list of what can be produced on a local basis even with the best possible use of human imagination. If only one factor of production is missing or in inadequate supply, the production will not take place. The solution to this problem is, of course, exchange, trade. And this is where self-reliance spills over the local borders and becomes international and global interdependence. Nothing in self-reliance is against trade provided it takes place according to the following two rules:

1   The exchange should be carried out so that the net balance of costs and benefits, including externalities, for the parties to the exchange is as equal as possible. In practice this will point in the direction of intrasectorial rather than intersectorial trade; in other words exchange of primary products (raw materials, commodities, agricultural products); or exchange of secondary products (manufactures, industrial goods including high technology); or tertiary products (services). The moment one exchanges primary products for secondary products or tertiary products there is a problem: the externalities may be extremely different and very difficult to compare or equalise. Provided that the parties to the interaction stick to exchange within a single sector of production, they need not necessarily be at the same level of technical economic development. But if they are at the same level, the proportion of primary/secondary/tertiary outputs is more equal, and equitable exchange would come more easily. A useful rule of thumb is that the total degree of processing involved in the items for exchange should be at about the same level in both directions.
2   One field of production – production for basic needs – should be carried out in such a way that the country is at least potentially self-sufficient, not only self-reliant. This includes the production particularly of food, clothing, shelter, energy, and whatever is needed for health, education and home defence. If production exceeds consumption, then there is no problem – provided one does not make others dependent on oneself through trade in this field of basic needs. If production is short of consumption, there has to be exchange according to the preceding rule, which again would be in order provided steps are taken and concrete plans are made so that in times of crisis society can nevertheless be self-sufficient. The crisis planning of Switzerland is a good example of such plans.

Fourth, typical of the theory of self-reliance is its scope for transcending the nakedness of economic relations. There is a strong normative injunction, based on a feeling of compassion and a will to resist threats and the actual exercise of violence, direct or structural, from the outside. At the same time, it puts some limitations on the kinds of contractual relations that should legitimately be entered into. Self-reliance is psycho-politics as much as economics; it presupposes, and builds, self-respect. It does not mean more or less splendid isolation, but spins a web of interaction that is mainly horizontal rather than vertical.

Finally, self-reliance is not a theory only for nations, but equally for local communities and regions. This is where the theory of global interdependence starts, as part of, and not separate from, the theory of self-reliance, which thus aims to avoid being or becoming dependent by fostering both independence and inter-dependence.

On the economics of global interdependence

The world does not merely consist of nation states; it consists of many things. One simplistic perspective is to see the world as Chinese boxes: first, as a set of regions, the First, Second, Third and Fourth Worlds (the last, in my use of that term, being the world south-east, east and south-east Asia, Japan and the countries surrounding it); inside the regions are the nation states or countries; inside the countries are the local communities. One might talk about the regional, national and local levels, or spaces. The concept of global interdependence sews all of this together in as equitable a manner as possible, 'horizontally', avoiding dependencies, but also seeing independence as a last resort in crisis, as something one should be able to withdraw into. But in general human beings are social, so are local communities, countries and regions – or at least they should be – extending outwards, embracing others, but in a friendly, not a deadly embrace.

The key to global interdependence is simple: practise the principles in the preceding section not only for countries, but also for regions and at the local level. Thus I am not advocating a regional self-reliance which is based on the strength of the strongest country (Brazil for Latin America; Nigeria for Africa south of the Sahara; the richest OPEC countries for that part of the world; India for South Asia), making all the other countries in the region dependent on it. Nor is it desirable that a country should become self-reliant in the sense that all local communities are dependent on the centre, the capital with its high concentration on the three more refined factors: capital, research and administration (or, in other words, bureaucracy, corporations and intelligentsia, the BCI complex).

Rather, the self-reliance which is advocated here is derived by reasoning outward from the innermost Chinese box. A local community may be self-reliant, producing for its own needs, trading with suitable communities defined by the vicinity and/or affinity. But if the nation – seen as a protective shield around the local communities – is not self-reliant, the local community may not have sufficient strength to withstand economic aggressiveness from without. Similarly, considering the Chinese box that lies at the national level, a country might have difficulties surviving economic penetration from the outside if not protected by regional arrangements. By the latter I do not mean a hierarchy of bureaucratic arrangements, in the sense that any willing seller or buyer from outside the region will have to negotiate first with the region, then with the country, and in the end with the local community. What I mean is simply that the local community which wants to be self-reliant should be able to find suitable trading partners within the country, or if not within the country, at least within the region. It should display some local identity first – then some national identity, then some regional identity – reasoning now above all from the point of view of the weakest region, the Third World. Other regions, higher on the scales of power and privilege, might relax this rule of solidarity and give the benefits of exchange to somebody who needs it.

Concretely, this means that of the three types of trade in the world today, centre-with-centre, centre-with-periphery, periphery-with-periphery (or in UN jargon, North-North, North-South, South-South), whether within or between regions or countries, this theory of global interdependence does not point, necessarily, to a reduction in intra-national and international, intra-regional and interregional trade, but to a *restructuring*. Centre-periphery exchange should be reduced, periphery-periphery exchange should be built up; centre-centre exchange will probably be built up anyhow. Note that what is being said is 'reduced', not eliminated.

However, the rule of self-reliance starts with the idea of producing things yourself rather than getting them through exchange. In some ways exchange is the lazy way out: 'I have something in excess, send it down to the storehouse, ship it out, get in return something somebody else has in excess provided we both agree on the prices,' and that is it. This is simplistic to the point or irresponsibility – it does not ask what additional impacts the agreement reached might have on both parties, on nature and on the rest of the world. We should be able to do better than that.

In fact, these suggestions are neither particularly radical nor original. They are already practised in many parts of the world, among communities and countries that feel related to each other, tied by bonds of solidarity that do not appear in any economic theory but nevertheless may be a part of psycho-political reality when joint agreements are reached. One example may be the Nordic countries: in general, two Nordic countries would not just drive for any agreement with each other. They would each be concerned with what impact that agreement had not only inside their own country but also inside that of the trade partner. The community is normative, not only contractual. As such, the concern with the welfare of the other goes beyond maximisation or optimisation in one's own cost-benefit analysis. There is some effort, however clumsy, to make an analysis of all the cost-benefit analyses of the parties involved. The problem would be how good the representatives of the various countries or communities are at articulating costs and benefits, not only of their own class. They may engage in the usual traders' tricks of being very explicit about the costs and silent on the benefits. Or, just as likely, they may be simply unaware of the hidden costs and benefits, never having studied them, never having been told about them by economists, who have so many blind spots embodied in their thinking from their early days of training onwards. In short, if things go wrong, it might be more fruitful to seek for reasons and possible solutions in lack of theoretical understanding than in lack of honesty. This is also a more hopeful perspective.

Self-reliance and global interdependence: a balance sheet

Self-reliant communities, nations, regions rolled together in global interdependence sounds beautiful even if not all of it is small. The reason for this is that although much of what is small is beautiful, not everything small is beautiful, and, similarly, some big things may be both beautiful and necessary. Consequently, the sketch of economic relations given here is more complex. It is not the sketch of a world consisting of very many and very small, not only self-reliant but actually self-sufficient communities. I do not think such a world will come into being, nor do I think it is desirable that communities should deprive themselves of exchange, one of the most powerful ways of communicating, learning the habits and thoughts of others and expressing one's own.

But another criticism can be raised against the division just presented: would it not lead to a two-tier world, centre in exchange with centre, periphery in exchange with periphery? One possible answer to that would be that we are already living in that world, to a large extent, due to centre-periphery interaction of a non-equitable nature. Furthermore, a two-tier world of economic cycles that do not tie in too much with each other might be preferable to a two-tier world where the cycles do interlock but in an exploitative manner, making the upper tier rich because the lower tier is poor and vice versa.

A more positive argument, however, would be that it may be easier for the peripheries to develop their autonomous technical and economic capacity if they are only left free to do so, benefiting from all the challenges and positive externalities and being themselves responsible for the negative externalities they create. Is it not our experience that children develop best, not by being perennially dependent on their parents, all the time receiving 'advice', ready-made products (food, shelter, pocket-money) and services (care) and never having to fend for themselves, but through self-reliance with some ultimate self-sufficiency? Why should our theory of communities, countries and regions be different? Could it be because we *want* periphery communities to remain dependent on the capital cities, we *want* periphery countries to remain dependent on centre countries and periphery regions on centre regions? Are we afraid that otherwise we in the centre might ourselves decline?

That is not to say that self-reliance and global interdependence is the formula for the centres' premature demise. Except for those at the very top, I think it is a formula for their regeneration. Thus I see no reason at all why the rest of the world should be dependent on Japan for electronics of all kinds, cameras, watches, cars and motorcycles. Why should others deny themselves the growth they could obtain through their own production of these challenging goods? And even those at the very top may contemplate whether it is not also in their interests to seek arrangements with some built-in stability, being neither dependent on somebody, nor threatened by somebody dependent on them in a situation from which, sooner or later, they may want to withdraw, possibly in a very violent manner. Ultimately, dependency is very unpleasant to everyone involved. Yet it is the consequence of conventional economic theory and practice. A new economic practice based on self-reliance has to be based on a whole new economic theory. Here we are only at the beginning.

●   ●   ●

The shift from dependency to self-reliance, involving individuals, communities, countries and regions endeavouring to meet as much of their consumption from their own production as possible, will reverberate through every aspect of economic and social life: working patterns, food production, the use of energy and other resources, education and training, technology, communication, entertainment and politics.[2] All these areas can be subjected to the Chinese box analysis, working outwards from the 'box' of the individual, and seeking maximum internal self-reliance at each stage before looking to the next level for the provision or exchange of resources beyond the capacity of the stage in question.

An emphasis on self-reliance has special implications for public expenditure, especially that part of it which is communal expenditure at an outer level (e.g. the national level), designed to meet needs at an inner level (e.g. the inner city), which that level was unable to provide for itself through its own self-reliance. With self-reliance as its objective, this expenditure would be subject to every different evaluative criteria than at present. It would seek to serve three main purposes.

Firstly, it would be exclusively geared towards the satisfaction of basic needs, as agreed in the context of the society in question. Second order wants and, even more, luxuries, which a level could not provide directly for itself, would have to be obtained through the exchange of surpluses, through trade. Secondly, it would be expenditure that was either especially appropriate to the outer level, i.e. providing goods and services which, by their nature, an inner level could not provide for itself, or was redistributive, i.e. resulting in a transfer of resources from a richer inner level to a poorer one. Gone would be the wholesale levying of taxation on an inner level by an outer level, for the outer level either to give the money back with strings attached or to provide, for the purposes of outer level, central control, a service which the inner level could perfectly well have provided for itself.

A serious example of this in the United Kingdom, which has led to much political controversy, is the system of rate-support grants. Local authorities in the UK themselves raise only about one-third of the funds they need for local services. The other two-thirds comes from the general taxation raised by the government, and is paid to local authorities via these grants. Inevitably political strings are attached to these grants, to the extent, in the 1985 rate-capping legislation, that every local authority in the country was told by central government what it may or may not spend. Clearly this is a denial not only of self-reliance but of local democracy, as the choices of electors voting locally are overruled by the dictate of central government. The only remedy for such an abuse of power is to ensure that inner levels, such as local authorities, raise through their own taxation the revenue they need for the services their electorate has mandated them to supply, except where their relative poverty justifies redistribution of resources, rather than having to rely on claw-backs from the centre, which will never be unconditional.

The third main purpose of public expenditure would be to be 'enabling'. The emphasis would shift away from public expenditure on the delivery of benefits and services to dependent clients, towards measures that enabled people to meet their own needs more self-reliantly. Thus welfare benefits would be of such a form as to reduce the recipients' need of them. They would, as far as possible, increase the ability of recipients to make future provision for themselves. The basic income guarantee, to be discussed later, is one such benefit, positively encouraging those unable to find a full-time job to engage in any part-time or voluntary work of their choice, and to enhance their income or their skills. This is in sharp contrast to unemployment benefit, which, in the United Kingdom at least, actively discourages people from doing anything but looking for possibly non-existent full-time employment.

Such enabling public expenditure may well need initially to be greater than the 'crisis management' pattern of current benefits. But, in a very real sense, it would be, and would need to be evaluated as, a *cost-saving investment*. Its 'return' would become apparent as enablement worked through to greater ability and diminished dependency, reducing the need for such expenditure in the future. This is quite different from the current mode of operation of the welfare state, which seems to cultivate dependency on its institutions to such a degree that the demand for its services increases far faster than the availability of resources to satisfy them. Thus we see the paradox in many industrial countries of a record amount being spent on public welfare of one form or another, while the inadequacy of such expenditure, reflected in waiting lists for hospital beds, dole queues or straight poverty, becomes increasingly obvious. Until public expenditure seeks actively to reduce dependency rather than inducing it, the public exchequer will never have enough to go round.

In no area is the dependency-creating nature of much public expenditure more evident than in the field of health, with health spending reaching new records in many countries, and still being clearly inadequate to meet perceived needs. As the Black Report (Townsend and Davidson, 1982) made clear:

> Rich industrial countries like the United States, Canada,
> Western Germany, France, Sweden and the UK have been
> spending an ever-increasing percentage of their national income

on health services, and at the same time have been unable to demonstrate satisfactorily to themselves that much higher spending is clearly related to much better health.

In fact, because of its crucial importance to human welfare generally, the whole field of health is of special importance to the New Economics, and it is to detailed consideration of health that we now turn.

NOTES

1   For more of Galtung's writings on self-reliance, see Galtung, 1979; Galtung, O'Brien, Preiswerk, eds, 1980; Galtung, 1982.
2   The implications of local self-reliance in many of these areas were explored by Ken Penney in 'Aspects of local economic self-sufficiency' (TOES, 1984).

5 HEALTH IS WEALTH

The impact of economic policy on health is so pervasive and profound that health comprised one of the main subjects of The Other Economic Summit conference in 1985. Sponsored by the World Health Organisation (WHO),[1] papers were commissioned from leading public health advocates from several countries, and it is quotations, extracts or summaries from these papers[2] that make up this chapter.

We start by analysing some of the direct effects on health of economic practice, and then explore some of the conceptual contradictions and inconsistencies underlying much current thinking about health, wealth and economics, going on to indicate the new attitudes and policies that would resolve these inconsistencies.

It is as well to begin from a realistic assessment of our present situation as it relates to health and economics. The fact is that many people and countries around the world are richer than ever before in terms of monetary wealth and that, in general terms, it has been the case that the greater such wealth nationally, the better the national health; and the greater such wealth personally, the better the personal health (Townsend and Davidson, 1982; Wilkins and Adams, 1983). Moreover, new tools, inventions and technologies of great potential further benefit to humankind are continually being researched and developed.

It is extraordinary indeed that, given this bright prospect, progress and development seem to have run into the ground, economic and health problems seem increasingly intractable, and pessimism about the future is the order of the day. This situation is directly traceable to political and economic priorities, which systematically divert resources from those in greatest need, use or squander resources in an increasingly counter-productive fashion and deploy new technologies in ways that actually intensify both health and economic problems. Many examples of these misguided priorities have already been encountered. The most important from the health point of view are briefly recapitulated by Peter Draper:

1 *The continued existence of mass hunger and poverty in the Third World.* It is calculated that 800 million people, one sixth of the world's population, still live in absolute poverty. (Commonwealth Secretariat, 1982).

2 *The persistence of poverty and serious inequality in industrialised countries.* The Black Report (Townsend and Davidson, 1982) recently documented the adverse effects of poor socio-economic conditions on accidents, illness and mortality. In Britain and many industrialised countries the inequalities are actually increasing; for example, from 1979 to 1982, U.S. citizens below the poverty line increased from 26.1 million to 34.4 million, reflecting a 28% growth rate, when population changes are taken into account.[3]

3 *Paid work is not shared equitably and much socially-useful work remains undone.* High rates of unemployment create poverty and thus damage health as discussed above, but there is also mounting evidence of the adverse effects of involuntary unemployment itself on the workers affected and their families, not only on mental health, but also on physical health.[4] The pioneer work of Harvey Brenner (Brenner 1976) showed that increasing rates of unemployment are associated with increasing rates of overall mortality, heart-disease mortality, suicide, infant mortality and psychiatric hospital admissions. A recent Canadian review (Kirsh, 1983) listed a large number of health problems resulting from unemployment, including heart disease, psychiatric and emotional problems and violent deaths. A review of German research for the Council of Europe (Schwefel, 1984) also points out that, whilst death rates of the affected workers and their families are raised from, for example, cancer and heart disease, unemployment is a non-specific burden and that pathological consequences are produced at the weakest point; 'there is no specific unemployment disease'. The maldistribution of paid work particularly affects women and socially-disadvantaged groups such as ethnic minorities and the disabled. On the other hand, much of the socially useful work that remains undone would make a positive contribution to public health, e.g. better care of the old and handicapped and the improvement of homes and public facilities.

4 *Investment too often funds unhealthy products and processes.* The clearest and most outstanding example of unhealthy economic development is investment in armaments. Nuclear war, of

course, would be the final epidemic (Petersen, 1983; World Health Organisation, 1984a), but the mere manufacture of weapons at present levels has severe health implications in terms of resources available for other purposes. Three examples from statements by the United Nations Secretary-General illustrate the point:

I am told that in 1983 world military spending was rapidly approaching $800 billion . . . . The total amount of official development aid to all developing countries from all sources in an entire year is now equal to eighteen days of global military expenditure.[5]

and

We spend more than $1 million per minute on the arms race in a world where 40,000 children in the developing countries die – not every year or month, but every day.[6]

and

The conquest of the dreadful disease of smallpox, which used to kill millions of people every year, cost the world about $300 million. This is less than what the world spends on the arms race in one day.[7]

But investment and trade in unhealthy products and processes is not of course restricted to the military-industrial complex. Unhealthy products, which too often receive government grants for agriculture or manufacture, range from tobacco and opium to sugar. And the long list of unnecessarily hazardous mining, manufacturing and agricultural processes ranges from uranium- and coal-mining to crop-spraying. Sometimes the problem is lack of investment in health and safety, sometimes it is investment in operations which are intrinsically hazardous and in no way essential, for example, aerial crop-spraying over people. Sometimes it is the export of potentially hazardous products and practices, e.g. dried milk for babies (Muller, 1974), pharmaceuticals (Muller, 1982), pesticides (Weir and Shapiro, 1981), dangerous jobs and production (Castleman, 1979). Pollution problems in the work-place, for local neighbourhoods and for the public at large, still continue and often increase. The polluter typically does not pay and all too often continues to pollute. Whether the issue is acid rain, toxic waste dumps, radiation, pesticide residues or a host of other pollution problems, it is true to say that independent researchers into their health significance are still mainly impressed by what we don't know about subtle or long-term effects. The very slow recognition and acceptance of the asbestos, lead and food-sensitivity problems illustrate the research, organisational and political difficulties.

5   *Finite resources are used irresponsibly.* The most obvious health implications of our myopic use of natural resources are probably those that affect food supplies, such as over-fishing and the destruction or impoverishment of agricultural land, through soil erosion, reduced soil quality and nutrient content, the widespread use of poisons and artificial fertilisers (Marks, 1984).

6   *Massive advertising promotes unhealthy products and lifestyles.* Instead of informative advertising, we are increasingly subjected to persuasive advertising, not only for products like tobacco, alcohol and sugar, but also for unhealthy lifestyles and diets. Above all, we are brainwashed with the myth that human fulfilment lies in the increasing consumption of goods and services. As problems of obesity graphically illustrate, more of what is good is certainly not always better as far as health is concerned.

•   •   •

In all these ways, current economic practice runs directly counter to people's health interests. Yet it is clear that this practice derives from economic theory and a conceptual base which either ignore health completely or which deal with health issues in a positively perverse fashion. James Robertson examines some of these deeper issues.

'THE MISMATCH BETWEEN HEALTH AND ECONOMICS'
by James Robertson

Health and economic growth

The principal objective of economic policy in industrialised countries is 'recovery', by which is meant growth. Yet as Peter Draper has been particularly persuasive in arguing (Draper et al, 1977; Draper, 1984a, 1984b), the pursuit of economic growth is, in many instances today, actually bad for health. For most sophisticated economies, evaluation of economic activity is now necessary in order to seek only that growth which is beneficial and to achieve other benefits that do not count as growth.

Health as an economic minus

Conventional economics makes an artificial distinction between the creation of wealth and the creation and maintenance of health. Not only are conventional economic policies and conventional business goals uninterested in the promotion and maintenance of health, but, as we have seen, they are often positively damaging to health. Yet, even when the need to safeguard health is accepted, for example by introducing safety measures and pollution controls in chemical plants and power stations, it is treated by conventional economics as a cost, and regarded as a constraint and a drag on economic and business growth.

The idea that the development of healthier people, and the creation of a social and physical environment which enables people to be healthy, might be treated as productive investment in a society's capital assets, as the development of its most important resources (its people), is alien to conventional economics. The New Economics, in contrast, redefines the creation of wealth to include the creation of health.

Sickness as an economic plus

The more we spend on doctors, drugs and disease, in any one year, the higher will register that year's Gross National Product. In other words, conventional national accounts regard the expanding activities of the 'health' sector as a positive addition to national well-being. But the main concern of the health sector as it functions today is with ill-health, and its main task is remedial. As is widely acknowledged, the National Health Service is really a national sickness service. No one denies the need for sickness care and a drug industry. But it is odd to count the growth of activity needed to deal with accidents and sickness as an indication that greater general well-being has been achieved. It hardly makes sense, except to conventional economics, to suppose that the more a society has to spend in response to accidents, sickness and disease, the better off it must be. What is needed is some clear evaluative distinction between the social benefits and social costs of economic activity, so that economic policies can be devised which maximise the former while taking into account and minimising the latter.

Limits to conventional health policies

All parties to conventional political debate believe that the economic department of life is separate from health and must be given priority over it. They share the assumption that 'wealth' must be created before it can be spent on 'health'. They share the assumption that only after economic growth has been achieved can improvements be made in health-service provision. They share the assumption that improvements in health-service provision are synonymous with improvements in health.

The conventional left-wing view is that the state should employ paid workers to provide health services and health care for all. The conventional right-wing view is that people should be encouraged to pay for their own health and medical treatments, that a national sickness service should provide a safety net for people who cannot afford to pay, but that its cost should be kept down by pushing as much responsibility as possible on to voluntary workers (mainly women) to provide unpaid health care in the community and in the home.

Unfortunately for the conventional left-wing view there is no prospect, either short-term or long-term, of restoring sustained expansion of the conventional welfare state, as a spin-off from sustained economic growth of the conventional kind. The 'Crosland model' of socialism – and of a mixed economy – may have been valid for the industrialised countries in the 1950s (Crosland, 1956). But, as I have said elsewhere (Robertson, 1982), the conventional growth engine has now turned from a miracle-machine capable of meeting continually growing demands into a disaster-device programmed to generate aspirations which it cannot fulfil, and programmed, moreover, to stunt people's capacity to fulfil their aspirations for themselves. Even in Sweden, where the Crosland model had its outstanding success, the writing is on the wall (Swedish Secretariat, 1984).

The problem about the conventional right-wing view is that it is one-eyed. It expects people to be more self-reliant in what it sees as the 'social', or welfare, department of life, but not in the 'economic', or wealth, department. Conventional right-wing policies actually increase most people's economic dependence on others more rich and more powerful than themselves, for such things as their work and incomes. They reduce the economic power of the state, not by enabling people to become economically more self-reliant, and therefore abler to provide for their own and one another's health care and welfare, but by increasing the dominance of financial institutions, industrial and commercial companies, and rich individuals. For that reason, whether by failure of understanding or by deliberate deceit, whether by accident or design, the conventional right-wing rhetoric of self-reliance often runs the risk of appearing exploitative, disabling and corrupt.

The economic/social divide

Conventional economics is based on an artificial separation between the 'economic' and 'social' departments of life. This reflects an artificial model of human activity as consisting of separate 'wealth creation' activities, which must come first, and 'wealth consumption' activities, which can only come second. The redefinition of wealth creation to include the creation of health will tend to blur this divide. In this context an instructive parallel can be drawn between health and work.

Conventional economic policies have assumed that money spent by the state on unemployed people, either in the form of benefits or in the form of Manpower Services Commission (MSC) training, work experience and community projects, is money spent for 'social' purposes – representing 'wealth consumption' required to maintain unemployed people during their unemployment. These expenditures are not seen as investment in the creation of new wealth and new resources. For that reason, unemployed people receiving social benefits or participating in MSC projects are not, with certain specific exceptions such as the Enterprise Allowance Scheme, allowed to build up personal earned incomes or revenues from projects without forfeiting their benefits or MSC grants. This effectively prevents unemployed people from graduating step by step from economic dependence on the state to economically viable self-employment or to economically viable employment in new enterprises which they themselves have brought into existence. But, if the conventional uses of 'social' expenditure have not included enabling unemployed people to create work for themselves, nor has 'economic' expenditure been thought appropriate for this purpose either. 'Economic' expenditure has taken the form of investment grants and tax incentives to existing employers and tax incentives for comparatively rich people to take an equity stake in new commercial businesses. Unemployed people are eligible for payments from the state only on condition that they remain economically sick, i.e. unemployed. Their restoration to economic health must depend on their being offered a 'real' job by a 'real' employer. Neither 'social' nor 'economic' expenditure is considered appropriate for enabling them to develop economic health for themselves. The conceptual apparatus of conventional economics cannot handle the idea that enabling unemployed people to create useful and viable work for themselves might be an investment.

Similarly, conventional economics and economic policies assume that money spent on health is money spent for 'social' purposes. With marginal exceptions it is seen as wealth consumption required to deal with sick people during their sickness. 'Economic' expenditure is not thought appropriate for health–creating purposes. The conceptual apparatus of conventional economics, based on the artificial distinction between 'social' and 'economic', cannot handle the idea that money spent on enabling people to be healthy might be an investment.

This false economic/social divide needs to be ignored in favour of addressing the common-sense tasks of clarifying which activities create well-being, and directing resources to, or otherwise enabling these activities to be chosen in preference to, activities which do not create well-being.

Health, lifestyles and living conditions

People's health is bound up with their personal lifestyles and with the economic, social and physical conditions in which they live. Three issues of current concern in the health field are connected with this.

First, the action needed to enable people to improve their health falls largely outside the 'health' sector. In rich and poor countries alike, it is action of kinds not expected of conventional health professionals and health institutions: doctors, nurses, hospitals, government health departments, manufacturers of drugs and other health products, and so on. It is action in other spheres: to improve the availability and conditions of work, the nutrition value of easily-available foods, housing conditions, the availability of transport and heating in bad weather, money incomes, family and local support networks, a sense of personal and social esteem, and the multitude of other factors that help to determine the level of lifestyles and conditions of living.

Second, it must be stressed again that people's health is directly related to their economic status. The Black Report (Townsend and Davidson, 1982) brought out clearly that the poorer people are, the lower their chances of good health. Carol Buck, 1984, too noted that poverty

brings in its wake all the obstacles to health . . . . It is the poor
people above all others, who live in dangerous environments,
who lack the necessities and amenities, whose work, if they
have any, is stressful and unfulfilling, and who are isolated from
sources of information and encouragement. On top of all this,
poverty is intrinsically debasing and alienating.

But the poorer people are, the lower also are their chances of
making the changes, and getting the changes made, that would
help to improve their health. This reflects the Catch 22 of
conventional economics: the greater people's needs, the weaker
their 'effective demand'.

Third, people's lifestyles are conditioned to a very considerable
extent by the social, economic, built, and natural environment in
which they live. On the other hand, it is also within most people's
power, at least to some extent, to adopt a healthier lifestyle and to
improve the conditions in which they live. There is a dilemma
here. If health promotion and health education concentrate too
much on individual behaviour and personal responsibility for
health – stop smoking! take exercise! eat healthier food! and so on
– they will ignore the fact that many people are trapped in
unhealthy lifestyles imposed on them by society. That approach
to health promotion and health education all too easily turns into
'blaming the victim'. On the other hand, to deny that people can
do anything to improve their own or their families' health and the
conditions in which they live, will help to keep them powerless.

Third World

In Third World countries the introduction of a westernised model
of health care, including prestige hospitals, high-technology
medicine, and doctors trained in western medical schools, has
made it even more obvious that the conventional health sector
cannot undertake the kinds of activities needed to improve the
health of the great majority of the people. It is now widely
recognised that the injection into the Third World socio-economy
of an expensive westernised health sector no more enables health
to trickle down to the people, than the injection of a capital-
intensive high-technology industrial sector enables wealth and
well-being to trickle down. For some years now, in an increasing
number of Third World countries, 'Another Development in
Health', aimed at enabling people in their villages and towns to
create better health and healthier conditions for themselves, has
been gaining momentum, and there are encouraging signs that

much can be achieved even in low-income countries. For example, Morley, Rhode and Williams, 1983, cite the Indian state of Kerala:

Though one of the poorest states in the country, Kerala has the highest levels of life-expectancy, literacy and utilisation of health services, as well as the lowest levels of infant and child mortality. Kerala demonstrates that equitable socio-economic and health policies are not necessarily incompatible with democratic government and that a high Gross Domestic Product is not essential for health: fair shares for the many are better than large shares for the few.

Another Development in Health, both in the Third World and in industrialised countries, needs to be seen as an integral part of a comprehensive strategy of decentralised, participatory development, based on the recognition that the only real development is human development – personal, social and political as well as economic – and that, if it is to be effective, people must be enabled to do it for themselves.

Health needs, human needs

When WHO was founded after the Second World War, it defined health as 'a state of complete physical, mental and social well-being, and not merely the absence of disease or infirmity'. Today, forty years later, many of us regard health not just as a state but also as a process or a capacity. Valentina Borremans has defined health as 'autonomous coping with the environment'. Katherine Mansfield defined it as 'the power to live a full, adult, breathing life in close contact with what I love – I want to be all I am capable of becoming'.[8]

But, whether one takes a static or a developmental view of health, health needs are virtually synonymous with human needs. An economy that promotes health will be an economy directed to meeting human needs. The following are, in fact, among the basic needs recognised by WHO in the context of Health for All.[9]

Food Access to enough of the right kind of food. Elimination of hunger and malnutrition.
Education A basis for developing individual potential, participating in society, and for looking after personal and family health.
Water and sanitation A continuous supply of safe drinking water and effective means of sanitation.

Decent housing   Housing conditions that contribute to physical, mental and social well-being.
Secure work and a useful role in society   This is identified by WHO as a fundamental need.

It is worth stating categorically that people and the planet have the skills and resources to enable these needs to be satisfied for the entire human population of the world. That they are not is a failure not only of our economic system, which could be changed, but of our political priorities and vision, which do not effect such a change.

Secure work and a useful role in society

Emery (1984) suggests six requirements for healthy work. Three are related to the intrinsic nature of the task:

1   The task allows room for the individual to make decisions;
2   The task allows the individual to learn (and the learning task is challenging);
3   The task presents variety.

The other three requirements are related to the nature of the work interaction:

1   Mutual respect and support between peers and supervisors;
2   Work that is meaningful;
3   Work that is directed towards a desirable end.

Seeking to meet these requirements obviously has the profoundest implications for all aspects of economic activity, from the choice of technology to business goals and aspirations.

Dependency/self-reliance

The conventional path of development creates dependency. That is one of its essential features. Historically, it starts by excluding people from access to land, and therefore from a subsistence way of life. It thus makes people dependent on paid labour or cash handouts for the money to meet needs formerly met by ownwork. It goes on to make people dependent on organisations and professions to provide for all needs, including health needs, and for a continually widening range of additional wants which become transformed into needs. It also makes localities dependent. They become dependent on outside agencies: to organise their work; to supply their needs for food, energy and other necessities of life, including health; and to take the political and economic decisions that shape their future development and affect their future health for better or for worse.

Dependency shades into addiction. Up to high-school leaving age the average North American child now spends 12,000 hours in front of a television set.[10] Addictions to tobacco, alcohol and drugs may be cases of especially unhealthy dependency, but they are a natural feature of a society in which the whole momentum of development is geared to dependency-creation. A dependency-creating society is not a health-creating society.

The dependency/self-reliance issue is related to the relative values given to the formal and informal sectors of the economy. The blindness of conventional economics to the value of the informal economy is an instance of the metaphysical assumption, derived originally from the philosophy of Descartes and now underlying conventional science, that only the material, tangible, measurable side of the material/non-material duality can be scientifically understood. In the sphere of health this finds expression in the idea that the human body is best understood as a machine, whose only essential characteristics and functions are those that can be quantitatively measured; that health consists of the proper functioning of this machine; and that the way to improve its functioning is by intervention – by, for instance, drugs, surgery, transplants – from outside.

That idea has encouraged people to feel dependent for their health on medical scientists and medical mechanics more know-ledgeable than themselves. But awareness is now growing both of the importance of the informal economy and of the psychoso-matic element in health. This can be seen as one aspect of an incipient swing, both in economics and in health, away from the old paradigm based on dominance/dependency towards a new paradigm based on self-reliance.

•　　•　　•

In fact, a concern with self-reliance 'alternatives' in the health field has been a significant factor in industrial societies for some years now, yet it does not seem to have reduced the role played by medicine and, in some cases, medicine has actually co-opted the alternatives. John McKnight explores this paradox from a US perspective.

'DEMEDICALIZATION AND POSSIBILITIES FOR HEALTH'
by John McKnight

The central health question in industrial societies is 'How did we ever get so distracted by medicine?' Perhaps this point is made best by Dr Lewis Thomas, an eminent medical author and past President of the Sloan-Kettering Cancer Center. He recently noted that 'less than 1% of the US population dies each year and the life expectancy is over 72 years.' Thomas says that this is 'not at all a discouraging record once you accept the fact of mortality itself'.[11] None the less, there appears to be an obsessive commitment towards medical technology and a growing demand for 'health' care. It is this demand that Thomas calls an 'unhealthy obsession'.

For the middle and upper classes, the utility of the tools of modern medicine has largely disappeared, through the radical decline of infectious diseases. For lower-income people, the modernized poor, the primary causes of physical malady are distinctively environmental and obviously irremediable using medical tools. There is no medical prescription to cure poverty, slums, and polluted air, water and food. However, this reality has not affected the tremendous allocation of public wealth for medical solutions to the problems of the poor. In New York City, for example, over half of all public and private program dollars specifically designed to assist poor people are spent instead on expanding ineffectual medical care. Indeed, only one-third of these 'poverty' allocations reach the poor in income, thus assuring their continued poverty while providing the justification for financing a monumental medical system that has become a monkey on the back of people without adequate income.

Modern technological medicine is so peripheral to our health that it is best understood as a tool in search of a use. Mark Twain said, 'If your only tool is a hammer, all problems look like nails.' One can hear the medical hammer's beat growing louder as it medicalizes more and more of everyday life. Indeed, it is now pounding away at anything remotely associated with health, including those activities that were once called 'health alternatives': initiatives to escape the medical model.

It was only a decade or two ago that the idea of alternatives to medicine or the medical model became popular. The idea of health as a condition of life rather than a product of medicine was discovered anew. We began to hear words like 'holistic', 'fitness', 'self-care', 'home birth', and 'hospice'. Unfortunately, these new definitions and alternatives have increasingly been revealed as nails for the medical hammer, which turns 'holistic health' into holistic medicine and 'fitness' into the development of sports medicine and doctor-directed diet centers. 'Self-care' has simply tended to teach people how to be their own medical prescribers. The home birth movement has laid the groundwork for hospital 'birthing centers', and the hospice movement, initiated a decade ago in the US to wrest death from hospitalized exile, has become inverted so that hospital-based hospices are growing while community hospices atrophy. How is it that, as we open each door to health, we find we have re-entered the medical chamber at the end of the corridor?

The reason we have failed to find another way is that we have not adequately comprehended the basic structure that guides the modern medical system, the three essential elements of which are:

Management, a system of hierarchical control that breaks human activity into tiny pieces. I know of no culture that believes health is the result of oligarchic control and fragmented life. How could a method predicated on these values conceivably allow a healthful way?

Commodification, the creation of a 'health consumer'. There is, of course, no possibility that health could be consumed. There has never been a 'health consumer'. None the less, this mythical being has been medically engineered as the necessary commodity to meet the needs of the medical sector of our economic system.

Curricularization or 'health education'. Once health is taken to school, it can be managed and commodified. The transmutation of cultural knowledge of healthful coping into a coded lexicon of expert knowledge is the function of curriculum. It is the 'new order' of this curriculum that disorders popular capacity to cope and celebrate, the essential doorway to healthful ways.

Most of the inventions or traditions that avoid the hammer-power of these three elements of the modern medical system are to be found in popular activities, in citizen efforts to release the healthful possibilities of citizenship and community when social space becomes unmanaged, uncommodified and decurricularized. There are many such efforts[12] and their result will *not* be an alternative. Rather, their direction is to open a door towards the thousands of other ways that grow when the monopoly of medicalized health is pushed aside.

There remains the question as to whether there are public policies that might support citizen efforts to allow health in these other ways. It is a perilous question and one to be approached with great hesitation. However, there are four tentative policy guidelines that might enhance the possibility that healthful space could be enlarged in contrast to the medical way.

First, all increases in expenditures for therapeutic medical services should be faced with a 'burden of proof'. Medical advocates should be required to demonstrate that their therapies will be more healthful than applying the same budget to the income of people, their community organizations or an alternative preventive approach.

Second, all medical or health proposals should be tested in terms of their capacity to strengthen local community authority and legitimize the competence of popular activities. This is a test that can only be applied by the community. Its legitimacy is demonstrated when community decisions are *decisive* rather than advisory or 'participative'.

Third, the non-medical tools and techniques that public health advocates claim will improve health should also be evaluated in terms of their empowering capacity. Are they usable by their 'beneficiaries'? Understandable? Controllable? Or are they mystifying, mega-scale, manipulative devices and methods – large school systems, mass media, etc., that necessarily require outside dominance to achieve their 'healthful' effect?

The fourth guideline is at once the most important and the most difficult to understand: health is basically a condition and not an intervention. The basic 'healthist' misunderstanding is best understood by the modernized poor. Injected, treated, cured, cared, educated, and manipulated towards 'compliance', these people know better than anyone else that these interventions are not the source of their health. Instead, each day their lives are physiologically sickened by their impotence, which is confirmed by their intervenors. They are reduced to being 'health consumers,' the raw material of 'health providers'.

Health is a condition, an indicator, a sign. In post-industrial societies, health status measures the power, competence and justice of a people and their communities.

Our research indicates that it is impossible to *produce* health. It is possible to *allow* health by avoiding the maladies of a managed, commodified, curricularized life and the ersatz society they create in lieu of communities of care.

•   •   •

It is, perhaps, surprising that one of the largest health institutions in the world, the World Health Organization, has shown an interest in developing some of the new approaches to health that have been elaborated here. Moreover, it is seeking to do so in a cautious, integrated and balanced way, mindful of the hazards of big institutional activity in the health field. Its programme of health promotion is a vital part of its strategy 'Health for All by the year 2000'. The programme, accepted by member states of the European Region in 1982, warned against quick and easy solutions,[13] while in the 'Dilemmas' section of a later document (WHO, 1984b), four main dangers of the health promotion approach are pinpointed and cautioned against:

1   There is a possibility with health promotion that health will be viewed as the ultimate goal incorporating all life. This ideology, sometimes called 'healthism', could lead to others prescribing what individuals should do for themselves and how they should behave, which is contrary to the principles of health promotion.

2   Health promotion programmes may be inappropriately directed at individuals at the expense of tackling economic and social problems. Experience has shown that individuals are often considered by policy-makers to be exclusively responsible for their own health . . . Thus, when they are ill, they are blamed for this and discriminated against.

3   Resources, including information, may not be accessible to people in ways which are sensitive to their expectations, beliefs, preferences or skills. This may increase social inequalities. Information alone is inadequate; raising awareness without increasing control or prospects for change may only succeed in generating anxieties and feelings of powerlessness.

4   There is a danger that health promotion will be appropriated by one professional group and made a field of specialisation to the exclusion of other professionals and lay people. To increase control over their own health, the public require a greater sharing of resources by professionals and government.

However, notwithstanding this sensitivity to possible pitfalls, the WHO approach to health promotion is robust and vigorous.

Health promotion is the process of enabling people to increase control over, and to improve, their health. This perspective is derived from a perception of 'health' as the extent to which an individual or group is able, on the one hand, to realise aspirations and satisfy needs; and, on the other hand, to change or cope with the environment. Health is, therefore, seen as a resource for everyday life, not the objective of living; it is a positive concept, emphasising personal and social resources, as well as physical capacities (WHO, 1984b).

In the same document, five objective areas were identified for 'integrated action':

1   Increasing access to health, by reducing inequalities in health and increasing opportunities to improve health. 'This involves changing public and corporate policies to make them conducive to health, and involves reorienting health services to the maintenance and development of health in the population, regardless of current health status.'
2   Development of an environment conducive to health, 'especially in conditions at work and in the home. Since this environment is dynamic, health promotion involves monitoring and assessment of the technological, cultural and economic state and trends.'
3   Strengthening of social networks and social supports. 'This is based on the recognition of the importance of social forces and social relationships as determinants of values and behaviour relevant to health, and as significant resources for coping with stress and maintaining health.'
4   Promoting positive health behaviour and appropriate strategies to improve health and cope with stress.
5   Increasing knowledge and disseminating information related to health.

Such a strategy for health is clearly inextricably linked to economic and social policy. It is also the key to a healthier future, defined by James Robertson as:

a future in which more people have more power to determine their own lives, to create well-being (i.e. genuine wealth) for themselves and one another, to undertake what they themselves regard as valuable work, and to take a positive part in shaping the society in which they and their children will live. It will be a future that greatly reduces the inequality and injustice which today condemns many millions of people all over the world to short, unhealthy, unfulfilling lives. It will be a future that treats planet Earth with care, and restores a healthy natural environment for humans and others to live in.

NOTES

1   The purpose of the WHO sponsorship was to stimulate debate, and the views expressed here or in the papers do not necessarily reflect those of WHO.
2   See the 1985 TOES papers by Peter Draper, Trevor Hancock, Ilona

Kickbusch, John McKnight, James Robertson and Mira Shiva.

3   *New York Times*, 26 February 1984.

4   K.A. Moser, A.J. Fox, D.R. Jones, 'Unemployment and mortality in the OPCS longitudinal study', *Lancet* (ii) 1324–1329, 1984.

5   Statement of the UN Secretary-General to the second 1983 session of the Economic and Social Council, 6 July 1983.

6   Statement of the UN Secretary-General to the Opening Meeting of the Assembly's Special Session on Disarmament, 7 June 1982.

7   Statement of the UN Secretary-General to the University of Pennsylvania, 24 March 1983.

8   'Another Development in Health', *Development Dialogue*, 1978, 1, Dag Hammarskjöld Foundation, Uppsala, Sweden.

9   See for example 'Regional targets in support of the regional strategy for health for all', *WHO European Region Working Paper*, 14 July 1984.

10   This figure comes from Pam Hall, Memorial University of Newfoundland.

11   L. Thomas, 'An unhealthy obsession', *Dun's Review*, June 1976.

12   Further information about such efforts and initiatives can be obtained by contacting the Center for Urban Affairs and Policy Research, Northwestern University, Evanston, Illinois 60201.

13   'Proposed programme budget 1984–85 and preliminary targets for 1986–89', WHO Regional Office for Europe, Copenhagen, 1980, unpublished document EUR/RC34/7.

6 INDICATORS OF ECONOMIC PROGRESS

It should by now be becoming clear what constitutes economic progress in the context of the new economic framework described in this book:

- increasing satisfaction of the whole range of human needs, with the emphasis on personal development grounded in social justice; good health for all, conceived as the ability of the individual or group to satisfy their needs, achieve their personal aspirations and change or cope with their environment;
- more equitable sharing of work, both in the formal and informal economies, with due value being given to each and with a new emphasis being put on the quality of work (the skills it uses and develops, the satisfaction it gives and its social usefulness) and on the quality of the technology which helps a person to do it;
- greater economic self-reliance at the individual, local, provincial, national and regional levels;
- conservation and ecological enhancement of the environment and sustainable use of natural resources, based on the realisation that increased consumption in a context of sustainability can only be achieved by making better, more efficient use of a sustainable quantity of resources, rather than by increasing overall throughput.

It need hardly be further stressed that conventional economic indicators are both inadequate and inappropriate for measuring progress towards these complex, multi-dimensional goals. Enough has already been said about how the panacea commitment to economic growth cannot succeed even in its own terms; far less can GNP indicate the sort of economic achievement described above. New indicators are needed, especially tailored to measure the kind of progress that is being sought, and this chapter both defines the sort of indicators now required and elaborates some of them in more detail. It examines in turn:

- resource indicators and resource accounting;
- a new indicator of national product, called here the Adjusted National Product (ANP), basically consisting of GNP with the social and environmental costs deducted from it, rather than added to it;
- indicators of health;
- social indicators;
- ways of taking the informal economy into economic account, so that its contribution to the national economy can be fully appreciated and valued.

Improvement across this range of indicators really would show that overall progress in terms of wealth, health, well-being, economic security and the fulfilment of obligations to future generations had been achieved.

An important general point is that, as far as possible, the data for these indicators should be collected and the results published and updated at the local level. They would serve a vital purpose in enabling communities to know exactly what resources were available to them, how they should proceed to utilise them for maximum benefit and maximum self-reliance, and what progress their local economy was making. Obviously the indicators from each locality could then be compared and aggregated as appropriate for overall national co-ordination; but the prime purpose of the indicators would be to enable people locally to understand how their local economy was faring and what individual and community action was necessary in the future to redress any shortcomings.

RESOURCE ACCOUNTING

There is a pressing need for resource indicators and resource accounting to become standard practice in economic management. It is extraordinary, even in terms of the present economic system, that there is no 'capital' accounting at the macro-economic level, but only a monitoring of income flows, when, as Lester Brown has written (Brown et al., 1984), 'glowing economic reports are possible even as the economic policies that generate them are destroying the resource base.'

No business would be run along such lines, yet national governments[1] proceed blithely on the basis of monthly figures of aggregate growth, with no systematic analysis as to whether that growth has come from greater employment, from greater utilisation of capital assets, from increased use of natural resources or from greater productivity, whether of labour, capital, land or of other natural resources, such as energy. Nor do the national accounts systematically show depreciation of national assets, such as depletion or pollution of natural resources, or the deterioration of industrial or social infrastructure (e.g. roads, sewers, schools) or housing stock. Just as important as this physical capital, and similarly unanalysed in the growth figures, is the nation's human capital, its people, their state of health and the wastage of investment through underemployment or unemployment of their skills.

The data for most of these indicators is already extant in one form or another, but it is often the result of irregular, one-off studies, which, whatever their impact when they are published, are soon forgotten in the run of everyday economic life. What is lacking is any thorough on-going monitoring of trends in these areas, and their publication on a regular basis by government, as is done with figures of national product, inflation, employment, etc., as a normal part of economic assessment of comparable importance to these other indicators.

These resource indicators would need to include all natural and human resources, as well as the capital built up by past labour, on which future economic activity depends. Natural resources include energy sources, mineral deposits, soil, plant and tree resources, the resources of the rivers, ocean and lakes, and fresh water itself. The figures would include the degradation of these by the pollution of earth, air and water. Important distinctions would be drawn between renewable and non-renewable resources, the former to be managed for sustainable yield, the latter maximally conserved. Productivity tables for agricultural land would be drawn up, showing its dependence for that productivity on chemical inputs. Figures for the resource contents of imports and exports, whether of raw materials or finished goods, would be computed, so that progress towards self-reliance could be monitored. There would be no attempt to convert these natural resource measurements into monetary units for the sake of aggregation or comparability; there would be no attempt to develop a Gross Resource Indicator, because of a recognition that each major resource is of crucial importance in its own right. For those interested in self-reliance, no amount of oil can fully compensate for a lack of drinking water, nor can great mineral wealth replace the need for soil to grow food.

As regards infrastructure, an enormous amount is known about the condition of roads, railways, buildings and other capital assets, but there has been little assessment as to how this infrastructure contributes to or detracts from the new priorities of sustainable resource use and environmental conservation. Do we need to maintain all our roads, built with indiscriminate economic growth in mind, when greater local economic self-reliance may cut out the need for much freight transport and when resource-efficient public transport will be promoted instead of private travel? In the reconstruction of our sewage system, how can we ensure the recyclability of human wastes free from industrial and other contamination? Thus, as with normal business decisions, there will be no blanket commitment to 'maintain infrastructure'. Rather the resource accounting will facilitate decisions as to how to develop our capital assets in pursuit of our economic goals, which to phase out and in which to invest.

Assessment of human resources is, of course, much more difficult because one is not merely dealing with a factor of production, one is talking about people. There can be no simplistic relation of education and training to some anticipated future production, for education is as much about personal development as about training people for particular tasks. Yet there must be some recognition that all the parental and community care, education and training that goes into the rearing of children and the development of adults is, in a very real sense, investment in the human resources of the future. As such, it can certainly be expected to yield a 'return', even if that return is not primarily a financial one. Some of the human elements in that return will be indicated in the health and social indicators to be discussed later in the chapter, as well as in the health or otherwise of the informal economy.

Thus informed as to the state of natural resources and the environment, the nature and condition of capital infrastructure and the human skill available, the decision-makers and other people, largely at local level, could then address the task of allocating these resources for production to maximise the wealth produced without undermining the resource base. In short, they could turn to informed consideration of the Adjusted Local Product and its national counterpart.

● ● ●

'FROM GROSS TO ADJUSTED NATIONAL PRODUCT'
by Christian Leipert

A large proportion of the outcome of the production process expressed each year in GNP does not represent any benefit to the quality of life and of the environment. On the contrary, it is an actual cost of production and consumption. The deficiency of the GNP concept becomes particularly obvious when it is recognised that GNP can be increased by methods of production which involve environmental destruction and social costs. The more environmentally damaging and spatially concentrated the production process, the greater the price to be paid in environmental protection and social costs, called here 'defensive expenditures'. These costs are then added into GNP and this higher level is hailed by economists, politicians and the business community as an achievement.

For the interest groups who see no future economic strategy other than the pursuit of growth, the expansion of defensive costs offers a new and certain growth mechanism in the context of industrial decline, allowing the problem-generating industries to be complemented by the new problem-solving industries. The damage-control and damage-repair sector thus becomes a new opportunity for growth for national economies, but, far from indicating an increase in human well-being, this sector could be interpreted as representing a decline in the quality of life to a level which now made defensive expenditures essential.

A more appropriate perspective for the future can be described as differentiated development, in which different sectors would experience either growth or contraction depending on the substantive goals of an ecologically- and socially-sound economic development. Such development would no longer be the chance result of following a profit-oriented policy of non-selective growth.

In order to organise this qualitative development, differentiated criteria of measurement are needed. More specifically, ways must be found of differentiating within GNP, and identifying defensive production and consumption activities, so as to arrive at an empirical demonstration of the full costs of industrial activity. In this way it will be possible to differentiate between types of production in terms of the concepts of defensive and autonomous, i.e. beneficial, expenditures.

The analysis of the costs of industrial growth which is developed below is systemic. The costs of production are not only those of the actual consumption of resources at prices set in the market-place, and thus included in the accounting system, but also those economic and other burdens which are brought about by production activities. The aim is to draw up a balance sheet of costs and returns of production, which is as comprehensive as possible, which does not concern itself only with defensive expenditures, but which also takes into account all the various categories of social cost. Difficult though such an objective might be to achieve, such a broad approach is vital if a meaningful welfare adjustment is to be computed. No real alternative exists for the future, given the accumulation of damage which has occurred to date, brought about by inadequate consideration of the consequences of economic activity, and the related practice of maximising or optimising partial indicators.

Statements on the actual impact and rate of growth of damage in many areas – such as human health, plant and animal life, ecological systems, the built environment, production equipment, etc., are still surrounded by considerable uncertainty. The chief reason for this is the uneasy position of research in the frontier region between the major fields of study – natural systems, medicine, economics and society. The failure in this area is one of the consequences of the market-centredness of economic thinking and the resulting blindness of economics to social costs. Today, in view of the general public interest in an alternative economic policy which is both ecologically and socially sustainable, the possibility exists of successively diminishing the blind spot – namely the lack of knowledge about the type, extent and growth-dynamics of social costs and damage, whilst maintaining the critical systems and theory perspectives.

The concept and classification of defensive expenditures

In the following, only the external costs category of defensive expenditures are dealt with. It is important to clarify two important points in relation to the time-factor involved in the production and consumption under consideration. Firstly, given growth over time of the national product, has this resulted in a parallel growth of consumption opportunities, has the increase in production permitted a comparable increase in net consumption, or has more product been necessary per unit of net consumption? Secondly, the positive and negative effects of the production and consumption process on the living, environmental and working conditions of the population will change over time, as a consequence of the growth in industrial production. In particular, some of the negative side-effects may come to require economic activities to eliminate, reduce or neutralise them. The expenditures associated with these activities are actually additional and essential costs of production, in contrast with the initial period on which the comparison is based. Parts of the production performance indicated by the Net National Product (see Figure 6.1) are therefore not outputs but inputs, i.e. production costs. These have to be deducted from the Net National Product before a figure is reached which actually shows the surplus of production over costs.

It must be emphasised that defensive expenditures are certainly not superfluous costs. Under the given socio-economic and ecological conditions, they are both necessary and useful. If these expenditures have increased over time, it is because the given conditions have deteriorated, effectively increasing production costs.

The fact that defensive expenditures are time-related means that different patterns of development and settlement will result in different defensive expenditures. In certain cases it is even possible that the attempt to generate more production through a certain development pattern will actually be counter-productive, i.e. it will generate more defensive expenditures, now or in the future, than extra product. Thus, in these cases, more can actually lead to less, while changing the development pattern to reduce defensive expenditures could result in less gross product actually leading to an increase in the net product available for consumption.

Knowledge of the social costs of production is therefore of

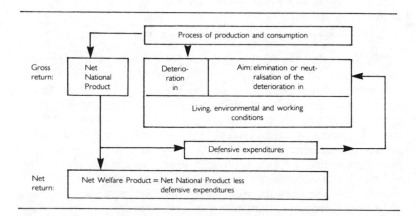

Figure 6.1 The transformation from gross to net production returns

primary importance for those who are responsible for economic policy. As a rule, the individual can only contribute a little to the reduction of defensive expenditures and other external costs of the economic process, for these costs are an expression of specific production, consumption and settlement *patterns*. It is these patterns that have to be altered, if the burden to society of defensive expenditures is to be significantly reduced, and this demands radically different policies from those currently being implemented.

Defensive expenditures have increased in recent years because of the great increase in the scale of economic and social processes, reflected both in the general growth in the Western economies, especially since the Second World War, and in the spatial centralisation of production and its concentration in larger and larger businesses in an increasingly urban society. As Leopold Kohr has shown (e.g. Kohr, 1978), such expansion and concentration in a finite natural and human environment are a cause of increasing stress. Thus production and consumption can no longer be harmlessly processed by the surrounding ecological system, by the limited spatial capacity and human assimilation ability, but have instead led to a rapid increase in damage, deterioration and reduction in well-being.

A classification of categories of defensive expenditures is given in Table 6.1, distinguishing those whose relationship to the specific pattern of industrialised production is very close (I, II, III) from those where the causal relationship is less direct (IV, V).

Table 6.1 Categories of defensive expenditures

I External costs of the general growth process of production and consumption (or of production stagnating at a high level)

   A Expenditure on environmental protection
      1 Investment in environmental protection (disposal and integrated complexes)
         a) manufacturing industry
         b) government
      2 Current running costs of environmental protection
         a) manufacturing industry
         b) government (including administration costs for the implementation and monitoring of environmental controls)
      3 Expenditure on research and development

B   Expenditures as compensation for damage caused by
environmental pollutants
1   Repairs
a)   to domestic and commercial buildings for exterior
paintwork, guttering, etc.
b)   to production facilities
c)   to motorway and railway bridges, high-voltage and other
pylons
d)   to historical monuments and works of art
2   Additional cleaning costs (windows, textiles, cars, etc.)
3   Additional costs as a result of damage to crops (fertiliser,
afforestation, etc.)
4   Consequential costs of damage to health

II   External costs of spatial concentration, centralisation of production
and associated urbanisation

A   Costs of getting to work
1   (Increased) expenditures on car use and purchase and/or
alternative transport as a result of increasing spatial
differentiation of functions
2   Costs of road accidents on the way to work

B   Increased expenditure on rents, accommodation and land use

C   Increased expenditure on security (state and private)

D |Increased expenditure on transport of goods, processing and
packing because of the increased distances between the location
of production and consumption

III   Increasing risk-susceptibility of the industrial system

A   Expenditure arising from increased crime and growing insecurity
in urban areas (II.C)

B   Increased expenditure for defence purposes arising from the
arms race

C   Expenditure on emergency provisions, technical security and
risk-minimisation

IV   Other costs of car transport (not included in II.A.2)

A   Costs of accidents
1   Treatment and rehabilitation costs
2   Repair costs or costs of premature purchases of new
vehicles

B Costs of environmental damage, e.g. costs of emission-reducing measures (catalysts, conversion to lead free petrol etc.)

V Costs arising from unhealthy consumption and behavioural patterns as well as living and working conditions

A External costs of smoking

B Costs of unhealthy nutrition

C Costs of excessive alcohol consumption

D Costs of drug-taking

E Costs of industrial diseases and accidents

F Costs of psycho-sociological health effects arising from unemployment

Category I The appearance and rapid increase of environmental damage is the unavoidable result of an excessive and long-lasting growth process in an *economic* world, in which the exploitation of limited natural resources is taken to be virtually cost-free. Expenditure on environmental protection and on compensation for damage caused by environmental pollutants is the price – without doubt still too low – which since the beginning of the 1970s has been demanded for the excessive use of the environment by the economy.

Category II These have their causes in (amongst others):

– the overuse of land, other natural resources and infrastructural installations associated with the agglomeration of production;
– the extension of centres of agglomeration into ever more remote areas (settlement of the surrounding countryside, urban sprawl) as individual private transport came to be the chief determinant of the transport system as a whole;
– the spatial differentiation of urban functions;
– the growing spatial separation of production and consumption;
– the rapid increase of criminality in urban areas.

The realisation of income objectives in urban areas is made more expensive by the rapidly-increasing distances to the work-place for more and more people who have to move into the surrounding areas away from the centres of concentration. In the

Federal Republic of Germany, for example, more than 4.2 million workers have to commute more than 10 km per day. It can be assumed with certainty that they require their cars for employment purposes. In other words, for them the question of whether or not to buy a car is no longer one of free choice. Whether they consciously realise this or not, the purchase of a car is forced on them by the spatial organisation of functions – the increasing distance between homes and work-places. Further costs result from the relatively high rents and living costs in urban areas and their peripheries. This scarcity-determined price for living in large agglomerations is due most significantly to the high increase in land prices, but also to the relatively rapid increase in building costs.[2]

Growing communication, co-ordination and regulation costs also burden industry and the state. These are the originally unplanned consequences of the micro-economically-determined process of specialisation, growth in business size and technological scale, as well as spatial concentration.[3] High distribution, packaging and advertising costs, too, result from the increasing distances between consumption and production and the increasing specialisation and standardisation of production.

Category III The growing significance of risk in industrial systems results in a rapid increase in defensive expenditures. As a reaction to the fact that criminal behaviour has increased continuously with industrialisation and urbanisation, expenditure on *internal* security in industrial society has increased over-proportionately in relation to GNP. The same applies to state expenditure on the maintenance of *external* security. The absolute and relative increase in expenditure, against the background of the very expensive arms race, is not associated with an actual increase in external security. And, finally, a significant part of the large increase in insurance can be blamed on the increase in burglaries and break-ins, as well as on the increase in transport risks and the technological risks of large industrial plants. The same is valid for emergency preparations and in the area of technical security and risk-minimisation: dangerous and exposed large-scale technologies increase the demand for protective installations, from technical and police security to insurance and emergency protection.

Category IV The external economic costs of car transport involve the costs of traffic accidents and damage repairs.

Category V A collective characteristic for the external economic costs of unhealthy consumption and behaviour patterns, as well as living and working conditions, is that the resultant treatment costs are damage-limiting expenditures, which could have been avoided to a large extent by more preventive and health-oriented behaviour.

The move from Gross National Product to Adjusted National Product

On the basis of the classification given above, the ANP can be calculated from the GNP by subtracting from the latter the defensive expenditures of all sectors, both the goods and services which are contained in the 'final use' components of GNP as apparent end-products, and the intermediary environmental expenditures which result from the vertical integration of production.[4] However, the work on the empirical transformation of the concept presented here has only just begun.

It is unrealistic to expect too high a level of precision from the increasingly significant qualitative social and political indicators, which can provide empirical insights into the socially irrational and counter-productive processes of the industrial system. It is largely the high methodological demands on the level of precision of empirical constructs, that have kept back economic research from investing further efforts in this area of identifying the complex and hard-to-determine external costs of industrial production. Juster, for example, writes on this: 'Concern with environmental damage from air pollution . . . evidently must be based on data that are more speculative in nature than many that economists are accustomed to dealing with.'[5]

• • •

The rest of Leipert's paper for TOES 1985 detailed preliminary statistics and calculations for West Germany of part of the defensive expenditures listed in Table 6.1. Because the figures are only partial, the main work still needing to be carried out in the future, they are not reproduced here, but they give a striking impression of the scale of defensive expenditures imposed on society by current industrial practices. They make clear that we are talking about tens of billions sterling each year. Leipert concludes by stating baldly:

> The development of a comprehensive indicator of the economic external costs of the industrial production process is both scientifically possible and politically important. The continuing use of aggregated GNP as a measure of economic welfare will only aggravate the environmental, social and economic problems of industrial countries. The shift to an Adjusted

National Product instead is a precondition of economic progress.

It is, of course, debatable how comprehensive any indicator of defensive expenditures could hope to be. Leipert himself acknowledges that 'there are still difficult theoretical, methodological and data-collection problems to be assessed and resolved'. But the elaboration of a useful first estimate of the necessary adjustment is certainly achievable in the near future. However incomplete, such an adjustment would be an improvement on the current GNP measure, giving at least some guidance to people and policymakers as to whether increases or otherwise in production were adding to the costs or benefits of society as a whole.

However, even an accurate Adjusted National Product would say nothing about how production is distributed in society, whether it is satisfying human needs or not, or whether it is contributing to the achievement of social goals. Progress in these areas needs to be measured directly by indicators that are more concerned with how the ANP is used, more with its social results, than with its mere monetary value.

As far as the satisfaction of needs is concerned, we have seen that human needs are largely identical with health needs, so that a careful choice from the many health indicators and targets in current use would provide a good indication of needs-satisfaction.

'HEALTH-BASED INDICATORS OF ECONOMIC PROGRESS'
by Trevor Hancock

There are certain key health status indicators that reflect broad social and environmental conditions, and that are therefore suitable as indicators of economic progress. In considering four of them – infant mortality rate, life expectancy, health expectancy (which combines mortality and disability experience) and coherence – an attempt is made to point to some of the problems that the use of these indicators may present.

Infant mortality rate

A recent review of the infant mortality rate was published by the Worldwatch Institute (Newland, 1981). This points out that the infant mortality rate is a composite of a genealogy of hazard, in the form of low family income, lack of sanitation, ignorance, discrimination, crowding, high fertility, or exposure to toxic substances. Many of the direct and indirect causes of death in the very young interact, so that it is difficult to pinpoint a single fatal factor.

It is the multiplicity of causes that contribute to infant mortality, and the complexity of their interaction, that make it such a useful indicator.

The sensitivity of the infant mortality rate as an indicator of social progress can be seen in the inconsistency of a direct relationship between income and infant mortality. Newland points to the dramatic variations in infant mortality rates among countries with similar incomes, and within countries. As an example she points to Kerala, which though one of the poorest states in India has one of the lowest infant mortality rates, less than half the national average. Similarly, in the United States, Washington DC has one of the worst infant mortality rates of any major metropolitan area although it has one of the highest per capita incomes. As she comments:

> the co-existence of low infant mortality with poverty is an encouraging demonstration of the fact that decent health need not await universal affluence. But the persistence of high death rates among the very young even in wealthy surroundings should act as a red flag to policy-makers signalling that beneath the surface of economic progress something is seriously wrong.

For these reasons alone, infant mortality rate would be a useful economic indicator. It has several other advantages, including the fact that it reflects the experience of particularly sensitive and vulnerable subjects who might be expected to be the first to be affected by detrimental changes (meaning, of course, the mother, the fetus and the infant). It is also a useful indicator because any major impacts will be felt within one year, since the infant mortality rate reflects death within one year of birth, unlike such indicators as the cancer rate, life expectancy, etc., which reflect health effects with a long latency period and thus reflect the cumulative experience of a population over some decades. A further advantage to the infant mortality rate is that although there are problems with the data it is one of the better-collected health-related statistics, relatively simple to collect, and amenable to analysis at the level of small areas or small groups. Thus differences within communities can be fairly readily measured. Perhaps its biggest drawback is that it tells us little of the emotional and social well-being of the community.

Life expectancy

This indicator is similarly a composite, and reflects and integrates the experience of whole populations. Many of the comments about the infant mortality rate apply to life expectancy, but there are certain drawbacks. The first is that life expectancy is a somewhat artificial statistic. In essence, life expectancy says that if individuals born this year experience the same patterns of mortality as individuals dying this year they can expect to live a given number of years. The problem is that individuals dying this year are dying because of their life experiences over a period of a number of decades, and therefore life expectancy tells us more about the history of our social progress than it does about our current social and economic state. Furthermore, detailed age-specific mortality data are required, and this is considerably more difficult to collect than infant mortality data in many parts of the world. The statistical manipulations required to calculate life expectancy, while not particularly difficult, would make it somewhat more inaccessible to individuals in a community than infant mortality, with its simpler calculations.

None the less, life expectancy has been used in at least one study (Herrera *et al.*, 1976) as the key outcome variable for a world economic model. The goal of this model was to optimise life expectancy, rather than maximise GNP, because, among many other reasons, of its good reflection of the level of satisfaction of basic needs. According to the authors, the world model that they constructed, based upon optimisation of life expectancy, 'demonstrates that, if the policies proposed here are applied, all of humanity could attain an adequate standard of living within a period of little longer than one generation'.

Health expectancy

While life expectancy is a useful indicator, it does reflect only those personal, social and environmental influences that ultimately cause death. But, in addition to death, we are also interested in the extent to which a population is disabled, either physically or mentally. Clearly, a society in which people live to a ripe old age, but experience severe disability for much of their lives, is not a very desirable society. One attempt to overcome this problem has been the development of the concept of 'health expectancy' and 'quality-adjusted life expectancy' (Wilkins and Adams, 1983).

What Wilkins and Adams found suggests that if we are to use indicators such as life expectancy as indicators of social and economic progress, we might be wiser to use disability-free life expectancy or quality-adjusted life expectancy, because these indicators highlight the disparities in and between societies to a greater extent than life-expectancy alone. Thus, while Canadian males from the highest income quintile can expect to live 6.3 years longer than their counterparts in the lowest income quintile, they can expect 10.3 years more quality-adjusted life, and 14.3 years more disability-free life. Similar results hold true for females. As Wilkins and Adams comment:

> In spite of their short life, low-income males must endure almost twice the number of years of disability, and low-income females an additional 40%, compared to their high-income counterparts . . . a shorter life is not compensated for by less disability. Rather than cancelling each other out, the differences on one scale are added to those of the other, thus aggravating rather than reducing the disparities already observed.

While the use of such health-expectancy indicators may prove more useful than life expectancy, the problems that this indicator poses are substantial. In addition to requiring detailed mortality data, calculation of this indicator requires detailed knowledge of minor and major disability rates for the country as a whole, as well as for geographic and social sub-units. A sophisticated health information system is required, together with frequent and consistent community surveys of disability. It has proved difficult enough to persuade policy-makers in the developed world that the expense of these undertakings is worthwhile, and it is hard to see how the required data could be collected with sufficient accuracy, ease and economy throughout the world, at least in the foreseeable future. None the less, health expectancy may prove to be a useful indicator in the long term.

Coherence

Neither infant mortality rate nor life expectancy tell us very much about the emotional and social well-being of the community, except in the most indirect fashion. The health expectancy or disability-free life expectancy do tell us about the lack of mental and emotional well-being, as far as this creates disability. But in view of the importance of these aspects of human need and health, it would perhaps be preferable to have a composite indicator. Such an indicator may be Antonovsky's concept of 'coherence' (Antonovsky, 1979).

Coherence has three major components, namely:

comprehensibility 'the extent to which individuals perceive the stimuli that confront them as making cognitive sense';
manageability 'the extent to which people perceive they have resources at their disposal adequate to meet the demands posed by stimuli' (manageability is not the same as control – it is 'a sense that aided by their own resources of by those of legitimate others, they will cope');
meaningfulness 'life makes sense emotionally, people care, at least some of the problems and demands posed by living are worth investing energy in, are worthy of commitment and engagement' (Antonovsky, 1984).

The concept of coherence is appealing on several levels. First, it is concerned with the creation of health, rather than the creation of illness. Second, the evidence, though not conclusive, seems to suggest that 'the stronger the sense of coherence of individuals and groups, the more adequately will they cope with the stresses immanent in life and the more likely are they to maintain or improve their position on the health-ease/dis-ease continuum' (Antonovsky, 1979). Third, Antonovsky has developed an easily administered questionnaire involving a twenty-nine item scale to measure the sense of coherence.

The concept of coherence as an indicator of socio-economic progress is not without its problems. Perhaps the most important one is that, while a sense of coherence may be good for health, it is not necessarily good in, and of, itself. As Antonovsky has said, 'a person with a strong sense of coherence is quite capable of being what many would consider to be thoroughly insensitive, unpleasant, inconsiderate and exploitative.'| Furthermore, one would have to be certain that any such indicator was not culturally biased, and therefore only of use in the modern industrialised Western democracy within which the concept has been developed and measured.

None the less, the relative ease of administering the questionnaire, the ability to generate an indicator of coherence for a group or community, the wide range of experiences and feelings that the concept integrates and, above all else, the fact that it is a measure of health and not a measure of disease, make it attractive as an indicator of socio-economic progress.

●   ●   ●

The four indicators detailed above – infant mortality, life expectancy, health expectancy, coherence – are obviously not equally appropriate to all societies, but some combination of them is both appropriate and immediately feasible for the vast majority of countries. As has been seen, their use throws light on aspects of economic and social progress that are quite invisible to ANP and other monetary indicators, and their use should become a standard part of economic assessment and feedback for policy-making at the local, national and international levels.

But health indicators, however necessary, cannot by themselves give a full picture of social trends and conditions. For these, specifically social indicators of wide relevance and application are required.

'SOCIAL INDICATORS FOR POPULAR PLANNING'[6]
by Roy Carr-Hill and John Lintott

Background

This paper describes work which was made possible by a small grant from the Nuffield Foundation. It is a small part of a large project, which is concerned with producing an alternative to the British Government's *Social Trends* (an annual compendium of significant social statistics with some basic commentary) by attempting to develop measures of individuals' well-being across a broad range of social concerns. This introduction summarises the approach we have adopted in selecting 'social indicators' of well-being. This approach is then illustrated by concentrating on some specific data.

The social indicator 'movement', of which *Social Trends* is one manifestation, arose in the mid-1960s, in response to new social movements and ideas: decline of the work ethic, breakdown of the family, concern about the physical environment, dissatisfaction with the Welfare State, and others. For social statisticians this translated into dissatisfaction with Gross National Product and other narrowly economic measures being treated as indicators of well-being, and with traditional econometric modelling as a tool of state management and control.

A number of proposals were made. Some economists suggested modifications and expansion of the national accounting framework, on which GNP is based, so as to produce a more comprehensive measure of welfare (e.g. the Net National Welfare proposed by Nordhaus and Tobin, 1971).[7] Another proposal was for an accounting-type framework for social statistics parallel and linked to the national accounting framework of economic statistics (e.g. the system of Social and Demographic Statistics proposed by R. Stone, 1975). The first proposal leads to absurd contradictions, especially when it involves trying to put a money value on people's time, and the second concentrates on the time spent in a status and ignores the quality of the activities carried out. It therefore seems to us that both make the mistake of proposing a technical solution to the fundamentally political problems of assessing the relative importance of different aspects of the quality of life.[8]

The social indicator movement

The most promising approach, in our view, was that taken by the social indicator movement. While subject to different interpretations, this generally implied the choice of a number of aspects of well-being, or social concerns, either deduced from a social theory or in the course of a political process, to be measured as directly and validly as possible by social indicators. This would imply, for example, devising and applying direct measures of health, in contrast to conventional *policy* indicators such as the number of doctors or hospital beds per thousand population. Also important is the idea that social indicators should provide as complete a view of well-being as possible, including aspects such as people's relationships, their sense of security, and the productiveness of their activities, which while difficult to quantify, are clearly as important for human well-being as more obviously measurable aspects.

Another strand of the social indicator movement, however, was more concerned with social control. Here the ultimate aim was to devise measures of crucial social variables which would be part of a model of social change, similar to, but broader in scope than, the conventional economic models. In this way all the consequences of social change could be monitored, predicted and controlled.

Of course, both these approaches, perhaps particularly the second, are very ambitious, and they also frequently came into conflict with each other. Largely as a result of this, the social indicator movement reached something of a stalemate in the second half of the 1970s. But while the recession has made some of the problems worse (in particular, difficulties of monitoring structual change compared with gradual expansion, and lack of funds for collecting new data), it has also made their solution more urgent. There is clearly widespread interest in assessing the likely outcomes of the present restructuring for the well-being, broadly defined, of the population as a whole, and of various sections of it.

A less ambitious, intermediate outcome of interest in social indicators was the development of a number of national reports presenting social data across a broad range of concerns. The first of these was the British Government's *Social Trends* (Central Statistical Office, London, 1970), originally designed to stimulate public discussion of social issues through the presentation, with commentary, of a broad range of available statistical data. While *Social Trends* has been published annually since 1970, its form has narrowed in the last few years; its use of data is more conservative, there is less commentary, and it is presented as a 'descriptive brief for government', rather than for a broader public.

Yet the social indicator approach seems to us fruitful, and the original purpose of *Social Trends* – encouraging public discussion of social issues through the presentation of appropriate statistical data – more valid than ever. In this project we present, together with illustrations, a possible formula for developing social indicators of well-being. In this respect, our project may face fewer difficulties – though they are still very considerable – than official attempts, since we are not concerned with the conflicting objective of developing a model of social change as an aid to state control.

From social indicators to a satisfaction index?

We have adopted an approach to social indicators which conceives of them as measures of individual well-being. This implies that the indicators should be direct measures of aspects of well-being, rather than measuring some factors influencing it; they should be valid in the sense that they should never increase when well-being decreases, or vice versa; and that they should be part of a set of indicators which between them do not neglect any important aspect of well-being.

Of course, this is an ideal to be aimed at, rather than a practical proposition, given both the conceptual problems of quantifying well-being, and the limitations of existing data. In practice we are likely to find that any available social data are ambiguous in what they tell us about well-being. None the less, we have found the criterion of measuring well-being useful as a guide.

One question, which has to be resolved before developing a set of indicators, is whether or not we are aiming for an overall social satisfaction index. In general, we are wary of such aggregation, for it often tends to obscure the detailed reality of the issues. For example, in the approach that concentrates on the satisfaction of basic needs, we believe that, however basic needs are defined and differentiated, it is essential to retain these different aspects of civilised living as identifiably separate dimensions. Thus the ILO Basic Needs Programme, which started out with a list of basic needs, carries through most of its analysis in terms of a Basic Needs Income, defined as that income which can buy the Basic Needs 'ration'. Now the cost to an individual of such a 'ration' will depend on the prevailing system of production, distribution and exchange; with appropriate policies and subsidies, it could be zero. The price of the ration is therefore largely arbitrary. Much more important is the ration's content. It is this latter exercise, defining the content, that is the purpose of our project.

Another approach to indices of satisfaction is to ask people whether or not they are satisfied. This has been the general tendency among American writers (e.g. Andrews and Withey, 1973) and has recently been taken up by Social and Community Planning Research (SCPR) in Britain (Jowell and Airey, 1984). We realise that the sentiments behind such attempts are democratic. But we believe that the evidence argues overwhelmingly that the answers to surveys are only very vaguely related to people's 'objective' conditions, whether those are defined externally or in terms of what people are actually prepared to do to maintain or remedy their current situation (see, for example, Marsh, 1979). Moreover, once again, we are chary of an approach which assumes that every aspect of life is potentially 'satisfying', viewed as a unitary concept.

Finally, we think it is important to acknowledge a plurality of visions of humanity, by which some argue that people are defined by what they are, others by what they do, others by what they have, others by how they relate and others by their chance of survival. We see these different world views as leading to very different patterns of weighting the multifarious aspects of well-being.

For all these reasons, we have preferred to concentrate on elaborating indicators for the various aspects of human well-being seen as relatively independent of each other. Nevertheless, despite our distaste for aggregation across kinds of need and across people, the basic needs approach, and to a lesser extent the satisfaction approach, have a crucial implicit message: that what is important is the proportion of people who do *not* have the basic minima or who are *not* satisfied. The argument for indicators in terms of the proportion of haves and have-nots has been proposed several times in recent years (e.g. at the Pugwash Conference, 1971, in Smith, 1984). We endorse this argument in general, and indeed use it frequently in developing our own indicators, but see it as neither necessary nor desirable to aggregate the indicators in order to play against the GNP game. We believe that the political choices implict in all consideration of indicators will emerge more clearly from the individual indicators as they stand.

Our approach

In order to get from the general idea of individual well-being to specific social indicators, we have had to decide what are the important aspects of well-being, and within each of these is a number of more specific social concerns. While such an exercise is fraught with value judgments, the framework we have chosen seems in practice to correspond broadly with a number of other attempts. Thus, as a first step we divide well-being into the following aspects: being, doing, having, relating and surviving.

Being is concerned with the state, both physical and mental, of the individual. It thus includes health and knowledge, both considered as aspects of well-being, rather than as part of the functioning of the health-care and educational systems.

Doing is concerned with the nature of people's activities in all spheres (leisure, paid employment, household tasks).

Having is concerned with individuals' access to the material conditions necessary to satisfy their basic needs. It thus includes items of individual or small group consumption (food, housing, heating) and aspects of the wider physical environment (pollution, resource depletion, etc.).

Relating is about the nature of people's relationships to each other, both on a micro level (households, friendships) and on a macro level (functioning of the wider social and political system).

Finally, *surviving* is concerned with threats to the security of individuals from other individuals, groups or the state. It includes harm to individuals arising from a range of accidental and/or unexpected events, as well as the functioning of the state's policing and judiciary role.

This framework seems to us reasonably coherent, but its main justification is pragmatic. It seems possible to include all the concerns generally regarded as aspects of well-being; and while there are bound to be overlaps among the different aspects, these do not prove serious in practice.

Having established this general framework, the procedure we have adopted is to start from these broad aspects of well-being, break them down into narrower social concerns and sub-concerns, to arrive at particular indicators of well-being. These are then matched as far as possible to existing social data. While the first stages involve various conceptual problems, the last stage – matching data to the indicators specified – requires all kinds of compromise if any actual data are to be presented at all.

We illustrate here this approach to measuring the quality of life by concentrating on one specific area: the pattern of human activity.

Human activity patterns

In structuring the area of human activities, we have tried to get away from the traditional dichotomy of 'work' – understood as paid employment – and 'leisure' – largely taken to be passive entertainment. Not only does this dichotomy ignore unpaid production, the productive uses of 'free' time, and the destructiveness and/or purposelessness of much paid 'work'; it is inappropriate as a description of the experience of most women, children, those who are 'retired', the inmates of various types of institutions, and the growing number of 'unemployed' men.

But although we would like to consider human activities together, however they may conventionally be classified as 'work' or 'leisure', it is conditions of paid employment that have been of increasing interest to government for a century, and statistics about other activities are comparatively scattered and few. A valuable source, although an irregular one and one which only provides crude breakdowns, is the time budgets produced by the BBC.

Thus clearly we have had to compromise between the ideal indicators that we would like and the data that is available. The tables we present here are a selection of data based on the following broad divisions:

1   *The use of time.* We present data showing the distribution of the population among different statuses – in paid employment, at school, etc. – which are relevant to the use of time (Table 6.2A) and a breakdown of total population time among paid work, unpaid work, discretionary time, etc. (6.3A). These data are difficult to interpret in terms of well-being, in so far as it doesn't tell us what people actually do in the course of paid work, discretionary time, etc.

Table 6.2 Changing patterns of work and leisure, 1951-81, Great Britain

	1951			1971			1981		
A Percentage of the population in:	Total	Women	Men	Total	Women	Men	Total	Women	Men
1 Paid employment	45.8	27.1	66.1	44.0	31.3	57.4	42.7	33.3	52.7
1a. of which part-time	1.7	3.1	0.2	6.9	11.3	2.2	7.3	12.9	1.4
2 Full-time education	14.4	13.5	15.4	19.9	18.6	21.2	21.0	20.0	22.2
3 Pre-formal education	8.2	7.7	8.7	7.5	7.1	7.9	4.5	4.3	4.8
4 Other (including 'housewives', 'unemployed', 'retired')	31.6	51.8	9.8	28.6	42.9	13.5	31.7	42.5	20.3
5 In institutions[d]	3.9	N/A	N/A	3.0	2.8	3.2	2.5	2.5	2.6
B Self-employment (thousands)	1649	306	1342	1744	361	1383	2148	N/A	N/A
C Accidental deaths									
1 Workplace	1802	N/A	N/A	860	N/A	N/A	457[a]	N/A	N/A
2 Transport	6286	N/A	N/A	8182	N/A	N/A	6230[a]	N/A	N/A
3 At home or in residential accommodation	6522	N/A	N/A	6917	N/A	N/A	5468[a]	N/A	N/A
D Potential leisure									
1 Average weekly hours worked to buy household's food	14.76[b]	—	—	11.28[c]	—	—	8.74	—	—
2 Average weekly hours worked to buy household's housing	3.92[b]	—	—	5.42[c]	—	—	6.35	—	—

Notes: a 1982
b 1953-4
c 1968-70 average
d Those included in 5 are also included in 1-4. Hence 1-4 comes to 100%.
It should be possible, for the final version, to align the dates better and fill in some gaps.

Table 6.3 Changing patterns of time use, minutes per day, population aged 15+

| | 1961 | | | 1974/5 | | |
	Total	Women	Men	Total	Women	Men
A Breakdown of total time						
1 Paid work, travel to/ from work, full-time education	263	144	394	245	153	347
2 Unpaid work (house- work, child care)	208	313	92	183	269	89
3 Recuperative	658	674	641	658	668	646
4 Discretionary time	310	303	313	353	350	358
B Passive leisure						
– as percentage of total leisure	48.0	45.4	50.8	40.4	38.5	42.3
C Time spent visiting	43.0	46.0	39.8	73.6	71.4	76.0

Note: The new BBC survey should make it possible to add figures for 1980s.

2 *The quality of activities.* This is closer to what we would ideally like to measure, but unfortunately it is difficult to conceive of a broad, general indicator. For the moment we content ourselves with accidental deaths (6.2C) and with the extent of passive leisure (6.3B).

3 *Social aspects of activities.* This is an essential aspect of many activities, but is largely considered in the 'relating' area. Table 6.3C gives information on visiting.

4 *The productiveness of activities.* A major concern here, and one which we are working on, is the extent to which people are employed in useless or harmful kinds of work. Another focus is on self-sufficiency, one possible output of activities. Self-employment (6.2B) is also of some relevance here.

5 *Access to activities.* This may be viewed in a number of ways. One rationale is that if the available data allows only a partial picture of what people do with their time, we may at least be able to measure how much choice and flexibility they have, on the basis that they will then have more chance to increase their well-being. Table 6.2D attempts to give an idea of the potential for leisure, by measuring the hours of paid work required to buy certain necessities.

Sections 6.2 A and B are drawn from census data and show the division of the population among different statuses which are related to the pattern of activities. 6.2C shows an extreme aspect of activities, accidental deaths. 6.2D aims to give an idea of potential leisure, by showing the average weekly hours of paid work required to buy the essential goods, food and housing. Table 6.3, on the other hand, is derived from time budget data, and gives a broad impression of how time is spent.

Although each of the above is subject to inaccuracy, some broad conclusions can be drawn:

Paid employment has steadily declined since the war, whether we consider the proportion of the population in paid employment (1951, 1971, 1981, table 6.2A) or the amount of total population time spent on paid work (1961, 1974/5, table 6.3A).

- But this results from a sharper decline in men's paid employment, while women's paid employment has increased. Again this is true for both proportions of the population, and for the amount of total population time.
- Among those in paid employment there is a substantial increase in those employed part-time, especially among women. After 1971 there is also a sharp increase in the number of self-employed.
- The 'others' category in table 6.2A – essentially 'housewives', the 'unemployed', and 'retired people' – after declining, started increasing substantially after 1971, but this increase took place entirely among men.
- Time spent on housework and child care has declined, but much more so among women.
- As a result of this and the decline in paid work time, the amount of discretionary time has increased by some three-quarters of an hour daily, among both women and men.
- This is consistent with the view of 'potential leisure' suggested by table 6.2D. The amount of paid work required to buy the average household consumption of food has declined steeply. In the case of housing the amount of paid work has increased substantially, and this may reflect both the move towards house ownership (and the resulting mortgage repayments) and urbanisation (resulting in higher prices).
- Although the amount of discretionary time has increased substantially, the proportion of it spent on 'passive' forms of leisure has declined, and in fact the absolute amount of passive leisure has declined. On the other hand, the amount of time

spent visiting has increased by about half an hour daily, and more so among men.

- The number of fatal accidents has decreased. This is particularly the case for workplace accidents, consistent with the decline of manufacturing and mining employment. The decline in transport accidents is more recent; it followed a substantial rise up to 1971.

Data of this sort about human activity patterns are far more useful than bald statistics of 'employment' and 'unemployment'. They convey qualitative as well as quantitative information and, most importantly, they are whole-economy indicators and are thus much less subject to political abuse. People are not included or excluded as a result of political expediency. Rather they shift from one category to another, staying in the picture the whole time and thus giving a much clearer idea of overall trends.

The area chosen above is for illustration only. The full project proposes indicators, as far as is possible, across all the dimensions of human well-being which we have identified. We think that such a set of indicators will be a useful tool in debating on, and deciding about, policy on a human scale.

• • •

Consideration of human activity patterns as social indicators brings us naturally to the informal economy. It has already been seen how conventional economic indicators neglect and misrepresent informal economic activity, and this neglect in measurement leads inevitably to a neglect in policy. One of the most serious results of this is described by David Ross (TOES, 1985):

> The formal economy is heavily supported by legitimized public incentives, subsidies, tax loopholes and self-interested regulations, because it alone is interpreted as producing society's wealth and jobs. The informal economy also produces wealth and jobs; however, it is supported not by 'economic' incentives, but rather by so-called social expenditures – transfers, social insurance benefits, and subsidized social services. These payments are often referred to as the 'safety net'. But the true safety net, in part supported by these benefits and services, is informal economic activity conducted within the household and neighbourhood. Ironically, however, when the formal economy turns down, and greater numbers of people are forced to reply on informal activity, government and business invariably call for restraint in social spending, citing phrases like 'the real engine of economic wealth – the formal

economy – can no longer bear the unproductive cost of social expenditures'.

Clearly the only way of rectifying this situation is to make informal economic activity economically visible, so that it can be taken into account and policies devised to support it. Ross identifies two key characteristics of much informal activity, which can serve to differentiate it from the formal economy: its predominantly small scale of operation; and its use of social, rather than financial, accounting procedures. (Social accounting is defined by Ross as the 'consideration of the full and ultimate consequences of economic activity on the individual, household and community'.) Ross then analyses the whole economy with regard to these two characteristics, dividing it into nine sectors, and goes on to consider how this approach might be developed to yield an indicator of informal economic activity.

'MAKING THE INFORMAL ECONOMY VISIBLE'
by David Ross

In what follows, a whole economy perspective is developed to make sure that no economic activity is excluded from observation and measure. The economy is divided into nine clearly identifiable and measurable sectors of activity, which can then be categorised *a priori* as being guided primarily by either a commercial or social operating rationale. At this stage, it should be remembered that the judgment about the rationale concerns the particular sector taken in aggregate, acknowledging that within each sector there will be exceptional units not properly detailed by the label applied to the sector.

Big Business When people refer to big business, they usually mean large corporations, both public and private. Most large

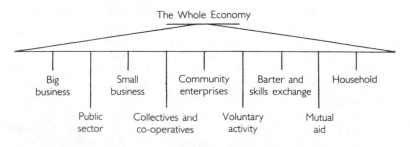

Figure 6.2 The whole economy divided into nine sectors

corporations operate on the fundamental principles of commercial profit and growth. They may also, to some extent, 'socially account' if it is 'good business'. Some publicly owned corporations are expected, by virtue of their charter or by parliamentary direction, to serve some social as well as economic functions. But both private and public corporations are primarily in business for strict commercial reasons and this is well understood by shareholders, management and employees. There is little expectation, therefore, that such businesses pay much attention to broad human or social issues beyond those that affect the bottom line: profit.

Public sector This type of activity – representing education, health care, policing, defense, social services, administration of social assistance, roads and highways, parks and recreation, inspections and regulatory action, and so on – is primarily based on a social accounting rationale. We do not normally think of governments as being in the business of making commercial profits. Yet there is obviously a strong political factor in decision-making, which determines whether the style of government reflects more the operating values of commercial enterprises or more socially oriented values. The supply-side based governments of President Reagan and Prime Minister Thatcher appear to be guided primarily by the same values that guide big business. The main casualties of administrations bent on privatizing former public sector activities are people-oriented programs.

Small business Some of the behaviours associated with big business are reduced or absent in small business activity. For example, owners and employees have daily contact, headquarters and plant are usually in one place, owner-managers have contact with final consumers, and so on. There are different types of small businesses: traditional, franchise, family, and not-for-profit.

Traditional and franchise operations tend to be guided by the pursuit of commercial profit. Social questions, if considered at all, are distinctly secondary. Family small businesses can be either traditional or operated somewhat along the more social lines of a household. Family farms, for example, in many cases may be extended household operations where surplus produce is marketed. Not-for-profit small businesses will also generally be based on a social operating rationale. However, because they depend on sales in the marketplace, they must have one eye on their commercial balance sheets and heed the market's warnings. Consequently there are limits on actions prompted solely by social considerations.

Collectives and co-operatives The basis for much collective and co-operative activity is a strong social purpose which is the rationale of the 'co-operative movement'. But in reality, many co-ops are established simply to save money for members and for other co-ops. As they grow, a co-operative's operations frequently become indistinguishable from those of larger commercial enterprises, even though co-ops and businesses may retain structural differences. Some of the large credit unions in Canada resemble chartered banks; some of the large food co-ops resemble chain groceries; and some of the large farm marketing co-ops resemble their corporate agribusiness counterparts. While there is still some element of social accounting (even if it is only that each owner, regardless of number of shares, has one vote), the pursuit of profit often reduces social accounting to a bare minimum.

Small neighbourhood, housing, day-care, food and worker co-ops and collectives are where we are most likely to find co-operatives strongly guided by social accounting. Within these structures, what and how things are produced, as opposed to how much is produced, take precedence. Activity is often undertaken only after an unfulfilled community need is strongly and clearly articulated. Satisfaction of that need, and not commercial profit, guides these co-operative activities. Individual members can freely discuss aspects of the operation; be a part of it and not feel they are simply factors of production; and maintain close contact between workers and those being served in the community. The original need for the operation is never dropped from sight. But like small businesses, co-ops and collectives rely on the market for most, if not all, of their operating revenue, and the market tempers the type and extent of their purely social endeavours.

Community organizations and enterprises Many of these organizations are often referred to as voluntary, charitable or non-profit. Because this type of social and economic activity is sponsored and controlled by the community and dependent on public donations and grants for its operating revenues, the structures to carry it out are associated with a social accounting rationale. Community organizations and enterprises usually spring up through volunteer efforts and are the result of unmet needs, the satisfaction of which it would not be profitable for commercial enterprises or co-ops to undertake. The public sector may also not meet these needs because of ignorance, a different set of priorities or lack of funding. The interests of the volunteer boards that guide small community organizations are virtually identical with the community served, although the presence of strong professional management can weaken this identity. And, in certain cases, this may also lead to the organization adopting some of the characteristics associated with commercially-run enterprises.

Generally, smaller community organizations have proportionately larger volunteer components while bigger voluntary organizations have proportionately large paid employee components. Unlike small businesses and co-ops, a community organization need not have its activity heavily influenced by commercial considerations. This is because revenue from the sale of output is usually not a major source of operating revenue. Community organizations can pursue activities which are socially necessary but not necessarily commercially profitable. This is why most are strongly supported by public funds, through donations and/or the tax and transfer system.

Voluntary activity Little organized voluntary activity is likely to take place outside of collectives, co-ops and community organizations and enterprises. Volunteer activity mostly aids charities, cultural and amateur athletic programs and is founded on social accounting. Commercial profit is seldom behind voluntary activity, which is not to say that volunteers do not sometimes act out of self-interest. How volunteers are treated by the organizations they work with and how closely they work with the owner/community, management and the people the organization directly serves, depends heavily, as in former instances, on the size of the particular organization. If the organization is small, volunteer activity may be informal. If the unit is large, then the activity may be more formal.

Barter and skills exchange The unorganized or loosely organized non-monetary exchange of goods – known as barter – and services among neighbours can be guided by either social or commercial objectives, but mostly the former. Most highly organized barter arrangements and the exchange of skills through large computer-aided networks would most likely have a commercial rationale. Commercial barter among large enterprises or between states is completely guided by a commercial profit interest.

Mutual aid This type of economic activity is still found to some degree in small rural and northern Canadian communities; in stable, established urban neighbourhoods; and in intentional co-operative communities. The trading and exchanging which occur among neighbours is not done for profit, but for reasons of kinship and alliance. The special social relationships engendered and permitted by these arrangements are primary for many people. The output of the economic activity is important but secondary.

Household activity The operating rationale of household economic activity is considered to be guided by social accounting. Most family decisions are guided by the full and ultimate and human consequences of their actions and not by short-run commercial profit motivès. Food is not allocated to the highest bidder or hardest worker. Nor is the minimum in food and shelter requirements necessarily sought in order to maximize savings as they would in a commercial enterprise.

Towards an operational definition of informal

Having outlined a specific sectoral approach for better identifying operating rationale, the task is now to break down activity according to scale of operation and attempt to assess all economic activity as formal, informal or 'mixed'.

Figure 6.3 illustrates how units of economic activity can be classified according to scale and rationale. On the horizontal axis is located the operating rationale, extending from extremely social to extremely commercial – with gradations in between. On the vertical axis is located scale of operation with the small-scale extreme being represented by a single-person productive activity and the large-scale extreme representing large corporations or centralized public bureaucracies.

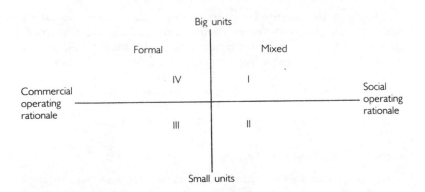

Figure 6.3 Scale and rationale of economic units

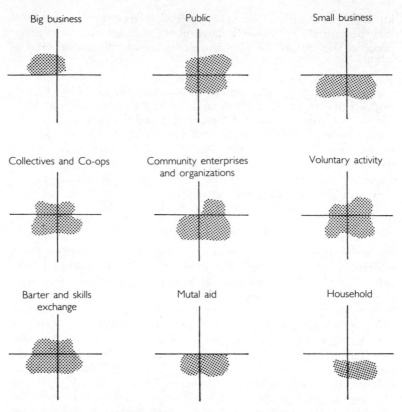

Figure 6.4 Sectional approach to scale and rationale

Adopting the sectoral approach for identifying operating rationale, all economic units (firms, organizations, households, etc.) can be arranged in configurations as in Figure 6.4, where individual dots represent hypothetical configurations of economic units, and not the number of participants or the dollar value of output. At this stage, the diagram is intended to show only the relative positioning of units within sectors, not the relative number of units among the different sectors.

Towards indicators of informal activity

If we accept that the definition of informal proposed here offers a realistic starting-point for developing indicators of informal activity, two major areas need to be further researched. First, economic data need to be collected and ordered according to the sectors of the whole economy and the scale of operation. This would overcome two major shortcomings of current output and labour force measures, in that

all economic activity would be included;
it would represent a way of separating out informal economic activity.

This is not to imply that current measures exclude all informal economic activity. For example, much co-operative, collective non-traditional small business and community-based economic development activity is included in GNP and employment totals. But the data are gathered and reported in ways that bury it and make impossible any later disaggregation for further study. Consequently, under the present system it is impossible to obtain estimates of informal activity, because not only is much of it excluded from measurement (household, mutual aid, volunteer effort), but what is included is done in a way that blends it with formal economic activity. A breakdown of whole economy activity by sector would also permit us to observe and document trends and shifts between formal, informal and mixed activity.

Second, it is to be hoped that, from this data, reseachers will be able to spell out the detailed relationships between informality, scale and operating rationale. For example, even though scale is fairly easy to measure, are there any important differences between units with fifty participants and those with twenty-five? Or are there critical thresholds – less than five, twenty-five, a hundred, etc.? The same applies to operating rationale. Even if the extent of social accounting can be measured, how does this translate into informality? And how do scale and rationale relate to each other – is one more important than the other, is there a constant linear relationship between the two? And are the relationships constant over different sectors?

It will also be important to assess the economic activity in different sectors in some kind of quantitative terms. The first impulse is to ape GNP methods and construct dollar values of output. Some work has already been done to convert non-monetized activity (e.g. household, mutual aid, volunteer effort) into dollar values, and add them into GNP.[9] While this work is important for enhancing the visibility of neglected economic activities, and can be useful in dealing with people who think only in economic terms, it is an inherently inadequate measure for estimating the value of activity (output) in the informal sectors. If informal activity is measured only by estimated dollar value of final output, it will always underestimate the true output and level of activity *vis-à-vis* formal economic activity.

The formal economy produces only for final output, that is its sole purpose, and any direct consideration of social value is nil or coincidental. The informal economy produces final output as well, but within a much more constrained and community-sensitive production framework. And the value of social and environmental 'outputs' cannot be measured in dollar terms. Consequently, only a fraction of the informal economy's total output is measurable and measured, if at all, by dollar values, but virtually all of the formal economy's total output has a dollar value placed on it. In the informal economy, the social benefits of how, and for whom, and not just how much is produced, are important but largely unmeasurable in direct financial terms (though neglect of these questions can lead directly to financial costs, as we have seen).

Consequently, to compare the real net benefits to society, or the level of human activity between formal and informal activities on the basis of the dollar value of final output alone, is erroneous and biased in favour of showing a greater contribution by the formal economy. Therefore, there is a need to look for a better indicator of levels of activity in the different sectors. The one proposed here is 'time-activity' (number of participants multiplied by hours spent at economic activity), and is an elaboration and an extension of current employment and hours of work indicators into the informal sectors. [See Carr-Hill and Lintott's Table 6.3 earlier this chapter.] Time-activity measures will not represent a dollar value measure of a nation's output, but will show the distribution of human effort among the different formal and informal sectors.

The outlook for change

In Canada today, there are signs that informal economic activity is becoming more visible, and attempts are afoot to measure both time-activity and output. In 1980, the government's central statistical agency performed for the first time a national survey on volunteer effort.[10] This is now being followed up by an ambitious proposal to survey all volunteer effort and organizations using volunteers – including co-ops, community-development organizations and so on. If this becomes a reality, it would ultimately produce a very comprehensive data base encompassing much informal economic activity. Several years ago the government began collecting small business statistics, with breakdowns of information according to more useful interpretations, e.g. the number of franchised businesses.

The Co-operative Union of Canada (CUC) is now producing annual estimates of output and employment within co-operatives – with some breakdowns for different types of co-ops. While the coverage of smaller and emerging co-ops is not adequate, this information is being extended and improved annually. The CUC is currently examining the feasibility of doing a separate survey on small worker co-ops.

The Canadian Council on Social Development (CCSD) has proposed an extensive survey of 'local economic initiatives' existing in Canada. And already several partial inventories exist, e.g. one of community development corporations, and another of local initiatives in British Columbia. Several other surveys are currently under way. A directory of intentional communities in North America, with annotated descriptions of their economic activity and numbers of people, now exists. Within the Native communities of the North, and in rural Newfoundland, important and rigorous studies have documented the extent and value of certain outputs (food, clothing, shelter, heat, transportation) attributed to household and mutual-aid activity. And several studies based on time-use surveys have documented the enormous amounts of time devoted to, and the value of, household economic activity.

Thus informal economic activity is assuming both increasing importance and visibility, and with continuing high unemployment there is every likelihood that this trend will persist. What is crucially important is that informal activity should be more highly valued for the productive and socially cohesive enterprise it represents, and that it escapes from the second-class status which it currently undoubtedly has *vis-à-vis* the formal economy. Measuring its performance more systematically can only help that process.

•   •   •

That completes the outline of a possible new framework for indicators of economic progress, involving resource-accounting, an Adjusted National Product, health and social indicators, and a due awareness of the importance of the informal economy. Much of the data for such a framework is already available, so that the framework could be given practical reality, in a crude and preliminary form at least, within a relatively short period of time. Bringing the data together in this way would ensure that important facts were not overlooked or brushed under the carpet in the heat of the political moment or for commercial or other expediency.

Before leaving indicators, it might be worth posing for this new framework the questions asked in Part I, which threw so much light on the inbuilt failings of GNP.

- What does the framework measure? The indicators together measure the costs and benefits of a society's system of production and consumption, both in capital (resource) and income terms. The measurements are of the whole economy, formal and informal, and also indicate the distribution of the national product through the inclusion of social indices, carefully chosen to correspond to desirable social goals.
- How are the indicators derived? Wherever possible, by direct measurement of the quantities involved, in whatever units are most appropriate. Care would be taken not to over-aggregate the indicators.
- Who takes the measurements? A wide variety of agencies, some of which might be governmental, but many of which would be independent of government and expert in their individual fields, and would be commissioned to carry out this task on behalf of the public. Wherever possible, data would be collected and primarily collated at the local level.
- What for? As a guide, firstly to local economic and social progress and, secondly, at a national level, to any need for redistribution or special support within the nation. The indicators would be comprehensible to people generally, as well as of use to policy- and decision-makers, and would be an invaluable aid to informed participation in the democratic process.
- What significance is attached to this framework of indicators? Very great, though obviously different parts of the framework would be assigned more importance by different people at different times. The framework could therefore act as a significant focus for political discussion, as, in fact, one would expect from something that was explicitly concerned with economic and social progress.

What assumptions underlie the framework?
1 That natural resources and the environment are neither infinite nor, at current levels of usage, 'free'.
2 That all costs and benefits of production and consumption should be accounted for and, wherever possible, internalised into the process concerned.
3 That the distinction between 'economic' and 'social' values and

motivations is both false and misleading. They are in fact inextricably interlinked and should always be considered together.

4   That paid work, *per se*, is neither more valuable, nor should it have higher status, than unpaid work.

Finally, it must be stressed that indicators are only as influential as the extent of their publication and the significance attached to them. The hegemony of the comparatively meaningless GNP and unemployment figures will continue as long as their monthly publication attracts headlines, and people and politicians continue to grant them importance. It is only by constant questioning of these measures and exposing of their failings, and by the practicable development and publication of the sort of alternatives detailed here, that economists and politicians will be weaned off their narrow and counter-productive obsession with 'growth' and 'jobs'.

That concludes the main exposition of the theory of the New Economics, as it has so far been developed through the work of The Other Economic Summit. Its concern with the satisfaction of human needs, with the nature of work, with the promotion of self-reliance, with the creation of health as well as of wealth, and with resources and the environment, sets it sharply apart from the economics of growth and effective demand. Part III of the book describes the New Economics in action: some of the initiatives that are already putting the theory into practice, or some of the policies and reforms that are necessary before such initiatives can realistically be expected to flourish.

NOTES

1   The Norwegian Government is an enlightened and honourable exception to this statement, having developed a system of accounting for its natural resources a decade ago and implemented it ever since.

2   Bundesminister für Raumordnung, Bauwesen und Städtebau, 1983.

3   On this argument, see for example Henderson, 1974 and 1981.

4   Even with the production of goods which do not serve to protect from environmental damage and which are part of net production or net consumption, environmental protection activities are required to varying extents in the production stages (e.g. steel and electricity production). For the calculation of the monetary cost of this environmental protection, see Leipert, 1984, pp.249ff.

5   Juster, 1981, p.2. Juster draws here on a study by Gianessi, Peskin and Wolff on the estimation of emission-related damage costs in the USA.

They write: 'It is impossible to proceed with such a task unless one is willing to make several assumptions, all of which can be criticised' (Gianessi *et al.*, 1981, p.201).

6   This paper draws much of its material from R.A. Carr-Hill, 'Social indicators and basic needs: who benefits from which numbers?' in S. Cole and H. Lucas, *Models, Planning and Basic Needs* (Pergamon, Oxford), and F. Nectoux, J. Lintott and R. Carr-Hill, 'Social indicators: for individual well-being or for social control' in *International Journal of Health Services*, 10, 89–113, 1980.

7   The Net Welfare approach was also explored by Japan Economic Council, 1973, and by Zolotas, 1981. A more detailed explanation of the unsatisfactory aspects of this approach is given in J. Lintott, 'National accounting and beyond' (TOES, 1985).

8   Again, see J. Lintott, ibid., for more details.

9   For a summary of this work in Canada, see Ross and Usher, 1985.

10   Statistics Canada 'An overview of volunteer activity in Canada', *The Labour Force*, May 1981.

PART THREE

The new economics in action

Many of the more general characteristics and concerns of the New Economics will by now be becoming clear, and the rest of this book will be devoted to elaborating these and indicating how they may be given practical effect. Fundamental to much of the preceding discussion has been the idea of democratising the economy, of increasing personal control over the forces that shape people's lives, over the work they do, over what is produced and how.

Such a transformation would be a complete reversal of the dominant economic trend of this century, which has seen unprecedented centralisation of production, concentration of economic power and globalisation of economic influence. Confronted with the mammoth economic agents of today, interlocking in a global economy of unparalleled complexity, it is little wonder that most people experience the economic system as remote and incomprehensible, and themselves as, at best, passive raw material within it. Yet, while the economy was perceived to be working tolerably well, in the rich countries at least, there was little public concern at this situation – if the bus is taking you in the right direction, why worry whether or not you can influence the driver?

But it is now becoming clear that the economic system is not taking most people in the right direction. It also appears to be going towards its unknown destination increasingly fast and with worrying momentum. Shouts to the driver sometimes don't even produce any acknowledgment. When they do, it is not at all clear that the driver either has control of the bus or that he knows himself where it is going. Some passengers are even beginning to suspect that the bus is on automatic pilot and that the voice coming from the cab is synthesised speech programmed with the conventional wisdom of the sixties, which offers little reassurance for the troubled mid-eighties. Under such circumstances, people start to take matters into their own hands.

It is bound to be an unco-ordinated and even incoherent process at first, characterised by a ferment of ideas and a welter of practical experiments and innovations. This part of the book describes many such experiments, generalising and drawing conclusions from them where possible and relating them to the theoretical concerns of Part II. It also explores policies which will help the promising experiments to prosper, policies of different sorts. Some involve putting brakes on the bus. Others entail enabling those who so wish to get off the bus and strike out in a different direction of their choice. Some are intended to help people who stay on the bus to find out where it is headed. All have the objective of re-establishing control over the bus, by forging a comprehensible connection between people and the economy.

The pattern that emerges is far from being a blueprint or manifesto for the future. There are still many unanswered questions and unresolved problems. Moreover, the exploration crosses some pretty unusual country. This is to be expected. If the old terrain had solutions to our problems, it is likely that economists would have unearthed them by now. The first subject to be investigated is that of land itself.

7 ACCESS TO LAND

From its profile on the public agenda in many Western countries, one would never imagine that land was a fundamental factor of production of comparable importance to labour or capital. Current systems of ownership and tenure of land in these countries are overwhelmingly taken for granted across the political spectrum. Yet holdings of land have also undergone great concentration, and, if only because land is the source of food, it can be argued that this concentration is at least of comparable public significance to industrial agglomeration.

For the New Economics, with its emphasis on personal and local self-reliance, land is of prime importance. Access to land is actually at the root of self-reliance, not only as far as home food production is concerned, but for virtually any productive activity, for workshop, office or storage space as much as for agroforestry or energy production, where appropriate. At both the local and national levels, the methods and efficiency of agriculture are obviously of crucial importance to the quest for potential self-sufficiency in food. Greater self-reliance inevitably involves more people having productive access to land and communities having more control over their land. Just as inevitably, this entails a significant measure of reform in virtually all countries in how land is owned, farmed and used in other ways.

The approach to land reform outlined here has three main elements. Firstly it outlines changes in agricultural policy and support, with special reference to Western agriculture, to change the direction of agricultural development and give far more people the chance of being involved in it. Secondly it explains a possible means of enabling and encouraging joint holding and working of land – the co-operative land bank – which combines private ownership of improvements to land with community ownership of the land itself. Thirdly this quest for a balance between private and social ownership of land, seeking its efficient use according to ecologically sound, socially agreed criteria, is taken further in a discussion of land value taxation. Underlying each of these three elements is a perception that land is not just another financial asset. It is the basis of food, work and life. As such, the whole concept of ownership of land needs to be replaced by that of stewardship, seeking the management of land not just for the benefit of the person who owns or works it, but also for the community as a whole, while safeguarding it for the future.

Land reform for people and social justice is traditionally one of the hardest political changes to achieve. For the New Economics, it is also one of the most important.

FARMING WITH NATURE

There is now widespread agreement on all fronts that European and, to some extent, Western farm policy generally, is seriously defective. Bateman and Lampkin (TOES, 1985) identify the chief issues thus:

> It used to be easy, then it became more difficult, and now it is virtually impossible to find anyone who will provide a coherent defence of existing policy. What used to be considered cranky criticisms have become the conventional wisdom, and we do not expect much disagreement with the following list:

> We waste resources producing surplus food and we waste resources again when we dispose of it.
> - Farm policy, supposedly designed to lead to fairer income distribution, is in practice highly inequitable: it is inequitable as between the agricultural sector and society as a whole which subsidises it; it is inequitable as between landowners, tenant-farmers, owner-occupiers and farmworkers; and it is inequitable as between different types of farmer, large and small, livestock and arable. The fact that, in the long run, probably the main consequence of farm support policies is higher land prices, with the returns to farmer and farmworker unaltered, is only the most ludicrous example of the inequities involved.
> - Farm structure policy, either deliberately or by default, has been geared towards larger farm size: associated with this has been the fall in the chance to enter farming both because of rising land prices and because of falling numbers of tenancies, and also a continuing and unabated fall in rural population (which is not the same thing as the population living in rural areas).
> - Farming has ceased to be complementary to or even

compatible with some other rural activities because of its side-effects on wildlife and on the beauty and amenities of the countryside; we have come to take it for granted, but it is in fact quite remarkable that this has become so serious that it has led to the development of a specific body of people whom we have learnt to call conservationists.

- The nutritional problems of developing countries are obvious, and it is equally clear that the agricultural policies of developed countries can worsen them. Even in developed countries themselves nutritional problems (though of a different kind) are now receiving more attention. The main areas of concern are: the make-up of our food in terms of fats, proteins and so on; the extent to which it may contain pesticides, herbicides, etc., which may be harmful to humans; and the extent to which water supplies, and even food itself, are affected by nitrates.

- Other problems about which concern has been expressed include: the dependence of agriculture on fossil fuel supplies; soil erosion and other factors affecting the long-term productivity of the soil; animal welfare; and the problem of competition between agriculture and other rural land uses such as forestry.

It is important to emphasise that the forces that have produced this situation have nothing whatever to do with the free market. In fact agriculture in Britain and elsewhere in the EEC has been the recipient of unprecedented financial support from public funds, which Richard Body, a Conservative Member of the UK Parliament, has estimated to amount to some £3 billion annually (Body, 1982).

Bowers and Cheshire have no doubts about the impact of this level of public subsidy (Bowers and Cheshire, 1983):

It is the import levies and artificial prices that cause the surpluses and it is the surpluses that cause a large part of the necessary subsidies from public funds, storage costs, restitution payments, denaturing costs and others . . . . we have a scandalous level of support creating extreme riches for big farmers and still leaving poor ones poor; generating shameful waste; ravaging the countryside and degrading the rural environment; and disrupting international trade.

Newby (TOES, 1985) has analysed the economic forces at work as follows:

The State regulation of agriculture has profoundly altered both the structure of the industry and the day-to-day nature of life and work in the countryside. The encouragement of fewer, larger and more capital-intensive farms has resulted eventually in the catalogue of changes which we associate with rural life today: the mechanisation of agriculture, rural depopulation, the urban middle-class invasion of rural villages and the widespread changes in the rural landscape and other environmental aspects of the countryside.

These changes have not been the result of some immutable natural law, but of policy decisions in Whitehall or Brussels. The Ministry of Agriculture (MAFF), for example, has promoted technological change, both directly through its grants and subsidies for farm capitalisation and amalgamation, and indirectly through its complex manipulation of commodity price supports and guarantees which have protected farmers from the consequences of chronic over-production (for details, see Self and Storing 1962; Donaldson and Donaldson 1972; Beresford, 1975). MAFF has also provided direct assistance through its advisory service (ADAS) and its own research establishments. It also finances research in universities and other autonomous research centres and influences the priorities of the Agriculture and Food Research Council. A large and complex network of institutions has thus been erected in the public sector in order to effect the technological transformation that post-war agricultural policy has ordained. The policy itself remained a central tenet of faith while its wider implications remained entirely unconsidered. MAFF, at least, adheres to the 'technological fix' in the drive towards cost efficiency.

The increasingly capital-intensive nature of British agriculture has had one further effect which deserves serious attention: it has made farmers more and more dependent upon non-farm inputs such as machinery and agro-chemicals, while drawing them into the embrace of a much wider complex of industrial companies involved in food marketing, processing, distribution and retailing. Agriculture is being slowly incorporated into sectors of the engineering, chemical and food-processing industries which are collectively known as 'agribusiness'.

The rise of agribusiness implies not only the increasing rationalisation of agriculture, but the growth of a food production system only a small proportion of which may actually take place on farms. Agribusiness companies are, of course, frequently in the vanguard of multi-national organisation and, particularly in the Third World, pose acute problems of national sovereignty and market power. Under these circumstances it becomes tempting to weave conspiracy theories around the exercise of oligarchical corporate power, but there is no need to invent conspiracy theories in order to discern the lack of public accountability embodied in the agribusiness conglomerates. They are actively involved in changing dietary habits, the structure of agriculture, food marketing and retailing, and wield enormous market power. Yet they often remain impervious to control by politicians and consumers.

Along with the state, agribusiness corporations represent one of the most important agencies involved in the restructuring of rural society. The processes involved are often instrumental and indirect, but are none the less effective and far-reaching. In Britain few agribusiness companies have attempted the restructuring of agriculture directly by farming land themselves. They have preferred instead to work their transformation by proxy, through large-scale involvement in farming, which controls the conditions under which farmers operate. The tendency in Britain is for farmers to become the equivalent of eighteenth-century outworkers for major agribusiness companies.

It seems likely that agribusiness influence over the structure of agriculture will continue to proceed in this indirect manner, with agribusiness companies seeking out highly market-oriented agribusinessmen farmers with whom to place contracts. Sufficient numbers of farmers have, indeed, proved sufficiently flexible to the needs of agribusiness companies for the latter not to feel the necessity to vertically integrate and take up farming themselves.

In this manner agribusiness companies have accelerated the trend towards the rationalisation of agriculture and the concentration of the industry on fewer, larger farms. Smaller farmers, who do not participate in such contractual arrangements, find themselves becoming increasingly marginalised, while the larger farmers find their enterprise gradually transformed by the relentless 'industrial' logic of agribusiness. As a result agriculture becomes organised according to non-agricultural criteria, on the assumption that agriculture is merely a disguised form of manufacture. This has implications, not only for farming entrepreneurs, but also for farm workers, the employees of food processors and ultimately all of us as consumers.

The changing pattern of consumer demand for food is also encouraging the growth of agribusiness in Britain. More of the food that we purchase is processed food and, given current trends such as the increasing proportion of women participating in paid employment outside the home, the demand for convenience food is likely to increase, quite aside from the encouragement given to it by agribusiness companies' own advertising campaigns. Since the value added from processing food is much greater than that which is accrued from growing it, the agribusiness domination of food production in Britain is likely to increase for the foreseeable future. Although farmers are likely to retain their nominal independence, their share of retail food prices seems destined to decline further and they will find themselves even more vulnerable to agribusiness marketing policies. So, according to this scenario, the British countryside of the future will contain fewer farms, fewer people employed in agriculture, a more industrialised system of production, and a rural social structure – and even a rural landscape – which takes all of these factors into account.

One of the paradoxes of the situation is that, despite the feather-bedding of agriculture as a whole, farmers themselves, except the very large ones, are being increasingly squeezed, as Vogtmann (TOES, 1985) has shown:

The basic problem a farmer has to cope with is the decreasing margin between costs and product prices: the costs are rising quicker than product prices, especially labour. This means the farmer has to live with a relative or absolute decrease in income, if there is no way to escape. Three ways out are offered to the farmer in this struggle: mechanization, intensification, or specialization.

Mechanization helps to lower the cost-to-yield ratio and enables the farmer to extend the area of farming or to do the work with less people. But it means at the same time that the landscape and the land have to be adapted to mechanization to make it work better. Examples are lowering of ground water tables, elimination of ditches and hedgerows, building of new roads, creation of larger parcels of farm-land, etc. All these changes had and still have environmental impacts, but the farmer often has no choice.

Raising the yield per hectare means *intensification* through increased inputs of fertilizers and pesticides in plant production and increased use of concentrates and medical treatments in animal production. The consequence has been a drastic regression of plant and animal species, dependent on the local conditions.

In the past, most farms combined several kinds of agricultural land use, for example arable farming and animal husbandry or horticulture. This mixed system of farming disappeared to make room for a more *specialized* type. This change has led to considerable problems. Where there are large numbers of animals, manure is causing environmental problems. Where mineral fertilizers have to be used extensively, combined with pesticides, problems arise. In countries like Belgium, Holland and England this is very much the case. Holland for example has the highest use of chemical fertilizers (Noirfalise *et al.*, 1974) and at the same time the highest production of manure due to imported feed.

The process of extracting agriculture from this cul-de-sac, which has only the agribusiness corporations and a few large farmers as winners and everyone else as losers, has to go back to first principles. Bateman and Lampkin have proposed objectives for future agricultural policy:

1 To produce in each region that part of the region's food that it is desirable to produce in that region having regard to:

- the needs of other rural land uses, in particular forestry,
- conservation and recreation;
- the stability and prosperity of rural areas and equity of
- income distribution within them;
- the nutritional needs of the population;
- the long-term productivity of the soil;
- environmental damage and the use of non-renewable resources;
- animal welfare.

2 To achieve this without imposing an undue burden upon tax-payers or consumers within the area, and having regard to the agricultural and nutritional needs of people living in other areas.

Vogtmann considers that the solutions to the agricultural problems mentioned, and the achievement of objectives such as those above, lie in adopting a radically different kind of agricultural development, which he calls 'Sustainable Agriculture':

Sustainable Agriculture does not necessitate a return to a backward way of farming, using uneconomic, old-fashioned methods, but looks forward to a modern type of ecological agriculture, which utilises scientific knowledge for the development of appropriate technology and advances traditional farming practices that are applicable for an agriculture not based exclusively on short-term economics, but which also takes ecological considerations into account.

The principles of Sustainable Agriculture can be summarised in the following way:

1 Organisation of the production of crops and livestock, and the management of farm resources, in such a way t' at they harmonise rather than conflict with natural systems. This does not mean that one must always decline to use man-made or synthetic resources.
2 Pursuit of optimum (not necessarily maximum) production through planned diversity.
3 Pursuit of optimum production, through the achievement and maintenance of high soil fertility, relying primarily on renewable resources.
4 Development of new, small-scale technologies, based upon a better understanding of biological systems.
5 Pursuit of the optimum nutritional value of staple foods.
6 Development of locally-based systems of processing, distribution and marketing.
7 Concern with the social well-being of the people who live and work on the land and of their communities.
8 Creation of a system which is aesthetically pleasing both for those working within it and for those viewing it from the outside. Thus, it should enhance rather than scar the landscape of which it forms a part.

Bateman and Lampkin analysed the extent to which their objectives would be met by organic farming, defined by the US Department of Agriculture as follows (USDA, 1980):

Organic farming is a production system which avoids or largely excludes the use of synthetically compounded fertilisers, pesticides, growth regulators and livestock feed additives. To the maximum extent feasible, organic farming systems rely upon crop rotations, crop residues, animal manures, legumes, green manures, off-farm organic wastes, mechanical cultivation, mineral-bearing rocks and aspects of biological pest control to maintain soil productivity and tilth, to supply plant nutrients and to control insects, weeds and other pests.

Bateman and Lampkin conclude that:

there is evidence that an extension of organic farming would, compared with conventional farming, offer quite clear advantages in relation to some of the objectives: output would be lower, the environment would benefit, soil erosion would be reduced and some nutritional fears (particularly those associated with the use of pesticides) would be allayed.

They go on to argue that a modest expansion of organic farming is in fact likely in any case, but its poorer overall financial performance *vis-à-vis* subsidised conventional farming makes it unlikely that this expansion will be significant without positive policy changes to redress the balance. First and foremost such policy changes should include research and advice. As they point out:

In the past, there has in effect been positive discrimination against organic farming – no doubt by default rather than by design. Research has been directed towards varieties that are dependent on chemical inputs and the use of artificial fertilisers. Advice has been similarly oriented. The high rate of technical change which is the obvious feature of British agriculture since the war is the direct result of these activities, and it is they, much more than those other elements of policy which generally receive most attention, that have been influential in shaping our agriculture. It is from changing attitudes in this area that the biggest change in the competitiveness of organic agriculture is likely to spring. A reorientation of research is the aspect of policy change that should be pressed hardest by those who wish to see an extension of organic farming. The provision of advice directly relevant to organic systems must also be considered as an urgent priority.

In addition to provision of suitable research and advice, policy changes to promote organic agriculture could also include:

Higher farm product prices. Premium prices already exist for many organic products, but the significance of these for farm income can be overstated. More important, and in line with much of the thinking earlier in this book, is the recognition that organic farming in fact internalises many of the costs (e.g. pollution, resource depletion, food contamination, environmental destruction), which conventional farming externalises and passes on to society at large. Thus organic farmers should be paid premium prices, because they are in fact saving society from the payment of these costs later on.

Income support. In the past, farmers have been given a variety of incentives to use more capital to increase output and labour productivity. With unemployment and food surpluses, such incentives now make no sense at all. Switching them to income support would make a switch to organic farming easier and have a positive impact on unemployment and the problems of rural communities.

Taxes on fuel and chemical inputs. Just as premium prices for organic farmers should reflect their internalisation of their costs, so taxes would compensate society for the external costs of conventional farming. Some sources (e.g. Schulte, 1983) suggest that a nitrogen tax, for example, would in fact not bring about any large change in nitrogen usage or in output, while substantially affecting farmers' incomes, but Bateman and Lampkin point out that 'such a tax might do much to improve the relative competitiveness of organic systems' and thus significantly encourage a shift towards them.

Quotas. In many cases, quotas, by encouraging farmers to minimise inputs for a fixed output, have made the shift to an organic system more feasible than was previously the case.

Subsidies for farm conversion. This would directly benefit organic farming and is an immediately practicable option. In particular, it would require capital grants to introduce appropriate mechanisation and livestock-waste handling systems as part of a development plan, as well as an annual payment during the conversion period, to alleviate the risk of serious fluctuations in farm income.

Conservation grants. The fact that much previous farming practice coincidentally resulted in a pleasing landscape has led to a rather unreasonable expectation that farmers have a duty to be unpaid conservers of the countryside for society at large. A fairer principle would seem to be that where farmers incur conservation costs for the public good in the maintenance of countryside diversity, beauty or amenity, they should receive grants for such work. This is very different from, and not to be confused with, recompense for notional lost income, which is not being advocated. These grants would be of obvious relevance to small farmers in many upland and 'less favoured' areas, whose farms are desirable both socially and environmentally, but where farming is sometimes marginal financially.

The exact mix of these policies and detailed costings for them have yet to be produced, but it is clear that together they comprise a package of agricultural reforms that would both eliminate the waste and destruction of the present system, and set a people-based agriculture on a sustainable course for the future.

CO-OPERATIVE LAND HOLDING

It can be expected that the agricultural policies just outlined would result in a significant increase in the number of those involved in farming. Many of the new units would be in family farms, but it is likely that there would also be a demand for joint land holding. Moreover, it is not just a question of increasing access to agricultural land. Measures are also needed to enable those with low incomes and little capital to build their own houses and to plan and build their communities. In Britain, two such current schemes are the Lightmoor Project at Telford New Town[1] and the Greentown Project at Milton Keynes.[2] One possible mechanism for facilitating these developments is the co-operative land bank, described below, which seeks to strike a balance between individual ownership of property on the land and community ownership of the land itself.

'CO-OPERATIVE LAND BANKS'[3]
by Shann Turnbull

Inequity and inefficiency in private and public ownership

The conventional methods of owning land and houses are either inequitable or inefficient, or both. The result is that they inhibit universal access to housing and provide the means for those with access to exploit those without access. This paper suggests an alternative method of owning urban land and shelter which, I believe, could reduce the inequities and inefficiencies of the present systems and facilitate both self-financing development and greater access to housing by the poor.

The inequities of private land ownership are generally widely understood. Existing private owners obtain benefits both in terms of monetary wealth and exploitative power from improvements and increases in value created by others. The alternative – public ownership – introduces gross inefficiencies, as neither the tenants nor their bureaucratic landlords have sufficient incentive to diligently maintain and improve the housing stock.

The same inefficiency arises with concentrated private ownership, which requires a private bureaucracy to manage the tenants and the housing stock. The results of such inefficiency are dramatically illustrated in the United States of America, where extensive urban areas have become devastated due to the alienation between tenant-occupiers and owners of property.

There is no shortage of examples of regressive social and economic effects of public ownership, many of which are to be found in the Union of Soviet Socialist Republics. During the last decade the Soviet authorities have embarked on a program of selling government-owned apartments to tenants, assisted by the provision of very low-interest mortgage finance.

The Soviet initiative is based on the realization that owner-occupation of dwellings provides the most efficient method of maintaining and improving the housing stock. Without private ownership there is no incentive for individuals to contribute either their funds or their labour to improve the value of their Owner-occupiers are in the best position and have the greatest incentive to enhance both their standard of living and their equity through their own labour. Such 'sweat equity' is often the only means available to the poor to either build or maintain their shelter. Indeed, on a global basis, this is how the majority of the world's housing stock has been created and maintained.

Any system for owning land and housing must mobilize sweat equity if it is to have any significant practical effect on a global scale. Sweat equity is not only the most universal and efficient means of creating or enhancing the housing stock, but it also creates the most satisfying shelter for the consumer. Ideally, then, all occupants of housing should also own their houses. The tenure system proposed here allows this to occur. But human settlements still require public expenditure to improve community facilities and services. This introduces two problems: how to fund such improvements, and how to overcome the new inequities created by the public expenditure generating windfall gains for owners.

The common theoretical answer to these problems is to fund public expenditure by imposing rates and taxes on those owners who benefit from the public expenditure. By this means, the inequities created by the expenditure should be offset by the charges imposed to finance them. This may be true in theory but it is difficult to implement in practice. The most serious problem is cash flow. The public expenditures create diffuse capital gains rather than offset cash flows.

The unrealized capital gains may or may not be convertible into cash. If they cannot be fully converted into the cash required, then the charges imposed on property owners to recover the cost of community improvements may introduce unreasonable financial burdens. This is especially so in poorer communities. Indeed, it is a fundamental problem in financing public services in any low-income area. It is commonly overcome by resorting to a higher level of government, which is then asked to pay for the improvements as a subsidy. This in turn can create political tensions within the government.

Even when it is practical to impose community charges to recover community expenditures, the charges imposed may not relate to the benefits. As a result the basic inequity of the public authorities creating windfall gains for some is further complicated by the added administration costs of assessing the charges and making collections.

The windfall benefits accruing to private property owners, or for that matter to long-term lessees, are not just created by public expenditure but also by all private expenditure in the neighbourhood. Shopping, commercial and secondary industries are the most obvious examples. Less obvious but more pervading is the extent of home maintenance and improvement undertaken by other property owners. Another benefit is the sense of community created in the neighbourhood by residents.

External factors, especially government regulations and public utilities may reduce rather than enhance property values. Such reductions are referred to as wipe-outs and create further inequities. Various proposals have been put forward to capture windfall gains and to use them to offset wipe-outs so as to mitigate the inequities of both (Hagman and Misczynski, 1978). The capture, pooling and sharing of all windfall gains and wipe-outs within a community is an important feature of the tenure system of a co-operative land bank.

Features of co-operative land banks

A cooperative land bank is in many ways similar to a condominium or company title system for owning apartment buildings. In both condominium and company tenure systems two related interests in property are created. One defines the ownership of improvements to the land which may be used exclusively by the owner and this would represent his or her particular apartment. This interest could be considered to be in the nature of a perpetual lease. The other related interest represents an ownership share in all the common areas such as hallways, stairs, laundries, garden, swimming pool and other amenities which the owner of a leasehold title has the right to use on a non-exclusive basis. This joint interest could be represented by stock units or shares in the corporate entity which owns all the rights to the land.

A co-operative land bank has a number of features which distinguish it from most condominium and company title systems. At this stage I will only mention those necessary to introduce the concept:

1   A co-operative land bank operates on a larger scale than a typical condominium, representing a neighbourhood or a community containing roads, gardens, schools, hospitals and commercial activities with a residential capacity of 3,000 to 50,000 people.

2   The owner of each perpetual lease representing her house or apartment obtains shares in the co-operative and so in all common areas, proportional to the area occupied by her leasehold improvements.

3   Unlike condominium and company title systems, there would be no restriction to whom a member of the co-operative could sell her shares and lease. The price of the property she owns (the leasehold improvements) will be directly negotiated with the buyer. The price of her shares will, however, be determined by the land bank. The aggregate price paid by the purchaser for both the shares and the leasehold improvements would be determined by the market price paid elsewhere for similar types of residences.

4   Only real persons (not corporations, institutions, or governmental bodies) would be allowed to hold either titles or shares. Corporations, institutions, governments and their agencies would only be able to obtain leases from title holders or the co-operative land bank for a time period of less than fifty years. This would allow any residual values in improvements made by such organizations to revert to individuals on the termination of the lease. In general, such organizations do not need the capital gains on property in order to operate efficiently. Traditional private ownership systems usually provide them with economic rewards in excess of the necessary incentives.

Since a house and its plot in a co-operative land bank could not be sold without its shares, the price received by a member for her house would depend upon the price at which the buyer had to purchase the associated shares in the co-operative land bank. While these shares represent the pro-rata share of the land value, their cost could be considered to be of the nature of 'key money' representing the cost of entry to the community. This would be a fair representation as the cost of land is really the market value of its location and this, in turn, depends upon the nature of the physical and social environment of the neighbourhood. The services, amenities and facilities creating the physical and social environment of the community would be created and managed by the co-operative land bank. The price received by the vendor for her house would be determined by how much the purchaser had to pay in key money to enter the community. The total proceeds received by the exiting member would be the price she obtained for her house, plus the price she obtained from the co-operative land bank for her shares. The price paid by the co-operative land bank for the exiting member's shares could be considerably less than the price at which the bank sold the shares. It is by this means that the bank obtains cash from the development gains it captures.

As a co-operative land bank would own all the land in a sizeable community it would have a substantial asset base and income-earning potential. It would thus be in an excellent position to compete in the capital market for long-term debt funds. This would overcome the cash-flow problem inherent in financing community improvements. By financing community improvements with debt finance their cost can be repaid in the future from the cash flows generated by the improvements.

The self-financing capability of a co-operative land bank would be considerably greater than the traditional type of local government organization found in western societies. This arises from a number of income-generating activities in such an organization, in addition to the income from the sale of shares, mentioned above. These include:

Income from all commercial enterprises, which would be only able to lease their premises;
- Savings on community improvements, because of the incentives in the structure of a cooperative land bank for residents to contribute their own labour and enterprise;
- The ability to levy a rate, as commonly already pertains to local government bodies.

These means of income generation can be adjusted as necessary to ensure an adequate cash flow for community improvements.

Building co-operative land banks

The tenure system of a co-operative land bank can be created wherever a sufficient area of land can be aggregated and vested in a suitable legal entity such as a co-operative, company, or a common law trust. In order to assist in land aggregation the entity could be formed to create not just two types of equity interests but others which may be required during the formative period of the co-operative land bank.

Rather than borrow money to pay cash for land aggregation, the co-operative land bank may wish to issue redeemable participating non-voting preference shares in exchange for land and/or its improvements. Such shares could also have special conversion rights if required. In this way the vendor of the land can participate in the development profits but not in the management of the co-operative land bank. The co-operative, on the other hand, can minimize its immediate requirements for cash. If the vendor is a low-income home-owner or a squatter whose home has to be relocated then her preference shares could be redeemed not into cash but into a new home in the co-operative. This would be represented by a perpetual lease over her new living area and a pro-rata issue of shares in the co-operative.

In both examples the need for cash is avoided by bartering property rights. The second example has many similarities to the land pooling/readjustment techniques described by Doebele (1976) and Archer (1976). These techniques can be used for aggregating either bare land or land with improvements.

There thus exists a number of possibilities for converting any area of land and its improvements into a duplex tenure system to form a co-operative land bank without any cash consideration. Like the land pooling/readjustment procedures in South Korea and Australia, this may require the authority of government.

Indeed, such arrangements would appear to have considerable political attractions compared with other proposals for making land available for low-income housing. In particular, proposed land ceiling legislation in South and Southeast Asia, aimed at limiting the size of unused land holdings in and around cities, would appear to be far more contentious both politically and technically. The transformation and aggregation of such land into a co-operative land bank tenure system would immediately make land available at no cost to the government or to the poor, who could be allowed to build their own homes on the land. This, in turn, would create development values for the existing land-owners to share. Existing landowners would not have to find the funds to develop their land and would be assured that their land would not be bypassed for development.

Another possible mechanism for building co-operative land banks is dynamic tenure. Dynamic tenure can increase the efficiency, equity, effectiveness, and self-governance of a co-operative land bank. Dynamic tenure is created when property rights are defined to flow from one party to another with the passage of time at a prescribed rate. There need not be any cash compensation paid or received by the parties involved.

The rationale for adopting the concept in a co-operative land bank is that it is the occupier of property, and not the owner, that maintains and creates property values. Thus, if the owner is not an occupier, the rights of ownership should flow from the landlord to the tenant. In practice I would suggest a twenty-five to fifty year transfer period for rental housing. This would involve a 4 per cent to 2 per cent transfer of equity each year by the landlord to the tenant. The landlord would consequently increase her rental charges by 4 per cent to 2 per cent. However, the tenant would be acquiring without cost a pro-rata share in the land occupied by her home. In a co-operative land bank, this land would already be owned by the community.

The pragmatic effect of such an arrangement is to ensure that all residents of a co-operative land bank will automatically, with the passage of time, become owners of leasehold improvements in the co-operative. It should thus increase development values by mobilizing sweat equity. By this means it should protect itself from the destruction caused by the alienation between landlords and tenants as demonstrated in the dilapidated areas of American cities.

Capturing development profits

The ability of the co-operative land bank to capture and obtain cash from land development profits is one of its most valuable features in terms of both efficiency and equity. The price at which the shares in the co-operative may be purchased by new members is determined in the same way as the price for shares in a real estate investment trust, that is, by dividing the number of shares, units or stocks on issue into the total value of land owned by the co-operative land bank. The valuation of the land would be tempered by pragmatic pressures in much the same way as countries now manage their exchange rate. If the price becomes too far out of line, market pressures would force an adjustment to more realistic levels.

The price at which the co-operative land bank would buy shares back from members would be discounted according to a formula. This formula would need to be embedded in the constitution of the co-operative land bank so that it would require no less than 75 per cent of the members to agree on a change. The formula would need to maintain equity between short- and long-term members of the cooperative and to inhibit speculation.

The appreciation in the land value of the co-operative land bank and its shares would be created by consumer demand for its sites, services and facilities. The greatest contribution to consumer demand for both public and private goods and services in the co-operative land bank would be the long-term residents. The members who suffer the greatest discount (or exit tax) should thus be the short-term members. There could well be a zero discount for long-term residents. A suitable formula would therefore be a sliding scale discount reducing with years of residency. A twenty-year period, for example, could reduce the discount applied by 5 per cent for each year of residency.

In Australia and the United States of America, the average period of owning a particular home is only around six years even though purchase finance is obtained for twenty-five to thirty-five years. Such a rapid turnover of members would make a co-operative land bank self-financing simply from this mechanism alone, as illustrated in appendix IV of my paper 'Land Leases without Landlords'.[4]

Conclusion

The co-operative land bank concept is designed to combine the efficiency of private property rights with the equity of public ownership. It is, however, more than just a land tenure system. It is also a grassroots structure of community self-management in the tradition of Sir Ebenezer Howard's concept of self-governing garden cities (Howard, 1902). As such, the co-operative land bank is a basic building block of a new type of political system which I have called 'social capitalism' in my book *Democratising the Wealth of Nations* (Turnbull, 1975). The ability of the co-operative land bank to become self-financing provides the basis for it to become financially independent of higher levels of government. It thus provides a means for creating a grassroots local government structure on a decentralized democratic basis. It is important, therefore, that the constitution of the co-operative land bank should prescribe that only individuals may have the right to vote so as to exclude corporations. All individuals who meet residency requirements and are of voting age would obtain only one vote, no matter how many shares they own in the co-operative.

The self-financing feature of a co-operative land bank is especially important in low-income areas and in developing nations. In low-income areas a co-operative land bank can provide land without cost to its initial or pioneer members who build or buy their home with the security of tenure provided by a co-operative land bank's perpetual lease. Squatter settlements often have a strong internal organization and the co-operative land bank concept provides a means to institutionalize and reinforce such informal social organization and cohesion.

Indeed, the operating and financial efficiency and effectiveness of the concept is very much dependent upon a strong grassroots social organization and sense of community. Local self-government is traditional in many countries. The co-operative land bank provides a means of building an economic structure on these traditions. Typically, development along either the capitalist or socialist path has resulted in an expensive organization, while breaking down traditional cohesion. Self-governance, on the other hand, is a most economical way to organize society, as it substantially reduces government costs. The co-operative land bank concept provides a non-exploitative private alternative to communes, state co-operatives and collectives for building a decentralized society.

•　　•　　•

One of the most important features of the co-operative land bank is its ability to capture for the community any increase in land values due to development. This is also one of the principles underlying the next mechanism of land reform to be discussed, land value taxation.

'LAND VALUE TAXATION'
by Fred Harrison

Land value taxation enables the community to benefit from the value of its land, and to profit from any increase in such value, by taxing land on the basis of its economic rent, that is, the surplus wealth earned by the land over and above the income earned by labour (wages) and capital (interest from assets on the land). It is, in fact, the oldest fiscal mechanism employed by human societies and would reinstate ancient principles in the modern context (George, 1979). It would fulfil the roles formerly played by custom and moral suasion, in preventing people from possessing more land than they needed for production and recreation; and it would ensure a fair and equal distribution of the value of nature, through the public sector.

The valuation of all land at free market rates is the first step, an exercise that could be swiftly performed in the UK by District Valuers once Parliament had sanctioned the reform of the rating (property tax) system. The Land Register should be opened to the public and the process of compulsory registration of titles to land should be accelerated to cover all land, including hereditary holdings. The next decision is to fix the rate of taxation as a percentage of the annual economic rent. Some, for example the United Nations (1968), have advocated a tax rate well below 100 per cent. I believe that the rate ought to be 100 per cent. Anything less leaves a margin that encourages speculation and waste. A full capture of rent would enable governments to reduce taxes on labour and capital, which penalise people who work or invest.

This fiscal reform would force speculative hoarders to relinquish vacant land in favour of those who wish to use it. Both unemployment and the speculatively high level of rents would be reduced, thereby increasing the real living standards of many people who are today trapped in poverty and lack the means to break out of the institutionalised cycle of deprivation.

It would encourage individuals to use the land that they possessed to produce the best returns consistent with the expressed wishes of consumers and society at large. In the agricultural sector, land value taxation would lead to a break–up of inefficiently large agricultural estates in favour of smaller, family–sized holdings. In the cities, high–value vacant land would be brought back into use. Buildings would be constantly renewed, which is the way to recycle urban land and so prevent the premature spread on to greenfield sites. Compact living environments would reduce the capital costs of infrastructure (thereby reducing the need for government revenues on the present scale), reduce the private costs of transportation (thereby increasing the real standard of living without having to push for higher money wages), establish integrated communities (thereby reducing psycho–social stress), and conserve the rural environment. It is a bright prospectus for just one change in the system of taxation.

The planning system

The current planning system is welcomed by land speculators. It helps to identify the areas of prospective development, and so reduces the level of risk speculation. Planning by itself is helpless to prevent inner-city dereliction and urban sprawl, as is all too obvious. Land use regulations provide untold spoils for owners.

For example, the designation of Sites of Special Scientific Interest in Britain, and conservation easement laws in the US, reward the owners of affected land while raising the value of adjacent sites. The controls placed on river pollution are another example.

Vast resources are marshalled by the public sector to clean up rivers, much to the gratitude of owners of waterfront sites in New York and St Louis. For as the Urban Land Institute in Washington, DC, has reminded us, 'the waterfront revival owes its existence to one easily overlooked factor: water-pollution-control efforts. Most major river systems have improved in terms of the fecal bacteria, phosphorous and dissolved oxygen they carry. Without relatively clean water, even the most appealing waterfront project can't succeed' (Guenther, 1983). Landowners, alas, capitalise the net benefits into higher prices, which the absence of land value taxation enables them to pocket.

None of this is to argue against land use planning *per se*. Planning laws are easily incorporated into the land value taxation model. Where regulations alter market prices, tax obligations are automatically adjusted up or down. For example, a preservation order on an historic building would restrict the economic use to which the land could be put. The economic rent of that land would be assessed downwards by the market, and the tax collector would have to follow suit. The re-zoning of land to an apparently more valuable use would not automatically raise the tax obligation, however. If the planner was ahead of the market, that is, if people did not express a *need* for the alternative use through the price mechanism, taxes would not rise.

Advocates of public sector planning and spending should in fact be among the first to recognise the benefits of land value taxation. Justice surely requires that the community as a whole should be the net winner of increased values arising from investments in infrastructural and social amenities and the enhancement of the ecological environment: schools, highways, pollution-control, open space conservation, etc. Indeed, this fiscal instrument would provide scope to undertake more of those projects, because the projects, through the increase in land values that they generate, would be self-financing.

Land value taxation is an eminently practicable reform and is used by countries in both the developing (Taiwan) and developed (Australia) categories. In its pure form (all buildings exempted from taxation), it can be seen in Johannesburg, South Africa. Its two-tier variant (tax rates for land values are higher than for those that fall on buildings) is used by Pittsburgh, Pennsylvania, and five satellite cities. The United Nations had advocated this tax for agrarian-based Third World countries, and two studies sponsored by the Land Institute in the English town of Whitstable, in Kent, have shown that site value taxation provides a buoyant revenue while cutting the costs of collection. [Titles listed in the Bibliography, which give more details of the practice of land value taxation, include Becker, 1969; Harris, 1984; Harrison, 1983; Lin, 1974; Lindholm and Lynn, 1982; and Prest, 1981.]

The empirical evidence, however, shows that the dynamic economic effects have not been as great as the theory would predict. This is because tax rates are either very low, or because large parcels of land have been arbitrarily exempted from the tax. In Jamaica, for example, where the tax came into existence in the 1970s to raise revenue and deter land speculation, the government decided to grant favourable exemptions or reduced tax rates to the tourist and agricultural sectors on economically ill-founded grounds.

None the less, there is now a large enough body of evidence to prove that this fiscal policy is both practical and socially equitable. The political power of landowners guarantees that the introduction of land value taxation will always be a difficult process. Yet the 100 per cent recovery of economic rent resurrects the ideal principle that individual possession of land should be based on both need and use. At the same time, it ensures that, through the redistribution of that portion of wealth that is attributable to the intrinsic value of land (the locational attributes or fertility of soil), everyone is the benefiting owner because he or she has an equal stake in the revenue received and spent by the public sector in a democratic society.

•   •   •

Policies to encourage organic agriculture; co-operative land banks; land value taxation – these are, of course, not mutually inconsistent. Nor is it claimed that these policies will act as panaceas for all problems of planning and development, many of which will still require specific imaginative solutions along the lines sketched by James Robertson (TOES, 1984):

> Planning, housing and development policies all assume today that people's work will be done on employers' premises and will be organised by employers. So planning regulations often prevent people from working in and around their homes, and building regulations prevent them from adapting their homes to productive purposes. Architects design homes as places of

consumption and leisure, providing no space for productive work to be done there. Development policies perpetuate local vulnerability by seeking to attract outside employers into a district, instead of helping local people to organise their own work. All these policies need to be reviewed. Higher priority will have to be given to enabling people to organise work for themselves in their own households and localities.

Such policies, allied to sustainable agriculture and a sound system of land tenure, such as those described, would provide real impetus for self-reliant and equitable community development in both town and country.

NOTES

1   Information from Town and Country Planning Association, 17 Carlton House Terrace, London SW1Y 5AS.
2   Greentown Group, Urban Studies Centre, Milton Keynes, Buckinghamshire.
3   This is an edited verson of Turnbull's paper 'Cooperative land banks for low income housing', published in Angel, Archer, Tamphiphat, Wegelin, eds, *Land for Housing the Poor* (Select Books, Singapore, 1983), Section IX, 'There are even alternatives to private or public ownership', p.512. The paper is reprinted here by kind permission of the original publishers.
4   C.S.S. Turnbull, 'Land leases without landlords', unpublished seminar paper, UN Habitat Forum, Vancouver, 1976.

8 FINANCIAL FUTURES

Resources, land and labour have all now received some attention. It is time to turn to the fourth major factor of production, which gives its name to the economic system that dominates the world economy: capital, and money generally.

David Weston (TOES, 1985) defined money as 'a readily acceptable claim against resources and/or wealth'. In similar vein, the well-known Dutch economist Jan Pen has defined money as 'a good, any good whatsoever, irrespective of its physical nature or further properties, which is generally accepted by people in exchange for other goods' (Pen, 1965, p.126). Pen goes on to identify three separate functions of money: its use as a medium of exchange, as a unit of value and as a store of value.

As a medium of exchange, money permits the trade of goods and services far more easily than systems of barter, which perform the same function. Using barter, someone with a car to sell who wanted to buy a washing-machine would need to find someone who wanted a car and had a washing-machine for sale, and would still be left with the problem of making the transaction into one of equal value for both parties, most cars being worth more than the best washing-machine. With money, the car can be sold to one person for its market-price and the washing-machine bought from another with the proceeds. This obvious example illustrates an important aspect of money as a means of exchange – it is an *enabler*. It enables transactions to take place much more easily than would otherwise be the case. By the same token, lack of money exerts a severe restraint on exchange. Even when there is no shortage of goods and services to be exchanged in a community, if those with the goods and services to offer have no money, the exchange can be prevented and the economic activity of the community stifled. This point will be returned to later.

Money as a unit of value enables comparisons to be made between goods and services of a different kind. The value of a good or service is supposed to be reflected in its price, which, according to classical theory, is determined by the invisible hand of the market. The price will be somewhere between a minimum set by the cost of production (a lower price would drive the producer out of business) and a maximum determined by competition and the relation between supply and demand. The equity of the market mechanism has already been extensively criticised in this book. More important here is the fact that it has become an unsound, unrealistic model of economic activity. Several of its major assumptions are simply not operative today because:

- it envisages competition among many small producers, when in fact many markets are dominated by a handful of huge producers;
- it envisages free entry to markets, when in fact the costs of entry to many markets can effectively prohibit new entrants;
- it envisages perfect information among consumers when, in fact, producers themselves are not aware of some important side-effects of their products, and consumers are increasingly subject to manipulative sales techniques that are essentially persuasive and can be counter-informative;
- it envisages a transaction between producer and consumer that does not involve any external effects on those outside the transaction. This book's detailed analysis of externalities indicates just how far today's methods of production and consumption are from this assumption.

In all these ways, the market price misleads as to the true costs involved, quite apart from the even deeper flaw in the market equation of price with value, succinctly expressed by Oscar Wilde in his celebrated identification of a cynic as 'someone who knew the price of everything and the value of nothing'.

Nevertheless, it is useful to have a unit of value, providing its limitations are borne in mind. It does not have to be the same unit as the means of exchange, although it usually is. The relation between the two will be an indicator of the stability of the economic system. A unit of declining value in terms of the number of goods and services for which it can be exchanged is, of course, the condition of inflation.

Money as a store of value is the raw material of capital and of investment. Such capital is partly accumulated through savings, by foregoing present consumption and storing the surplus. Usually this surplus is invested, hired out to those wishing to produce in the future, or used to buy goods that are thought to be likely to increase in value. Partly capital is accumulated through credit creation: the banks creating credit against future production. This credit can be thought of as future savings. It is often not appreciated that banks have this power and that the credit they create is greatly in excess of their deposits. Wealth stored as money is, of course, particularly vulnerable to inflation.

Money used as a store of wealth has also led to the creation of the money market, that is, the treatment of money as a commodity, somthing to be bought and sold in its own right, in the hope of profit, using the national currencies and their exchange rates. The huge sums involved in this market and the speed with which transactions can be electronically effected has led to great instability in these exchange rates, and to enormous difficulties for domestic economic management for any economy which depends significantly on international exchange. This, of course, includes the great majority of countries.

This very brief introduction to money obviously does no more than scratch the surface of an extremely complex subject. It is merely intended to serve as a background to a more intensive exploration of three financial innovations – local currency, saver sovereignty, decentralised banking – which could remove some of the drawbacks and inequities of the present financial system. They are not presented as a complete agenda for financial reform, but as indications of some of the ways in which financial practice will have to change if money is to operate equitably and efficiently as society's scoring system as to who is entitled to what, which is its ultimate function.

LOCAL CURRENCY

Weston (TOES, 1985) identifies two major drawbacks in the use of a national currency as far as a local community is concerned:

1   National currency, as a store of value, is exported out of communities by persons who have interests elsewhere within the nation. If it is re-imported into the community, it is as externally controlled capital. In the process the community loses control of its economy.
2   National currency is subject to the vagaries of international financial markets that treat money as an item, to be brought and sold like sheep, apples, or shares. It therefore becomes susceptible to speculation and devaluation.

National currency is, therefore, subject to manipulation at the international, national and local levels. Indeed it is at the local level, where the wealth has been generated, that it appears most vulnerable. 'Regions of sacrifice' are created, as capital cities suck wealth from local communities, and rich countries from poor countries. Weston makes the further point that some of the wealth then circulates as 'stratospheric money', giving the impression of a vigorous economy, but with the benefits actually being limited to a conspicuously consuming minority.

Not only does this process result in the impoverishment of communities and poor countries, in the sense that they lack money as a store of value, but also in the sense that they lack money as a means of exchange. If their goods and services become redundant to the rich outsiders on whom they have become dependent, they can no longer even exchange these goods and services between themselves. Large-scale local unemployment results, with local skills and local assets (e.g. buildings, machinery, land) lying idle, at the same time as many local needs are unmet, because of a lack of a means of exchange to bring these needs and resources together.

The purpose of establishing a local currency is, therefore, threefold:

1 To keep the flow of local money within the community concerned, preventing the export of its wealth and retaining greater local control of the local economy;
2 To prevent speculation and trading in the means of exchange;
3 To ensure that all those in the community who have goods and services to offer are able to participate in a local market-place that has an accessible means of exchange that is available to all.

The idea of a local currency is far from being a new one. There have been literally hundreds of monetary and quasi-monetary systems developed round the world over the ages. Galbraith, 1975, explores some of them, while Nobel Laureate Professor F.A. Hayek gave intellectual and academic respectability to the modern use of the historical concept of privately issued concurrent currencies in two 1976 monographs *Choice in Currency* and *Denationalisation of Money* (Hayek, 1976).

Weston mentions several currencies, and his description of three of the most important is given here.

The Labour Exchange Bazaar, 1832 to 1834

Robert Owen, the nineteenth century social reformer, proposed

the formation of a Labour Exchange principally for the
unemployed and partially employed (Lloyd Jones, 1905).
Labour was to be accepted as 'the natural standard of value and
the principal source of wealth'. Wealth, he argued, is the
'combined manual and mental powers of [people] called into
action'. For this, he drew upon the ideas of Adam Smith, who,
in his introduction to *The Wealth of Nations* says: 'The annual
labour of every nation is the fund which originally supplies it
with all the necessaries and conveniences of life which it
annually consumes, and which consists always either in the
immediate produce of that labour, or in what is purchased with
that produce from other nations' (quoted in Lloyd Jones, 1905).

Owen therefore asked the question: if labour be the parent of
wealth, why were workers of the country compelled to starve
when they were able and anxious to work? The statesmen and
politicians gave no answer. The political economists spoke of a
falling off in demand; of the unremunerative condition of the
markets. Owen argued that 'the producer was also a consumer,
and that some intelligent effort should be made at least to
produce as much by the labour of the unemployed as would
enable them without injury to others to keep life in themselves.'

To facilitate the process of exchange, he devised National
Equitable Labour Notes in denominations of one, two, five,
ten, twenty, forty and eighty hours. The money values of the
raw materials used was then calculated by appraisers according
to the market price of the day and then converted into Labour
Notes.

A Labour Exchange Bazaar was set up in London on Gray's
Inn Road. Materials were brought in, purchased with money
loaned by Owen. At this point, it appears that, with the need to
'prime the pump', external 'capital' currency could not be
avoided. There are interesting parallels between this problem
and those of current Third World and local economies who
cannot obtain capital goods and/or raw materials without using
'external currency'. At the Bazaar, Owen was the external/
internal financial broker.

The process, therefore, consisted of three major steps:
1 The 'importation' of the initial stock of raw material: the
'pump primer'.
2 Within the Bazaar, workers formed those raw materials into
goods, which were then priced by evaluators, using 6d = one
hour as the conversion rate. When the goods were sold, minus
an 8.5 per cent transaction charge, the workers would receive
hourly based Labour Notes. The Labour Notes, in turn,

would be used by the workers to purchase food and
manufactures produced by other workers, and also the raw
materials for the next day's work.

3   Some of their products were sold to other workers, the Labour
Notes acting as internal currency, and some were sold outside
to raise money (external currency) to replenish the raw
material stock.

Within a very short time the Bazaar was turning over about
£1000 per week. Workers who had been unemployed and unpaid
for months and years were now using their skills and receiving
good (alternative currency) income. The Labour Notes currency
had helped in solving the unemployment 'problem'.

The Guernsey experiment, 1815-36, 1914 to the present

The effect of the Napoleonic Wars on Britain had been very
hard. On the Channel Islands, including Guernsey, it was even
harder. Invoking its ancient prerogative to produce its own
notes, the state issued £4000 in Guernsey State interest-free
notes. They were eagerly accepted by the islanders. Within
months their 'community economy' included the improvement
of roads, repairs to buildings, and in 1826 led to a further issue
to rebuild Elizabeth College. Issues were made with great care,
so as to avoid inflation. Over a period of twenty years, Guernsey
evolved from a depression to a position of real prosperity.

As is the experience of innovative no-interest or low-interest
ventures, the interest-charging banks tried to undermine or
crush, legally or otherwise, these successes. Guernsey was no
exception. Fortunately, through the determined perseverance of
the Channel Islanders, and the respect of the British
Government for history and precedent, the issuing of their
community currency is still intact. As is well-known, they also
pay low or no taxes.

The Worgl experiment, c.1929 to c.1934

In the town of Worgl, Austria, there stands a bridge whose
plaque commemorates the fact that it was built by debt-free,
locally created money. This was just a small part of a significant
experiment that transformed towns and whole areas out of
poverty within three months and into prosperity within one
year, at a time when there was widespread unemployment in
the national economy.

It appears that the Mayor of Worgl proposed a plan to issue local currency to the value of 30,000 Austrian schilling notes in denominations of one, five and ten schilling, which were called 'tickets for services rendered'. They were decreased in value by 1 per cent per month, but 'revalued' by the simple purchase, from the local authorities, of a stamp. The proceeds went to the poor relief fund. The result was that the notes circulated with unheard-of rapidity. They were first used for the payment of wages for the building of streets, drainage and other public works by men who would otherwise have been unemployed. During the first month, the money had circulated twenty times. Taxes were paid, unemployment greatly reduced and local shopkeepers prospered.

A nearby town, Kirchbichl, followed suit with a similar program. A meeting of 200 Austrian mayors decided unanimously to follow the Worgl example. Prominent people, including Daladier of France, visited and were enthusiastic. But when the example threatened to spread, the Austrian national bank took legal action against it. After a long legal battle the Austrian Supreme Court decided in favour of the bank, and the innovation was prohibited.[1]

These last two examples illustrate the way in which a local currency can be linked to interest-free credit creation for the purpose of funding public works. This aspect of local currencies will be explored in more detail in the later discussion of decentralised banking. First it is worth studying in some detail a system of local currency operating in several communities in British Columbia, Canada: the Local Exchange Trading System, or LETSystem, which was established by a consultancy, Landsman Community Services Ltd, in Courtenay on Vancouver Island.

The first and so far most developed of the twenty or so LETSystems currently operating was established in the Comox Valley, British Columbia, in January 1983. In the first twenty months of its operation about $(green) 250,000 worth of trade was carried out. Its unit of currency is the green dollar, which is tied to the Canadian dollar. Landsman defines the LETSystem[2] as follows:

A LETSystem is a self-regulating economic network which allows its members to issue and manage their own money supply within a bounded system. Its essential characteristics are:
1   The agency maintains a system of accounts in a quasi-currency, the unit being related to the prevalent legal tender;

2   Member accounts start at zero, no money is deposited or
    issued;
3   The network agency acts only on the authority of a member in
    making a credit transfer from that member's account into
    another's;
4   There is never any obligation to trade;
5   A member may know the balance and turnover of another
    member;
6   No interest is charged or paid on balances;
7   Administrative costs are recovered in internal currency from
    member accounts on a cost-of-service basis.

The accounts are serviced in the office of the LETSystem and
transactions are entered on the telephoned instruction of the
member whose account is to be debited. Chequing and credit-
card-type procedures are also available where necessary to
prohibit fraud, but these are comparatively rarely used. There is
no credit limit in the system. Members may decline to accept
further money from a non-performer and, because a seller is
entitled to know the balance and turnover of a buyer's account, a
buyer in significant green dollar debit should find it increasingly
difficult to obtain goods or services. There is also no provision for
deposits or credit creation. Thus the accounts always sum to zero:
one person's credit is another's debit.

Landsman considers that green dollars are subject to taxation, as
ordinary currency, and is seeking the right to pay taxes on green
dollar earnings in green dollars, a step which could have profound
implications for decentralisation.

Some have wondered whether the establishment of a local
currency in this way is, in fact, legal. LETSystem transactions
depend on simple promissory statements by its members of the
form: 'I received $48 worth from Joe and I promise to contribute
that worth to others.' It is hard to see how a government with
even the scantest regard for free speech and freedom of action
could make such transactions illegal.

There is also provision in the LETSystem for the establishment
of a LETSfund, which can be regarded as a community bank. It
would derive its capital from membership fees charged principally
to participating businesses, who would derive considerable benefit
from the information service rendered by the LETSystem and the
increased trading activity brought about by it. This could provide
a source of national currency for the LETSfund, depending on the
size and nature of the business concerned. The LETSfund would
be a locally managed non-profit society, incorporated under

customary local regulations to provide finance to its members, who would be the members of the LETSystem. It would:

make finance available to individuals, commercial, and community organizations for projects considered likely to contribute positively to the real economy of the whole comunity. A LETSfund will therefore preferentially support: projects which are labour rather than capital intensive;

- resource enhancement and maintenance rather than exploitation and extraction;
- conservation of energy;
- sustainable agriculture and ecologically appropriate industry;
- community development in all social, cultural, and economic aspects.[3]

The crucial difference between a LETSfund and a bank is that a LETSfund does not make loans. It provides finance on a partnership basis, sharing the risks and the profits of any investment. The question of interest, therefore, does not arise.

The LETSystem of local currency is an important tool for local economic development. Because transactions have to be between members, and members have to be locally based, the green dollars can only circulate in their local community; the means of exchange cannot be siphoned off by powerful interests elsewhere. Moreover, there is a strong community incentive to economic activity, because every transaction represents an instance of local skills and local resources meeting local needs. Its simple relation to the national currency facilitates national taxation questions and also simplifies dual pricing in the community, by which each good or service could eventually come to have two components in its price: the green dollar component, representing the resource or added value which had come from within the community, and a national currency component, representing that proportion of the product which had had to be imported from outside. Buyers would therefore be able to tell simply from the price of an article the extent to which they were supporting their local economy.

The tie-up with the national economy is, however, a disadvantage as far as the green dollar as a unit or store of value is concerned, for it would effectively import any national inflation into the transactions of the local community. Thus those with their green dollar accounts predominantly in debit would benefit from the devaluation of their debit. Those with their accounts predominantly in credit would suffer similar devaluation. Looked at another way, this means that long-term creditors would be repaid in cheaper dollars than they earned.

Because green dollars could not be transferred outside the community, they would not be subject to speculation on the international money markets. But this means that the community would have to trade in national currency for all imports and exports, so that its dependence on external currency fluctuations would remain insofar as it remained dependent on outside exchange.

The LETSystem is by no means the only innovation in the local currency field and there is continuing active debate, both as to desirable currency controls within an area operating a local currency, and with regard to the most desirable relationship between that currency and others, especially, of course, the national currency.[4] But despite their experimental nature, the LETSystem and other local currencies provide a simple yet effective means to encourage local economic self-reliance, an innovation that can make a real difference to the level of economic activity and prosperity in a community that has been impoverished and disempowered by its exclusive reliance on the national currency for its means of exchange.

SOCIAL INVESTMENT AND SAVER SOVEREIGNTY

The LETSystem operates as a means of local exchange. The LETSfund allows for local finance and investment. This leads to consideration of facilities for personal saving and investment, for providing means for those with significant credits in their accounts to make those funds available, through investment, for the use of others. Before exploring what sort of channels might be appropriate for such investment, it is clearly relevant to examine those patterns of saving and investment that are currently established.

•   •   •

'MONEY AS IF PEOPLE MATTERED'
by David Cadman

Postwar investment in the UK has been marked by a separation of saving and investment: personal saving and institutional investment. Rising disposable incomes and relative prosperity have enabled and encouraged a growing number of people to set aside a part of their income as savings. However, this increase in personal saving has not led to an increase in personal investment. On the contrary, such investment has decreased in Britain during the postwar period. In 1940, for example, some 80 per cent of all ordinary share capital was owned by private individuals. By 1980 this had fallen to less than 40 per cent. Increasingly, either voluntarily or as part of their contracts of employment, private individuals have passed their savings to financial institutions to be invested on their behalf by professional fund managers. The principal beneficiaries of this transfer of funds have been the building societies, the insurance companies and the pension funds. Building society deposits grew from £2.2 billion in 1957 to £56.7 billion in 1981. In a similar period, the savings handled by insurance companies and pension funds grew from £7.0 billion to £85.0 billion.

This phenomenon has been encouraged both by the idiosyncracies of the British tax system, which has favoured a selected range of assets such as houses, pension fund investment and life assurance, and by the method adopted for the provision of old age pensions. Britain has a funded system, now under review, for the provision of pensions which, unlike the pay-as-you-go system adopted in other countries, provides for employers and their employees to meet the future cost of pensions by saving up in advance. This has encouraged the growth of the large institutional investors.

In the search for investments that would provide both a secure stream of income and that would out-perform inflation, the institutions have operated both in the traditional markets of the City – shares, gilts and commodities – and in the more recently developed markets of fine art, farm land and commercial and industrial property. Inevitably, these markets have become marked by centralised decision-making and by the somewhat narrow and standardised criteria of institutional investors. This can be seen, for example, in commercial and industrial property markets which reflect increasing selectivity and standardisation.

There are no doubt advantages in the institutional model. The great majority of the managers of the building societies, the insurance companies and the pension funds are most careful and responsible in their work. Their evidence to the Wilson Committee in 1980 made it clear that they see themselves as the trustees of other people's money and act accordingly. But it is almost inevitable that in accepting this responsibility they have created an impersonal system. The essential personality of saving and of enterprise are separated by the impersonality of institutions.

As the shift in saving and investment has taken place, there has emerged a new financial ethos. Not only have the rules of economics come to be regarded as sacrosanct, determining rather than being determined by human activity, but a sub-set of rules, the rules of accountancy, have come to be regarded as of particular importance. Thus, increasingly, the particular measure of the money rate of return has come to be seen as not only the principal but also the only true measure of the worthiness of human endeavour.

This can be observed not only in the market place but in the realm of such social activities as education and health. Schools and hospitals must conform to the accountant's rule and, indeed, must concentrate on financial targets. As a consequence, those activities and products that can best be measured by price, such as the manufacture of goods or the provision of services for consumption within the market mechanism, that is, those activities normally regarded as private-sector activities, are favoured; whilst those that seem to deny the measure of the market place, the convivial and caring activities, are either disregarded or put into the category of subsidy. Private-sector market activity is then artificially separated from public-sector activity. The former is regarded as essentially good and to be encouraged, whilst the latter is regarded as inherently bad and to be discouraged. The myopia of measuring by money alone makes it virtually impossible to measure, other than by reference to the accountant's rule, the extent to which enterprise and activity, whether public or private, is appropriate or inappropriate to individual and social well-being. Yet it is becoming increasingly obvious that, whilst the rules of finance are useful in the part, they are inadequate as a means of determining either individual or social well-being as a whole.

● ● ●

This analysis leads to two conclusions. The first, tying in with much that has gone before, is that financial performance alone is an inappropriate and misleading indicator of the overall success of an investment. Many investments have social costs or benefits which are left out of account by financial measures, and which can significantly affect the extent to which the investment has been successful overall. Two innovations need to be introduced into the economic infrastructure to give weight to such factors:

1 The concept and means of *social accounting*, so that the social effects of investment and development can be evaluated and taken into account;

2   The concept of *social investment*, so that possible social, non-financial returns accruing to a future investment can be estimated. Investments for social benefit will never hold their own in the investment market with those that are more narrowly geared to financial gain, until social returns are also taken into account.

The second conclusion is that there is a need for new financial institutions that subscribe to the principle of *saver sovereignty*, by which they encourage and expect their investors to have a personal interest in and commitment to the projects in which they are investing. Several such institutions already exist, such as the Mercury Provident Society in the UK and its sister organisations in Germany and Holland. These are banks which match the saving criteria of investors with appropriate projects. The Financial Initiative (UK) is a new venture capital company with similar objectives: the Ecology Building Society (UK) only lends on properties that fulfil certain ecological conditions; the Ethical Investment Research and Information Service (UK) gives advice on the ethical nature of the activities of many companies, to aid would-be investors with a conscience, while the Stewardship Fund of Friends' Provident in the UK, and the Calvert Social Investment Fund in the US, offer investors a portfolio which has been similarly checked against social and ethical criteria.[5]

Many of these initiatives are still very small, but they are attracting increasing interest from investors. All too often, however, government or professional regulations limit the extent to which non-financial considerations can be taken into account. An example is the proposed UK legislation on building societies, which would effectively limit to 10 per cent of its mortgages the ability of the Ecology Building Society to apply its ecological criteria. It has said it will close if the legislation goes through. Clearly investors need protection from fraud, but equally clearly there are valid non-financial criteria to which investors should be able to give weight when they invest. The law needs to acknowledge these criteria, while providing appropriate safeguards based on the recognition that savers have a right to be sovereign in the investment of their savings.

DECENTRALISED BANKING

Finally in this chapter we turn to the process of credit creation by the community. It should be kept in mind that credit creation at present is the prerogative of the banking system; that the credit the banks generate goes far beyond the sums they have on deposit; that the interest they charge on credit reflects a monopoly price on access to liquidity and is far in excess of their administrative or other costs in providing the service, nor is it based on the risks involved in the investment; and that the debt thus incurred by the borrower, who is often a local or national government, is correspondingly burdensome. The decentralised banking system described here gives the power of credit creation to democratically-accountable community organisations.[6]

The logic of these banking arrangements is based on the ability of technology to increase productivity to pay itself off and so to become self-financing. In fact, there are only two ways in which a community or nation can increase its production: either its people work longer hours or they adopt new technologies to increase their productivity. The development of such technology generally requires money and credit, to mobilise the necessary labour, resources and know-how. The efficient and appropriate provision of this credit is the prime function of the decentralised banking system.

The ability of self-financing technology to pay for itself in the future means that it need not be financed out of past savings, whether in the form of private deposits or taxation. The credits to finance it can be generated in respect of future savings, thus satisfying the economic dictum that savings must equal investment. As the technology comes on stream, the credits that were used to finance it will gradually be cancelled and, once this process is complete, there will be as many new goods as there was new money in the first place. It is for this reason that credit creation for the development of self-financing technology is inherently non-inflationary.

This process of development is quite distinct from the financing of new technology through the investment of past savings because to achieve such savings consumption must be foregone in other sectors, and this acts as a brake on the growth of those sectors. In a poor society, such foregone consumption can also result in real hardship. However, it must be stressed that the creation of new money in respect of future savings should only be used to develop self-financing technology, because it is only such technology that will generate these future savings and so prove non-inflationary.

There is, in theory, no limit to the self-financing technology that can be developed in this way, because the creation of credit simply requires the entry of figures in a book and the self-financing nature of the process ensures its monetary soundness. However, in practice there will, of course, be limits to labour, resources and expertise, and overall social and environmental limits. Increasingly in a society where resources are depleted and the environment is under stress, self-financing technology will be the technology that makes the most efficient use of resources and has minimum impact on the environment, especially when all the external costs have been internalised as far as possible to the account of the technology concerned.

The process of granting these credits to a project thus has two separate components: the first concerns the social and environmental desirability of the project, and this can be assessed through a combination of market-forces and local strategic planning. The second concerns an assessment as to whether the project really will be self-financing, and this can be calculated using standard risk-assessment procedures. The credit would be obtained in the first instance from a community bank, which would rule on the project's overall desirability. The credit would then be refinanced through a credit insurance institution, which would charge a fee to guarantee the self-financing nature of the project.

This approach to financing new technology can well be effected through a local currency, using new locally based, locally guaranteed money especially created for the purpose. This has several powerful advantages, from the community's point of view, over the alternative option of borrowing the credit from outside. With the latter there are the direct costs of the foreign transaction deriving from the fact that the interest charged on the foreign loan may well be in excess of that justified by the investment's risk, and also the fact that the future savings element of the new technology will be exported from the community to pay the return on the foreign funds, instead of circulating in the community and fuelling the development process. Thus the main beneficiary of the self-financing technology ceases to be the community at all.

Even worse, should the investment fail to become self-financing, the community or country concerned can easily spiral into the debt trap, where more funds have to be borrowed from abroad simply to service past debt. The international economy today amply illustrates the dangers of being in debt to other countries. All these dangers are bypassed if a local currency is used to finance the development: future savings stay and circulate in the community; the risk of failure is accepted internally and, while failure will still lead to loss of consumption, it does not result in the debilitating cycle of debt and dependency.

Another advantage of creating credit through a local currency is that it enables the community concerned to decide its pace and direction of development. It can choose the self-financing technology that is most appropriate to its own culture and conditions. When the introduction of new technology is financed externally, bankers who are alien to the community may determine or influence the choice of technology. Indeed, the financial colonisation of communities by higher levels of government, by foreign governments and/or international agencies is all too common. From the perspective of the community, technological imperialism may be little different from political imperialism. It can be just as socially disruptive.

The introduction of new technology must always result in social change. Any change in the mode of production or modification in working patterns – the inevitable results of new technology – must affect how, when and where people work. There are bound to be both winners and losers in this process, which should form an important aspect of local political debate. However, the community concerned will only have the power to choose which new technologies it will develop and how fast if it is financially independent. Such financial independence depends on it having control of its currency, and a banking system through which it can finance its own development.

In conclusion, it is clear that the decentralised banking system outlined here, and the ideas of saver sovereignty, social investment and local currency explored earlier, are radical reforms as things are today. Yet the financial institutions of today do not exist by natural law. They are, in any case, continually undergoing change. Whether or not they change in the directions discussed here will depend purely on the political pressures on them to do so. The directions themselves are entirely practicable.

NOTES

1 For further details of the Worgl experiment, see Cole, 1930.
2 Landsman Community Services *Announcement of a LETSystem* (TOES, 1985). More information about LETSystems, including printed material and computer software to aid their establishment, can be obtained from Landsman Community Services Ltd, 479 Fourth Street, Courtenay, B.C. V9N 1G9, Canada.
3 Landsman, op. cit.
4 Relevant to this debate is a monograph by Shann Turnbull *Selecting a Local Currency*, Australian Adam Smith Club, New South Wales, 1983.
5 The addresses of the institutions named here are given in Appendix 2.
6 This banking system derives from a paper by Shann Turnbull, 'Financing world development through decentralised banking', published in Mtewa, ed., 1985.

9 WORKING LIKE WOMEN

Much has already been said in this book about work. In Part I, Sparrow exposed the reality behind the unemployment statistics, estimated the true costs of unemployment and identified the extent of unvalued work. Fleming showed that the formal economy has no answers to mass unemployment and drew attention to the vulnerability of transfer payments with so many jobless. Chapter 3 in Part II examined more deeply the nature of work and advocated a revival of the local and household sectors. Chapter 6 investigated human activity patterns as an alternative to unemployment statistics, concluding that they give a far better picture of the distribution and nature of work, as well as of informal economic activity.

It must be stressed that these ideas are not being floated as of relevance to some distant future. They are actually necessary to describe working patterns now, which are far more complex, flexible and dynamic than the blinkered, binary language of 'jobs' and 'unemployment' would have us believe.

'FLEXIBLE WORKING PATTERNS'
by Sheila Rothwell

Few people in Western industrialised economies now predict a return to full employment. What is much less commonly realised is the extent to which full employment has, in any case, been historically more the exception than the rule, and that it is the period 1950–75 which might be the one to be seen as aberrant by future generations. The 'future' has in fact begun and the seeds of it exist in present practices; nevertheless it is not predetermined, it will be created and shaped by the decisions of individuals and organisations – not only at international and national levels, but also at local, family and personal levels.

If these decisions are not to be made by those 'who spend their lives looking forward to the past' (John Osborne), but by those who seek to achieve a more humane, balanced future, it is important to start from an analysis and understanding of current patterns of work from a wide perspective. Some of the trends of what is happening to work both 'inside' and 'outside' formal employment will be outlined and an attempt made to see who is being affected by these in the UK, and in what areas. Some future options are finally proposed: changes in attitudes and in sources of income may both be critical, if it is accepted that there is no shortage of work, only of the means to pay for it as previously organised in employment.

Employment: paid work

Three million unemployed has concentrated British concern over the future of work in the 1980s, although the origins of this concern can be found earlier, and were not entirely unforeseen.[1] Very briefly, this rise in unemployment is conventionally explained by the simultaneous increase in labour supply – for demographic reasons (the birth bulge of twenty years before) and because of the growing increase in women's economic activity – and decrease in labour demand arising out of changing patterns of world trade, government policies, including deflation, employers' needs to reduce labour costs and the rapid substitution of capital for labour. Apart from the demographic factor and, possibly, government policy, none of the above factors seem likely to diminish, but rather to intensify, by the end of the century.

What effect is this having on work in employment? Are the 88 per cent of the working population who are in employment still working in the same way as previously, and are they becoming increasingly isolated from those who are without a job? What is the nature of the million new jobs being created each year?

There is no doubt that changes are taking place in the type of work that is being done, the time spent at it, and perhaps in the attitudes towards it. Yet those changes are largely gradual, not necessarily spread equally over different industries, age groups or geographical areas, and not all visible in official statistics.

Occupations and industries
Many studies and forecasts indicate the decline in semi- and unskilled manual occupations, especially those involving physical lifting and handling, or routine work such as repetitive assembly, especially in manufacturing industries. Routine clerical and some

service jobs are also diminishing as automation begins to be applied to office work and distribution on a far greater scale than previously. While a higher proportion of remaining jobs are expected to be 'knowledge-based', that is, technical and managerial, involving higher qualifications and/or greater interpersonal and relational skills in personal service occupations, the 'new' jobs that are currently being created (apart from electronics engineers, computer programmers and systems analysts) appear to be low level jobs in service industries such as fast-food chains, or keyboard operations.[2, 3]

With the decline of many traditional craft skills and of many supervisory positions, there is some sign that jobs are becoming polarised into high-level, high-overload, high-stress ones and low-level, low-variety low-discretion ones. Despite the considerable amount of research into job design and people's work requirements, there is very little sign of any utilisation of this in the design of computerised systems of working, despite the new opportunities available. Traditional control hierarchies and engineering 'simplification' assumptions still tend to predominate so that employment is not necessarily becoming more attractive or people-centred, even in service sectors.[4] The aim of automating people out of employment in manufacturing seems likely to be realised in certain areas such as cars or machine tools, but this may also mean the end of many particularly unpleasant and degrading jobs as well.

Hours of work
Patterns of working time are steadily changing as, despite employer resistance, the length of the working week diminishes. By April 1983, over half the full-time labour force had a normal basic week of thirty-eight hours or less, and holidays were extended (most now have over four weeks). With early retirement becoming more widespread, and the increase in time spent in education, the length of employed lifetimes is diminishing. Total annual working hours of men diminished by one-third between 1890 and 1975, but by 7 per cent in the decade 1971-81. Male life-hours of work fell by 15 per cent between 1951 and 1971.[5] One calculation showed that in 1981 only 14 per cent of the year was spent in paid work by people of working age.[6]

Shift-work has also increased, and while some will need to reject the unsocial hours of working, and the disruption this implies, its increasing calculation on an annual basis and the use of four- or five-crew working can mean more regular and more predictable patterns and more scope for individual choice and greater blocks of leisure time.

The increase in varieties of part-time or less than full-time working is, however, the most striking change in patterns of employment in the last decade.[7] One in five of those in employment are now working in this way, and the proportion could rise to one in four by the end of the decade, as many (possibly two-thirds) of the new jobs in service industries are in this category. The extent of the change has been described as 'the quiet revolution nobody noticed' by one labour economist.[8] Employers seeking to adjust labour forces so as to reduce costs and to meet peak customer demands have increasingly utilised it in a variety of ways. As full-time working declines so the distinction can become blurred, if part-time is defined as an average of less than thirty hours per week.

Employment contracts are beginning to change, too. Since, for a variety of reasons, wages have shown little downward adjustment in response to demand, labour costs have been contained, after contraction, by companies making greater use of short-term, fixed-term or temporary contracts of services of specialist managers and professionals; or of self-employed contracts for services of consultants; as well as the use of agencies not only for office workers but increasingly for those with computing and engineering skills.

Places of work
Self-employment and home-working are also increasingly evident trends. The distinctions between employment and self-employment and working from or at home are often blurred as people move from one category to another, operate in different ways (e.g. the much publicised Rank Xerox networkers), or as legislative interpretations alter. While forecasts of the extent of computer-related work from home, dubbed 'the electronic cottage', appear so far to be exaggerated, with more being written about it than appears to exist in practice, there are definite signs of growing trends in that direction. Whether it will develop further, once the infrastructure is more widespread, remains to be seen; company and individual resistance to the isolation of home working may mean that it is unlikely to become more than a part-time feature of many people's work. A 1981 survey of the 'out work' labour force found 1.68 million workers, with roughly equal numbers of men and women, men tending to work from home, women at home.[9]

Taking the statistics of part-time working and self-employment together, the Manpower Services Commission (MSC) observed that in 1980 over a quarter of the labour force were not involved in the 'standard' pattern of full-time work for an employer. This proportion has probably increased in the last four years.[10]

Non-employed: unpaid work

Since the official unemployment statistics do not include the large number of married women who would like employment if it were available, nor full-time housewives, nor for various reasons the working unemployed, the term non-employed is better used to describe the proportion of the population who are not 'in employment' or formally self-employed, but who may nevertheless work. What happens to those who are not in employment? Are they idle, at leisure, or active in ways not formally measured as 'economic activity'? Comparatively little is known, by the nature of their situation; if their activity were measurable, it might well be included in the above category. GNP estimates could similarly show a big increase.

Black economy

Work most akin to conventional employment is, in the UK, labelled as 'the black economy', since the remuneration for such work is not recorded in the formal system.[11] Estimates of its extent in the UK put it at $7\frac{1}{2}$ per cent of GNP; in Italy it is thought actually to sustain the economy; while in Belgium increasing attempts have been made to control by legislation any form of service performed, whether the exchange is transacted in goods, cash or kind. Many people are surprised to learn that this is 'criminal' activity, and there appears generally to be higher toleration of it as 'tax evasion' rather than 'social security scrounging'.

Community work

Little is known, too, of the extent of useful community or voluntary work, or of the distinction between some of this and 'leisure' activity, although the reductions in public expenditure on welfare, health and education have necessitated reliance on self-help groups to a far greater extent than previously. In some cases this has been ideologically necessitated by a conscious decision not to be dependent on state assistance and therefore control. In many instances, however, new links are being forged between local voluntary activities (by the unemployed, the 'leisured' classes, trade unionists, Rotarians, etc.), government initiatives (local, central or MSC) and large private companies or nationalised industries. 'Employed' and 'non-employed' are working to provide services or even set up new employing businesses. Personal initiatives and services performed out of kindness or a sense of citizenship are obviously also included in this category.

Domestic work

The third major category of non-market activity is that which covers shopping, cooking, laundry, housework, child care, and do-it-yourself house and garden maintenance. The dividing lines between these activities, leisure pursuits and mere 'personal maintenance' time are difficult to draw, but the aggregate amount of time spent on them and the 'purposeful activity' (not to mention routine drudgery) involved justifies their classification as 'work'. The availability of small-scale, power-driven tools has meant that many activities have now returned to the home which might previously have been performed outside it. With the simultaneous increase in home-based leisure activities, it is likely that the volume of domestic work has actually increased, even if semi-automation has made it possible to decrease the amount of time and energy spent on certain tasks.

Education and training

Increasing proportions of young people are in education or training, and while this is encouraged by public policy in the sense that it both takes people out of the labour market and equips them subsequently to function more productively within it, it increases the problems of providing them with an income. Moreover, public expenditure cuts are reducing education provision. Unemployed adults seeking to use their time to qualify for future employment, or simply to make up for the further education they never had, are likely to find their unemployment benefit cut. Places on Training Opportunities Scheme (TOPS) college-based courses in the 1970s, which were filled by women seeking to acquire some skills and prepare themselves for a return to work, have been drastically reduced. New 'return to study' or 'return to work' short courses are only available in a few areas. Local authority adult education and evening classes, largely dominated by men in vocational subjects and women in non-vocational subjects, have also been reduced. Nevertheless new schemes for more self-managed and self-directed training such as the Open Tech or the 'Drop In' skill centres may offer newer opportunities.

Otherwise, in Britain, most continuing education has tended to be employer-sponsored: only those in employment get it, and only at certain times in their career. Hitherto this has mainly, except for managers and a few specialists, been at the 'beginning' rather than 'continuing'. Much more lip-service is now being paid to the need for retraining and for continuous modular training, but the practice so far tends to be fairly narrow and specific, largely related to the acquisition of computer skills, and available to men more than women. The practice of sabbaticals for employees at any level has largely disappeared.[12]

People

Which people are being most affected by the changing patterns of employment?

Young people

Young people of both sexes are much less likely to be in formal employment than any other age group except the over-fifties. While Youth Training Schemes will provide temporary occupation for 16–19 year olds not in employment or education, the 18–25 year olds are most likely to be without either. Those that seek to obtain further education may find that they lose benefits as a result. Black young people are even less likely than white to be in formal employment or in higher education or training. Studies of attitudes of the young unemployed, both white and black, show apathy and alienation from society on the part of many, rather than aggression; but the outbreaks of inner-city violence in London, Liverpool, Birmingham and Bristol have shown the dangers of latent hostilities.

Whether young people should be prepared to expect 'proper' full-time jobs or to cope with life on the dole remains a controversial issue. Some research seems to support a suggestion that in certain areas of the North a youth culture of unemployment has developed which enables young people to cope satisfactorily without missing what they have never had, although this perhaps conceals considerable despair, frustration, and 'privatisation' of existence. There are some signs that people are not necessarily prepared to accept a job of any sort at any price, and that adjustment to time-keeping routines of formal employment is no less difficult than for those in newly industrialising societies. Growing current emphasis on education and training schemes in creating self-reliance and skill adaptability, in acquiring computer-related skills, or in becoming self-employed, suggests that there are a few attempts being made to help people to cope with the future rather than past society.

Young people in employment, however, are largely treated in

fairly traditional ways in working hours. Only in retailing are they now likely to be working part-time, and although the 'Job Split' scheme originated in the EEC attempts to alleviate youth unemployment, it does not appear to have widespread appeal.

In occupational terms, those working most closely with computers at all levels are most likely to be young, and in some of the computer companies, the average age of employees is under thirty.

The sex-stereotyping of jobs is largely unchanged, despite isolated examples of girls obtaining non-traditional manual skills.[13] Even in computer-related work, the more technical it is the less likely it is to be done by women.

The likely shortage of school leavers by the end of the decade should mean that a significantly higher proportion will be in formal employment, while the 'missing generation' moves into its late twenties and early thirties.

Older people

Older people, both in and out of employment, are increasingly affected by current trends. There are also proportionately more of the 'older' old now than in recent periods. Those in employment may be increasingly likely to move to some form of part-time employment (even men) or self-employment as early retirement takes effect. Increasing numbers are even welcoming this as an option. Pre-retirement education is developing both in extent and concept to enable people to cope more creatively with transitions.[14]

Older people outside employment by reason of redundancy or ill-health are increasingly unlikely ever to obtain formal employment again, but while some are setting up small businesses or as consultants, others may be working largely in 'domestic' or community activities.

Women of course have always done this and have been assumed to have no 'problems' with retirement. They have in fact tended, even in the past, to 'phase out' retirement and to do so earlier than men; this was one reason for Beveridge fixing differential state pensionable ages.

Adult men

Adult men's working patterns have probably changed less than those of other groups, despite the decline in manual employment in manufacturing industry. Those in work are more likely to be working full-time, and certain groups will still be working six to eight hours overtime a week. Certain young or middle-aged specialist managers, professional engineers or computer experts may, however, now be more likely to be working on fixed-term contracts, or on a self-employed basis, than previously. Higher proportions than previously are setting up their own businesses.

The more highly visible work in the 'black economy' has tended to be largely male, some of it being 'moonlighting' or 'double jobbing', as men seek to maximise the earning capacity of their mechanical, electrical, building or other skills, or professional expertise. In some areas, however, as Ray Pahl found in the Isle of Sheppey, traditions of formal full employment have never been strong, and men are accustomed to moving in and out of jobs, which may be full- or part-time, temporary or 'permanent', legitimate or 'black' in payment. The recession may only have accentuated certain aspects of this pattern.

Adult women
Women's working lives have perhaps always shown greater variety, and many of the current changes can be seen in women's paid and unpaid work.

Women now represent over 44 per cent of the labour force; and 40 per cent of them are working part-time. Over half of working women are married. Women with the youngest children are those least likely to be in employment at all, but very few are never employed at any stage. Breaks in employment for child-rearing tend to be fewer and shorter than previously. Part-time working provides the flexibility that many seek in order to combine their paid and unpaid work, and employers are sometimes persuaded into providing it.[15] Full-time work is often seen as a less than optimal alternative. 'Twilight' shift-working is another form of part-time work that seems to meet the needs of both employers and women workers.

While the variety of and reasons for the growth of part-time employment are wide, it has in general remained low-paid and low-status work. Those working less than eight hours a week (sixteen hours for the first five years) and/or earning less than £32 (in 1985) may not be entitled to legal employment protection rights or National Insurance benefits. Even those who are paid the same rates pro rata as full-timers often have lower fringe benefits (sick pay, holidays, pensions) or opportunities for promotion, and EEC proposals for equalising these were widely opposed by employers, despite ignorance as to productivity levels of part-timers. Employer resistance to part-time professional and managerial jobs, or to job-splitting, remains strong, despite the feasibility for many, if not all, jobs.

Home working or out-working has traditionally been seen as

women's work, but while this has tended to decline along with the manufacturing industries involved, computing work and that for other service industries has increased.

Women made redundant, too, have set up their own businesses, sometimes with redundant husbands, often in services, but also in clothing or food, sometimes as cooperatives. Again, the motivation has often been the need to combine family care and income-generating activities more flexibly; but sometimes also frustration with the blocked career paths experienced by women in big companies has been the driving force.

Women's share in the black economy in domestic services, typing, waitressing, provision of lodgings, may be as widespread as that of men, but is less visible, and of a more casual, short-term nature. This too may well have increased as the possibility of obtaining other employment has diminished, or where the husband's unemployment has resulted in the wife giving up her job.

Domestic work has remained largely women's responsibility, regardless of whether they are in or out of employment. Questionnaire responses still show little male domestic assistance, other than occasional washing-up or driving to the shops. Media-publicised examples of 'swapping lifestyles' still appear to be isolated examples, even if increasingly numerous, rather than a widespread pattern. Some couples have done this deliberately as part of a conscious design to seek a different and more equal lifestyle. Others have been pulled into it by the man losing his job, and once having been forced to adapt, then chosen to continue it or adopt a modified form of it. In the majority of cases, however, women have continued to carry most of the domestic burdens, unemployed men regarding taking on house-work as a further diminution of status besides losing the 'breadwinner' role. Some women appear to have deliberately given up employment for these reasons, as well as because of loss of benefit entitlements. Even in couples who claim to divide domestic chores between them, more often where both are in employment, the woman tends to retain those that need to be done on a daily basis. Car, gardening, decorating and repair work is more likely to be done by men, although women also do an increasing amount of these sorts of work too.

The care of young children and most of the non-leisure activity connected with school-age children is still largely the mother's responsibility, although some of the transportation of children to school or social activities is undertaken by fathers. Holidays, flexible working hours and other days off are increasingly chosen by male, as well as female, employees to coincide with school holidays or special events. Care of elderly dependants has also largely remained a woman's responsibility, even if she is employed, but reductions in state welfare services are increasing the stress such women experience, or causing them to resign their jobs.

Since higher proportions of middle-aged women have returned to employment, participation in organised community work (e.g. meals-on-wheels, hospital visiting) has tended to become the responsibility of the early retired or of young mothers, although part-timers may still be active. The considerable informal voluntary help to old or sick neighbours, or those with family crises, is still largely done by women, although husbands also help with repairs and gardening. Young people are also undertaking this on a more organised basis in some areas.

What of the future?

While some of the factors underlying the present state of employment may well change, as they have done cyclically in the past, reversion to traditional patterns of industrial society seems unlikely. Too many features of that – sustained population growth, occupational structure, economic growth, welfarism, urbanisation – have already changed. 'Work' and 'income' may well have to be organised more flexibly and appropriately, and while many would predict that changes will be sufficiently gradual to enable social adaptation, the growing polarisation between 'haves' and 'have-nots', between 'North' and 'South' in British society alone, let alone other critical threats to the world's economic and political stability, could mean that time for adaptation is more limited than optimists allow.

Much will depend on attitudes, both to the need for change and the nature of that change. Before we seek too far for dramatically new patterns, however, the patterns of women's working lives should be examined more closely. In many respects the greater flexibility of these, the balance of responsibilities between employer, family, local and personal needs, between extra income and other priorities, demonstrate different 'opportunity-cost' trade-offs, which may vary at different stages of the personal, job and family life-cycles, but are more fitted to the needs of society and individuals at the present time.[16]

Moving away from assumptions of traditional male working lives as the assumed norm does not imply any desire for a woolly domesticity, utopian 'small craft' society or subsistence economy.

Needs for income, for the creation of surplus and added value, for the use and development of high technology will still be important but could be less likely to be seen as ends in themselves. Nor is this shift advocated at the cost of continuing low-level second rate part-time employment status for most women, and the extension of it to more men. It does mean up-grading, reducing and/or balancing out the quality, quantity and rewards of paid employment and seeking for much greater variety and flexibility of both work-sharing and pay-sharing, by which couples or individuals can, for example, opt for contracts of employment offering certain packages of percentage reductions in hours or income for a certain period, leaving more time for other unpaid work. Otherwise it is logical for feminists to reject part-time solutions as an acceptance of inferior status, and to demand an 'equal wage slavery, equal stress syndrome' with men, regardless of its effects on children (if any), the community and themselves.

The contradictions of the present time are apparent when many men in stressful management positions are asking 'need success cost so much?'[17] and ambitious young women who feel pressed to choose between career and family ask 'need loving cost so much?' If it can be assumed that the majority of both young men and young women will want time for education and training, worthwhile paid employment, parenthood, domestic work, community recognition, and recuperative and re-creative leisure, then public policies and private attitudes should facilitate it – in particular to put a new emphasis on the practical responsibilities of fatherhood and the responsibility for each individual to support his or her self and their children jointly.

Thus the basic shift in attitudes needed may be the shift away from sex-stereotyped thinking. So much 'alternative' thinking still, like Marxism, takes traditional patriarchal norms for granted, however innovative and insightful it may be in other ways. Yet it may be questioned whether those who cannot think outside traditional sex role paradigms can think through other new paradigms. Liberation from sexist thinking represents an opportunity for human liberation and values which can provide a new starting point for radical change. It may enable us to think differently in terms of people, when we think about ways in which 'things are not going to get better: they are going to get different' (Naisbitt, 1984) and how we intend to shape this different future.

●　●　●

Even at the risk of repetition, it is worth appending a warning postscript to this general advocacy of flexible working patterns. There is a danger of this flexibility being applied to low-paid, low-skill, low-satisfaction, part-time workers on the margins of society, while a small core of high-tech, high-skill professionals work long hours for high pay and control the bulk of the output from the formal economy. Professor Charles Handy has vividly expressed this fear of a split society:

> My nightmare is one of managers in their middle-class ghettos resenting having to pay exorbitant taxes to provide the blue-collar workers with bread and circuses, while the latter live in a derelict wasteland, bitterly envying the lifestyle of the former.[18]

It is but a short step from economic marginality to political impotence. It is hard to imagine that the professional elite in such a split society would not become dominant politically, irrespective of whether there were nominally votes for all. To avoid such social division, it will be essential to ensure that work itself is shared equitably, as well as the fruits of work, reducing the norm of hours worked by any one person in the formal economy, so that more people have access to it. There are a wide range of fiscal arrangements available to encourage such work-sharing, from overtime disincentives to labour subsidies or tax allowances for each employee, encouraging employers to employ more people, rather than work their existing labour force for longer hours. Such measures, involving a wider distribution of work, should be part of a broad package of fundamental reform, concerned also with a redistribution of income and a redirection of the tax burden away from jobs and work and onto the use of capital and resources. It is to consideration of these aspects of the package that we now turn.

NOTES

1 R. Taylor, 'The future for jobs', *Management Today*, December 1982.

2 Institute for Social and Economic Research, *Review of the Economy and Employment*, University of Warwick, Summer 1983.

3 C. Purkiss, 'Unemployment: perspectives on the debate', *Manpower Studies*, no.7, Winter 1983-4.

4 C. Clegg, 'The derivation of job designs', *Journal of Occupational Behaviour*, April 1984, vol.5, no.2.

5 B. Williams, *Technical Change and Life Hours of Work*, Manchester Statistical Society, 1983.

6 S. Mason and B. Martin, *Annual Leisure Review*, Leisure Consultants, September 1982.

7 G. Clark, 'Recent developments in working patterns', *Employment Gazette*, July 1982.

8 C. Leicester, 'Part-time Britain', *Personnel Management*, June 1982.

9 C. Hakin, 'Homework and Outwork', *Employment Gazette*, January 1984.

10 Manpower Services Commission, *Manpower Review 1982*, MSC, 1982.

11 J.I. Gershuny and R.E. Pahl, 'Britain in the decade of the three economies', *New Society*, 3 January 1980.

12 A. Steel and S. Rothwell, 'Manpower matters: shorter working time', *Journal of General Management*, vol.9, no.1, Autumn 1983.

13 C. Hakim, *Occupational Segregation*, DE Research Paper no.9, November 1979.

14 C. Handy, *Taking Stock*, BBC Publications, 1982.

15 S. Rothwell, 'Women returning to work in the UK', in A. Yohalem, ed., *Women Returning to Work in Five Countries*, Allenheld Osmun, 1980.

16 S. Rothwell, 'Women and work', *Resurgence*, May–June 1981.

17 F. Bartoleme, 'Need success cost so much?', *Harvard Business Review*, March 1980.

18 Quoted in *Business in Society*, New Initiative, London, 1984.

10 Taxation, Benefits and the Basic Income

Flexible working patterns may already have arrived in society at large, but they are still largely unrecognised by governmental systems of social security, which continue to base their operations on assumptions of full-time working as the norm. In the UK, the system of income maintenance is based on Beveridge's proposal for a social insurance scheme (Beveridge, 1942). While there is widespread acceptance that this system is in urgent need of reform, proposals to achieve this rarely go beyond seeking to tidy it up. Such proposals do not recognise that the assumptions on which Beveridge's system is based have ceased to apply (and perhaps never did) and that these have been a major factor contributing to its complexity and inefficiency. Any simplification of the system which does not challenge its assumptions can only compound its inadequacy and in addition will further impoverish the poor, as the recent social security review of the British Government has shown.

Anne Miller (TOES, 1984) has identified the assumptions underlying Beveridge's thinking which bear least relation to contemporary reality:

1 That paid employment is an effective instrument for preventing financial poverty;
2 That a rigid formal employment structure of 'full-time' work is the norm;
3 That full employment for men during their working lives (16–65) is desirable and feasible;
4 That married women are, or wish to be, merely financial appendages of their husbands;
5 That high growth rates in the economy are desirable and feasible;
6 That those who are unable to support themselves out of earnings or national insurance benefits are a very small minority.

Much evidence has been cited in the previous chapter to demonstrate the fallacy of these assumptions, and it is not difficult to add to it. With regard to assumption 1, the Low Pay Unit has consistently shown that earnings can be so low as not even to guarantee subsistence, and a recent publication of the Unit estimates that in 1983 'seven and a half million adults, or one-third of the entire workforce in Britain, suffer from low pay', with 'low pay' here defined as £5 per week less than the 'official poverty line' of the Supplementary Benefit earnings equivalent.[1]

Assumption 2 is contradicted by the growth in part-time work, and 3 by the growth in male unemployment throughout industrial countries, which, in the UK, has actually resulted between 1961 and 1982 in a reduction of 200,000 in the number of men in jobs. In contrast, the number of married women in paid work grew by 70 per cent over the same period, invalidating the 'financial appendage' assumption 4.[2] Enough has been said in earlier chapters to question the desirability and feasibility of economic growth assumed in assumption 5, and 6 is ruled immediately out of court by the current numbers of people living on supplementary benefit.

Given the invalidity of these key Beveridge assumptions, it is not surprising that the benefit system based on them is close to collapse. First there is the poverty trap, by which a pay rise for someone on a low wage can actually result in loss of income through the withdrawal of benefit. Even where there is a net income gain, the effective marginal tax rate (defined as the amount of income forfeited by the wage earner from each extra £1 earned, on account of tax or benefit withdrawal) can be greater than that experienced even in the highest income brackets. Then there is the unemployment trap, whereby if only low-income jobs are available, working at all can entail a drop in income for some people due to withdrawal of their benefits. There is also an idleness trap, involving the effective prohibition on unemployed people doing voluntary work or anything else except 'looking for a job', even when there obviously are no jobs, which is a recipe for despair, alienation and depression. And there is the spendthrift trap, which discourages from saving people who think they might become unemployed, because supplementary benefit is denied to those who have financial assets of more than £3000.

In addition, the present system often involves means-testing, always a repugnant process, and sometimes involving the investigation of the most intimate details of people's private lives, as with the cohabitation rule. Moreover, the system is so complicated that many of those who need the benefits most miss out on them, because they do not know their entitlements nor how to claim them.

There is no point trying to tinker with the superstructure of a system with such fundamental structural flaws. It needs to be rebuilt from first principles that have their roots in the realities, lifestyles and aspirations of the present day. Such a rebuilt system is the Basic Income Scheme:

> A Basic Income Scheme would aim to guarantee to each man, woman and child the unconditional right to an independent income sufficient to meet basic living costs. Its main purpose would be the prevention of poverty, as opposed to mere poverty relief.

These are the opening sentences of the Constitution of the Basic Income Research Group (BIRG), based in London, which seeks to encourage an informed debate about the desirability and practicability of the Basic Income idea. Miller is a member of BIRG's Research Panel and describes the scheme as 'an instrument for guaranteeing unconditional minimum economic rights for all individuals'. She adds:

> Such schemes are not new. An early proposal was put forward by Major C.H. Douglas (1920, 1922) and many variations have been suggested since then. An excellent short history and bibliography is to be found in Roberts, 1983, to which may be added reference material by Parker and Rhys-Williams[3] and Vince.[4] Interest has prevailed in Canada, the USA, New Zealand and the UK, and is growing in Europe, particularly in Belgium.

The Basic Income Scheme does not start from Beveridge's discredited assumptions. It grants an unconditional right to an independent income to all citizens, irrespective of other income, work status, sex or marital status. It advocates that such income should be adequate to meet basic living costs. For the sake of fairness, consistency and simplicity, it further advocates that it should replace existing benefits and tax-relief, being administered through an integrated tax-benefit system.

In the UK in 1983 the House of Commons Treasury and Civil Service Committee recommended that the government put work in hand to examine the feasibility of the Basic Income approach with respect to the reform of personal income taxation and income support. It also recommended that 'changes to the present system should be compatible with an eventual move to an integrated structure of tax and social security'.[5]

The beneficial effects of a Basic Income Scheme are wide-ranging and profound. It would obviously abolish the poverty, unemployment, idleness and spendthrift traps: because the basic income is not withdrawn, people are free to take what work they can find, earn what they can and save what they wish. This would positively encourage the flexible working patterns discussed earlier, doing much to break down the distinction between the present stark alternatives of 'employed' or 'unemployed' and so diminishing the stigma of the latter. As Miller has pointed out:

> If the government stops using its artificial categories of full-time work, part-time work, unemployment, retirement, then employers should be able to desist from using these terms too, and the opportunities for 'part-time' employment on the same basis and conditions as 'full-time' employment might increase. The concept of 'unemployment' as currently defined (the number of people claiming unemployment benefit) would be redundant. The alternative concept of underemployment (the short-fall between the number of labour hours that all people would like to offer at their current wages, and the number that they are able to offer) would be relevant, especially in some deprived areas, but there is every probability that it would be less acute, because of the greater freedom in the labour market which the basic income would introduce.

Much work that is currently not done, because of its inability to compete with benefits, would become viable, because even the low wage involved would represent an addition to the basic income. Some marginal employers who find difficulty paying the subsistence component of income would be able to employ people at a wage-rate determined purely by the value added by the work involved. From the point of view of labour, a worker would be able to negotiate a wage with subsistence already assured, so that people would not be forced by hardship into unpleasant work, but could hold out for the decent pay that such work should entail. A real choice would exist as to the mix between paid, unpaid, voluntary and domestic work which people wished to do, and the basic income would also make a reality of wages for housework, giving financial independence for the first time to those who were rearing children, keeping house or caring for dependent relatives. It would be society's acknowledgment of the vital importance of these tasks, without undermining their human, social component by seeking to bring them formally into the monetary economy as such. The lack of means-testing would end investigations of personal circumstances, and the simplicity of the scheme should ensure that no one slips through the net because of ignorance or confusion.

Given these advantages, which are largely uncontested, one must look at the objections which have so far prevented the implementation of basic income schemes. The first is that a basic income, being a universal payment, is thought to be impossibly expensive and to entail very high tax rates, if it is to give adequate help to those who need it. Yet the alternative of selective payments can involve very high marginal tax rates on low income earners, as we have seen. Hermione Parker makes a powerful case for:

> a judicious combination of both universality and selectivity. The exact mix can only be discovered by comparing tax rates under each system, assuming given benefit levels, and working out the numbers of people likely to be affected by high marginal tax rates . . . . [Shared prosperity] is incompatible with a system which imposes high marginal tax rates on large numbers of people. Therefore means–tested benefit ceilings should be kept as near as possible to the bottom end of the income range (half to twice the average), where most incomes are concentrated.[6]

One detailed scheme outlined later in her article proposes a 1984/5 basic income of £21.50 per week (£15 for children) and the retention of housing benefit and the payment of basic income supplements to expectant mothers, widow(er)s, single parents, those over sixty-five and to invalids and those with handicaps, with disability costs on top. It also involves a starting rate of effective marginal tax of 73 per cent (composed of income tax, levied on all income, of 40 per cent, plus 33 per cent due to the withdrawal of housing benefit), the abolition of National Insurance and a new 10 per cent employers' payroll tax. In contrast, the UK Green Party's scheme[7] has a Basic Income of £28 per week (£12 for children), similar supplements and a starting rate of income tax of 50 per cent on all income after £10 per week.

These two schemes illustrate quite well the various political and economic trade-offs that the payment of a basic income to all inevitably involves, but they both illustrate that, *per se*, basic income schemes need not involve prohibitive costs. Even the present system in the UK is intended to give a guaranteed income (though with many strings attached and with the notable exception of 5 million married women) to those who cannot earn one. Formalising this in a basic income scheme need not entail any increase in taxation, if the basic income is set low enough. In fact, David Chapman, another member of the BIRG Research Panel, has put forward a minimum-cost, minimum-change scheme, which might well be able to be operated within the present social security budget, without requiring any increase of tax on higher incomes, while yet not reducing the incomes of those not in work. Both the other schemes quoted above are, however, significantly redistributive from those with high to those with low incomes, and surely it is right that the fruits of modern technology should be shared more widely in this way. But the point is that this is a political decision. With the political will, it is economically perfectly possible.

Notwithstanding the redistributive potential of basic income schemes, some, especially on the political left, resent a scheme that guarantees an income to the rich as well as the poor. This is a peculiar blind spot, for those with high incomes will more than pay for their basic incomes through the higher tax rates involved in schemes such as those above.

A potentially more potent criticism is that the payment of a basic income would erode the incentive to work, at the low-wage end of the scale, by encouraging idleness, and at the high-wage end through the disincentive of high tax rates. In countering this suggestion, it must be pointed out again that, for those currently on unemployment benefit or on low pay, the payment of a basic income would significantly increase the incentive to work by abolishing the poverty and unemployment traps. For the rest, there are probably few people who would relish a life of idleness on £28 per week, and the basic income could always be indexed to the national income if this proved to be necessary. Higher incomes are already subject to higher tax rates and, in any case, the necessity to share work, especially highly paid work, which was emphasised at the end of the last chapter, means that it may be no bad thing if over-stressed executives were given some encouragement by high tax rates to work less hard at their jobs and spend more time with their families in their informal economies.

Tax-collecting could be more difficult with a basic income scheme, especially if increasing numbers of people opted for part-time, flexible working for several employers or through self-employment, and tax-collecting procedures (such as Pay-As-You-Earn in the UK) and obligations would doubtless have to be altered to take account of this. Such a consideration opens up the whole question of taxation, because flexible working patterns become a taxation problem only if income remains the primary source of taxation. There would, in fact, seem to be very good reasons why this should not be the case.

In days of full employment, the taxation of income was a logical way of raising money. Those who earned most contributed most to the public purse and were the most able to do so. Those not earning were relieved of tax liability which, in any case, they would not have been able to meet. However, an undeniable result of placing the tax burden most heavily on income, and therefore on jobs, through income tax and National Insurance, has been discrimination against labour with regard to the other factors of production – capital, land and resources. This discrimination has been compounded by the fact that capital investment attracts tax relief, whereas employing people involves tax liability. This in turn has contributed to mechanisation, the replacement of people by machines, and to more intensive resource use, especially that of energy, as fossil fuels undercut human energy, and must even now be contributing to automation. Mechanisation and automation are, therefore, not mechanisms that are powered by free market considerations alone. They receive a powerful boost from a taxation system that increases labour costs by up to 40 per cent, as it does in the UK, when National Insurance is taken into account.

When the labour market was able to absorb those made redundant by rising labour productivity, it may have been that the distortions introduced by taxing jobs did not matter. Now, however, with mass unemployment, and in the people-rich and resource- and capital-lean economy of the 1980s, it is hardly sensible to continue putting people out of work simply because employers get bigger tax breaks if they invest in plant. It has become an urgent priority to find ways of shifting the tax burden from labour onto the use of capital and resources, not to increase it overall, but to allow fairer competition between people and robots.

Little detailed work appears yet to have been done on this issue. The ideas put forward here are still very much on the drawing-board, but they will have served their purpose if they show that there are alternatives to income-based taxes, which could raise the bulk of government revenue in their place.

Chapman[8] has identified three kinds of taxes – nuisance taxes, conservation taxes and taxes which are primarily for raising revenue. The first two are expressly designed to discourage the economic activities on which they are levied, and to give incentives to alternatives, as well as to raise revenue. They thus act as fiscal instruments of damage prevention.

Nuisance taxes are most obviously relevant to pollution and to the protection of the environment and society generally. Their aim would be to internalise to the production process the costs incurred by society at large due to that process, so that the price of the product reflected its full costs both to present and future generations. Chapman contends that the admitted difficulties of estimating taxes on this basis, of putting a monetary value on illness, pollution and other environmental and societal damage, do not constitute an excuse for not trying to do it at all. On the other hand, there is a danger that this difficulty will result in taxes being set too low, so that they become, in effect, a licence to pollute. Thus, accepting the principle of nuisance taxation in no way replaces the necessity of banning some activities and production processes completely, where the evidence so warrants.

Conservation or resource taxes are levied on the first use of resources, whether by domestic industry or in imported products, to encourage their efficient use and, because recycled resources could be exempt, to promote recycling. Energy is obviously the prime candidate for such a tax, but it could equally be applied to other resources, renewable or non-renewable. Where desirable, some of the revenue derived in this way could be used to boost production of some renewable resources, e.g. timber, in the interests of self-reliance and increasing the sustainable yield. Daly (TOES, 1984) has proposed an alternative to resource taxes, which he calls a 'depletion quota auction', in which the resource market would become two tiered:

> In the first tier the total amount to be extracted or imported of each resource category would be set by a government agency, and auctioned off in divisible units as rights to purchase or extract the resource up to the specified amount. Purchase of the depletion quota allows entry into the second tier of the market which would be a private competitive market. In addition to paying the market price to the extracting/importing company, the purchaser must present the previously purchased depletion quota rights, which the firm will present to auditors at tax time. The scheme sets total quantity centrally, but leaves the decentralised price system to determine allocation of the fixed total among alternative uses.

Clearly indirect taxes of this sort bear most heavily on those with low incomes, but there is no reason why this inequality should not be ironed out by progressive distribution of the tax receipts, such as through the basic income. Conservation taxes could also be extended to specific industries, such as taxing the building of new houses, to encourage the repair, maintenance and conversion of existing buildings, or through giving incentives to manufacturers to extend the guarantee of life-expectancy of their products, to encourage durability. Import taxes could be imposed to promote self-reliance and this is discussed later in Chapter 14.

All the above taxes are fiscal instruments geared to policy objectives, most of which have been advocated in this book. In so far as they were successful in achieving their objectives, they would raise progressively less revenue, although some, like resource taxes, would always remain significant. There are other taxes which, while continuing to have social objectives, would tend less to diminish their tax base.

The most important of these is probably land value taxation, which has already been discussed. All that will be added here is to note that such a tax would have no disincentive effect on production, rather tending to bring land into use, by preventing speculative gains from holding it idle, and by being payable whether land was in use or not. The potential revenue of land taxation is very large – a recent calculation in the United States has indicated that the annual rent of land plus resources there was 28 per cent of national income in 1981. If collected by the government, this would be enough to replace all taxes on labour and capital, apart from user charges, according to the author of the study, Professor Steven Cord.[9] In addition to advocating land value taxation, Chapman has also put forward proposals for a Luxury Housing Tax and a Progressive Value-Added Tax.[10]

Whether the extra taxation to fund a comprehensive and redistributive basic income scheme were to be raised from income tax or from some combination of the alternatives discussed here, the additional tax burden would, as has been seen, be substantial. However, in a society like the United States, any taxation on this scale would prove politically difficult to introduce, yet a basic income is no less necessary there than in other countries. Ward Morehouse explains why, and outlines a means of guaranteeing a basic income, which does not depend on transfer payments. It is closely related to the principle of decentralised banking explored earlier.

●　●　●

'UNIVERSALISING CAPITAL OWNERSHIP'
by Ward Morehouse

The US economy is the largest in the world. It is also one of the most productive. But its record on one of the other critical planes of economic performance – namely, equity – is much less satisfactory. Indeed, given its enormous productive capacity, I would argue that its performance on this plane is positively dismal.

This critical dimension involves the equitable distribution of income and assets. Although equity is a relative concept, meaning simply 'fairness', and what may be perceived to be fair to some persons in one situation may appear to be quite unfair to others in different circumstances, the table of relative incomes given in Table 10.1 shows that the US distributes the fruits of its economy

Table 10.1 The fairness ratio: income distribution in selected countries

Country	Relationship of income of top one-fifth to bottom one-fifth
Finland	4/1
Denmark	5/1
Japan	5/1
Netherlands	5/1
Sweden	5/1
United Kingdom	5/1
Bangladesh	6/1
West Germany	6/1
Norway	6/1
Sri Lanka	6/1
Yugoslavia	6/1
India	7/1
Indonesia	7/1
Spain	7/1
South Korea	8/1
Tanzania	8/1
France	9/1
United States	10/1
Malaysia	16/1
Turkey	16/1
Venezuela	18/1
Mexico	20/1
Peru	32/1
Brazil	33/1

Source: World Bank, *World Development Report 1983*, New York, Oxford University Press, 1983.

far less evenly than many other countries. Among societies at roughly comparable levels of per capita productive capacity, the US stands at the bottom of the heap. It is also well below far poorer countries like Tanzania and India.

Poverty is also a relative concept. Every society does – and should – define poverty in relation to its own economic circumstances. But by US definitions, there is plenty of poverty in the United States today, especially in a society with such a productive economy. Moreover, after a period of relative decline, US poverty is increasing again. Thus, from 1979 to 1982 (the latest year for which such data are available), Americans below the poverty line increased from 26.1 million to 34.4 million, reflecting a 28.2 per cent growth rate, when population changes are taken into account.[11]

One of the critical determinants in the inequitable distribution of income which such poverty levels in an affluent society reflect is in the ownership of productive assets. Here the picture is even more sharply skewed. Less than 6 per cent of the population derive substantial benefits from their ownership of roughly 95 per cent of the country's productive assets (Speiser, 1984).

Given the way in which productive assets are financed in the corporate sector of the US economy, this concentration of ownership is inevitably going to be perpetuated. The accompanying bathtub diagram (Figure 10.1) tells why. 95 per cent of capital expansion is funded by retained earnings and by debt (the latter paid off by future earnings from the new assets). The increase in equity in the company that results is distributed proportionately to the existing ownership, with the pinnacle class of less than 6 per cent receiving 95 per cent of the increased value from the fresh investment in productive assets.

There are at least two principal ways of remedying this situation in terms of working towards a more equitable social order. One is by redistributing income through a series of transfer payments that involve taxing the better off for the benefit of those less well off, using the government as the transfer mechanism.

In the United States at least, many Americans feel the government has not been a particularly efficient mechanism, whether rightly or wrongly. And there is increasing political resistance even to maintaining, let alone increasing, such transfer payments in order to reduce poverty and diminish the gap between the top and the bottom, calculated in economic terms, in US society. (The absolute level of transfer payments in constant prices has in fact declined during the Reagan administration.)

This situation prompts consideration of an alternative approach

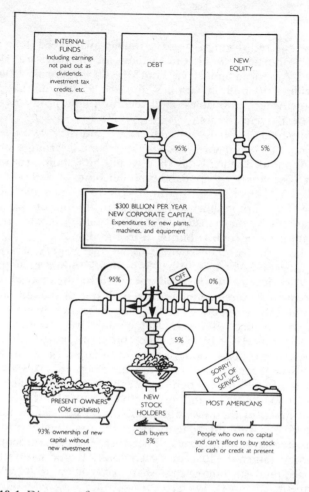

Figure 10.1 Diagram of present system for creating new productive assets by US corporations

Source: Stuart M. Speiser, 'A $100,000 Stock Portfolio For Everyone', *New York Times*, 5 June 1977

– namely, working towards a more equitable distribution of productive assets. Note the lack of mention of any *redistribution of existing* assets because that would be politically impossible on any significant scale in the United States today. But the more equitable distribution of new assets is politically more feasible and a plan to achieve this has been proposed by Stuart Speiser (Speiser, 1984), which envisages that every American family would acquire (through a government-guaranteed loan which would be repaid through the earnings of the assets) a $100,000 share in American industry. The $100,000 figure is determined by dividing 50 million families into the $5 trillion that Speiser estimates American business will spend on new productive assets in the next twenty years.

This $100,000 share in American industry would yield, assuming that companies no longer retained earnings but paid them all out as dividends (as they would be required to do under Speiser's scheme), an annual family income of $20,000, which would thus constitute something akin to a guaranteed annual income, but without the politically difficult role of the government serving as the transfer mechanism, taking income from the more affluent and redistributing it to the poor.

At the heart of the scheme, called the SuperStock plan, is democratization of credit. What SuperStock would make possible for all Americans is the method now used by the pinnacle class of 6 per cent to acquire productive assets. If one of the old capitalists wants to buy some new stock and does not have sufficient cash lying around to do so, he or she goes to the bank to take a loan on relatively more favorable terms, since it is secured. They use as collateral some of their existing stock. And they pay off the loan through earnings from the assets they are acquiring. Under the SuperStock scheme, everybody would be able to use this method for acquiring productive assets. However, many, perhaps most, of the new capitalists (the 94 per cent who do not now derive significant benefits from the earnings of productive assets) have few or no assets. Therefore, the government would have to guarantee the loan that each family would in effect secure as it acquired an increasing share of equity in new capital investment.

Hence, the method being proposed for more equitable distribution of new productive assets is certainly not new or radical. It is the one already being used by the old capitalists. Nor is government guarantee of credit on such a wide scale new or radical. It is the method that was introduced after the Second World War to help veterans returning from the war to acquire housing, i.e., the GI mortgage, which was guaranteed by the government.

The Speiser scheme advocates that SuperStock should be confined to the 2000 largest corporations in the US. I feel that this would undesirably reinforce the existing concentration of power in the US economy, and, in any case, there is no guarantee that these companies are going to perform better in the uncertain time ahead than younger, smaller and perhaps more flexible and dynamic business firms. Thus I would advocate that SuperStock include from the outset all companies with publicly traded stock and satisfactory earnings records.

In contrast to an employee stock ownership plan or ESOP (discussed further in Chapter 12), SuperStock is a universal stock ownership plan or USOP. In an effort to determine the feasibility of USOPs from the point of view of mainstream academic and business economists, a Seminar on Policies for Capital Diffusion through Expanded Equity Ownership was held at the Brookings Institution in Washington, DC in September 1977. The general conclusion, as set forth by Professor Lawrence Klein of the University of Pennsylvania and moderator of the seminar, was that there was no economic reason why the plan could not be made workable. Moreover, on the crucial point of inflation, Klein confirmed that the expansion of credit under the plan 'will not be inflationary if the funds made available flow into investment that raises national productivity.'[12]

The full scale programme for introducing USOPs would involve their creation in three tiers – national, state and local or municipal. SuperStock would become the national tier. States and localities would be authorized, but not required, to establish USOPs if they so desired. As the attractiveness of USOPs became apparent, there is little doubt that more and more states and localities would do so.

Equally voluntary would be the participation of companies but with the powerful incentive of relief from federal corporate income tax and access to capital for expansion. The federal government would provide the same facility of guaranteeing loans with which to acquire USOP equity in the state and local as in the national or SuperStock plan.

There are still many details of the SuperStock idea to be explored and settled, such as the circumstances under which SuperStock could itself be used as collateral, like other stock, or could be alienated, and the critically important queston of how broad public interests, reflected in the ownership of SuperStock equity, would be introduced into the management of companies in the SuperStock plan, without hamstringing the ability of management to manage. As to who would make the capital investment decisions, and how business failures would be dealt with, it was suggested earlier that banks with community representation should undertake the former, while credit insurance institutions should spread the risks of the latter, but more still needs to be done to firm up these ideas.

It is anticipated that in a fifteen to twenty year transition period, most, if not all American families would acquire a significant equity stake in productive enterprise in the United States. From the present skewed distribution in which less than 6 per cent have the lion's share of such assets (1 per cent of the US population hold some 50 per cent of all privately held corporate stock[13]), the other 94 per cent would have acquired about 50 per cent of productive assets towards the end of the transition period. Thus, while there would still be rich people in America, there would be no really poor people, if the overall strategy was successful, and the US would have achieved a much more equitable distribution of income, with a ratio of the top 20 per cent to the bottom 20 per cent more like Finland, Denmark and Japan, with 4/1 and 5/1 ratios.

USOPs would also have important and beneficial side-effects. They would reduce the need for transfer payments as the stock began to generate income. They entail wide participation in the fruits of new technology, and the worker whose job was now being done by a robot would at least have the satisfaction of thinking that he or she was the partial owner of that robot. Local USOPs could be used to create local currencies along the lines described earlier.[14] The state and local USOPs would also open up access to capital markets to community-based enterprises and small businesses operating at those levels. As matters now stand, such undertakings are at a strong disadvantage in competition for scarce capital in financial markets that have become increasingly national in character and that are dominated by the requirements of government and large corporations. The non-profit sector, too, could seek the financing of productive assets through USOPs, which could provide a boost to the informal economy.

Finally it is important to emphasise that, with universal capital ownership, there will still be plenty of scope for risk-taking and innovation, and successful entrepreneurs will still be able to reap the rewards of their entrepreneurship. Citizen-owned equity through USOPs will never exceed 49 per cent of the total equity in a given company, nor will USOPs be a suitable vehicle for high-risk new business start ups. Venture capital would still be very much in demand, and the rewards for enterprise would be untrammelled by the high taxation that, without USOP, might be necessary to finance transfer payments.

But these are bonuses. More fundamentally, universalizing capital ownership involves a fundamental redistribution of not only ownership of productive economic assets but also of political power. More and more this power would begin to shift from its concentration in the pinnacle class of some 6 per cent of the US population who are now capitalists to the 94 per cent who are not. Only through this shift in power will it be possible to build a just and more equitable social order in the US in the decades ahead.

•   •   •

In conclusion, it is worth noting that the ideas underlying the USOP proposal are also being seriously discussed in the UK. In July 1985, the Working Party on Share Ownership of the Social Democratic Party (SDP) published a discussion paper on wider share ownership,[15] which advocated the establishment of a citizen's unit trust. This unit trust would eventually comprise a 10 per cent stake in all major UK enterprises and a large share of the nationalised industries. It would yield a dividend of about £100 per annum to each adult. The paper draws heavily on the arguments of Cambridge Nobel Laureate economist James Meade, which is a further indication of the degree to which the ideas of a basic income and wider share ownership are now in the mainstream of debate. It will, hopefully, be sooner rather than later that the growing realisation of their advantages results in their introduction.

NOTES

1   Low Pay Unit, *Low Wages and Poverty in the 1980s*, Low Pay Review no.16, Low Pay Unit, London, 1984.

2   BBC Education *Workforce*, BBC, London, 1985, p.3.

3   See H. Parker and B. Rhys-Williams in the Treasury and Civil Service Sub-Committee, 'The structure of personal income taxation and income support', *Minutes of Evidence*, Her Majesty's Stationery Office, London, 1982. See evidence on 21.7.82.

4   Vince, P., . . . *to each according* . . . , Liberal Party, London, 1983.

5   Parker and Rhys-Williams, op. cit.

6   H. Parker, 'Costing basic incomes' in *BIRG Bulletin*, no.3, Spring 1985.

7   Green Party, *Information About the Basic Income Scheme*, Green Party, London, 1985.

8   D. Chapman, 'Suggestions for the tax and subsidy system of a Green government', unpublished, 1985.

9   S. Cord, 'How much revenue would a land value tax raise in the US?', paper presented to the 16th Conference of the International Union for Land Value Taxation and Free Trade, August 1984. The paper is

available from Land and Liberty, 177 Vauxhall Bridge Road,
London SW1.

10   Chapman, op. cit.

11   'Either way they slice it, more are poor', *New York Times*,
26 February, 1984.

12   From unpublished notes of the seminar, available from the author at
the Council on International and Public Affairs, 777 United Nations
Plaza, New York, NY 10017.

13   Joint Economic Committee, US Congress, *Broadening the Ownership
of Capital – ESOPs and Other Alternatives: a Staff Study*, Washington,
1976.

14   See also Shann Turnbull 'Creating a community currency' in
W. Morehouse, ed., 1983.

15   SDP Working Party on Share Ownership *Wider Share Ownership:
Equality and Opportunity in an Enterprise Economy*, SDP, London, 1985.

11 INDUSTRIAL PRIORITIES AND TECHNOLOGICAL CHOICE

Greater responsibility for their investments by personal savers, a decentralised banking system, perhaps operating through a community currency and facilitating the development of locally appropriate, self-financing technology; the distribution of the ownership of this technology to the entire community; an integrated tax-benefit system, which guarantees a basic income to all citizens, and which taxes land and the use of capital and natural resources rather than labour – these are the chief fiscal and financial innovations being presented here. Their introduction would transform the economic landscape and would favour the pursuit of industrial priorities very different from the present obsession with economic growth.

Those who still regard production growth as the panacea for all economic and social problems have sometimes jumped to the conclusion that a critique of growth such as has been given here implies, firstly, a rejection of all growth *per se*; secondly, a lack of concern with poverty and economic development; and thirdly, a drastic decline in material living standards. No part of this conclusion is correct, and the purpose of this chapter is to map out the economic and social results of moving towards a conserver- rather than a consumer-economy, and to identify the technological growth points in such an economy, the areas that will need to be developed and expanded to give it social and ecological sustainability.

The broad outlines of the conserver-economy were much clarified by the completion of a recent study in the Netherlands, the results of which are published here by Roefie Hueting. The study details an economic scenario which gives top priority to the conservation of energy and the environment, rather than to encouraging production growth, but it still assumes a positive correlation between increased output and human welfare. It clearly shows that, over the twenty year period to the year 2000, production growth and conservation are not mutually exclusive, and that an emphasis on conservation generates considerably more employment than current economic policies. This growth, of course, arises from making much more efficient use of resources, including labour. These savings can only be made once, so that in the new century growth would fall away, while new conservation measures would still be necessary, but material living standards would then be some 20 per cent above 1980 levels, and, because they would be based on a lower overall consumption of energy and other natural resources, they would be far less vulnerable to external shocks to price and supply.

The study was funded by the Dutch Government as part of the broad social debate which arose out of opposition to the proposed expansion of nuclear electricity generation in the Netherlands in the 1970s. Initially the Conserver Scenario (CE) was to be compared with a low growth (one and a half per cent per annum) scenario, called the Reference Scenario in what follows; but, when it became apparent that the CE Scenario was going to perform considerably better than the Reference Scenario in terms of employment, an Industrial Recovery Scenario, envisaging two and a half per cent growth per annum, was also elaborated. The comparison between these three scenarios provides one of the clearest economic and political choices between expansion and conservation that has yet been formulated.

'AN ECONOMIC SCENARIO FOR A CONSERVER-ECONOMY'
by Roefie Hueting

[Editor's note: in the rest of this book, the term 'economic growth' has been used to mean growth in production or in GNP. In the paper that follows, however, please note that the term 'production growth' is used to mean growth in GNP, while economic growth is defined as an increase in welfare, which comprises much more than an increase in production, as the paper makes clear.]

Introduction

Between 1980 and 1983 a unique experiment was conducted in the Netherlands. Several scenarios were worked out for the Dutch economy for the period 1980–2000, some by the Central Planning Bureau (CPB), the official advisory body of the Ministry of Economic Affairs and the government, and one, composed by the Centre for Energy-Saving (CE), by the Foundation for Economic

Research (FER) of the University of Amsterdam. The scenarios worked out by the Central Planning Bureau are based on an economic policy in which growth or production is the central objective. In the scenario composed by the Centre for Energy-Saving, on the contrary, top priority is given to saving the environment and energy in the long term.

Theoretical points of departure

The theoretical points of departure are important because they describe the logical relation between the instruments introduced into the econometric model, used to elaborate the scenario, and the results yielded by the model. Such an analytical description of what may logically be expected as the result leads to a better understanding of what is going on in the model.

The CE Scenario is based on the concept of welfare as used in economic theory (see, *inter alia*, L. Robbins, 1952, and P. Hennipman, 1977). Welfare is defined there as the satisfaction of wants evoked by dealing with scarce means. Satisfaction of wants or welfare is a psychical category, an aspect of one's personal experience. The theory assumes that when choosing among scarce means – which is, in brief, the subject matter of economics – we try to maximise our welfare. The opposite is nonsensical.

Besides maximisation of welfare with given means, the desire to raise the level of the satisfaction of wants (welfare) in the course of time is also regarded as a motive for economic action. In so far as society succeeds in this, we have economic growth [see editor's note at the beginning of the paper]. As a psychical, subjective category of personal experience, welfare is not outwardly observable and thus not directly measurable in figures. So as nevertheless, to obtain an indication of the trend in the level of the satisfaction of wants, use can be made of the following approach, in which the factors which can be assumed to affect welfare and which *are* measurable are investigated. The following factors can be distinguished:

1   The package of produced goods and services;
2   The scarce environmental goods in the broad sense, thus including space, energy, natural resources, plant and animal species;
3   Time or leisure time;
4   The distribution of scarce goods or income distribution;
5   Working conditions, that is the conditions in which scarce goods are acquired or produced;

6 Employment or the degree of free choice between working and other ways of spending time;
7 The safety of the future insofar as this depends on our dealings with scarce goods.

In politics, and unfortunately also in part of the economic literature, economic growth is defined as an increase in national income, and therefore as growth of production. But production is only one of the factors influencing welfare. Moreover, part of the growth of national income does not form an increase in the quantity of scarce goods becoming available. Expenditure on treatment plants, on aid to victims of road accidents, on commuting over greater distances and the like must be interpreted as intermediate, that is as costs, and not entered as final deliveries, as happens now (Kuznets, 1947, 1948; Hueting, 1980). We increase activities burdening the environment and then we take steps to restore the original situation. In that case we again have exactly the same quantity of environmental goods as before, while the quantity of consumable goods, made by business *and* by the government, simultaneously has not increased as a result of the repair work, And yet by the present method of calculation national income has grown.

The point is that the factors determining welfare have constantly to be weighed against each other; this amounts to economic choices. Omission of a factor in the information on society's welfare means a distorted picture of reality.

The CE Scenario is concerned with scanning the effects on welfare that result from a policy giving top priority to environmental conservation. In the process, the above factors affecting welfare must be translated into precisely defined objectives. This is also necessary on account of the requirements made by the econometric model. A brief explanation follows of how those factors which are of crucial importance for the scenario study have been translated into objectives and what the political and theoretical considerations were in so doing. For the sake of brevity, discussion of the factors 3 and 5 is omitted here.

Production
The CE Scenario assumes a positive relation between production and welfare, so that it does not proceed from a 'Stop Growth' idea, but from a shift in productive and consumer activities in an environmentally acceptable direction. Improvements in productivity continue to be very welcome, except when they are at the expense of the environment. However, it may be expected before-hand that this reallocation will exert a severe check on the growth

of production. After all, about a quarter to one-third of the activities going to make up national income do not contribute to growth, because by definition no increase in productivity can result from them. In other activities the improvements in productivity are only slight. The growth of at least 3 per cent per year (a doubling of production in twenty-three years) desired by official policy must therefore be achieved by much higher growth percentages among the remaining activities. Unfortunately these are precisely the activities which by use of space or pollution, in production or consumption, do the greatest harm to the environment, such as the oil and petrochemical industry, agriculture, public utilities, roadbuilding and the extraction of minerals.[1]

The shift in economic activities towards conservation entails a sacrifice not reflected in the statistical results. For the pattern of consumption brought about by the need to conserve the environment differs from the first choice that people might have made independently of environmental considerations.

Environment

For an economic approach, the environment can best be described as the physical surroundings on which people are dependent in all their activities: production, consumption, breathing, leisure, and so on. Within this environment a number of possible uses, or environmental functions, can be distinguished. When the use of an environmental function by an activity is at the expense of the use of another (or the same) function by another activity, loss of function occurs; and losses of function are costs. In this competition between functions, a distinction can be made between qualitative, spatial and quantitative competition. Qualitative competition amounts, broadly speaking, to pollution: some activity introduces an agent (e.g. a chemical, heat, noise) into the environment, using it as a dumping ground for waste, as a result of which the quality changes, disturbing or preventing some other use. In the case of spatial and quantitative competition, the amount of space or matter is insufficient to meet the existing wants for it. Activity in the sense used here also includes the conservation of the natural environment on account of its present and future utility to people.

This approach is much broader than the traditional approach to the environment as a pollution problem that can be solved by building treatment plants. Tracing the competition between functions exposes the conflicts. Intensification and increase in scale of agriculture and fragmentation of space by roadbuilding and suburbanization thus logically fall under the environmental problem by their effect on plant and animal species: spatial competition with the function natural environment.

Competition between functions may occur in all kinds of forms. But in by far the majority of cases one can speak of use of the environment by present producing and consuming activities at the expense of other desired uses or, with a certain degree of probability, of future possible uses. We have now, roughly speaking, reached a situation in which the use of an environmental function is always at the expense of one or more other functions, now or in the future. Of course our environment is material, as are the things that we produce and consume with the aid of it, whether these are wheat, music, medical aid or books. In this situation, the subject matter of economics can be described as the study of the problems of choice that occur when arranging the dead and living matter of our surroundings in accordance with our wishes. Such a definition does justice to the fact that the environment is the basis of our existence, the foundation of our production and consumption and, in view of the competition between functions, finite.

On account of the obvious conflict between use of the environment for stepping up production and conservation of the environment for other use and for the future, calculations of shadow prices for environmental functions that are directly comparable with the market prices of goods and services would be most welcome. However, only exceptionally does it prove possible to construe such shadow prices (Hueting, 1980). Environmental functions and produced goods cannot be placed under one denominator, any more than the other factors influencing welfare; a balance cannot be struck. We shall have to make do with a description of the factors in different units.

In addition, the individual factors that determine welfare cannot always be expressed in one single indicator. This is immediately apparent with the factor of environment. Because of the often greatly differing and non-comparable action of activities burdening the environment – such as the discharge of all kinds of harmful substances, fragmentation of space and intensification of agriculture – in the scenario, environmental quality, on which the availability of the functions depends, and the changes in it are described in different units, in so far as that is already possible. The significance of all this calls for expert interpretation.

Notwithstanding these limitations, much information is provided in the scenario. The factors determining welfare are described in words and figures and where possible the costs of attaining the principal objective – environmental conservation – are estimated in terms of money.

Income distribution
Investigation of the subjective appreciation of income reveals that the absolute height and the growth of income are of much less importance to welfare, or satisfaction, than the place that a person's income occupies among the incomes of his or her peer group – the people with whom the person has contact and takes as his or her example (Van Praag and Spit, 1982). Moreover, to achieve the same increase in satisfaction more and more additional goods prove to be necessary as income rises. In other words, the effect on welfare of an additionally earned guilder falls sharply as income rises. According to the investigators, reduction of the differences in income leads to a (much) greater growth of welfare than an increase in income does. Since more real income is identical with more produced goods and services, this result casts strong doubt on the importance of perpetual growth of production.

The scenario takes as a starting point an equal distribution of the costs of the environmental measures, with compensation for those with lowest incomes.

Employment
For an industrialised and wealthy country like the Netherlands, the CE Scenario regards full employment, after a safe environment, as the principal objective.

The proposition that environmental conservation is at the expense of employment is at present probably the biggest stumbling block for a good environmental policy. However, this proposition ignores the simple truth that environment and energy are scarce goods; to obtain or maintain them factors of production have to be employed. In the industrialised countries 80 per cent to 95 per cent of national income goes to the factor labour. *The same amount of production and consumption requires more labour with environmental conservation than without.*[2] However, that labour is employed for non-market goods. And since wages are nothing more than a claim to produced goods, environmental measures amount to a reduction in the (growth of the wage) rate, at a given package of goods and services produced by the government. The conflict is not between environment and employment, but between production (plus consumption) and environment, whereby expenditure on treatment and the like is regarded as costs.

On the strength of this reasoning, in the econometric model in which the scenario has been worked out, wages have been simultaneously reduced in proportion to the estimated costs of the measures taken. In so far as environmental measures are the cause of bankruptcies now occurring, this is the result of the failure to draw the logical consequence for the wage rate.

Safety for the future
People derive part of the meaning of existence from the company of others. At the very least these others include their children and grandchildren. The prospect of a safer future is therefore a normal human need, and dimming of this prospect has a negative effect on welfare. In recent decades, the nature and extent of our activities has brought us to the point at which it is possible, even in peacetime, to cause dangerous environmental effects on a more than regional scale.

The most important feature of the environmental measures taken in the scenario is the reduction of risks. The objectives of environment and safety are extensions of one another; growth of production in accordance with the present pattern is in conflict with this. Reducing ecological risks without doubt means giving up some potential growth of production in accordance with the present pattern. This is an important economic choice, in fact the most important one confronting us today apart from the question of war or peace. The CE Scenario supplies information for that choice.

Measures and instruments

After having listed the major impairments of environmental functions, now and in the future, by kind and cause, measures must be formulated that reduce the burden, and the reducing effect per measure must be quantified or, if this is not possible, described in words. Finally the costs of the measures must be estimated. The data must be supplied as much as possible in the form of coefficients, that is to say, burden per unit of product, per £1000 added value, per kilometre driven, per ton of coal burnt as fuel; elimination per first, second and so on, £1,000 spent (here non-linear relations usually occur); shifts in the pattern of production and consumption per £1 million of the activity in question, with the effects brought about by this. Information in this form can 'follow along' in the calculation of the model in the period to be described (1980-2000), via links and feedbacks. Not all information could be supplied in this most ideal form.

However, its absence could be largely compensated for in the model.

This part of the work was farmed out by the CE to a number of scientific institutes. Most figures for the initial situation were provided by the Central Bureau of Statistics. The sub-reports of the institutes are stated in the summarising report.[3] Many measures reinforce one another. Thus energy-saving reduces pollution; the changes in physical planning, agriculture and transport to ease pressure on the environment also lead to less energy consumption.

As stated, the measures are directed towards environmental conservation in the broad sense: the prevention of air, water and soil pollution; increasing the chances of survival of plant and animal species, for example by the prevention of biotope destruction; reducing the risk of future worldwide effects such as change of climate, the erosion of the life-support functions of the ecosystems, and radioactivity; improvement of living conditions, especially in the cities.

The measures can be broken down into the following categories.

1 Measures for the prevention of pollution. These consist mainly of treatment. There are insufficient data on recycling and its cost, and this hampers processing in a model. The same applies to the residues of treatment and to the replacement of toxic and persistent substances. In the elimination forecasts allowance has been made for techniques not yet operational.
2 Energy-saving. This can be subdivided into the improvement of efficiency and the reduction of energy-intensive activities. Improvement of efficiency was obtained, for example, by insulation, and by combined heat and power generation, this being done in small units as far as possible to avoid heat losses during transmission. Reduction of energy-intensive activities was obtained, for example, by heating only the living room and the work-room, by switching from car travel to rail, bus and bicycle, and by shifts in the structure of economic activity occasioned by a changing pattern of consumption.
3 Developing and applying forms of energy derived from the sun.
4 Transport policy aimed at the reduction of passenger transport by car and reduction of the need for mobility.
5 Agricultural policy includes reducing the use of artificial fertilizers and pesticides; transporting surpluses of manure to areas with shortages of manure; reduction of the manipulations

of ground water level; reversal of the trend towards fewer and larger farms and fields; the use of smaller and lighter machines; more crop rotation; restoration and maintenance of hedges and the like.

6 A building policy aimed at restoring the residential function in cities, so as to avoid suburbanization and reduce commuting distances. Urban renewal activities in the model comprised accelerated replacement of irreparably decayed housing and extra renovation. In this, and in new construction, optimum insulation was applied.

7 Encouragement of the service sector, partly because services such as repair firms and corner shops fit into an environmental programme, partly so as to reduce expansion of environmentally unacceptable activities under pressure of high unemployment.

8 To cut back the unemployment still remaining after these measures, short-time working has also been introduced, with the hours of business being lengthened.

For the sake of realism these measures have been gradually introduced. Where elimination data were not available a fairly arbitrary, and in my opinion very modest, increase in the costs of elimination has been applied. Moreover, the measures have not been implemented to their maximum. Too abrupt shifts have been avoided and measures with extremely high costs have not been carried out. In my personal estimation saving the environment and energy will in the long run call for the use of more labour than finds expression in the scenario.

Calculation of the CE Scenario was delegated to the Foundation for Economic Research of the University of Amsterdam (FER).[4] The other scenarios were calculated by the Central Planning Bureau (CPB). The CPB uses the VINTAF-II model. In this model a macro-economic picture is first drawn that is then provided with a certain sectorial structure. The SECMON-C model used by the FER[5] proceeds from the developments per sector generated by the demand which are then totalled into a macro-economic development. In my view the latter procedure is much better suited to scenario exercises. This opinion is shared by Jan Tinbergen.[6] After all, the environmental effects, the employment and the energy consumption differ greatly by sector. Through the possibility of direct feedbacks per sector by means of the measures taken, on both the production side and the demand side, a more realistic macro picture is drawn than in the procedure of VINTAF-II. Moreover, the method fits in much better with the theoretical points of departure with regard to growth described on pp.243–4: in the environmental scenario changes are made in an environmentally acceptable direction, after which one waits to see what this means for growth of production.

The measures mean in essence internalization of the costs of the losses of function caused or expected in the future. The instruments used for this are price manipulation and direct measures. The effects on the pattern of production and consumption have been estimated with the aid of calculated or estimated elasticities. Thus for the effect of the transport policy use has been made of elasticities obtained from transport studies; the expansion of the service sector as a result of the intervention in VAT rates has been estimated with the aid of a recent consumption model of the FER forming part of SECMON-C. The effect on energy consumption of the changes occurring in the model has been calculated by the CPB with the aid of an energy model designed for this purpose.

To finance the measures, according to the CE Scenario's compilers, the greatest possible use must be made of the following set of instruments: *the costs of the measures are defrayed by charges levied on products (on the domestic market) of polluting activities from both home and abroad. These products therefore undergo a real price increase. For the sake of the employment effect wages are not compensated for this.* In the model the desired effect occurs endogenously because there real wages do not rise more strongly than productivity. The charge-levying procedure just described is probably less efficient than direct charges on the polluting activities, that is, the incentive for the polluter to seek cleaner processes is less. But this method obviates impairment of the competitive position on both the domestic market (by products from abroad) and foreign markets. Together with the adjustment of the wage rate, this forms a sufficient guarantee to render permanent the positive effect of environmental measures on employment. The method at the same time prevents the flight of polluting activities abroad, for instance to developing countries.

The following specific instruments may also be mentioned.

The government subsidies to encourage energy-saving and the development of forms of energy derived from the sun are financed by an increase in the price of energy and the introduction of progressive rates of charges. The lag in the increase of productivity in agriculture as a result of environmental measures leads to relative price increases for agricultural products; remuneration of the farmer's work undergoes no relative fall. In transport policy the point of departure makes the fixed costs of the private car as variable as possible. In addition serious parking charges are introduced and no new parking garages and roads are built. As a result of the insulation and the renovation policy, rents rise. The expansion of the service sector mentioned above comes about through a reduction of the VAT rate for the labour-intensive services involved that fit into an environmental policy (repair and the like) or impose little burden on the environment, and an increase in VAT rate for the capital-intensive firms that greatly burden the environment. This too amounts to internalisation of environmental costs that are spread out over society in such a way that certain groups do not make more sacrifices than others.

Table 11.1 Comparative survey of three scenarios
Results at the year 2000 (1980 = 100)

Aspects	Reference scenario (unchanged policy). RS	Industrial recovery scenario. IR	Environmental scenario. CE
Production			
GDP	129	164	127
agriculture	149	181	135
industry	187	321	177
services	145	181	145
available income per			
capita	106	116	104
unemployment	245	82	83
employment	98	110	111
tax burden	117	98	103
labour income share	98	88	98

Plant and animal species	Further deterioration by, among other things, increase of productivity in agriculture, more use of space, more use of persistent compounds. Only measures against pollution have been taken (estimated by R. Hueting)	Idem, but much stronger deterioration (estimated by R. Hueting)	Checking of deterioration or even improvement

Aspects	RS	IR	CE
Emissions			
Air pollution			
SO_2	102	154	24
NO_x	90	130	76
particulate matter	207	310	58
hydrocarbons	183	266	48
CO (total)	22[a]	29[a]	31
of which			
processes	—	—	75
stationary	—	—	48
transport	27	36	21
CO_2	—	—	83
lead	38	44	0
Water pollution			
mercury	53	53	29
cadmium	79	79	36
other heavy metals	95	109	57
persistent organic			
compounds	—	—	70[b]
phosphates	83	81	29
oxygen demand	29	35	17
thermal load	110	139	44
Solid waste			
total	139	152	108
of which			
harbour sludge	100		100
energy-related	1,400	1,400	467
gypsum	245	210	90
industrial slag	227	358	136
chemicals	—	91	64
Radioactive waste			
laboratory wastes	100	100	100
nuclear energy			
waste	300	300	0
reprocessing waste	598	598	0
fissionable material	633	633	0

Aspects	RS	IR	CE
Energy input			
total	114	123	81
of which			
coal	505(605)^c	505(605)^c	292
uranium	463(0)^c	463(0)^c	0
Landscape	Further deterioration (see plant and animal species)	Idem, but even stronger deterioration (see plant and animal species)	Checking of deterioration or even improvement
Livability of cities	—	—	Improvement

[a] This figure is not consistent, as the CO emissions of processes and stationary sources are missing.

[b] Very rough estimate.

[c] If nuclear energy is not used, coal input rises.

− Signifies that no data are available.

The results

The results are shown in Table 11.1. More detailed ones may be found in the reports listed under notes 3 and 4. Table 11.1 gives not only the results of the CE Scenario, but also those of two of the three scenarios elaborated by the CPB.

In the right conditions, environmental conservation creates employment. This is confirmed by the results. In my opinion this is the most important conclusion that can be drawn from the scenario exercise. In view of this I feel that the question 'Can industrial society develop into being less dependent on growth?' can be answered in the affirmative. The following additional comments can be made on the results.

Some of the positive environmental results attained in the CE Scenario cannot find expression in the figures. This applies to improvement of the climate of life in the immediate vicinity of the home by renovation of the inner cities, and to the greater chance of survival for plant and animal species as a result of the interventions in agriculture and physical planning. Scientific insight into the relation between human activities and their effect on plant and animal species is already sufficient to derive measures which may be expected with great probability to have a positive effect. However, our knowledge is insufficient to quantify this effect in advance. Nor can the improvement of the residential and living climate in the cities and the restoration of the landscape be expressed in figures. The results for the natural environment may be defined as follows: on a number of points the decline is halted, and on a few other points improvement occurs (see note 3 for details).

The environmental scenario aims at a much longer period than 1980-2000. Twenty years is a short time for developments in the natural environment. The measures have been introduced very gradually in the model. In the long run more changes will be necessary to restore a safe environment.

The growth of production occurring in the CE Scenario must be qualified, for the following reasons.

1 In the period under study employment is created for 400,000 jobless. The resultant additional production can be realised only once. A substantial part of the environmental measures can be said to have been carried out free of charge. After the year 2000 this will no longer be possible.

2 Part of the growth of production is generated by a pronounced increase in energy productivity. As long as such improvements of efficiency lead to a reduction of costs, there is a contribution to production growth. As soon as the costs of increasing energy efficiency arc equal to the cost reduction due to the higher energy efficiency, a limit is reached. A further increase in production due to a higher energy efficiency is then no longer possible, and production growth will then be accompanied by an increase in energy consumption.

3 Under the influence of price manipulations and direct measures, a shift occurs in the pattern of consumption. This constitutes a certain amount of 'negative growth', or loss of welfare, that the figures cannot reflect.

4 Part of the growth of national income (growth of production) consists of costs rather than of final deliveries. This also applies to the other scenarios.

5 Even in the CE Scenario the environment is not totally safeguarded, although a step has been taken in the right direction. After the year 2000 further measures will be required.

Why it seems necessary to implement the environmental scenario

The future is unpredictable, and apart from this platitude it cannot be shown for certain on scientific grounds whether a lasting emphasis on the growth of production leads in the long run to disastrous exhaustion of the environment. Of course not only the Netherlands is concerned. Overburdening of the environment is taking place in every country in the world, and the effects that are feared come about on a world scale. The environmental scenario is concerned with a distant horizon in space and time.

A scenario is not concerned in the first place with exact results. The uncertainties are far too great for that. It *is* concerned with scanning the possibilities of changing the direction that society is taking. With the aid of the techniques now available, the CE Scenario shows that change in an environmentally acceptable direction is possible. On account of the irreversibility of a number of effects and because the basis of life is at stake, if just one of the many possible risks becomes a reality, a choice in favour of increasing production rather than environmental conservation may lead to an unlivable future. The CE Scenario proves the feasibility of a conserver-economy. Its implementation is now an absolute priority.

● ● ●

At the CE Congress on 1 March 1983, the Dutch Council of Churches supported the CE Scenario, as did the trade union movement and the consumers' organisation, but on the strict condition that those on low incomes should not suffer. The employers, however, stated that they categorically rejected the scenario.

The lack of sympathy from industry and employers for the conserver approach is probably the most important obstacle to its acceptance and implementation. It is highly undesirable that a conservation-oriented economic policy should become yet another football in the political arena. Much depends on industrialists being persuaded that their current objectives and activities are actually cutting the ground from under their own feet, destroying their resource base as well as that of people in general.

One way of seeking to convince business leaders that conservation is not solely about retrenchment is to emphasise the business opportunities that it offers. Such is the approach taken by those who argue for the rapid growth of the new technologies that have come to be called the 'Sunrise Seven'.

'THE SUNRISE SEVEN'
by John Elkington

Europe, which depends on outside sources for 55 per cent of its energy and 75 per cent of its raw materials, has been plagued with slumping economic growth rates, soaring unemployment and persistent high rates of inflation. A central plank in any policy designed to address these problems in the long term must be the development of what have been dubbed the 'sunrise industries', which are perhaps best defined by their characteristic of producing a considerably higher value per ton of product than do the more traditional, and typically declining, industries.

Simultaneously, such a policy can help us address the ever-worsening environmental resource problems highlighted in *The World Conservation Strategy* (WCS).[7] As part of one of the most extensive environmental consultation exercises ever carried out in the United Kingdom, involving the preparation of the UK response to the WCS, the outlines of such a policy were developed in *Seven Bridges to the Future: Industrial Growth Points for a Sustainable Economy*,[8] which opens with the categoric assertion, 'There has been a striking convergence between the interests of industry and of conservation over the last decade, a convergence which is the subject of the present report.' The 'seven bridges' of the title are seven potential growth industries, whose future development will be critical if we are to improve industry's environmental performance, and hence safeguard its future.

In selecting seven such industries, or, more accurately, seven clusters of activity which are in the process of assembling themselves into industries, this report was not suggesting that they are the only potential growth industries. But the 'Sunrise Seven' are all, directly or indirectly, providing answers to the problems identified in the WCS.

Some, such as the pollution–control industry, are providing cures for environmental problems, while others, such as the tradeable environmental services sector, increasingly deal in prevention. Whereas many environmentalists have tended to see appropriate technology as low technology, viewing anything else as a 'technological fix', there are a number of appropriate high-technology industries, most of which are represented to some extent among the Sunrise Seven.

The seven are: microelectronics and information technology; the new biotechnologies; pollution–control technology; recycling and resource substitution technology; energy-efficiency technology; ecologically tailored energy-supply technologies; and the environmental services sector. Much detailed description of the challenges and opportunities facing these industries is given in the 'Seven Bridges' report and need not be repeated here.

Even without much government assistance, there is every reason to believe that the embryonic Sunrise Seven will contribute considerably more each year to the UK economy by the mid-1990s than will North Sea oil. Unlike fossil fuels, they are based on non-depletable, indefinitely renewable resources, including our imaginative, and other, skills. However, government support, both at the UK and EEC levels, will be vital in building up these industries, given that many of their markets are heavily shaped by government policies and spending, and because the lead times associated with many of the technologies are rather longer than the private sector can comfortably cope with, especially in relatively fragmented industries. As the EEC's Third Action Programme on the Environment, covering the period 1982-6, suggests, environmental policy must 'help in creating jobs by the promotion and stimulation of the development of key industries [based on] products, equipment and processes that are either less polluting or use fewer non-renewable resources'.[9]

In Europe around 1.25 million people already work in the emerging environmental industries.[10] The conclusion of the 'Seven Bridges' report was that industry should turn current logic on its head and view the WCS as a market brief for the 1980s and 1990s.

• • •

There is a tendency to think of the Sunrise Seven industries as predominantly based on high technology, and indeed new technologies can be expected to play a crucial part in their development. But just as important are what John Davis, National Secretary of the Industrial Christian Fellowship, has called the '4R' industries, those of repair, reconditioning, re-use and recycling. Davis vigorously attacks the mistaken notions either that these are low value-added industries, or that, by extending the useful life of products, jobs will be destroyed. Giving an example from the motor industry, Davis concludes:

> The more labour-intensive 'reconditioning' operation can be more productive than the 'production' operation . . . . It is very important that we should recognise and understand the high real-wealth-creating potential of many manual repair and reconditioning services. . . . The effect on the quantity of

employment arising from the substitution of 'reconditioning' for 'production' was indicated by a study made in 1977 by the Battelle Research Institute in Geneva for the EEC Social Affairs Commission.[11] It showed that when the average life of cars was doubled from ten to twenty years by means of reconditioning, although the amount of employment in production was nearly halved, there was an overall increase in employment of almost 50 per cent because of the labour-intensive reconditioning operation and the extra servicing required.[12]

As the 'Seven Bridges' report openly acknowledges, the prospects offered by the Sunrise Seven are not wholly devoid of problems. Concern was there expressed about the pattern of employment they are likely to promote, similar to the point about a dual economy to which attention was drawn at the end of the chapter 'Working Like Women' (p.222).

To build a sustainable society split into two camps, those who have work and those who will never have an opportunity to work, is clearly unacceptable. The new core industries will need promoting whatever happens, but we must simultaneously think very seriously indeed about ways in which the social implication of this process can be resolved equitably.[13]

Another issue raised is the fact that the new industries have tended to locate themselves near the economic centres of their host country, which could contribute further to regional decline. Both these points raise broader questions of technology in general, concerning technological choice, assessment and control.

All technological development is the result of choice. Those who claim that we must adopt a 'new' technology in order to remain competitive are simply saying that they are choosing to operate within the international market and accept its conditions. Put crudely, the conditions of the market are that the product with the lowest financial cost will win the day. Thus, by choosing to operate within the market, we are implicitly choosing those technologies that will make the cheapest goods. As far as the business that makes the product is concerned, it will invest in the technology that produces goods of the desired quality as cheaply as possible, so that competitors may be undercut, profit margins maximised and the business get the greatest possible return on its investment.

Enough has already been said about the importance of non-financial considerations in our economic life to suggest that the adoption of purely financial criteria with regard to the choice of technology will have the same sort of skewed consequences as measuring economic welfare purely by GNP, and in practice, of course, most societies modify market imperatives to some extent when new technologies are installed: the health and safety of workers are perhaps given some weight; some governments encourage or insist on environmental impact assessments or pollution controls; others take into account strategic issues – the armaments industry, for example, frequently escapes market disciplines altogether. Another good example of this last point is the UK Government's continuing enthusiasm for nuclear electricity, despite the fact that the free market, as represented by the American electricity companies, declared this technology dead some years ago: no new nuclear power stations have been ordered in the US since 1978, and many partially-constructed ones have been mothballed. We can be sure that a privatised Central Electricity Generating Board would retreat from nuclear power just as completely.

It is also worth pointing out that workers' conditions and environmental safeguards differ widely from country to country, as the Bhopal tragedy illustrated all too clearly. Generally it is true that the competitive advantage in the market will go to the company that exploits its work-force and environment to the maximum extent. Needless to say, this generates continual demands from business that environmental controls and legislation protecting workers should be relaxed, especially in times of recession, demands that have been particularly apparent during President Reagan's years of office with regard to the US Environmental Protection Agency and Office for Technology Assessment.

The fact that even our present money-centred economic system acknowledges, however grudgingly, the non-financial implications of technology indicates their importance. Adam Smith decribed the effects of the mode of production, and especially the industrial division of labour, on the work-force in an 'improved and civilised society' as follows:

> The man whose whole life is spent in performing a few simple operations . . . has no occasion to exert his understanding . . . . He naturally loses, therefore, the habit of such exertion and generally becomes as stupid and ignorant as it is possible for a human creature to become . . . . But in every improved and civilised society this is the state into which the labouring poor, that is the great body of the people, must necessarily fall, unless government takes some pains to prevent it.[14]

Schumacher expressed the same sort of idea by stating that technology affected 'how people produce; what they produce; where they work; where they live; whom they meet; how they relax or "recreate" themselves; what they eat, breathe and see; and therefore what they think, their freedom or their dependence' (Schumacher, 1979, p.41). It is no exaggeration to say that choices in technology play a considerable part in making us who we are.

Despite the importance of technological choice and the related questions of how to assess technologies, so that that choice is informed, and of who should make the choice and who controls the technology, these issues have slipped almost completely off society's agenda in recent years. In 1978 a Symposium was hosted by the British Association for the Advancement of Science (BAAS) and the Intermediate Technology Development Group (ITDG), entitled 'Technology Choice and the Future of Work'. Its report reads as freshly as if it had been written yesterday.[15]

James Robertson's definition in this report of appropriate technology as 'one which conserves resources, is kind to the environment, is good to work with and creates socially-useful products'[16] is still valid, but no progress has been made towards elaborating criteria for assessment based on this definition, nor have any of the main recommendations been implemented. They were:

> More public participation; new criteria to take account of socially-desirable factors; research and curriculum development to help designers to make better choices of technology; and a new code of practice for decision-makers, to ensure that decisions about technology and work systematically include consideration of wider issues.[17]

'Design for Recycling' and 'Designing for Overall Life', together with life-cycle costing which would give value to more durable products,[18] have made no headway, and the UK Alternative Technology Unit of ITDG, which in 1978 was being set up with great expectations, was wound up in 1984. We are no nearer to harnessing in a systematic way the vision and creative energies of ordinary working people, as expressed in the Alternative Corporate Plan drawn up by the Lucas Aerospace Workers,[19] nor have we found any answers to the de-skilling tendency of industrial technology, identified so long ago by Adam Smith and analysed in great detail by Mike Cooley in *Architect or Bee?* (Cooley, 1980).

We have, in sum, made little progress in distinguishing, and being able to choose between, two sorts of technology:

One which leads to specialisation of functions, institutionalisation of values and centralisation of power, and turns people into accessories of bureaucracies or machines; the other which enlarges the range of each person's competence, control and initiative, limited only by other individuals' claims to an equal range of power and freedom (Illich, 1973).

Technology is neither neutral nor static. Where its development is not democratically controlled and directed by people generally for their own benefit and that of society at large, it will be controlled by a few people for their own power and profit at the expense of everyone else. This applies crucially to the new technologies like information and biotechnology, for their scope and potential influence transcend that of their predecessors as the motor-car did the horse and cart. Whether these sunrise industries actually turn into twilight technologies of oppression and social control depends neither on the stars nor on themselves, but on who controls them, who develops them and by what criteria.

NOTES

1   This emerges from an analysis of the base material for the Netherlands National Accounts (of which the sectorial composition does not differ appreciably from that of the UK) over the period 1965-79. See R. Hueting, 'Some comments on the Report "A Low Energy Strategy for the United Kingdom" (compiled by Gerald Leach *et al.* for the International Institute of Environment and Development)', paper for the Working Party on Integral Energy Scenarios, The Hague, 20 May 1981).

2   This argument has been elaborated by R. Hueting in a number of articles and supported by examples. See, *inter alia*, R. Hueting, 'Milieu en Werkgelegenheid', *Economisch-Statistische Berichten*, 5 March 1975; 'Socio-economic effects of environmental policy', paper prepared for the Symposium on Quality of Life, Universidad de Deusto, Bilbao, 21-23 September 1977.

3   H.Y. Becht, R. Hueting, T.G. Potma, G.J. Ziljstra, *Het CE Scenario: Een Realistisch Alternatief*, Centre for Energy-Saving, Delft, January 1983. This is accompanied by a number of background reports.

4   For the report on the calculation of the Scenario, see W. Driehuis, E.C. van Ierland, P.J. van den Noord, *Economie, Energie en Milieu in Nederland, 1980-2000*, FER, Amsterdam, 1983.

5   Information on the model may be obtained from FER. An earlier version, SECMON-B, may be found in the report W. Driehuis, P.J. van den Noord, *Produktie, Werkgelegenheid, Sectorstructuur en betalingsbalans in Nederland, 1980-1985*, FER, The Hague, 1980.

6   Personal communication.

7   *The World Conservation Strategy*, International Union for the Conservation of Nature and Natural Resources, assisted by the United Nations Environment Programme and the World Wildlife Fund (WWF), 1980. Available from WWF. A popular version appeared as *How to Save the World*, Kogan Page, London, 1980.

8   John Elkington, *Seven Bridges to the Future: Industrial Growth Points for a Sustainable Economy*, World Conservation Strategy, London, 1982. A revised version of this report was published in *The Conservation and Development Programme for the UK: A Response to the World Conservation Strategy*, Kogan Page, London, 1982, pp.35-96.

9   *Third Action Programme on the Environment, 1982-1986*, The Commission of the European Communities, Brussels, 1981.

10   *The Environment Industry in the EEC: Employment and Research and Development in the Next Decade*, Joint Unit for Research on the Urban Environment, Aston University, Birmingham, 1982.

11   Reported in W. Stahel and G. Reday-Mullvey, *Jobs for Tomorrow*, Vantage Press, New York, 1981.

12   *Growth, Justice and Work*, Report of Industrial Committee of General Synod, Church Information Office, London, 1985.

13   *Seven Bridges to the Future*, op. cit., p.69.

14   Quoted in Schumacher, 1979, p.42.

15   British Association for the Advancement of Science, *Technology Choice and the Future of Work*, London, 1978.

16   Ibid., p.6.

17   Ibid., p.3.

18   Ibid., p.57.

19   Described by Mike Cooley, ibid., pp.97-105.

12 LOCAL ECONOMIC REGENERATION AND CO-OPERATION

Just as important as the industries and technologies to be developed in the future, and the overall priorities guiding that development, is the level at which it is envisaged that development will take place. Enough has been written about the importance of scale in human activity[1] for no detailed elaboration of this theme to be necessary here. The re-emphasis of the human scale in economic activity leads inexorably to consideration of the local economy as the driving force behind future economic development in general.

This chapter looks at three aspects of local economic regeneration. It explores some ideas for a new local economic order, in which enterprise is balanced by social responsibility. It looks in detail at the experiences of a network of small businesses in the United States, and it examines different kinds of business structure, with special reference to the co-operative movement.

'A NEW LOCAL ECONOMIC ORDER'
by Guy Dauncey

My instinct that we need to develop a new local economic order derives from several sources. Through many years of work in the unemployment business, I have observed the vacuums that have been revealed within local economies when major employers close down, and I have observed the spontaneous way in which groups of local people have sometimes formed to fill these vacuums. They seek to do what they can to help their own local economies, but they do so in a conceptual as well as a practical vacuum. There is no body of theory to draw on; there are no books on the subject;[2] there is not a single university economics department in the UK which has a specific lectureship in local economics.

I have observed how, unless a local economy contains a wide

range of varied, locally owned and controlled businesses, it stands at the mercy both of the international trade-winds, which can destroy a mono-crop economy overnight, and of the policy-makers in Tokyo or New York, who can close down a local branch without ever even knowing properly where it is. The experience of powerlessness is devastating. Unemployment can treble in a single day. I have seen that our local economies have no self-righting mechanisms, and apart from stepping up endeavours to attract a replacement branch from another distant giant, there has traditionally been nothing that can be done. Conversely, I have seen inspiration grow in the hearts of local people when they have begun to understand that they can taken matters into their own hands, and begin to have a significant impact on their own local affairs. Another strand of my inspiration for the development of this area of thinking has been the knowledge that we have to develop a model of local economic functioning which is inherently replicable right across the globe, and which does not rely upon exploitation of other lands for its prosperity. I have been excited to see how many of the initiatives that are developing as this new order emerges are truly transnational in their applicability, and are as relevant for a town in the Pennines of England as for a village in Ecuador.

Very few people ever stop to think about their local economies. We are aware that the local banks look after our money, and that a lack of jobs locally often leads to local unemployment, but that is usually the limit of it. We have no awareness, for instance, of the critical importance of local circulation. A myth is spread through the media which tells us that economic difficulties can only be sorted out by people in distant cities who can talk about economics in terms that nobody else understands. We are almost completely alienated from our local economies.

We have been out of touch with them for so long that we have lost the awareness that we have muscles there at all, that we have an intelligence which can inform them and a nerve which can control them. So when local people suddenly discover that they can set up a body which will help people to form co-operatives, such as a Co-operative Development Agency, or create a neighbourhood energy campaign to lessen the money and the work-energy that is lost to the community each year through the purchase of expensive imported fuels, they begin to get excited, in the same way that a person with a paralysed arm does when she suddenly discovers that she can use two fingers.

At the same time, we are horribly aware that the tropical rain-forests are being destroyed, that unspeakable things are being done to animals in scientific laboratories in order to get new products on the market, and that families in Brazil are watching their children die from simple diarrhoea caused by malnutrition. We know that all this is going on, we know that it is awful, and we feel the same powerlessness that we feel about our local economies. Nothing seems able to stop it all.

The timbers imported from the tropical rain-forests come through our ports. They are processed in our firms, presented to us in our hardware hypermarkets and end up in our living-rooms. The cigarettes, beauty-care products and food additives for the sake of which animals are made to suffer such pain are in our shops for us to buy. The meat which was raised in Brazil, encouraging the hunger which kills the little ones, is in the hamburgers which we buy from our local shops. There clearly is a connection. Instinct tells me that the alienation from our own local economies, which makes us feel that we cannot do anything about unemployment, also makes us feel unable to do anything about the famines overseas and the gradual destruction of the Earth's ecosphere.

In response to the ever-worsening problems that countries from Mexico to Mauritius are experiencing, the call has constantly been repeated for a new international order: a new set of rules to cover trade, aid and development issues. Once again, however, it is something 'out there', something that puts the responsibility for saving the world into the hands of government finance ministers. Not surprisingly, nothing has happened. Maybe in order for the new international economic order to become a reality, we have to take power into our own hands, and establish new local economic orders in the villages, towns and cities where we live, all over the world. Think global, but act local, the saying goes.

I believe that we are witnessing the first stages of the emergence of just such an order. All over the world, small isolated initiatives are being developed which, in their scattered ways, show the path forward. Some examples are:

San José, California Here the city council discovered that together they were paying out huge sums of money to remote fire-insurance companies 3000 miles away. By setting up their own insurance programme, they could reduce costs by $25 million, keep the revenue within the local economy and use it for local investment, and link the cost of fire insurance to the number of fires annually, thus providing a strong incentive for people to take better fire precautions.[3]

Newport and Nevern, in Dyfed, South Wales In these two tiny parishes, a group of local people carried out an energy audit, and discovered that between them they were sending £¼ million per annum out of the local economy to pay for imported energy. They therefore initiated a campaign to spread awareness about alternative energy sources and to insulate houses.[4]

Llewellyn County, USA The people here are embarking on a full county-wide programme to attain energy self-sufficiency, creating many new jobs locally and retaining large sums of money within the local economy for further circulation.[5]

Bury St Edmunds, UK This small town provides a further example of this type of thinking. The Town Trust, a body set up by local people to develop the sense of community in the town, put in a tender for a major development scheme, using locally raised money, with rents from the development accruing to the town itself. Over 100 years, the Trust's scheme would have kept £15 million in the town for further local investment. The Council rejected the proposal and accepted instead a tender from a firm of outside developers which will ensure that over the same 100 years £32 million will *leave* the local economy and accrue to the development company.[6]

One of the most obvious ways to increase local prosperity is to help local people to set up their own businesses, whether cooperatively, privately or as a community business. The UK is full of creative initiatives where people are taking up this responsibility. The traditional notion that only certain kinds of people can set up in business is being thrown to the winds. In Swansea, Roger Warren Evans and the team at the Centre for Trade and Industry, who are working with a clear conceptual grasp of the importance of the local, or 'city-regional' economy, have a particularly successful scheme called 'First Enterprise', which helps teenagers to start up their own businesses.[7] In Sheffield, the Manor Employment Project is enabling local people from a disadvantaged housing estate to generate their own permanent jobs – twelve different enterprises are now running.[8]

Nor is this impulse towards the taking of community responsibility limited to the UK. In Patea, Taranaki, New Zealand, the township responded to the almost complete collapse of the local economy when the meat-works closed down by forming the Rangitawhi Marae Trust, a federation of eleven different maraes. They have set up market gardens and several other cooperatives by pooling their local economic resources to create jobs for local people.[9] The importance of local banking has been demonstrated in Mondragon, Spain, where the Caja Laboral

Popular plays an important part in the great success of their co-operatives.[10]

The importance of cooperative action for the future well-being of the new local economic order is all-important. Local farmers in Mulkanoor, in India, were always at the mercy of money-lenders, who charged exorbitant rates, and fat middlemen, until they grouped together to form a powerful multi-purpose cooperative, which enables them to borrow money, purchase seed and other supplies and hire the necessary equipment to irrigate their land and develop their wealth. Before they formed the co-operative and reclaimed their power, the resources they needed for their own local development were constantly being siphoned off and away from the local economy.[11]

There are thousands of stories like these. They show the beginnings, but as yet they do not begin to add up to a new local economic order. One major common characteristic is their expression of enterprise. The spirit of enterprise is one of initiative, courage and creativity, which expresses vitality in a society. A major feature of the new local economic order is the deliberate encouragement and assistance of new enterprise. The harm begins to arise when owners and employers have no concept of democracy within their enterprises, when enterprises can be bought and sold without any concern for local or employee interest in the affair, and when the enterprise trades in goods or services that are not in the overall interest of the planet and its people as a whole.

Another important principle that emerges concerns circulation. Prosperity is a function of the circulation of wealth, not of the crude quantity of wealth, which could all be sitting in one person's art collection, having absolutely nil effect on the local economy. Local circulation can be stimulated by establishing new local businesses, by taking steps to increase self-reliance in critical areas such as energy, by establishing local banks to re-invest people's savings in the local economy and by deliberate attempts at import substitution, among other measures. The American Indian Movement, in its need to build up secure local economies on its lands, has voiced the concept that locally generated money needs to circulate three times within the local economy by purchasing goods and services from other local people, and thus stimulating further production, before it leaves the local economy in order to purchase an import. The discussion of local currencies in Chapter 8 is obviously relevant here.

The initiatives described above represent one dimension of the new local economic order. They are mostly concerned with encouraging local prosperity and creating jobs, as a response to unemployment. A second critical dimension, designed to enable the local economy to co-exist in peaceful harmony with the rest of the Earth, and its people, is described below. But first it is necessary to clarify the vision set out above. The picture formed by aggregating the huge variety of initiatives and putting them together into one as yet imaginary future community is one in which there is a highly creative, innovative, enterprise-supportive environment, and a strong overall sense that the local economy belongs to the people. Business is no longer seen as a means to get rich quick on the backs of other people, but as a vehicle through which personal visions can be realized, the local community and the planet as a whole can be served, and fulfilling, meaningful work can be created for all who desire it. The local economy has a *constant self-renewing ability* built into it through this new generation of community-based initiatives. This helps to ensure that it is able to ride the waves of growth, death and change, without its inhabitants suffering widespread poverty or unemployment. However, this is only part of the solution. If we are to make the local economy expressive of our compassion as well as of our vision, we have also to find ways to combat the evils that constantly flow through our hands.

My own home town of Totnes, that sits so comfortably among the small hills of south Devon, is a good example of the problem. An old market town of 8000 people, it lives by a healthy mixture of farming, timber processing, tourism, education (Dartington's schools, colleges and Trust are just nearby), crafts, small businesses, bacon-making and milk-bottling. It is an exceptionally pleasant place to live in, and as seemingly harmless a local economy as one might wish for. It also has a very wide range of creative economic initiatives, for such a small community. Schumacher would have loved the place.

Look more closely, however, and the obstacles to a new local economic order begin to emerge. The pigs that are killed in the bacon factory have been fed upon proteins grown for export in countries where the children are dying from a lack of food. The chemists' shops are full of beauty products in the preparation of which animals were tortured. Our petrol is as full of lead as anyone else's and the money that we put in our banks is invested in the arms industries. As for the innocent-looking timber yard, sited so attractively by the River Dart, it is importing hardwoods from tropical rain-forests.

To pursue matters further, I phoned to speak with the manager of the timber merchants. His secretary told me that on matters relating to policy he had to receive clearance from head office. The timber firm was recently taken over by Thomas Tilling, which was in turn taken over in 1983 by BTR Ltd, a huge multi-purpose corporation which owns Pretty Polly tights and Heinemann books, among other companies. The firm, which is probably Totnes' biggest single employer, does not even feature in BTR's annual report. This is the 'octopus economy' in full swing.

In order to tackle this kind of problem, I envisage the need for the new local economic order to have a second major dimension: one of legislation and control. Clearly a major shift of emphasis to local economic development would require a significant strengthening of local authorities, but even now local councils do have powers – through the levying of rates, the granting and denial of planning permission and the granting or withholding of permits of various kinds. For example, in Portland, Oregon, it will be illegal after 1985 to sell an uninsulated home. They predict that this measure and others will save some 35 per cent of the energy that the city will need by 1995. In Davis, California, a new building code was introduced in 1973 in order to optimise house insulation. Since then, total electricity consumption has fallen by 18 per cent.[12] The Greater London Enterprise Board, set up by the Greater London Council (GLC) in the UK, insists that any firm wishing to receive the benefit of its financial and technical resources must agree to a package of measures concerning industrial democracy, enterprise planning, wage-levels and non-discrimination.[13]

In order for us to begin to live in harmony with ourselves, with the whole natural world and with the rest of the planet in a long-term sustainable way, I envisage the need for three new 'Codes of Conduct' to which all enterprises in the local economy will have to adhere. I picture a situation in which, after agreement about the codes has been reached, there is an initial three-year breathing space, during which the codes are purely voluntary. This is followed by a second three-year period in which they are accompanied by financial incentives and penalities, and publicity, both good and bad. After this, the codes become fully binding on all local enterprises.

These codes would need to cover three specific areas of social and ecological importance:

- The relationship of the local enterprise with its work-force and the community as a whole, including its democratisation, an open accounts policy, provision for flexible working, and non-discrimination on any basis other than skill and ability to do the job;

- The relationship of the local enterprise with the natural environment and other living creatures, including bans on the import of endangered species of animals or plants into the local economy, strict curbs on pollution and animal experimentation, and incentives for conservation and positive ecological innovation;
- The relationship of the local enterprise with other people and communities in the same country and abroad, including the guarantee of fair trading relations, of socially and ecologically sound investment, and a prohibition on the export of goods of a poisonous or socially destructive nature.

These codes still need full elaboration but, when operative, they would ensure that the creativity and vigour of local enterprise did not degenerate into exploitation at home or abroad. Those firms that persisted in abusing the codes would have to cease doing so, close down or move out. This would produce unemployment in the present condition of the local economy, and this is why the earlier creative dimension is so important. We are not looking at a new order which is simply prohibitive of activities that are socially and ecologically harmful. We are looking at an order in which we are all able to lead nourishing and prosperous lives in an atmosphere of creative harmlessness. In order for this to happen, the local economy needs to be supported by a range of creative initiatives which will deliberately help people to set up their own businesses and cooperatives.

The unions at the Lucas Aerospace Company in the UK, through their shop-stewards combine committee, have already shown that it is possible to convert to new, socially useful products and to establish new businesses, when they faced large-scale redundancies back in 1975.[14] The firm knowledge that it is possible to convert from one kind of production to another lives on with the GLC's Popular Planning Unit, which helps neighbourhoods to think creatively about the future shape of their local economies, and the Technology Networks, which draw the skills of members of London's Polytechnics into the task of developing new, socially useful and necessary products, to be taken up by firms which are in need of product diversification, as an alternative to closure.[15]

When a people care strongly enough about something, they soon find a way to achieve what they want. For every creative initiative or measure that has so far been developed, there are a dozen more waiting for us to think them up. The voices who say 'it can't be done' are the ones who basically don't want it to be done. Once we begin to care enough, there is nothing that can't be done. We made all the rules. We can change them, too.

• • •

The codes of conduct of a new local economic order certainly might be important back-up instruments of regulation and control, but they are likely to have to be invoked far less often in a locally-based economy than in an economy with long supply and distribution chains, primarily conceived in terms of national and international markets. The reason lies in the reduced impersonality and greater accountability that automatically pertain to any enterprise that operates locally. A business that uses local resources, employs local people, impinges on the local environment and sells to local markets, experiences a degree of local pressure on its mode of operation, and the quality of its products, which diminishes markedly as one or more of these activities are externalised beyond the local community. We turn now to the experience of the Briarpatch Network in San Francisco, which shows that such local transactions turn much conventional economic theory on its head.

'WHAT SMALL BUSINESS EXPERIENCE TEACHES ABOUT ECONOMIC THEORY'
by Michael Phillips

The Briarpatch Network is an informal association of people and co-operative businesses that believe in open account books, honesty and information sharing. With this philosophy it has had phenomenal success on the West Coast of the US, where it began. Now its ideas have gained popularity in Japan and Sweden, and new networks are also being founded in Finland and Canada. Briarpatch currently has 315 active members, another 300 associate members and 200 former members. The market-behaviour and actual experience of these 800-odd different small businesses provides an empirical base for the development of a new and different approach to economics.

The association takes its name from the briarpatch in the folk tales of Uncle Remus, where the hero, Brer Rabbit, led a happy, safe life. The gentle rabbit was protected from predators by its humble and seemingly inhospitable home of thorns. Briar business people feel that, likewise, by keeping their lives simple and their businesses open and honest they will be protected from the problems of larger society.

The Briarpatch Network in the San Francisco Bay area includes nearly every kind of business, from high-fashion clothing design to massage-table manufacturing. Mixed in the assortment of members are a sheep ranch, an elegant $2 million restaurant, a family circus, and a unique and highly respected school which awards doctorates in human sexuality. There are special libraries of medical information available to the public, many holistic medical practitioners, clinics, and schools. A Japanese acupuncturist, an Irish bar, a Mexican weaving company, an Asian theater troupe, a tea ceremony school, and an immigration lawyer are also members. Almost any service or product you could possibly want is available through San Francisco Briarpatch, plus dozens of new, fascinating, innovative businesses.

The network differs from more traditional associations because it has few meetings and no officers. Instead it usually has parties or classes on how to improve business practices, and a group of financial, legal, and accounting advisers to help its members. All of these activities are coordinated by one or two people. The coordinators also put businesses with common problems or questions in contact with each other and publish a directory of members. One business may have a problem about writing a partnership agreement. It would be referred to a book on do-it-yourself partnerships published by another Briarpatch member who publishes self-help legal books. Another business, a small neighbourhood grocery store, may want advice on whether or not to expand into an adjacent vacant space. The co-ordinator would then arrange for a visit to the store by several Briarpatch financial advisers. For this range of services, Briarpatch members make voluntary contributions of money or services every six months. The fees and donations support the coordinator on a part-time basis and pay for the parties and periodic mailings.

The outwardly visible characteristics of all the people who run Briarpatch businesses are that most are under forty-five years old and the majority are women. Furthermore, in talking to Briars you find their values have been heavily influenced by the ideas and experiences of the social, political and environmental upheavals which occurred in the United States during the late 1960s and early 1970s. Today these successful entrepreneurs are determined to run their businesses in a way that reflects the new social justice.

Members of the Briarpatch fervently believe that business is a way to serve others. This value separates them from many other small businesses which exist to make money. Because of their environmental values, Briars engage only in businesses that preserve resources that allow the owners to seek simple life-styles and to enjoy their work. They definitely are not in business to make a lot of money. One of the heroes of the Briarpatch is Steward Brand, publisher of *The Whole Earth Catalogue*. This enormously successful book has enjoyed a net profit of over $1.25 million. Brand, however, created a board of directors to give the money to worthwhile environmental and political causes relevant to the issues discussed in *The Whole Earth Catalogue*. Today, Brand is also publishing the *CoEvolution Quarterly*, a Briarpatch magazine containing articles about current ecological issues.

Briars keep open books. In any Briarpatch business you can ask to see the financial statements and ask how much is paid for rent and for supplies. You will always be given a clear, understandable explanation. Many Briar businesses, in fact, publish their financial statements as a matter of course. Being honest people running open businesses results in better management, more community support, and an opportunity for friends and family to actively participate in the business.

Another characteristic of Briarpatch business is generosity with each other and with people outside the network. For example, the Down Depot, which cleans down-sleeping-bags, parkas, and jackets, has helped other Briar outdoor rental businesses to clean their used sleeping bags at a low price and on a rush basis. They have also trained dozens of people who wanted to start down-cleaning stores in other parts of the United States. Similarly, in Albany, California, Toy-Go-Round sells used toys and returns 50 per cent of the sale price to the original owners, usually children. Toy-Go-Rounds' owners have gladly trained others in how to open and run similar businesses.

Yet the most surprising fact about the Briarpatch way of doing business is its extraordinary success and survival rate. In the United States the average failure rate for most companies in the first three years of business is 80 per cent. Briars, however, have experienced less than a 5 per cent failure rate in three years. These figures are based on ten years of experience. The network was formed in 1974.

Direct observations derived from the Briarpatch economic database

1   Briars set their own prices with relatively little direct reference to 'the market'

Traditional economic theory states that for any supply of a good for which there is a demand there will be a price at which supply equals demand. In so far as this is a simplistic truism, our database cannot offer contrary evidence. In so far as it is treated as a realistic description of how markets work, it is quite incorrect and inapplicable. The simplistic notion suggests that an increase in demand will raise prices in the short run until greater supply is provided which will return the price to equilibrium.

The reality, based on ten years of observation on many hundreds of businesses with thousands of different goods and services is that traditional economic theory is incorrect. What is correct is that a seller has a wide range of freedom in setting the price on any particular good or service and on the whole set of goods and services offered. Further, that the object of most exchanges, which I call 'exchange/price', is not the significant occurrence in business. In the real world a 'transaction' occurs. The transaction includes an exchange/price in most cases, but it also includes non-price considerations. Transactions can have non-price components that range from 5 per cent to 95 per cent of the transaction.

Knowing that the fundamental unit of business is a transaction and not an exchange is important. First it helps us to understand what 'business' is; second, it sheds light on the error in supply/demand analysis. When a complete stranger buys a small amount of an illicit drug in a dark alley, that is close to the traditional economic model of exchange/price. When a shopper buys a loaf of wholewheat bread at the local bakery, takes the bread and leaves cash, that is a transaction.

The transaction can have a 5 per cent non-price component in it if the baker is a giant chain where the shopper knows no one and dislikes the merchandising and smell of the store, to one that has a 95 per cent non-price component if the bakery is run by friends and has a personally appealing environment. The non-price components of the chain bakery purchase probably include good parking, an accurate date on the label, refund for errors and the certainty that a lawsuit would recover damages if the bread were harmful. The non-price components of the transaction at the bakery run by friends are far more numerous and include a large component of warmth, happiness and fun.

It is quite clear from working with small businesses that transactions are the reality of business, and exchange is only a concept in economics. Let us call the non-price component factor N. Economic theory ignores or dismisses factor N. However, it is a fundamental business event of large magnitude.

Some of the transactions that involve high prices and very high proportions of factor N, are in the service and information domains. Therapists, bodyworkers, attorneys, publicists, business consultants, health workers, etc., charge prices that are unrelated to any known supply costs and can find themselves overloaded with clients or starving, without any correlation with the prices they charge. The type of services offered in the market increasingly have a large factor N, and traditional price equilibrium theory becomes less and less appropriate.

2 Pricing, merchandising and marketing are more successful in attracting customers when they contradict prevailing business values
Prevailing business attitudes favour greed, competition, dishonesty wherever feasible, personal gain wherever possible, and also seriousness and boredom. Economics has a bias in this direction too. On these points the Briarpatch database provides the most conclusive contrary evidence. For a small business to grow and be healthy in the environment of our database it must provide goods and services that are appreciated by the buyer and generate word of mouth recommendations. Such businesses must be actively supported by the friends, acquaintances, suppliers, employees and customers of the business. This support in turn is contingent on superior attention to good service and products, human relations and honesty.

Every reader can immediately think of many examples. Most businesses that don't rely on word of mouth recommendation rely instead on deceptive advertising and practise the prevailing greed-based way of doing business. Our database clearly shows that this is an inferior way to do business, and that such practices can exist only in an environmental niche filled with other similar misanthropes. When an honest business enters such a market it readily succeeds.

3 Profit as a primary goal or value in business has a detrimental effect
Profit as defined in economics is the net revenue to the proprietor after all expenses have been paid, including reasonable salary compensation at 'market rates', and return on invested capital at appropriate rates for that level of risk. Most of the database businesses did not have this as a target and were happy to earn a

return comparable to a salaried job; most invested little capital, only sweat equity, so this was never an issue after original lenders to the business were paid off. The two most serious problems with profit as a primary business goal are that it isn't sufficient for most human beings, and that it leads to incorrect decisions.

First, small business is very hard, it is fraught with crises and late hours alternating with long periods of boredom. It would not be unusual for a small retailer to face a leak that damages merchandise, a spouse who leaves home in anger, a lost invoice and a serious lease problem all at 5p.m. on Saturday. Only love of the business and the support of friends will carry a person through this. Rarely will greed suffice, especially since greedy people learn quickly that small businesses very rarely lead to riches.

Second, profit is a poor guide for what a business needs to do to improve. The goal of service to the customers, held strongly and pursued aggressively, is the goal that most often works and leads the proprietor to muster the necessary energy to improve merchandising, marketing and accounting controls, and to pay sufficient attention to customer suggestions, whims and desires. Or, in the case of a financial advisory business, to give the required harsh or candid response that is undesired but may be in the customer's best interest.

The empirical data bear out this reasoning. As observed earlier, Briarpatch businesses, where profit is not a major goal, have a far better survival rate than new US businesses in general, in the majority of which, according to survey data, profit is almost always one of the top three reasons for starting the business. The conclusion is inescapable: in small business the pursuit of profit doesn't pay.

4 *Social costs are rewarded when included in the business pricing structure*
Traditional economic theory suggests that businesses trying to maximise profits will pursue policies that push costs on to the public, such as polluting the air and water. In fact this is probably true in most instances but it is not the behaviour of businesses in the database and the opposite behaviour is rewarded by their customers.

Small businesses that make a point of appealing to customers by serving the common good are rewarded by getting more customers. Such is the case with numerous bicycle-repair businesses that train customers to make their own repairs, with food suppliers that use the finest ingredients and openly disclose their food-handling procedures, with health practitioners who generously and patiently instruct their clients, with manufacturers who strive for very durable products, and with publishers that sell up-to-date books and allow older editions to be traded in for current editions at no extra cost.

The same pattern appears to apply on a larger scale in the rare instances where good research has been done. The Council on Economic Priorities in New York has done extensive research on the same issue and found many times that even large corporations which pursue socially beneficial policies in pollution control and employment practices are the most profitable.

5 Infrastructure costs are the prime determinant of final consumer prices

Is there really a free market, with an invisible hand efficiently allocating resources? A fundamental premise of economics holds this to be true, but the evidence suggests the contrary.

Even cursory experience with real businesses indicates that infrastructure costs and policies are so pervasive in the market-place that the concept of a free market is not meaningful. The price of each good and service offered is thoroughly tainted by the costs and subsidies of the infrastructure. Infrastructure refers to institutions, practices and resources that are provided by the government. Examples include highways, education, retirement benefits, tax subsidies and import duties.

Robert Heilbroner of the New School for Social Research in New York has pointed out just how dependent all business is on such infrastructure. The success of whole industries depends largely on the extent to which they are able to persuade or bribe governments to underwrite their infrastructure costs. This, of course, is the reason why many industries, at great expense, finance huge and sophisticated lobbies in capital cities to put pressure on legislators.

Small businesses cannot compete in this field and for them the paperwork and bureaucracy to meet minimum legal requirements are highly intrusive and represent an important aspect of the way in which infrastructure exerts direct control over businesses: sometimes to subsidise them, sometimes to restrain them. Many a US business has got off the ground by hiding in the institutional cracks and emerging years later to become legitimate, when it finally has the skills to cope with the complexity of the infrastructure.

6 Competition is a poor model of the real world; cooperation and 'niches' are more accurate

Among the many hundreds of businesses in the database, virtually none of them consider themselves to be in competition with any other businesses. Why?

This relates to the factor N mentioned earlier. Where this is high and reflects a personal, distinctive quality in the good or service offered, the product is clearly unique and, if desired at all, will be purchased irrespective of the competition. It is only when the factor N is low, or based on considerations that apply to many businesses in that field, that the exchange price becomes an important basis for competition.

7 Monopolies can occur in ordinary circumstances and arise from superior service

Economic theory has long suggested that there are 'natural monopolies' such as power, gas, water utility companies and telephone services. The theory says there are physical economies of scale, such as the advantage of one wire or line going to each house. The evidence in fact suggests that there are other kinds of monopolies, ordinary ones where the business does such a complete job of serving customer needs that other businesses in the same field aren't needed.

One such example is *Common Ground*, a quarterly newspaper listing all the health, spiritual, educational and related businesses and institutions in the area. 60,000 copies are distributed in the Bay area. All advertisers have the same format: a small logo and a written description. The finances of *Common Ground* are published in the front, and every quarter when the printing is finished the final copies are brought to a large space where a party of advertisers is held and each takes a bundle to distribute. The advantage to the suppliers is that they get to meet each other and exchange information on how to improve their ads. There is also a share of the profits that the advertisers get to use for their common interests. The net revenue after paying all expenses is $4–6,000 per quarter. No one has succeeded in producing anything similar in ten years, because so many of the readers and advertisers are so delighted with the service that they have no need to use another one.

8 Honesty is a major positive factor in business efficiency; dishonesty has negative effects and is geometrically harmful the greater the degree of dishonesty

Retail business has a high degree of dishonesty in the US, but wholesale business has very little. The reason is simple. Retailers can get away with it; they have a large flux of strangers to do business with. Wholesalers have a very limited list of customers and potential customers, and word gets out very fast about dishonest practices.

The advantages of honesty are many, but the clearest reasons are that repeat business is more economic than generating new business; and that a wider range of people will participate in the decision-making and advising of an honest business, thus allowing greater business wisdom and relevant feedback. Moreover, the costs of protecting against dishonesty are very high. In fact the costs of dishonesty tend to rise geometrically. No society can have more than about 20 per cent dishonesty, because dishonesty requires some degree of trust, otherwise deception isn't possible. In a situation where 1 out of 5 statements or actions are deceptive it is easier to assume that all are deceptive and act accordingly.

The best way to test this is to consider a shopping centre where you experience a dishonest act by one merchant. You will probably not be much more careful in future shopping. If it happens at two separate merchants you will become very careful, and should it happen a third time with still another merchant in the same shopping centre, you will probably go elsewhere altogether.

9   Ownership of resources doesn't make any difference to business efficiency

The database businesses consist of many ownership forms, including cooperatives, sole proprietorships, partnerships, corporations, non-profits where the control is in the hands of a board of directors and the State is the ultimate owner, and 'collectives', a special version of non-profit where all workers have an equal vote.

The evidence is simple. Each of these legal structures requires the same skills and practices to stay in business. No particular form has been more or less successful than any of the others. Who owns the business makes no difference in its efficiency or its survival. There are examples of highly efficient worker collectives, and hopeless authoritarian corporations, and vice versa.

The issue of ownership has given rise to wars and revolutions. As far as business efficiency is concerned, the evidence of Briarpatch does not support any side when all forms of ownership are given an equal chance.

•   •   •

The Briarpatch experience provides a useful counterweight to many of the nostrums of conventional economic wisdom, and such business networks offering mutual support are likely to be an important part of any locally based economic revival. The question of ownership needs clarification, however, for it cannot be dealt with simply in terms of business efficiency. Ultimately issues of ownership resolve into issues of benefit, power and control.

The traditional business structure of Western industrial economies is the limited liability company, a productive unit with three more or less distinct groups of people: shareholders, who contribute the capital to the company and who hire managers, headed by the Board of Directors, who hire workers. The workers and managers are paid a wage for their labour. Profits, the surplus over the costs of production, are either reinvested in the company, boosting the value of the shares, or distributed to shareholders as dividends. Either way, profits benefit shareholders rather than workers, which can be viewed as a structural recipe for industrial strife.

This shareholder/manager/worker relationship can be seen as the producer side of the business equation. On the consumer side, those who are affected for better or worse by the company's operations, there are the consumers of the company's products, the suppliers of the company, the community in which the company operates and society at large.

As far as responsibility goes, the limited-liability company in its crudest form has workers responsible to managers. Managers are responsible to shareholders, with a view to bringing them the maximum return, via profits, on their investment. The company itself is not seen as having any responsibility to its workers beyond their wages or to its suppliers beyond paying their bills. It has no formal responsibility to the community or to the society at large, and its responsibility to its consumers is perceived as being discharged through the price mechanism: if the price is too high or the quality too low, the firm will go out of business.

This simple framework of responsibilities has, of course, been much modified in most industrial economies: employment legislation has given rights to workers; fair trading legislation has given rights to consumers; pollution legislation has sought to protect a company's community and society at large. Moreover, many companies now perceive that they have responsibilities beyond minimum legal requirements, which they may seek to effect through company policy, their own charitable trust, or through an initiative like Business in the Community, which channels business resources and expertise into worthy community projects.

Sir Peter Parker, Chairman of Mitsubishi UK, the Rockware Group and the British Institute of Management, has given strong expression to this shifting view of a company's role in society:

> Managers are beginning to look at their organisations and ask questions: 'Have we got an established social policy, flexible, unembarrassed and unequivocal? Has the Board succeeded in getting this philosophy down the line, so that the individual manager knows that if he acts like a human being he will not only not lose marks, but actually gain them? Has it got an employment, educational and training aspect that is adapting to the new, imaginative patterns that are about to burst through? And, in particular, have we got a community programme?'[16]

Obviously this sort of attempt to think beyond the bottom line is greatly to be welcomed and, some would say, long overdue. Those who encourage businesses to evolve in the direction of broader social responsibility sometimes even claim that such enlightenment can have a positive spin-off for the bottom line.[17] But clearly the structure of the limited-liability company discriminates against these efforts. Its separation of owner and worker from each other, from their consumers and from the society in which they operate, together with the tendency of such companies to pursue purely financial goals, makes the grafting of social objectives onto the structure extremely difficult, and sometimes only serves to give benefit to the unscrupulous at the expense of the socially-responsible. Enter the co-operative.

'CO-OPERATION: WHERE THE SOCIAL MEETS THE ECONOMIC'
by Paul Ekins

Co-operatives have been variously defined as follows. 'A group of persons pursuing common economic, social and educational aims by means of a business enterprise.'[18] 'A group of people, small or large, with a commitment to joint action on the basis of democracy and self-help, in order to secure a service or economic arrangement that is at once socially desirable and beneficial to all taking part.'[19] 'Other movements have a high social aim: other movements have a broad business basis. Co-operation alone has both.'[20] 'The real differences between co-operation and other kinds of organisations resides precisely in its subordination of business techniques to ethical ideas.'[21]

The objectives of the co-operative movement are encoded in the six fundamental principles ratified by the International Co-operative Alliance in 1966, which can broadly be summarised as:

- open membership without discrimination;
  democratic management, particularly embodying equal voting for shareholders irrespective of shareholding or other qualifications;
- a strictly limited return on share capital;
- equitable distribution of any surplus earnings, to develop the co-operative business, to provide common services for members, or simply among the members in proportion to their transactions with the society;
- provision of education in co-operative principles and techniques;
- co-operation between co-operatives at all levels.

Of these principles, the two which distinguish co-operatives most radically from limited liability companies, apart from the explicit commitment to social and educational objectives already mentioned, are the equal voting among co-operative members and the limited return on share capital. This last characteristic is sometimes regarded as the corner-stone of the co-operative financial framework, embodying the belief that just as the risks of shareholding are limited, so should be the rewards.

Co-operatives exist for many purposes, with agriculture, producer, consumer, credit, housing and marketing co-operatives among the most important. They also come in all sizes, from fewer than ten to thousands of members. World-wide, the International Co-operative Alliance has affiliates in sixty-five countries with a combined membership of 355 million,[22] making Co-operation the largest socio-economic movement in the world.

It can be seen that, both through the objectives and structure of co-operatives, co-operation tends to break down the traditional division noted earlier between producers, consumers and society at large. As far as producer or worker co-operatives are concerned, this integration of previously conflicting functions goes even further, because in a workers' co-op, workers and managers are shareholders of equal influence, who share both in the decisions about the future direction of the enterprise and in any profits generated by its success. Thus worker co-operatives provide an organisational model which explictly recognises the social aims and impact of economic activity and which seeks to heal the conflict between workers, managers and shareholders by vesting each of the three functions to some extent in each of the people involved in the enterprise and ensuring that all get a share of its fruits.

Worker co-operatives comprise only 1.6 per cent of the members of the ICA's affiliated co-operatives,[23] and still account for an insignificant proportion of overall employment and output. Yet in the UK they have experienced a significant revival in the past decade. In 1975 only a dozen enterprises were registered by the Industrial Common Ownership Movement (ICOM). By the end of 1982 there were over 600, with new co-operatives being formed at the rate of one a day, and failing at a rate of only two and a half per cent of those formed, a far lower rate than for small businesses as a whole.[24] Moreover, these co-operatives are now promoted and sustained by a network of seventy local Co-operative Development Agencies supported by local authorities.

Such growth reflects the fact that co-operatives in the UK and, in fact, world-wide, enjoy very broad political support. Socialists regard them as a form of 'social ownership', whereas Conservatives think of them more in terms of 'partnership', but most political groupings pay them generous lip service. Not all of this finds expression as active support, however. Co-operatives in the UK still suffer from tax discrimination and other disadvantages with respect to private companies, such as high registration costs.

The main financial problem of co-operatives is the raising of capital, both in the formation of the enterprise and in the achievement of adequate levels of investment from surplus earnings durings its operation. This problem stems directly from the co-operative principle of only giving a limited return on share capital, so that most initial co-operative capital comes either from the workers in the enterprise or from outside loans. The ICOM-model rules actually prohibit outside shareholding altogether. Thus a major expansion of public funds available for loans to co-operatives is a political priority if the current co-operative impetus is to be maintained. It is worth noting in passing that the record of repayment of such loans by co-operatives to the Co-operative Bank and Industrial Common Ownership Finance (ICOF) has actually been better to date than the loan repayment of conventional companies.[25]

Because the return on capital is limited, surplus earnings in a workers' co-operative tend to be distributed to the workers in proportion to work contributed. This is sometimes done in the form of bonus shares to enable workers to reinvest in the co-operative, thus participating in the growth of its assets. Private companies can also issue such bonus shares to employees, a form of profit-sharing known in the US as ESOPs (employee stock ownership plans), which also attracts wide political support because of the incentives it gives for workers to identify with their company.

In 1978 a law passed in the UK gave personal tax relief in respect of bonus shares issued by companies to their employees, but specifically excluded co-operators from the personal tax concession. This is a major discrimination against co-operatives and constitutes a significant disincentive, *vis-à-vis* private companies, for co-operators to plough their earnings back into their business. The granting of the tax concession on bonus shares to members of workers' co-operatives is a second priority for political action.[26]

A further tax concession which could do much to promote capital formation in co-operatives and provide a powerful incentive for private companies to convert to co-operatives is the exemption of co-operatives from Corporation Tax. This has been frequently proposed by co-operators,[27] most recently in the UK by ICOM in their memorandum to the Chancellor of the Exchequer prior to the 1986 Budget. So far, however, these proposals have only had a negative response.

Another way in which the UK government could help co-operatives is to close the loophole which allows their residual assets, after winding up, to be distributed to shareholders. The problem here is that the limited return on co-operative shares, and the associated fact that these shares therefore do not increase in value, means that the value of a successful co-operative's assets can be greatly in excess of its share values, giving a clear incentive for the co-operative either to be wound up or taken over. The best known example of this is Bristol Printers Ltd, which was wound up in 1977 after sixty-eight years' successful trading, whereupon each of its shares, redeemable for £1 during the company's operation, realised the £28 that the co-operative's assets warranted. The distribution of such assets to shareholders is in clear breach of the co-operative principle of a limited return on share capital.[28] In France and other countries such distribution of residual assets by co-operatives is illegal. It should become so in the UK.

Despite the wide political support enjoyed by co-operatives, and the growth in employee shareholdings in the UK since the tax relief legislation in 1978, and in ESOPs in the US since tax concessions were granted in laws in 1975 and 1981, outright conversions to common ownership companies, whether in line with the co-operative principles or not, remain rare. But it is a rarity that has nothing to do with failure. John Lewis converted his stores business to a partnership in 1929. In 1984 the John Lewis Partnership employed 25,000 people and distributed £25 million in bonuses to its employees. This and the successful Scott Bader chemical company, converted to common ownership in 1951, remain shining examples of what common enterprise can achieve.

In 1983 Baxi Heating, with 1981-2 pre-tax profits of £5.8 million and a labour force of 900, became the latest substantial company to embrace partnership. It had two main motives in mind:

The first is *job security*. Once it had been decided that Baxi Heating would not continue indefinitely as a family business, a partnership was seen to offer greater assurances of employment than either sale to another firm or turning it into a public company.

The second is to achieve a *dynamic balance*. The partnership structure is reckoned to offer the chance of striking the best balance between business and management on one hand, and democratic participation and accountability on the other.[29]

In the current economic system it takes visionaries like John Lewis, Ernest Bader and Philip Baxendale to give effect to the obvious good sense of these arguments, and such visionaries are inevitably few and far between. If conversions are to increase in number, so that partnerships and co-operatives can fully realise their potential, it is the system that must change. Ways must be found of giving real value to the social and educational aims of co-operation.

It has been a recurrent theme of this book that economic activity has a social as well as a financial dimension. Co-operatives recognise this explicitly and pledge themselves to pursue social and educational, as well as financial, objectives. The pursuit of such objectives inevitably takes resources – resources which a private company might well use to improve its financial competitiveness *vis-à-vis* the co-operative. Thus a co-operative operating in an economic system that gives no value to social and educational objectives, which leaves such objectives, in fact, exclusively to the 'public sector', is bound to be uncompetitive with the private company, other things being equal. So producer co-operatives will remain economically marginal until the economic system within which they operate takes into account their social and educational achievements and makes them some corresponding financial compensation.

This is the real political challenge of the co-operative movement: to amend the very evaluation of economic progress and success to include its social and educational dimension. It is the political nettle that will need to be grasped before the Co-operative Commonwealth dreamed of by the pioneer co-operators can become a reality.

NOTES

1 See, for example, Kirkpatrick Sale's definitive work *Human Scale*, London, Secker & Warburg, 1980.

2 The journal *Initiatives* (Centre for Employment Initiatives, London) gives good regular coverage of creative local economic initiatives. So do the LEDIS sheets (see note 8).

3 From Paul Hawken, *The Next Economy*, Holt, Rinehart & Winston, 1983.

4 Newport and Nevern Energy Group, Dyfed, Wales.

5 Amory Lovins, *Soft Energy Paths*, Harmondsworth, Penguin, 1977.

6 Guy Dauncey, *Nice Work If You Can Get It*, Cambridge, National Extension College, 1983.

7 Centre for Trade and Industry, Swansea, Wales.

8 LEDIS Information Sheet A94, Local Economic Development Information Service, Glasgow.

9 Vivian Hutchinson, *Healing Unemployment: Some Keynotes for Community Initiatives*. Available from PO Box 4101, New Plymouth East, Taranaki, New Zealand.

10 John Burbridge, 'Lessons from Mondragon's success', *Initiatives*, February 1984.

11 BBC TV series, *Wheels of Fire*.

12 John Naisbitt,*Megatrends*, MacDonald, 1984.

13 Greater London Enterprise Board, London SE1 6BD.

14 Hilary Wainwright and Dave Elliott, *The Lucas Plan – a New Trade Unionism in the Making?*, Allison & Busby, 1982.

15 *Technology Networks*, Greater London Enterprise Board, London.

16 *Business in Society: a new initiative*, New Initiative, London, 1984, pp.17–18.

17 Ibid., p.31.

18 Charles Gide (1847–1932), an eminent French co-operator, quoted in International Co-operative Alliance's *Co-operatives in the Year 2000*, ICA, London, 1980, p.33.

19 Ibid., p.32.

20 The celebrated economist Alfred Marshall (1842–1924), from an address in Ipswich in 1889, quoted in ibid., p.68.

21 W.P. Watkins in the *Review of International Co-operation*, March 1962, quoted in ibid., p.68.

22 Ibid., p.9. This figure is now probably nearer 500 million. Chinese co-operatives joined the ICA in October 1984.

23 Paul Derrick, 'Co-operatives – the key to economic emancipation', unpublished paper, 1985.

24 *Towards Common Ownership*, Labour Finance and Industry Group, London, 1985, p.11.

25 Ibid., p.12.

288 The new economics in action

26   In the UK 1986 Finance Act the 1978 tax concession was finally extended to workers' co-operatives, so that they now can issue bonus shares to worker members free of personal tax.
27   See, for example, Paul Derrick, 'The taxation of co-operatives' in *Taxation*, September 1984.
28   See Paul Derrick, 'Towards a consensus on common ownership' in *Science and Public Policy*, April 1985.
29   Baxi Heating, *From Participation to Partnership*, Preston, Richard Baxendale & Sons, 1983.

13 LEARNING FROM THE SOUTH

The world has heard much of the problems of the South in recent times and, indeed, there is much to hear. Far less is heard about solutions to those problems, especially solutions which originate in the South and from which the North has much to learn. This chapter first describes two initiatives from different countries, one rural, one urban. Both are the more remarkable for the difficult context in which the initiatives were born and operate. The first is from Africa, that continent about which it has recently been written:

> Africa is dying because in its ill-planned, ill-advised attempt to 'modernise' itself, it has cut itself in pieces. The cities where the governments live have been torn from the countryside, and development budgets have gone to filling those cities with hotels, factories and cars. This has been paid for by milking the seven out of every ten Africans who live on the land, by taking much from them in labour and produce and giving back little in money or support. In these policies, Africa has been advised, financed and assisted by Northern governments and aid agencies (Timberlake, 1985, p.9).

If Africa is indeed dying, then it is such initiatives as that described below, originating in Africa and working with and for Africans, that will bring it back to life.

'THE GREEN BELT MOVEMENT'
by Wangari Maathai

Background

The term 'green belt' describes a mass movement of tree planting taking place in Kenya. It is an activity that has been developed steadily in response to local needs and capabilities. The idea was conceived in 1974 but the very first trees were planted on the occasion of World Environment Day, 5 June 1977.

The activity was developed within the National Council of Women of Kenya by a Standing Committee on the Environment. It was developed into a programme that approached the issues of development holistically and endeavoured to build on local expertise and capabilities so as to allow for intrinsic involvement and development.

The needs which inspired the movement

Fuelwood

About 90 per cent of Kenya's population live in the rural areas and depend on firewood as their source of energy. The greater part of the urban population also uses charcoal, which in most part is inefficiently converted into energy. What happens when populations who use fuelwood do not have enough of it?

Firstly, much time is used to collect whatever is the alternative. This is time that could be used more productively. Secondly and more seriously, the women change the eating habits of their families and use foodstuffs that require little or no energy to prepare, such as bread, rice, refined maizemeal, etc. All these foods are refined carbohydrates which promote kwashiokor and other diseases associated with malnutrition.

What is striking is the observance of such diseases in areas considered comparatively affluent, where cash from crops like tea and coffee is available, but where at the same time trees have been cleared to make way for such cash crops. The production of cash crops for export supersedes crop production. A malnourished society, no matter how rich, is a sick and a non-productive society, and a government may be forced to expand hospitals and other health facilities to cater for the large number of unwell citizens who need not be sick. Providing energy and teaching people proper nutrition, or encouraging them to re-adopt their former eating habits, may not appear progressive, but it is the right step in the right direction.

Food production

Food production has fallen in Africa and in some areas famine has become a recurrent phenomenon. Among the precipitating factors is the fact that the fertile soil has been eroded by water or wind and has been lost. The consequence has been that farmers, mainly

women, have had to produce food crops from highly impoverished soils. Even where soils are not heavily eroded many farmers
do not replenish the soil with manure, either because they have
none or because they believe in commercial fertilizers which they
cannot afford. Farmers must learn to relate soil erosion and over-
exploitation of the soil with poor crop yield and they must be
willing to rectify the situation.

Soil erosion
Soil erosion is closely related to the indiscriminate cutting-down
of trees, encroachment on forests and catchment areas by people
and livestock, and destruction of soil cover. Ordinary people need
to be taught the role of forests and catchment areas and be made
to see how their own survival is dependent on the survival of
those forests.

Population
Kenya has one of the highest birth rates in the world (about 3.8
per cent) and much of her land is arid, semi-arid or desert. Unless
her population is educated on the pending dangers and involves
itself in massive afforestation activities and reclamation, the
country could become desertified within a short period, resulting
in the usual disasters now prevalent in Africa.

Lack of community participation
Since about 90 per cent of Kenya's 19 million people live in the
rural areas and use fuelwood, and since the majority of the urban
population use charcoal, we will continue to witness the high
demand for fuelwood, timber, building and fencing materials and
charcoal. The only alternative is to work much harder and work
with Nature. Such work can only be effective if the whole community
participates. The financial inputs into such activities are comparatively low and comparatively more effective. It is one alternative
development strategy that would work for the poorer nations.

Lack of public awareness
The public must be aroused to an awareness that appreciates the
pivotal role played by a sustained environment and the interrelationship between such an environment and all the other issues
which form the basis for development. Without this understanding, policies are carried out in an unco-ordinated manner, and at
certain points a country moves in vicious circles which are difficult
to break because they are firmly supported by the traditional
economic systems.

To meet these needs we formulated short- and long-term objectives which guide our thinking and our operations.

The short-term objectives

Focus on women's role in development

Although women play a major role in development, their contribution is rarely given more than lip service and is, of course, not proportionately rewarded. We felt that the period for talking and complaining about the status of women had come to an end – it was time for women to talk around development issues and develop positive change in themselves, the environment and the country. Development issues provide a good forum for women to be creative, assertive and effective leaders and the Green Belt Movement, being a development issue, provided the forum to promote women's positive image. Therefore we would:

- Promote tree planting especially among small scale farmers in order to make rural communities self-sufficient in fuelwood, building and fencing materials.
  Promote informal environment education on such activities as preventing soil erosion and flooding. Environment education sessions consider desertification, cultivation along river banks and sloping areas, indiscriminate cutting-down of trees and clearing of bushes for crop-land.
- Create employment for the physically handicapped, young school leavers, the aged and those grossly handicapped by poverty. These are engaged to attend to tree nurseries and green belts and to promote the movement in the field. At the moment there are 250 persons in the field.
- Make seedling production an income-generating activity, especially for women and school-children.
- Transfer forestry techniques to ordinary people, especially women, and increase the rate of production of tree seedlings by the same people who will plant them, keeping the whole process within their communities, for ease of transport.

The long-term objectives

These can be summarised as:

- To halt deforestation, particularly of catchment areas and indigenous forests, and halt indiscriminate cutting-down of trees;

- To promote agricultural practices which enhance food production;
- To introduce practices for good livestock management;
- To promote the concept of agroforestry amongst small-scale farmers;
- To make the rural population self-sufficient in fuelwood, building and fencing materials;
- To establish tree plantations for charcoal production;
- To promote more efficient combustion devices in order to save energy both during production and combustion;
- To promote environmental education in schools so as to sensitise future generations;
- To raise public awareness on issues related to environment and development in line with the World Conservation Strategy and to utilise the forum to discuss the interrelationships between environment, energy, food production, population, political stability and peace.

Achieving the objectives

In order to achieve these objectives the Green Belt Movement has been allowed to evolve slowly and respond to the needs felt by the communities. Once a person or a group in the community feels the need to participate, a series of activities is initiated. These are:

- Each would-be participant must send an application to the headquarters indicating that he or she wishes to participate in the Green Belt Movement and indicating the desired area of participation, for example to produce tree seedlings or to plant them.
- Participants have to carry out certain work before they can receive trees, such as digging holes, preparing ground for tree nurseries, and so on. This work is checked by the Green Belt Movement field staff.
- For many months participants are followed by the Green Belt staff to ensure that the procedure is followed as laid down, so as to ensure survival of the trees. Here we must emphasize that participation is completely voluntary. The role of the Green Belt Movement is to stimulate, inform and motivate. Those who shut the door are neither persuaded nor coerced. The decision to work or not is still a free choice.
  In order for any group to produce seedlings, a one- to three-day workshop is organized to teach them forestry techniques and the aims and objectives of the Green Belt Movement. During

these workshops the women learn what is meant by the concepts 'environment' and 'development', and discuss the interrelationship between environment and all the other issues which affect development. They also learn how to collect seeds, how to handle them, how to establish a tree nursery in their backyard, how to plant seedlings and how to take care of them.

• While seedlings are being produced the community is persuaded to plant trees. Individual farmers and heads of institutions are instructed how to plant the seedlings and how to attend to them to ensure survival.

• When seedlings are ready to plant they are issued to those members of the communities who have accepted the scheme and have prepared accordingly. In this way over 920 public green belts of 1,000 trees each, and over 15,000 private green belts owned by small-scale farmers, have been registered with the movement.

The lessons learnt

As expected many lessons have been learnt, some wisdom has been rediscovered and appreciated and, in all these eight years, actions have spoken louder than words. The lessons are as follows.

First, many locally placed and ordinary persons have ideas which could contribute positively to our development. But most Third World leaders and those they lead believe in imported, ready-made packages to solve national economic woes. Even after two decades of political freedom, our economic freedom is still a dream. We have no shortage of good ideas. If we would give them a chance they could break the vicious circle and halt economic regression. The Green Belt Movement is an example of such ideas.

Second, the basic needs of the Third World communities remain very simple, and until these are met no real development will be realised. For the populations within which we work, food and fuelwood are primary needs and yet, surprisingly, more emphasis may be laid on export goods in order to import consumer items which are not essentials.

Third, we have to get our priorities right. It is not necessary to reach for the moon when we cannot even leave our village. We have to be realistic in our aspirations in order to realise most of the objectives, at least short-term, and be encouraged to pursued the long-term objectives. Economic priorities which do not cater for the needs of the majority are temporary and are bound to fail.

Fourth, the people must participate. Development is for the people, and must therefore also be by them. The direct participation of the community has been recognised as the correct approach but has not always been achieved. The Green Belt Movement has succeeded in making the community participatory benefactors.

Fifth, development is achieved only through courageous interactions with many persons and institutions. These inter-actions must be based on truth and a sense of accountability. Whether we are dealing with few or millions of shillings, unless there is a sense of accountability, targets remain unrealised and development lags.

In conclusion, the Green Belt Movement is endeavouring to promote through indigenous means the attainment of the new economic order that is being sought by so many who are seeking personal development and social, political and economic justice, in addition to the satisfaction of these basic human needs shared by all on this planet.

● ● ●

From rural development in Africa we move to urban development in India, where the Self-Employed Women's Association is greening the lives of tens of thousands of women workers throughout the sub-continent.

'PIECE-RATE WORKERS' ATTEMPT AT SELF-RELIANCE'
by Ela Bhatt

SEWA, which means 'service' in several Indian languages, is the acronym of the Self Employed Women's Association. It is a registered trade union, born out of the Women's Wing of the Textile Labour Union. Gandhian thinking is its source of guidance.

There are three categories of membership in SEWA: home-based producers, petty vendors, and providers of services, including manual labourers. It is said that 89 per cent of employment in India derives from these three categories, but our unions and our labour legislation have almost bypassed this mass of the work-force. Indeed, I would venture to say that most of our other formal systems have bypassed them as well, such as health, education, public distribution, the law, banking and town planning. Yet it is this work-force that should be in the mainstream of the labour movement in countries like ours, where most of the production of goods and services is done through the self-employed sector. We call them self-employed workers because they have no recognised employer-employee relationship. They have been described as unorganised, informal, marginal, residual, peripheral, undocumented, etc., by our economists. This may be the case in the industrially developed countries, but certainly not in our country where this work-force is absolutely central to our economy. Such a description shows the ignorance or negative attitude of the so-called experts. To underline their positive role, we call them self-employed workers, and this term is now slowly being accepted by the Indian Government in its documents and by the International Labour Organisation. These workers are the people who are the hardest hit in our economy today, and they form the vast majority of the population.

Of the population of working women, only 6 per cent are in regular employment; the rest are left to earn a livelihood by their own means. Therefore they remain poor. Also, women's economic contribution remains invisible to society and to the policy-makers. We believe, however, that these women should be playing a leading role in the women's movement of our country.

With these ideas in mind, we started the Self Employed Women's Association. It began with Ahmedabad workers, spread into villages, and is now in six states of the country. Our total membership is around 40,000. Along with the Textile Labour Union, the members have also organised their own Co-operative Bank in Ahmedabad. Some of the trade groups are further organised into their own co-operatives: handblock printers, chindi workers, bamboo workers, weavers, vegetable vendors and growers, rag pickers, cleaners, kerosene vendors, and in six villages landless labourers have formed village-level milk co-ops. Each co-op has a different story.

In short, SEWA tries to be both visible and audible, to bring into focus the self-employed women workers' economic role in society, to increase their income, and to assist them to be in control of their incomes and assets. Our strategy is the joint action of union and co-operative in the struggle for development.

Of the three categories of SEWA members described above, the vendors and labourers sell wares and services in the open market and, at least physically, are visible to the public eye. But the home-based workers are invisible to society, physically in that they work within their homes, and officially in that they hardly ever appear in censuses or other official statistics. For example, in the 1981 Census of India, the number of workers listed under household industry is 8.8 million. However, according to government labour statistics, the number of workers who roll bidis (a type of Indian cigarette) at home is 2.25 million. This number is an under-estimation, because no official agency has collected precise statistics. According to SEWA estimates, 10,000 million bidis are rolled every day, engaging 50 million workers and, out of these, 98 per cent are women. But even taking the government statistics, does this mean that one minor product like bidis constitutes one quarter of the household industry work-force? Then what about carpenters, potters, blacksmiths? What about 10 million handloom weavers? What about 5 million in the Khadu and Village Industries Commission? What about localised craft, such as half a million lace-makers in one District of Narsapur of Andhra State, and 50,000 embroiderers in the District of Kutch in Gujarat? What about the vast multitude of women workers in garment-making and food-processing? What about incense-stick rollers, coir weavers? Clearly 8.8 million is a gross under-estimation of home-based workers.

These workers can be classified into two types. First, those who are own-account artisans; second, those who are piece-rate workers.

Among home-based piece-rate worker members in SEWA, more than 5,000 are bidi workers, about 6,000 are stichers. For bidi rollers, there is legislation to protect their wages, working conditions, etc., though the implementation is weak. But for the stitchers there is no law. For bidi workers we are active on the union front, but for the stitchers we have had to evolve our own strategy. This was the first struggle of its kind in SEWA, so I would like to describe it in detail. It involved the joint struggle for development of a group of 600 chindi stitchers of the Daviapur area in Ahmedabad, a textile town with sixty-eight mills. These mills throw out various kinds of scrap, including rags, or 'chindi'. Chindi is purchased in bulk by big traders who give it out to women to stitch 'khols', i.e. quilt covers, and pay them by piece-rate. 600 women's lives depend on the income from khols. Our tale is as follows.

The year is 1977. Fatma is a home-based worker. She sews khols in her own house, on her own machine. The local khol trader gives her the chindi rags, while Fatma has to buy the thread, needle and oil for the machine. She gets paid by piece-rate. When her two daughters help and they work ten hours, they can earn Rs8 (50p) a day. During the slack season she earns two to three rupees. Whether she gets work or not, whether she gets paid or not, and what piece-rate she gets, all depend on the whim of the traders. The price of thread is continuously rising, the prices of essential goods rise higher than the inflation rate, yet Fatma's earnings remain the same. How can she defend herself against rising prices on the one hand and a consistently low piece-rate on the other? How can she defend herself against unfair dismissal?

There are many women in the cities, towns and villages of our country who either sell their labour or work as home-based producers at piece-rates. These working sisters themselves realise how much they are exploited. They see prices rising, but their own earnings remaining the same.

Fatma and others just talked amongst themselves, then as a group they gathered up their courage and went to the employer to say, 'All the prices have risen, will you increase our rates?' The employer, knowing well that this would cut into his profits, said a big 'NO'. He said, 'If I raise your rates, I will make a loss and I will have to stop production. Then you will have no work at all.' Hearing this, Fatma and the others got very angry. They had seen how much profit he was making. 'We have seen him grow richer. Earlier he had a small house, now he has expanded it and added on two more storeys. Earlier he rode a bicycle, now he and his family go around in a car!'

At this stage the women felt that they needed to get organised, and Fatma entered the SEWA office in 1977. They wanted to defend their rightful place in the economy. The first step in defensive action was to get all the facts. SEWA union organisers went with them to their homes, which are also their work-places. The organisers talked to them and obtained information on their working conditions. They were asked: What different kinds of work do you do? How many hours? How much work do you get per day? How many days are you unemployed? What wages do you get? How much can you earn per day? As the organiser talked to the women, talk turned into discussion. While discussing, they saw a wider picture of the areas where their rights were most under attack. During the series of surveys-cum-discussion-cum-union-meetings, Karima emerged as the group leader of the chindi workers of Dariapur.

During 1977-78, the union started taking shape under the leadership of Karima. With the help of the SEWA organiser, she and other group leaders went quickly from house to house and to the work-places, having meetings, talking to workers, listening to their opinions and suggestions, and enrolling them as members of SEWA.

Most people think that women are too shy or afraid to join a union. But no, even the Muslim women patchworkers, who are in purdah, came out of their houses, against the will of their men and elders, and unhesitatingly paid the union fees. They felt very strongly, and even came to the night meetings and publicly expressed their opinions.

When the majority of the stitchers had joined the union, they framed their minimum demands to present to the employer. SEWA then approached the employer to discuss the situation. The employer passed the buck to the Chindi Traders Association, who did not care to respond to the demands made by SEWA. So we were left to deal with the individual employers directly. Their usual first response, of course, was to disregard the workers' rights. They said that the employers were benevolent and the workers were lazy and ungrateful. They said that the SEWA organisers were wasting their time, because there was nothing to discuss. So SEWA had to prepare for action.

Now that we were organised and stronger, the employers could be threatened with strikes. They were therefore prepared to sit with us and negotiate. But although they signed an agreement to a pay rise, they did not abide by it. They started using their usual methods: making threats, bribes, bringing family and community pressures to bear on the women, harassing the workers by giving them bad material to sew, providing less work and, in the case of forty workers whose total income depended on chindi work and who were in some instances more active in union activities, giving them no work at all. The struggle had only just begun. The victimised had to be rescued, otherwise the union would face a fatal set-back. The union did not have a victimisation fund to support the victimised, so the SEWA Executive Committee decided to start a Production Unit to support the forty victimised members.

That was in 1978. To buy new chindi, we approached the textile mills. Here we had to face the very employers against whom we were fighting. They tried their best to exclude us from the chindi market by offering a higher price for chindi to the textile mills, and by getting the storekeeper to put materials like an old shoe, a wet blanket, even a dagger, in our bags of chindi. We had to struggle very hard against these attacks. Being women, we could not mix with the plant-level mill officials to convert them to our side. A market for the finished khols has never been a problem, because the khols are very much in demand by the common masses. But the struggle to buy chindi from the mills went on for a very long time, and is not yet fully over. It was only in 1981 that we established a business relationship with the

Government Textile Mills, who entered into an agreement with us for a fixed price and an assured quota of chindi during the year. SEWA representatives now also sit on the Price Committee that meets periodically to fix the price of chindi. However, there are only seven Government Mills in the state, while the rest of the ninety-three mills belong to private parties over whom there is no control as to the price-regulation of chindi. The supply of raw material is still a serious problem. In fact, we have taken up this issue at central government ministry level and also with the National Planning Commission, demanding as broad government policy that the first claim over the raw material should be that of the actual producer, whether for chindi or junk and scrap from big industries, or yarn, or bamboo, or forest produce.

Then, there is the problem of space. In a highly congested area of Dariapur, space is very scarce. The little space we had, had to be vacated when SEWA's parent body, the Textile Labour Union, ousted us from our premises.

In spite of all these difficulties, we survived and slowly grew. Our Production Unit realised that this was a profitable business and could directly link the urban poor, who are the producers of khols, with the rural poor, who are the consumers of khols, thus eliminating all the middlemen from the process. The Production Unit also realised that it was able to give higher wages all the year round, and assist the member producers to replace their old sewing machines with new ones by lending them credit facility. The most important lesson that we learned was that it was the Production Unit of the Union of Chindi Workers that gave us strength. No one is now victimised by her employer. Also, the workers have increased their capacity to fight and to acquire bargaining power.

Until 1983, the Production Unit was run by SEWA, in consultation with the member-producers. Having learned routine management and marketing skills, they decided to transform the Production Unit into a co-operative named 'Sabina'. Now Sabina has its own shop on the same road as the shops of the very employers against whom we have been fighting. Of course, we face a problem while negotiating workers' demands with the employers, who then call us traders, thus mixing up two images: that of trade unions with that of businessmen. The Sabina co-op has 200 members, and is financially self-sufficient. The members' income has increased from Rs100 to Rs400 per month. Sabina is largely managed by its members; however, there is still heavy dependence on SEWA in terms of space, product design, market contacts and training of various kinds needed from time to time.

The Sabina member-producers could work and earn still more if the problem of the supply of raw materials could be solved. In my opinion, the supply of raw materials is the biggest bottleneck faced by artisans in India. Because chindi is in short supply, we have had to diversify products in the co-op. The daughters of members took training in fancy patchwork, and now produce patchwork quilts reaching the higher market. So today the mothers produce quilts for the urban and rural poor, while the daughters do fancy patchwork quilts for the urban middle class. We are not very happy with the latter because of its inherent dependency on SEWA and on experts in product design. However, the members are content, because the combined income of mother and daughter can now amount to more than Rs550. The mothers and daughters have separate savings bank accounts in the SEWA Co-op Bank, as both wish to save for the future.

But the more they work, the more their home electricity bill goes up, and they are charged at the commercial rate. SEWA has to struggle with the City Electricity Board to change this policy. Stitching, also, is an occupational hazard in a poorly-lit slum house. We observed that by the age of thirty-five the women are not able to stitch, so the workload is shifted to their daughters at a very early age.

To sum up, what began with a survey led to a trade union, combined with a producers' co-operative, resulting in the joint action of union and co-operative to fight poverty and vested interests. In the process women learned many things. Those who had never before worked outside their homes started going to the mills to buy chindi, and to various institutions to take orders. They stood in the khol shop in the central market-place to sell the products, talked with strangers, went to the government offices and banks to clear their bills, conducted co-op meetings, dealt with constant internal fights and resolved them, and, all the time, faced the pressure of their husbands, the masters of the house, and the community.

What still remains to be fully achieved is the change of attitudes, of self-perception. Before, they were producing for an employer, regarding themselves as labourers. Today they feel neither owners nor labourers, but something in between. There is still a long way to go, but the women feel that they are developing the skill and the confidence in themselves to become owners. Running a business takes a different set of capabilities from being a unionist.

Certain conclusions have been drawn in the course of the

struggle. One is the advantages of home-work. There are several reasons why women workers actually prefer their home as a work-site over other worksites:

1   They can combine their other roles of wife, mother and home-maker with the worker role relatively easily;
2   They can save time, energy and expense in commuting to and from another work-site;
3   They can work at their own convenient time;
4   They can avoid facing social sanctions against going to work out of the house, or working with or under strangers, particularly males;
5   They can involve the family members in the work, or can involve themselves in the family.

All these are considerations from the women's point of view. But although they may be positive reasons, home-work also leads to negative consequences for both own-account and piece-rate workers. Their awareness of the outside world, of market forces, of dealing with money, of buying and selling abilities, of the nature of the exploitation to which they are subject, and so on, is very limited, because they are restricted to their homes. Their contact with co-workers is reduced, and their ability to work collectively for common goals is constrained.

Another preference concerns piece-rate work. In addition to the reasons listed above, we find that women workers accept piece-rate work because they are not tied down to any one person, they are free to produce as much as they want to, and they have freedom of choice over their work as they do in own-account work. The reason why piece-rate work at home is encouraged by the owners is because it does not fall under the legislation pertaining to factory workers and thus is more profitable for them.

The future of home-based work will depend on the kind of industrialisation policies that are adopted, on the nature of protection given to home-based workers, and on the support services extended to them, on the recognition of home-based work as real work. The future of home-based workers will also depend on the concept of a worker, of a work-site, of production relations, in the minds of policy-makers: is factory work alone to be promoted as work, or is home-based work also considered valid work? For women workers this question is a very significant one.

Obviously worker-organisation is the only way to fight exploitation, but pressurising the owners to improve the conditions of the workers leads to a series of never-ending struggles. However, this situation is created only if the sole option conceived for piece-rate workers is regularisation of their status along the lines of factory workers. But there is another option which can be pursued and practised: they can be enabled to become fully-fledged own-account workers. They were doomed to be piece-rate workers due to a process of pauperisation, which eroded their resource base. By reversing this process, piece-rate workers can be encouraged to become truly self-employed, with all the self-respect this brings. The preferred mode of working in our culture is self-employment, of course!

If this option is to be seriously pursued, then it is obvious that the first step is to become organised; the second is the provision of a package of services that deals with supply of raw material, capital, tools and equipment, space to work, markets, protection against mass-produced goods, and remunerative prices for goods; and the third is training in the skills of procurement of raw material, selling, understanding market forces, handling money, costing and accounting, and taking responsibility for one's own economic activity. Help on one or some aspects is not sufficient; often it is counter-productive, and this is particularly true of poor, home-based workers.

SEWA's three-faceted policy is therefore to have organising workers, who provide a package of inputs and strong protective measures, to help home-based workers to become self-employed. The relationship between the organisers and the workers, and the nature of the advice and protection they offer, need careful consideration. The illiteracy of the majority of home-based workers has to be borne in mind, and also the fact that most of them are women. Then there are the linkages with institutional credit, supplies, marketing, and skills training, all of which are very new to the workers, so they have to depend on the help of professionals and can again become subservient to these people. This tendency has to be safeguarded against. The workers have to be exposed to such transactions in order to become owners of their organisations. Unless they learn themselves how to monitor their whole range of business activity, they will simply end up being exploited by a different set of masters.

• • •

The Green Belt Movement and SEWA have directly improved the well-being of tens of thousands of the poorest people in the South in ways that increase their skills, increase their self-reliance and, in the Kenyan example, provide immense environmental benefits, in stark contrast to the results achieved by much official development assistance through bodies like the World Bank. Moreover, the cash costs of these initiatives have been tiny, compared with aid budgets. What, then, is the role, if any, of Northern aid and the Northern development professional in Another Development in Southern countries? Or should such people stay at home and concentrate on the poverties and inequities in their own countries? Timberlake gives a stark description of the reality of much of the development industry today.

> Advising Africa has become a major industry, with European and American consulting firms charging as much as $180,000 for a year of an expert's time. At any given moment Sub-Saharan Africa has at least 80,000 expatriates working for public agencies under official aid programmes. More than half of the $7-8 billion spent yearly by donors goes to finance these people. Yet in the two and a half decades since African independence, Africa has plunged from food self-sufficiency to widespread hunger . . . . The Sudanese Government, with the help of Northern aid, World Bank loans and Arab investment, has put vast sugar and cotton plantations on its best land along the Nile. It has ignored rapidly falling yields for small-holder farming in the 1970s. It seems not to have noticed that the land on which eight out of every ten Sudanese depend for their livelihoods is slowly perishing due to over-use and misuse. It invested little in dryland regions, where people like the Hadendawa live. So when drought came, these pastoralists and peasants had no irrigated settlements in which to take temporary refuge, no government agencies to buy their livestock, no sources of drought-resistant sorghum seeds ready for planting when the rains resumed. But neither have the government's investments in cash crops produced money to pay the nation's way through the drought. The result is starvation and debt: Sudan's external debt in 1985 was estimated at $9 billion. The Hadendawa face virtual extinction as a culture, due to hunger and dispersal (Timberlake, 1985, pp.8-10).

But development professionals, whether foreigners or nationals of Third World countries, are not going to go away and neither are the aid budgets with which they work. The very least they can do in the light of their past failures is to rethink the whole basis of their profession.

'PUTTING THE LAST FIRST'[1]
by Robert Chambers

Professional development these days takes place in a context of cores and peripheries of knowledge. Globally, there are gradients from extremes of wealth and power in urban, industrial cores to extremes of poverty and impotence in rural, agricultural peripheries. These gradients, between 'first' and 'last', exist both between rich and poor countries and within poor countries themselves. The wealth and power of the cores attract and sustain concentrations of professionals, resources and capacity to generate and spread knowledge. The knowledge of the cores is prestigious, and described as modern, scientific, advanced, sophisticated and high technology. It is also powerful, being supported by and supporting the machinery of the state and of commerce. As a colonising, unifying and standardising force, it pushes out into the peripheries, propagated through communications, commercialisation and education. In the receiving rural peripheries, there is an unconnected scatter of people who are powerless, low status and poor. They have many localised sets of skills and funds of indigenous technical knowledge particular to their communities and conditions, but these are rarely recognised or valued by the bearers of modernity from the cores.

In this system, the cores attract those who gain education and seek advancement. Like iron filings drawn by a magnet, they point and move inwards and upwards. During their careers, professionals move along the gradients as they strive for promotion, prestige, recognition, higher income and better living conditions. Within the Third World they transfer from rural to urban, and from urban to metropolitan centres. They then feed the international brain-drain to the richer countries. At the very centres are the black holes of defence and space programmes in the USA and USSR, sucking staff and resources towards them.

First modes of analysis fit badly with last realities. Critics such as Gunnar Myrdal, 1968, E.F. Schumacher, 1973, and Michael Lipton, 1977, have in their different ways attacked the unthinking transfer to Third World environments of the values, technologies and prescriptions of the urban industrial rich. It is now conventional wisdom among many development professionals that the first priorities of the affluent North (sophisticated armaments, diseases of the overfed and ageing, multiplicities of costly drugs, high-input mechanised agriculture, and so on) distract from priorities for the poorer majority of people in the

South. But curiously little attention seems to have been paid to how those who are first perceive, misperceive or do not perceive at all, those who are last and their conditions.

Errors and explanations

One starting point for trying to understand the application of core or 'first' thinking to peripheral or 'last' people and conditions is to examine past errors. Considering the manifest power of science and the vast human, financial and physical resources devoted to research, it is astonishing how often, and how badly, development professionals have been wrong. Many deeply held beliefs for which empirical evidence was mustered in their day have now largely been rejected. Some of these concerned the poor themselves: beliefs that the rural poor were inherently lazy and fatalistic and that small and subsistence farmers were ignorant and irrational. Others concerned agricultural practices: beliefs that the capital-intensive mechanised monocropping of temperate climates would be widely suitable in tropical conditions; that group or communal farming by peasants would work; that the intercropping of small farmers was uneconomic and inefficient; that on-farm post-harvest losses of cereals were high, with 30 per cent often quoted. Others concerned the nature of deprivation: the belief that the problem of hunger was mainly one of total food production, rather than mainly one of entitlement or effective demand, as is now understood (Sen, 1981); that malnutrition was more a problem of protein deficiency than lack of calories; that human calorie requirements were higher than is now believed. The list could be extended but the point is already made. It is alarming how wrong we were, and how sure we were that we were right. And it is humbling and sobering to speculate on how many of the 'first' beliefs of today may in their turn prove to be wrong.

There are several obvious explanations of past error: the arrogance of those with power, status and supposedly superior knowledge; the low prestige of professions and people close to the poor; the minimal resources devoted to research on 'last' subjects; the behavioural biases of rural development tourism, usually based on a brief and hurried rural visit by the urban-based professional to those who are better off and more accessible, to the neglect of the poorer and more remote (Chambers, 1983, pp.10-23); the human capacity to explain the misfortune and poverty of others in terms of moral turpitude and divine justice; the comforting stereotypes of colonial natives and post-colonial peasants as lazy, stupid, stubborn, ignorant and fatalistic; and the unwillingness, inability and lack of opportunity for first professionals to listen to, study and learn from those who are last.

Beyond these, there are two other levels of explanation: values and preferences of first professionals; and the structure of first thinking.

First values and preferences

The values and preferences of first professionals are typically polar opposites of last realities. These can be presented as two parallel and contrasting lists, as in Table 13.1. Most professionals see first values as sophisticated and scientific, and last realities as primitive and based on ignorance.

Table 13.1: First values and last realities

First values	Last realities
Urban	Rural
Industrial	Agricultural
High Cost	Low-cost
Capital-using	Labour-using
Mechanical	Animal or human
Inorganic	Organic
Large	Small
Modern	Traditional
Exotic	Indigenous
Marketed	Subsistence
Quantified	Unquantified
Geometrical	Irregular
Visible and seen	Invisible or unseen
Tidy	Untidy
Predictable	Unpredictable
Hard	Soft
Clean	Dirty
Odourless	Smelly

Professionals also have preferences for clients and contacts and for places and times of work, as shown in Table 13.2.

Table 13.2: Professional preferences

	First	Last
For contacts and clients	High status	Low status
	Rich	Poor
	Influential	Powerless
	Educated	Illiterate
	Male	Female
	Adult	Child
	Light-skinned	Dark-skinned
For place of of work	Urban	Rural
	Indoors	Outdoors
	Office, laboratory, research station	Village, homestead, field
	Accessible	Remote
For time of work	Day	Night
	Comfortable (dry, cool) season	Uncomfortable (wet, hot) season

(Adapted from Chambers, 1983, p.173).

The biases interlock. There is mutual reinforcement between first values, class, gender and ethnic preferences for contacts and clients, and the convenience, comfort, infrastructure and resources which determine places and times of work. Rural development is seen as extending the expressions of the first list into last environments. It takes the form of large exotic cattle rather than improvement to small indigenous goats; export cash crops sold by men rather than improved food crops sold by women; costly high-yielding packages of chemical fertiliser, purchased seed and irrigation for resource-rich farmers rather than cheaper organic technologies for farmers who have to rely on rain; scarce supplies of expensive 'sophisticated' drugs for the few rather than abundant supplies of cheap drugs for the many; urban curative hospitals and surgery more than rural health centres and preventive community health. Almost inevitably, first technologies are most readily adopted by and benefit most those who are least poor; for reasons of scale and cost they are best able to profit from them; for reasons of contact, communication, knowledge and influence, they are most likely to have access to them.

Conversely, the problems and needs of the rural poor tend to go unrecognised. Even today little attention has been paid to drudgery-reducing technologies for rural women in fetching wood, fodder and water, in food preparation, and in cooking. Until recently the diarrhoeas which kill millions of children each year were neglected. Subsistence crops like millets, sorghum, sweet potato and cassava (manioc, tapioca, yucca) have had low priority in agricultural research. Mortality of the young of small stock (goats, sheep, rabbits, hens, ducks and so on); the culture and productivity of indigenous multi-purpose trees; lopping regimes for tree fodders; the value of insects as food; strategies for surviving the worst times of the year; and sequences of disposal of assets to meet contingencies – these are examples of the sort of last realities which have tended to be ignored or accorded little priority by first professionals.

To be sure, there have been some reversals, and the picture must not be overpainted. Institutions have been set up which put more of the last first. Examples include the Intermediate Technology Development Group and others concerned with appropriate technology (McRobie, 1982); the International Centre for Diarrhoeal Diseases Research in Dhaka; the International Crops Research Institute for the Semi-Arid Tropics in Hyderabad; and the International Council for Research on Agroforestry in Nairobi. But even in these, biases can still operate. A technology for millet cultivation can still be relatively capital-intensive or large-scale, and appropriate technology can still sometimes be out of reach of those who need it. Even when research concerns things which are last, the methods, materials, and locations of work can still distance the technology from the poor.

The structure of first thinking

A second level of explanation is in the structure of thinking of first professionals. Linked to values, professional rewards, class attitudes and contacts, convenience, comfort and other first characteristics, are modes of learning and analysis which can be described as first thinking. These are liable to overlook or misinterpret the last. They affect choices of subjects for research, methods of research, interpretations of poverty, development priorities, and the generation and transfer of technology. They are basic to the thinking of most development professionals.

Three orientations or biases of first thinking are:

growth and spread;
science and quantification;
learning from above.

Growth and spread

'First' thinking identifies development with growth and spread. Development is seen as the intensification and spread of economic activity, with commerce, markets, cash crops, employment, roads and railways penetrating, activating and incorporating the peripheries. Most of those who emphasise the negative aspects of this process, and who see underdevelopment as an effect, nevertheless share the view that growth (only in a different form) is desirable and that services (only organised differently) for education, health, agricultural extension, communications and so on, should be pushed and spread into the rural peripheries where so many of the poorer people are to be found. Trickle-down may be largely discredited and few now believe that growth alone is enough. But it is basic to the thinking of most professionals that the growth and spread of economic activity and of services are essential elements in development.

Science and quantification

Reverence for science and its manifest power are part of first thinking. Measurement and quantification are especially valued. Facts with numbers are preferred to facts without numbers. There are several reasons for this: much scientific advance has come from precise measurement; the highest-status professions tend to be those which are strongly mathematical, with fundamental physics at the top; the softer social sciences aspiring to status and respectability have taken refuge in surveys and numbers; the analysis of figures has well-known techniques with which professionals can feel secure; numbers are needed for planners; and for some there is a basic aesthetic pleasure in mathematical manipulations.

Learning from above

Learning and training are organised hierarchically to face inwards and upwards towards those cores where knowledge is most readily generated. Sources of knowledge and learning are seen not in the rural peripheries but in the urban cores, not in rural women and men but in laboratory scientists and university professors. Much 'education' is a one-way transfer of 'knowledge' downwards and outwards. Learning is not horizontal, involving exploration and experience but vertical, from the top-down. In this vertical structure, the first modes of thought and values of the cores are projected downwards by those who have learned them. Rural researchers use their own first categories and thinking in designing questionnaires and imprint alien structures on rural realities. They see and find out what fits their thinking, reinforcing the vertical structure of knowledge. First values, constructs and experience are transferred to last situations and impose meanings on them.

These three orientations – growth and spread, science and quantification, and learning from above – together influence first perceptions of the last. From this perspective, Marxists, dependency theorists, structuralists, and neo-classicists all play variations on a theme. Their paradigms differ in detail but are similar in structure, applying similar core biases to the last. Thus, instead of open-ended empirical investigation of the last being allowed to generate last theory, first theory is imposed upon it. Core or first theories are thus self-sustaining. By imposing their categories and meanings on imperfectly perceived last realities, and by bending or ignoring what does not fit, they fabricate support instead of facing challenge.

The systematic exploration of first misperceptions promises to open up many domains and dimensions. By way of demonstration, two will be examined here: ideas of what the rural poor – the 'last' – need; and the generation and transfer of agricultural technology.

Analysing last needs

Basic needs and basic goods

The World Employment Conference of 1976 convened by the International Labour Organisation (ILO) adopted basic needs as an explicit goal of development planning. Basic needs were defined as having two elements:

- First, they include certain minimum requirements of a family for private consumption: adequate food, shelter and clothing are obviously included, as would be certain household equipment and furniture.
- Second, they include essential services provided by and for the community at large, such as safe drinking water, sanitation, public transport, and health and educational facilities (ILO, 1976, p.30).

A basic needs-oriented policy was also seen as implying participation of the people in making the decisions which affect them. In all countries employment also entered into a basic-needs strategy. Although the objects to be set would vary according to levels of development, climatic conditions and social and cultural values, the concept of basic needs was of universal applicability.

For all its critics, the basic-needs formulation made a useful contribution to development thinking; it focused attention on key issues and on poor people, those whose basic needs were not met. But the question can be asked whether the ideas of basic needs bore the imprint of the urban, industrial and formal sector of developed cash economies, and whether, reflecting first thinking, they neglected or misperceived the needs of people who were rural and poor.

In retrospect, it can be seen that basic-needs strategies did overlook the need for basic goods. First thinking assumes growth and spread, a market and goods available for purchase as they are in the rich world and in most urban areas in the Third World. The original ILO statement emphasised the need for the poor to gain the purchasing power to gain access to goods, tending to assume that the goods would be there. But the ILO basic-needs missions mounted at the invitation of governments in Sub-Saharan Africa sometimes found otherwise. In the rural areas of Zambia and Tanzania in 1980, many basic goods were either not available, very scarce, or very highly priced on the black market. The ILO mission to Zambia found widespread lack of soap, salt, blankets, cooking oil, paraffin, matches and the like (ILO, 1981a, pp.22-4). We are not concerned here with the causes of these shortages. But any doubt that the availability of basic consumer goods is a basic need should be dispelled by the conclusion of the Tanzania mission that 'There seems little doubt that if villagers were pressed to give priorities to their main needs the first place would have gone to the supply of essential consumer goods' (ILO, 1982, p.205). Yet they were not explicitly part of the 1976 statement; in first environments, and in first thinking, supplies of soap, salt, matches, paraffin and the like, are assumed. The reality in some last conditions can be that basic goods are basic needs: as was said to the Zambia mission, 'Without goods, money is nothing' (ILO, 1981b, p.22).

Employment and livelihood

Employment is a first concept, derived from formal sector employment in a job, with a regular salary or wage, at a workplace. The 1976 ILÒ conference was on world *employment*.[2] The Director-General of ILO wrote at the time that the basic-needs approach 'implies that each person available and willing to work should have an adequately remunerated *job*' (ILO, 1976, p.7). The Nigeria Constitution of 1978 included a statement that the State 'shall direct its policy towards ensuring . . . that . . . a reasonable national minimum living *wage* as well as social security benefits would be provided for all citizens'.[3]

Some limitations of these concepts have long been recognised. In his magisterial work on Asian poverty, Myrdal agonised thoroughly over the misleading preconceptions of Western economics when applied to Asian conditions:

> When new data are assembled, the conceptual categories used are inappropriate to the conditions existing: as, for example, when the underutilisation of the labour force in the South Asian countries is analysed according to Western concepts of unemployment, disguised unemployment, and underemployment. The resulting mountains of figures have either no meaning or a meaning other than that imputed to them . . . . The very fact that the researcher gets figures to play with tends to confirm his original, biased approach . . . the continuing collection of data under biased notions only postpones the day when reality can effectively challenge inherited preconceptions (Myrdal, 1968, pp.12-23).

And he called for behavioural studies founded on observations of the raw reality (Myrdal, 1968, vol.2, p.1027), which, for many of the rural poor, is very different. Their concern appears to be less with employment than with livelihood: a level of wealth and of stocks and flows of food and cash which provide for physical and social well-being and security against impoverishment. Most families of small and marginal farmers and of the landless are concerned not with a job or a work-place, but with sustaining and improving a repertoire of activities which will provide them with an adequate and secure level of living around the year. These may include cultivation, keeping livestock; collecting or catching and consuming or processing and selling, common property resources (firewood, charcoal, fish, grass, medicinal plants, wild animals, bamboos, reeds, tree fodders, etc.); casual labour; hawking; seasonal public relief works; seasonal migration; work as artisans (pottery, basket- and mat-making, earthenwork, blacksmithy, weaving, thatching and the like); and many other activities.

Starting from their stance, jobs or employment can make sense for one or more members of a large family if they can be obtained, but the prime opportunity is to strengthen and add to their existing repertoire, raising the productivity of their labour and filling in seasonal gaps when there is little or nothing to do. To better their lot can involve measures quite different from the generation of conventional employment. These include improving the management and productivity of common property resources and of their access to them (forests, common grazing, ponds and lakes, etc.); organisation to raise casual wages or to get better prices and surer markets for produce; seasonal employment programmes which fill in slack periods; and technology to improve the productivity of whatever resources they command.

Poverty and vulnerability

Another pervasive bias in first perceptions of last needs is the stress on poverty to the neglect of vulnerability. Five dimensions of deprivation are poverty, physical weakness, isolation, vulnerability and powerlessness (Chambers, 1983, ch.5). Any of these can be attacked, but first biases stress poverty in the sense of lack of income, to the neglect of vulnerability in the sense of lack of assets which can be realised to handle contingencies.

In three respects, this emphasis on income fits badly with last realities. In the first place, a high proportion of the 'income' of poor rural people is often in kind, for subsistence – especially crops and livestock which they grow or herd themselves. Economists have tried to accommodate this by placing a cash value on subsistence flows. Second, the method fits best with a regular wage or salary income which does not vary round the year – a characteristic of urban, industrial, formal sector employment which contrasts with the variations of rural incomes year by year, and within years, season by season.

Third, the income definition of deprivation overlooks vulnerability to contingencies. This is easily neglected by first professionals. Shielded by state social security, by savings or by other means, they underestimate the importance of contingencies for others less fortunate. But for the rural poor the position is radically different. They are vulnerable to many sudden unforeseeable needs, which may be great or small, or needs which are foreseeable but large. These include social conventions, such as dowry, bridewealth, weddings, funerals and other ceremonies; disasters, such as floods, fires, the collapse of a hut, theft of animals or tools, the death of an animal, a bad year for crops; physical incapacity, such as sickness, accidents, the child-bearing sequence; unproductive expenditure, such as children's education, bribes or investments, where these do not pay off; and exploitation by the rich and powerful.

In many places the costs of such contingencies have risen while the social supports which in the past helped the poor to meet them have weakened. Health treatment which once was cheap, through traditional remedies, increasingly opens up expensive options which impoverish those whose relatives are seriously sick. For those who are peripheral, the costs of transport add to the problems. While costs of contingencies have been rising, the mutual supports of patrons, the extended family, neighbours, and the community have generally been weakening.

Against this background, the income approach to poverty assessment, and the prescriptions and policies which follow from it, do not cover the needs of the last very well. The deprivation of a family is related to vulnerability as well as income. A family with a lower income but with more assets to meet contingencies may be better off than a family with a higher income but fewer assets. Families whose assets are mainly productive are especially vulnerable to impoverishment, since disposal of them to meet a contingency will reduce the family's productive or earning capacity. Government programmes, however, tend to overlook the implications of this point. The Integrated Rural Development Programme in India is an example. It is targeted to households below the poverty line and designed to raise them above it in income, usually through a subsidised loan to acquire an asset. But the asset itself may constitute an element of vulnerability. Milch buffaloes are often provided but they are large and indivisible, that is, they cannot be sold in less than single major units, and if they die all is lost.[4] Poverty, in income, may be reduced while vulnerability to impoverishment is increased. In contrast, recognition of the importance of assets which are small or divisible, which spread risks, and which can be disposed of readily without a conspicuously distress sale, points towards smallstock (goats, sheep, pigs, poultry, rabbits, guinea fowl and so on) and trees, which can usually be cut and sold at any time of the year. With these, income may be raised and vulnerability reduced at the same time.

First and last in agricultural technology

Agricultural research and extension present a case of applying first approaches to last conditions. Parallels could be found in engineering, medicine and other professions.

In the core, or first, model for agricultural research, high-yielding technology is developed by scientists in controlled conditions in agricultural research stations, in laboratories and in greenhouses. The technology is then transferred to farmers through extension organisations. This model worked well in the United States, and was transferred internationally to other countries. The green revolution in wheat in North-west India is its most spectacular success, encouraging attempts to apply it to other conditions. In practice, however, this 'transfer-of-technology' (TOT) model works well only with resource-rich farmers, whose conditions resemble those of the research station. Resource-rich farmers typically have fertile soils, controlled irrigation, tractors or strong draught animals, and good access to credit and agricultural inputs like improved seed, fertiliser and pesticides. They also face relatively low risks, and they produce for the market. Conversely, the TOT model works badly with resource-poor farmers. Typically they have poor soils, either no irrigation or irrigation they cannot rely on, no draught animals, or only weak ones they have to hire, and poor access to credit and agricultural inputs; and they face high risks and give priority to assuring their subsistence food supply. For them the high-input technologies generated by the TOT approach not only do not fit; they may be positively dangerous. In consequence, they do not adopt the new practices, and are then labelled conservative and uneducated. 'We must educate the farmer' is still a common cry among first professionals.

The inappropriateness of the first technologies, such as mechanical cultivation, exotic cattle, purchased inputs including chemical fertiliser and pesticides, for resource-poor farmers has been increasingly recognised. New approaches to agricultural research have been evolved[5] which reverse the sequence of research and start with farmers and farm households and their needs. An attempt is then made to identify or evolve technologies which will satisfy those needs.

Collectively, these approaches put the farm family first, and have been described as the farmer-first-and-last model,[6] which involves four reversals from first to last: explanation, learning, location and evaluation.

1 Explanation of non-adoption of new technologies needs to shift from deficiencies of the farmer and the farm level to deficiencies in the technology and in the technology-generating process, that is, from blaming the last to blaming the first.
2 The reversal of learning entails the transfer of technology from farmer to scientists, with scientists systematically adopting the

role of students of farmers' needs and practices.
3   The reversal of location is from research station cores to farm-level peripheries, requiring research and development on-farm and with-farmer, sharing farmers' conditions, management practices and risks, with research stations and laboratories in a referral and consultancy role.
4   The reversal in evaluation is from judgment of technology by scientists' peers to judgment by farmers. The indicator of success is not the number of professional papers published but the number of farmer adopters. From being peer-oriented, research becomes client-oriented.

The nature of these reversals is summarised in Table 13.3.

First defences: blame, distance and denial

Many professionals find reversals such as these threatening. Conditioned to learn from above and trapped in hierarchical organisations, their reflexes are to look upwards not downwards for authority, information, approval and priorities. But, again and again, the first technologies and categories which they seek to project and transfer do not fit and are rejected by the intended 'beneficiaries'. Faced with this failure, first professionals have three defences, used separately or together: blame, distance and denial.

Blaming the uneducated is the easiest and most automatic, of which many examples could be quoted.[7] Distance is the second defence. Avoiding direct contact prevents the embarrassment of facing discordant views and facts. Such avoidance may be deliberate or involuntary, or some combination of the two. Lack of contact with, and learning from, the rural poor is built into the spatial and other biases of rural development tourism, while the defence of distance from the poor has been reinforced by the poverty of Third World governments, which reduces rural travel by professionals. Denial is the third defence. Bunker Roy[8] has written about the inability of scientists to admit that they can be wrong, especially when a problem they have not foreseen is raised by someone they consider less intelligent than themselves.

Last thinking

The frequency and intensity with which first professionals defend themselves by blame, distance and denial reflects the depth of the threat presented by learning from the last. Part of the threat is the

Table 13.3 Contrasts in learning and location

	First approach Transfer-of-Technology	Last approach Farmer-first-and-last
Research priorities and conduct determined mainly by	needs, problems, perceptions and environment of scientists	needs, problems, perceptions and environment of farmers
Crucial learning is that of	farmers from scientists	scientists from farmers
Role of farmer	'beneficiary'	client and professional colleague
Role of scientist	generator of technology	consultant and collaborator
Main R and D location	experiment station, laboratory, greenhouse	farmers' fields and conditions
Physical features of R and D mainly determined by	scientists' needs and preferences, including statistics and experimental design research station resources	farmers needs and preferences farm-level resources
Non-adoption of innovations explained by	farm level constraints failure of farmer to learn from scientist	research station constraints failure of scientist to learn from farmer
Evaluation	by publications by scientists' peers	by adoption by farmers

paradigm of 'last thinking'. To adopt last thinking, first professionals have to suspend much that makes them feel secure. They have to do a 'flip' and see things from the stance of those who are last, taking hold of the other end of the stick, as psychologists sometimes call it. They have to learn from below instead of from above. They have to accept as teachers those whom they have been conditioned to regard as ignorant and inferior. Instead of working with and for the high-status rich, they have to work with and for the low-status poor. Instead of standing and lecturing, they have to sit down, listen and learn.

More, they have to accept the priorities of the last. These often differ from those of the first. Sadgopal[9] recounts how officials in a dry and barren area in rural India had planned an expensive (first) programme involving exotic cattle and an artificial insemination network. But local landless people, when consulted, suggested afforestation of barren land, and the allocation of contracts for minor forest produce to local small contractors instead of to large outside contractors who took most of the wealth. None of them mentioned a cattle programme, which it turned out was desired only by a few large farmers who would benefit. As so often, first values in a programme meant that the better-off would gain. The priorities of the poor were quite other.

Poor or not, farmers' priorities often differ from those of scientists. In a fertiliser programme in Colombia reported by Ashby,[10] scientists wanted on-farm trials to test the yield-response to different doses of phosphate rock. Farmers wanted to know responses to combinations of phosphate rock with the established last (indigenous, small, dirty, smelly) technology of chicken manure. The resulting research design took and tested the farmers' (last) questions using a conventional (first) statistical method.

There is a clue in this example. It was not a question of either first or last, but of a combination. It would be as foolish to place indigenous technical knowledge on a pedestal, as inherently always superior, as it is to consider modern scientific knowledge the only knowledge. The key is to get the best of both. But because modern scientific knowledge is so powerful, and so profoundly linked with the status and self-importance of first professionals, a major and often traumatic effort is involved in making the reversals needed for balance.

Last thinking entails:

1 Putting first what those who are last want and need;
2 Understanding their situation, resources and problems;
3 Combining these to determine programme and research priorities.

First knowledge can then be used in a referral role, to be tapped and adapted where it will be useful to the last. Putting the last first, and putting last thinking before first thinking, changes the agenda of research and action.

An agenda for research and action

To consult those who are last is the first step in seeking an agenda. In a sense, therefore, this paper should end at this point. To go further is, for me, as a first person, to project. Nevertheless, the argument points towards areas to explore, and these are presented here with the qualification that those who are last in any environment will generate their own, no doubt different, agenda.

Subjects for research neglected because of the structure and biases of first thinking include:

First bias	Neglected last subjects
Growth and spread	Economic decline and retraction from peripheries and their effects on last people Processes of impoverishment
Science and quantification	Indigenous technical knowledge Non-quantifiable qualities Individual household case studies
Learning from above	Methods of learning from the last Psychotherapeutic techniques for introspective insights and making 'last-first' flips
Employment thinking	Strategies for gaining rural livelihoods, including seasonal activities, migration, the use of common property resources, etc.
Poverty defined as low income	Vulnerability, contingencies, and the value and use of assets as buffers, including their characteristics, classification, usefulness, and sequences and manner of use by last people

Last thinking also identifies gaps where technology has not yet been developed between disciplines, professions, and government departments. Existing disciplines, professions and departments have often generated and disseminated technologies which have fitted the capacities of the less poor and have been appropriated by them. The opportunities presented by gaps may also be opportunities for those who are last, since they are as yet unappropriated. New energy technologies are one domain. Another is agro-forestry, involving the interaction of crops, trees and/or livestock. Agro-forestry relationships are familiar to many small farmers but have been neglected by the specialisations of agronomy concerned with crops, forestry with trees, and animal husbandry with animals. In many environments, agro-forestry may present a major opportunity for resource-poor families.[11]

Other research needs are presented by the 'last realities' list on p.307. They suggest many topics such as the unpaid tasks of women, subsistence crops, smallstock, organic manure, and non-timber forest produce, where sensitive research and development should benefit the poor.

These areas of ignorance or former low priority also indicate opportunities for action. There are programmes already designed to put the rural last first. Over the past two decades India has initiated a series of large-scale administered programmes intended for target groups of last people: small and marginal farmers, landless labourers, those who are seasonally unemployed, those in resource-poor areas, harijans, tribals, women and children. There have been successes, such as the Maharashtra Employment Guarantee Scheme, and also many disappointments. For the future, such programmes, in all countries, will be more successful if their design and priorities reflect more accurately the perceived needs and actual resources and capabilities of the poorer.

NOTES

1   This is an edited version of the article 'Putting last thinking first: a professional revolution', published in *Third World Affairs 1985*, Third World Foundation for Social and Economic Studies, London, pp.78-94. The paper was presented to TOES and is reproduced here by kind permission of Third World Affairs.

2   All emphases in this paragraph are Chambers'.

3   Clause 16(2), quoted in ILO, 1981b, q.v.

4   There is, however, an insurance policy as part of the IRDP.

5   Michael Collinson, 'A low-cost approach to understanding small farmers', *Agricultural Administration*, 8(6), November 1981, pp.433–50. Robert E. Rhoades and Robert H. Booth, 'Farmer-back-to-farmer: a model for generating acceptable agricultural technology', *Agricultural Administration*, 11, 1982, pp.127–37 (also available as Social Science Department Working Paper 1982–1, International Potato Center, Aptdo. 5969, Lima, Peru). J.B. Raintree and Anthony Young, 'Guidelines for agroforestry diagnosis and design', ICRAF Working Paper No.6, International Council for Research in Agroforestry, PO Box 30677, Nairobi, Kenya, November 1983.

6   Robert Chambers and B.P. Ghildyal, 'Agricultural Research for Resource-Poor Farmers: the Farmer-First-and-Last Model', *Ford Foundation Discussion Paper*, Ford Foundation, New Delhi, 1984.

7   Anil Sadgopal, 'Between question and clarity: the place of science in a People's Movement', Vikram Sarabhai Memorial Lecture, 12 August 1981, Indian Council of Social Science Research, New Delhi.

8   Bunker Roy, 'Science and the rural poor', *Indian Express*, Delhi, 1 November 1983.

9   Sadgopal, op. cit.

10   Jacqueline A. Ashby, 'Participation of small farmers in technology assessment', Report on a Special Project of the International Fertiliser Development Center, A.A. 6713, Cali, Columbia, 1984.

11   W.R. Bentley *et al.*, 'Agroforestry: a complex system for resource-poor farmers', Paper given at the Indian Society of Tree Scientists' Satellite Session on Agroforestry, Birla Institute of Technology, Ranchi, Bihar, January 1984.

14 TRADE AND THE MULTINATIONALS

Any concern for development, whether in rich nations or poor countries, or from the point of view of the World Bank or of Another Development, leads straight to consideration of trade: its quantity and quality; free trade and protectionism; its impact on poverty; and the degree to which it permits freedom of choice as to the path of development. In the past free trade has been almost universally extolled as the bringer of progress and prosperity. Today that assumption is increasingly being questioned, and alternative trading strategies, although as yet in embryonic form, are waiting in the wings.

'ALTERNATIVE TRADING STRATEGIES'
by Frances Stewart and Ejaz Ghani

In a sense the world is at a trading cross-roads today: there is a certain retreat from free trade, which might be intensified, or it could be reversed. This is true both for developed countries and developing countries. Developing countries are currently under considerable pressure from the international community (the IMF, the World Bank and the major donor countries) to move towards freer trade, but their financial crises reinforce protectionist tendencies, while giving the international community considerable leverage to secure liberalisation. This is a time, therefore, when a great number of countries are facing choices in trading strategy, based on three broad options: free trade; autarchy; and selective trade.

Free trade

One option is to aim to reverse the move towards protectionism, and promote freer trade. This option may be interpreted as involving freer trade for all, both the developing and the developed countries; or it might consist in freer trade for just some category, such as developed countries, and not developing countries; or it might be selectively operated by particular countries. The argument then becomes somewhat complex because what is best for any one country or group of countries depends in part on what policies other countries are adopting. From a developing-country perspective, genuinely free access to developed country markets would offer an enormous extension of markets: all middle-income countries, which have already established an industrial capacity, would be likely to benefit, as their lower wage-costs would enable them to undercut developed countries in many lines. The sheer size of developed country markets, which account for nearly two-thirds of world markets, means that developed-country markets offer significantly more potential in some respects than other possibilities, more, for example, than trade between Third World countries. Genuinely free trade extended to primary commodities, such as sugar and grain, would benefit a number of the poorer developing countries as well.

If such a policy led to a faster growth of manufactured exports among developing countries, it would be likely to raise incomes per head, as suggested by developments over the past few decades.[1] It would also, despite claims sometimes made to the contrary, be likely to be accompanied by some reduction in poverty. However, there are a number of qualifications that need to be made before concluding that this option offers most countries the best prospects.

One concerns political realism. The developed countries have resisted free trade in agricultural products and in textiles, even in the apparently free trade era of the 1950s and 1960s. While the new moves towards protectionism might be halted, it is extremely unlikely that totally free access would be permitted for Less Developed Countries' (LDC) exports. It is more likely that rich countries will seek to impose free trade on LDCs, while at the same time protecting the most vulnerable of their own industries. This sort of 'free trade' gives a particularly bad deal to LDCs.

Another qualifying factor is economic vulnerability. Even with totally free access to developed country markets, LDCs would become even more vulnerable to fluctuations in the world economy, since an increasing proportion of their markets would be external. Experience during recent world fluctuations has suggested: (a) that countries mostly dependent on exports of primary products, such as many African economies, are very vulnerable to world fluctuations,[2] more so than more inward looking countries; and (b) that countries which have been successful exporters of manufactured goods are better able to defend themselves against world fluctuations than less export-oriented economies, because their potential to adjust, into new markets, and into import substitution, appears to be high. South Korea and Taiwan provide examples. However, large countries, such as India and China, which do not trade or borrow a great deal internationally, are probably the least vulnerable, but this is not a realistic possibility for small economies.

From the point of view of reducing vulnerability, then, it appears that reduced dependence on primary products is desirable, but an increase in manufactured exports need not increase underlying vulnerability.

A third qualification concerns the need to protect infant industry. In order to compete in the world economy, countries have to build up a strong competitive base in manufactures. To do this requires time, both for industry as a whole and for particular industries. Hence some protection is essential; in the early stages of industrialising countries, the whole industrial sector needs protecting from competition from abroad; in the later stages, selective protection is necessary while a country builds up a capacity in particular industries. Consequently, developing countries must retain the ability to impose some protection. If the price of free access to developed country markets is completely free trade, then it will only benefit those countries which have already established themselves as industrial economies – the so-called Newly Industrialised Countries (NICs) – and will perpetuate underdevelopment in the less developed economies.

A fourth major qualification concerns dependence. It is often suggested that increased trade with developed countries also involves increased dependence. This may be variously defined:

dependence on markets;
dependence on Multi-National Companies (MNCs);
dependence on international banks;
dependence on advanced country technology.

We have discussed market dependence above. Whether or not a free trade strategy involves more dependence on MNCs and on international banks depends on the strategy adopted, and also on the alternatives considered. For example, many import-substituting countries, with high levels of protection, have used the multinational company as the vehicle of development and are highly dependent on it. It is also the case that many of these same countries became heavily indebted to the international banks in the 1970s. Consequently, an import substitution (IS) strategy does not necessarily mean reduced dependence. Moreover, the countries exporting manufactured goods – Taiwan, South Korea – have not been so closely involved with MNCs as some of the IS countries. Taiwan has not borrowed heavily, although South Korea did. So we may conclude that dependence on MNCs and international banks is neither a necessary nor a sufficient condition of an export-oriented strategy, nor of an IS strategy, since countries like India and China did not make use of MNCs nor borrow heavily.

However, a trade oriented strategy does involve technological dependence. This is a serious disadvantage. An open, trade-oriented strategy inevitably sucks countries into the trends of technology change, which are determined by the world technological leaders. This has some heavy costs.[3] Technological dependence occurs because it is necessary for countries to keep up with product changes, which means keeping up with technology change, if they are to compete internationally. Moreover, the result of importing freely is that domestic consumers follow internationally determined taste patterns. As time passes, countries are forced to adopt increasingly capital-intensive technologies to maintain competitive standards. Consumption patterns tend to switch to more and more sophisticated goods for high-income groups. There is a lack of availability of goods appropriate for low-incomes: poor consumers tend to adopt lop-sided consumption patterns, with expenditure on inappropriate luxuries, and inadequate expenditure on goods to meet basic needs.

The pressures towards competitive efficiency engendered by a free-trade strategy may lead to an increasing scale of production, and an increasing specialisation of work. Alternative styles of production – in industrialised countries as well as Third World countries – are much more difficult to justify economically, if international competitiveness is regarded as essential. Even where some appropriate technology, or some alternative in advanced countries, is proved viable in international markets, its viability could be short-lived unless it is subject to continuous technological change to maintain its competitiveness, since it will be competing with advanced technologies that are changing most of the time. While it is possible and desirable to devote resources to improving the efficiency of alternative technologies, perpetual pressure to do so could push the technical change in the very direction it was initially desired to avoid: towards increasing scale, specialisation and capital intensity. An example is the Intermediate

Technology Development Group's development of an egg-tray packing machine. The initial innovation was for a very substantial reduction in scale and capital cost, compared with the conventional alternative. Since then, all improvements to this machine have gone in the opposite direction: towards larger scale and heavier capital cost, because of competitive pressures. The final result is that the 'improved' egg-tray machine is hardly more appropriate than many inappropriate technologies.

The technological dependence engendered by free trade thus makes it more difficult to adopt appropriate technologies and to promote appropriate consumption patterns. In addition, it involves the country in very heavy costs to pay for the technology; these can amount to as much as 20 per cent of export earnings. Suppliers of the technology may also impose restrictions on the recipient countries, for example as to markets and use of the technology.

These are heavy costs, but how far they can be avoided depends on the alternative strategy. If the alternative is import-substitution using MNCs, imported technology and producing the latest products, then just as much technological dependence, with even worse effects in terms of choice of technique and inappropriate consumption patterns, would occur than with an export-oriented policy. This is not a hypothetical alternative, but one actually adopted by many countries. On the other hand, if the alternative is to adopt appropriate techniques, and produce and consume appropriate products, one comes to very different conclusions: the costs involved may be less efficiency and lower levels of output, but there would be important gains in terms of the creation of employment opportunities, a more even distribution of income, and a satisfaction of the needs of the poor.

A trade-oriented policy requires continual adjustments to a changing international environment, entailing increased competition from other nations, new technologies, and so on. Some countries may be less good at such dynamic adjustments than others, and therefore do less well; some may regard these adjustments as having a very heavy cost in terms of continual change and tension. Both these types of countries might well prefer to grow more slowly, with less rapid change. Countries which have already reached a reasonable income level, with all their people living well above some poverty floor, might prefer to choose a slower rate of growth involving less adjustment. This seems to be the implicit choice of many in the UK, for example. But it is difficult to make this choice in a free-trade environment, because the country adjusting less fast will tend to do progressively worse in international trade. Moreover, consumers tend to want to keep up with the most recent consumption goods; to do so, while growing less fast than others, means diverting resources away from some basic goods and services, especially in the public sector, such as health, education and public transport. Hence this is a difficult choice to make; and one that almost certainly requires a retreat from free trade. For poorer countries, it is an even more difficult choice because population increase requires continual change, just in order to maintain per capita incomes.

The final problem with a free trade approach lies in the political sphere. There can be strong political opposition to trade liberalisation, and strong support for restrictions, coming from all those elements in societies – usally special interest groups of both capitalists and workers – who would lose. The political opposition derives partly from a fear that there will not be alternative opportunities. If there are not, then the policy will be highly wasteful, simply resulting in increasing unemployment of resources. With good macro-policies, this should not be the case, and the long-run opportunities should be more productive; but in many countries, and at the level of the world as a whole, these 'good' macro-policies cannot be assumed. Opposition may also be inspired by a dislike of change, and of the heavy costs imposed on particular groups. Whatever the precise reasons – good or bad – political opposition is important because it may mean that it is quite unrealistic to assume that many countries will adopt a thoroughly free-trade set of policies. This brings us back to the very first objection: unrealism.

Autarchy

The main reasons for adopting this option – a complete retreat from trade – are:

1 To protect employment;
2 To reduce vulnerability to international fluctuations;
3 To permit the development and adoption of appropriate technologies.

These justifications apply to both developed and developing countries.

The disadvantage of this strategy is that it is likely to lead to lower levels of income for the countries concerned, and levels which become increasingly reduced relative to the rest of the world. Essentially, the option would involve giving up the advantages, in productivity gains, of international specialisation and economies of scale. These losses would be particularly great for small economies, and for economies lacking a large technological capacity. In a way this strategy has been followed by China, but that country is now turning away from it because of the costs involved; India, too, which had until recently taken a very selective approach to trade and technology, and had tried to develop its own self-reliant capacity for production of goods and technology, is also now opening the economy more to foreign technology and, to a lesser extent, specialisation in trade.

Trading blocks and selectivity

There are obviously a huge number of variants within this option. Basically, the reasons for selecting this approach may be twofold:

1 Because a free-trade policy is not possible, given the restrictions in trade and finance in the world trading system;
2 To permit countries to enjoy some of the advantages of trade without some of the disadvantages.

In practice, at this moment, both reasons apply. The many restrictions in being, especially in payments, mean that many countries in payments difficulties *cannot* afford to import because they have no ready access to foreign exchange. If two or more of such countries get together and offer swap arrangements, they will be able to expand their markets and their imports, resulting in increased incomes and employment for them all. The growth in countertrade[4] is a way in which this coincidence of interests among countries in difficulties may be realised in selective trading arrangements. For example, Brazil and Nigeria have made arrangements whereby Brazil exchanges machinery for Nigerian oil. Indonesia buys the refined oil products it needs, like kerosene and diesel, from Singapore, in exchange for other oil products where it has marketing difficulties, such as low sulphur waxy residue. Malaysia has bought two naval patrol boats from South Korea in exchange for crude oil, refined palm oil, textiles, timber and electrical products.

These are examples where the necessities of the international crisis have led to a variety of bilateral trading arrangements. But there is also a more positive case for trading within blocks of rather similar economies.

Trading within Southern economies, all seeking to develop and use appropriate technology and products, permits joint development of appropriate technology. This provides these technologies with some competition from similar economies, but does not force them to compete with advanced-country, inappropriate technologies. In addition, each economy may benefit from specialisation.

In a similar way, richer countries which wish to adopt alternative patterns of production and consumption may do so jointly, permitting joint development of the relevant technologies and modes of production, but not competing with the rapidly-changing, advanced technology. If there is to be any hope of controlling the direction and pace of technological advance, a joint approach of this kind will be essential.

Low- and middle-income countries which are aiming to use and master advanced-country technology still require infant-industry protection in the early stages. Yet if the smaller economies protect on a national basis, very high costs are likely to follow, because of the economies of scale and of specialisation in these methods. Joint trading blocks, with free trade within them but restrictions against competition from the rest of the world, may permit countries to benefit from specialisation and from some competition, and to produce a variety of goods without being swamped by competition.

Trading blocks may assist smaller countries to simulate the conditions of the larger economies, and may be organised in a number of ways.

Regional arrangements between economies of similar levels of development is one possibility. Problems often emerge in these arrangements due to differences in stages of development so that one member of the group may come to dominate the whole. These problems are compounded by political problems between neighbours. However, among developed countries these arrangements have been very successful (e.g. the EEC); and in some cases among developing countries also (e.g. the Latin American Free Trade Area).

Another method is trans-regional arrangements between economies at a similar stage of development; the countertrade examples above were of this type. More generally, payments unions involving a number of countries in the Third World would promote this type of arrangement.[5]

A third possibility is North-South blocks; the EEC arrangement with Lomé countries is an example, as are the US arrangement with the Caribbean countries and the old UK arrangements with the Commonwealth countries. These arrangements may benefit the richer countries, providing protected trade outlets; the poorer countries may secure a greater share of finance. Normally, the arrangements have not permitted less developed countries better market access to any significant degree. If they did, then these arrangements would offer the particular group of countries some of the advantages of market access to developed countries discussed above. Their advantage over more general free-trade arrangements would be (a) protecting the lesser developed countries compared with more developed ones (e.g. Africa in the EEC as compared with Asian products); and (b) they might be easier to negotiate than more general arrangements, but history does not give this hypothesis much support.

Arrangements also exist between countries of similar degrees of dynamism. Examples are trade arrangements between the more dynamic NICs and the more dynamic industrialised countries; and between the less dynamic developing countries and the less dynamic industrialised countries. This sort of arrangement would have a major advantage for countries in the 'less dynamic' category, permitting them to enjoy some of the advantages of specialisation and trade without forcing them to accept the pace of change of the most dynamic countries. But there are obvious practical problems about this sort of arrangement. How would more or less dynamic countries be defined? Would they agree to accept this categorisation? Would they consist of countries which make sensible trading partners, geographically and economically? Mostly, the less dynamic countries are trying to become more dynamic, so they would not wish to be tied indefinitely to a more slow-growing group. Moreover, they are also the most resistant to trade, even with non-dynamic partners; note, for example, the resistance of the UK to imports from Bangladesh. This type of trading arrangement would suit a changed political environment, where some countries have consciously chosen to pursue an alternative type strategy with respect to economic development – that is, a strategy involving a conscious decision to turn away from modern competitive technology and a fast changing economic environment, in favour of smaller scale, more satisfying and less changeable methods of production, with alternative patterns of ownership and control, and alternative patterns of consumption. In this context, the decision to pursue an alternative development strategy would have to come first. The trading strategy would then follow naturally.

In conclusion, the pros and cons of any strategy depend very much on the alternatives being considered. There is a strong case for arguing that trade between rich and poor countries tends to perpetuate a particular pattern of technological dependence and technical change that is undesirable. However, trade restrictions by themselves do not prevent this occurring. Many economies have followed restrictive policies, but combined them with heavy technological dependence, financial indebtedness, inappropriate patterns of technology, and extreme inequality. *Trade restrictions only permit more appropriate patterns of development in a political context in which this type of development strategy is favoured.* This type of political economy is very rare and cannot be assumed. In its absence, trade is actually likely to lead to a better situation in terms of employment opportunities, income distribution and independence, than heavy restrictions.

In general, trade should be the servant of development, not its master: that is to say the general strategy of development should be chosen first, including the desired technology, income distribution, mode of production, etc., and a trading strategy then chosen which fits in with this, rather than the trading environment dictating the choice of development strategy. In practice, this requirement is often not realised. One reason, of course, is that trading patterns influence the political economy of a country and consequently the choices it makes.

There are very strong grounds for favouring a *selective* approach to trade, especially one that promotes trade among countries at a similar stage of development and with similar objectives. This selective approach should permit countries to realise their objectives better, as compared both with an autarchic approach and a free-trade approach.

A selective approach is in fact emerging, to some extent, from the present crisis. It is not the most rational of selective approaches, in many cases; it needs investigation and rationalisation, but it may offer countries some potential for realising their development objectives.

• • •

So the choice of trading strategy, as so much else in economics, is actually a political matter, determined by those in power for the benefit of their constituency. Such a conclusion quite contradicts the attitude expressed by the then World Bank President, Tom Clausen, at a recent conference on world development, who ingenuously declared, 'I have no political case to argue. The only altar I worship at is sound economic management.'[6] There is, of course, a tendency for establishments to assume that their analysis is somehow more objective than opposing views and for believers of all kinds to consider that theirs is the only true faith, so we should not be surprised at such statements from the high priests of economics. For those who do not accept such determinism, the political as well as the economic implications of the international market are becoming increasingly clear.

'DELINKING FROM THE WORLD MARKET'
by Wolfgang Sachs

As questions of resources and the environment become increasingly prominent in public life, a new distinction is gaining importance. On the one hand are the environmentalists with their focus on overhauling industry and the welfare state, through remodelling and diversifying the range of products and services needed to meet the demand for cleaner and healthier products, and for less costly and more flexible social services. They are often able to stem the waste of resources and the inflation of the welfare apparatus, and enjoy an increasing acceptance, even in the centres of power; they are the avant-garde of eco-capitalism and self-help welfare.

On the other hand, those who might be called eco-decentralists insist on inverting superstructures and revitalising the self-reliance of local communities on a historically new level of knowledge and technology. They believe that it is only through the multiplication of self-reliant local economies, their subsistence made affluent through intelligence and information, that people will no longer be rendered economically redundant and vulnerable to the vagaries of international competition.

Local self-reliance has long been perceived solely in terms of conservation of resources. But it should be viewed more broadly as an inversion of market relations on two levels: first, to downscale the range of exchange relations so as to strengthen the local economy, closing more economic circuits within the regional space; and second, to stimulate unpaid work and a whole new variety of non-economic activities. In other words, a different model of economic security is proposed, one where wealth is not derived from specialising in export for distant markets, and sending the earned money to distant producers in order to import a large percentage of food, energy, materials, insurance, health care, but rather from reducing people's involvement in the national and international economy and providing more locally. In the long run, what we might call a market-enhanced self-reliant economy should enable people to live gracefully with less money, less consumption and less wage-labour, because an infrastructure which is geared towards self-sufficiency will compensate for losses in income.

These considerations may sound abstract, but all sorts of initiatives – striving for free clinics, community gardens, traffic-free zones, local radios, ecological agriculture, new-style cooperatives – implicitly converge on that vision. The fragile life of such initiatives leads us to ask whether the time-honoured conflict about who controls the means of production should not be rephrased as a conflict between centralized capital/labour and local autonomy. But perhaps this is going too far, and at this stage we should rather be asking whether the project of self-reliance really does have a place in today's context.

The present crisis did not put the dominant classes to sleep. On the contrary, microchips and gene splicing, satellites and cable systems, this new generation of technologies allows the elite of yesterday again to raise the flag of growth and progress. The protagonists of high tech have a vocabulary much like the boulevard press reporting from the Olympic Games: 'Germany (or France or Italy) is falling behind, we are overtaken by foreigners, let's hurry to join the race, to catch up and to take the lead!' What is at stake, in fact, is the dominance of the world market. With Japan and the Pacific Basin on the rise, the rush into super-industrialism can be seen as an attempt to shore up the crumbling empire of the West.

Super-industrialism attempts to pull the old industrialism out of the mud. Resource-intensive growth is suffocating under its own weight; plundered resources, inflated administrations and all sorts of waste have enormously increased the external costs of production and are stifling the economy. What had once given rise to the 'smoke stack economy', namely the transformation of fossil energy into labour and materials, is today leading to its decay, through the loss of capital caused by high energy costs and ecological destruction.

Micro-electronics and biotechnology claim to be able to rescue industrialism through a new age of efficiency by reducing the scale, the costs and the energy-intensity of a product, while industry-bred micro-organisms replace the petro-chemical base of many products, from pesticides to pharmaceuticals. The industries of tomorrow offer the glamorous prospect of turning today's heavy industry into a subject of interest only to industrial archeologists, while facilitating a new style of clean, efficient growth. To put computers in cars, to replace secretaries with word-processors, to monitor electronically the resource-flow in a factory, this is the expensive diet they prescribe to society to get rid of the overweight acquired by the old industrial expansion. The implicit ideal of the microelectronics revolution is a well-tuned society where all technical and social processes are electronically monitored so as to continually adjust them towards an efficient society without friction and waste.

This diet, moreover, will soon be prescribed to the service industries as well, in particular education and medicine. The prophets of the information age envisage learning programmes on home computers, supposedly rendering teachers and schools superfluous, and bio-medical devices for self-examinations that are said to make resort to doctors and hospitals less necessary. Service through administration-based stuff, we are told, will largely be replaced by self-service through technology at home, a solution to trim down the welfare state which will please the ministers of finance, since clients will have to pay for the devices and programmes themselves. It will also delight industrialists, since the needs for learning and caring can also finally be transformed into a demand for marketable commodities.

Much of this is still in its embryonic phase. However, what seems to be emerging are the outlines of a less polluting and material-saving capitalism, where the resource base is being changed (biotechnology, ocean research), where the cleaning up of environmental wastes is becoming a source of profit, and where non-material needs, hitherto not marketed, are being commercialized (communication technologies). A new generation of industrialists, planners and scientists are working hard to find a way out of the crisis while taking society more firmly into their hands. A capital-intensive, administration-intensive and research-intensive solution to the crisis of growth is looming on the horizon. But what nation will take the lead in modernizing its economy, what country will take the upper hand in a restructured world economy? These are the unsettling questions for politicians and economists who believe in the super-industrialist vision. How is the concept of self-reliance related to these concerns?

The single most important argument used against the eco-decentralists time and again, is that they collaborate to marginalise their country economically. When every other argument fails, the stick of declining international competitiveness is used to silence the protagonists of fundamental change. Recent debates in Germany provide us with telling examples: even the government recognised that the fast-breeder reactor promised to be an economic disaster, but it nevertheless decided to complete construction so as not to 'fall behind' in technological know-how; a moratorium on genetic research because of uncontrollable consequences, as requested by the Greens, was dismissed with laughter, since Germany could not afford to 'drop out' of the international biotechnology race; cable-TV is being installed against the will of the majority of the population to secure a domestic mass market for the export-oriented electronics industry; and finally a speed limit on the free-ways – the only immediately effective measure to reduce acid rain – was denounced as economic suicide since Germany is the leading world exporter of high-performance cars. The world market is used like a guillotine to cut off all discussion on the social use of certain products and technologies. The trouble is, however, that it is an argument with some validity.

Even within the rich countries, gearing the economy towards world market competition has become the categorical imperative which governs domestic development. Enterprises and nation-states are caught up in dynamic competition which renders every participant dependent on everybody else's choices. No country today seems to be capable of controlling its own development; the differences between countries are only a matter of degree. Germany has more influence than India but less than Japan. The European countries in particular, for better or worse, are condemned to rush into the super-industrialist race. In 1981, 26 per cent of the German, 22 per cent of the British and Italian and 15 per cent of the French GNPs were exported abroad. To renounce the competitive effort amounts to sacrificing not only the economic well-being, but also the political loyalty of their citizens. Capitalists in fear of lost markets, governments in fear of dropping revenues, workers afraid for their jobs, and retired people worrying about their pensions are rallying behind the trumpeters for higher exports: a powerful coalition for growth at whatever cost.

From the eco-decentralist perspective, it would seem to be necessary to scale down export-import relations for two reasons: first, to decrease the vulnerability of even the richest society to crises and collapses abroad, and, second, to open up a whole new range of choices in shaping domestic development. If there is no other way to ensure the economic and political ability to achieve these objectives, then we have to finally abandon the idea of a homogeneous, unified market from the village to the global level, where the factors of production can be freely moved around, and to conceive of restrained markets, where political norms limit the scope and the range of market activities without emasculating their potential for innovation and liberty. Following this line, two related concepts must be considered: protectionism for the sake of self-reliance and reconversion for the sake of export 'disarmament'.

In Third World countries, it appears that the magic question for a self-reliance strategy may be phrased as follows: how to avoid buying in the North? Imports from the North create consumption without inducing growth, and force export production to expand to pay for the increasingly expensive imports. Export production is the stronghold of the national power elite, and diverts valuable resources in terms of land, capital and technology away from the needs of the population at large. Selective dissociation from the world market, on the other hand, aims at escaping the notorious squeeze between falling export prices and rising import prices by reducing imports and focusing on the domestic production of non-sophisticated capital goods, and by reducing exports in order to free resources tied up in catering to the rich countries in the North. Two basic reasons – one more conventional, the other more radical – for such dissociation are: (a) there seems to be no other way to lay the groundwork for a self-sustained growth, which will eventually turn all strata of the population into market producers and consumers; and (b) it seems to be the only path open to a society that aspires to create its own style of development according to its own culture, rejecting a homogeneous norm of development imposed from the outside.

The cosmopolitan idea of one world based on free trade has fallen to pieces. It rested on the doctrine of comparative advantage, claiming that the general well-being would be enhanced if each nation specialised in doing the things at which nature and history had made it relatively most proficient: coffee beans from Guatemala in contrast to pharmaceuticals from Holland. This might be true from a static point of view; in the long run, however, it is the country offering more complex products which benefits by internalising the spin-off effects of more sophisticated production: pharmaceuticals stimulate research and complete processing technologies, whereas coffee beans don't! Thus the weaker party finds itself at a cumulative disadvantage, a downward spiral which can only be overcome, even under the condition of 'equal' terms of trade, by partially retreating from the free-trade arena.

There are even signs that in the future many Third World countries will simply have no other choice than to delink from export-import relations with the rich countries. Microelectronics and biotechnology are going to worsen drastically the bargaining power of many Third World countries *vis-à-vis* the North. To put it bluntly, the Third World is increasingly becoming redundant for the reproduction of industrial systems in the North. Their position as supplier of raw materials is weakening as the 'information economy' of the North advances, since the historical mission of the chip is precisely to relieve industrialism from dependence on squandering fossil and mineral resources. Furthermore, their position as supplier of agricultural products is threatened as biotechnology renders nature – climate, soil, maturity cycle – less and less important in the face of technological know-how. Finally, their position as suppliers of cheap labour is deteriorating as the automatization of production in the North progresses, reducing the relative importance of wage costs; the 'new' international division of labour has already grown old.

I can so far only conclude that delinking from the North (and reinforcing linkages within the South) is the only possible approach for many Third World countries seeking to defend themselves economically, to reassert themselves culturally and to transform themselves socially. Such a vision is implicit in the various grass-roots struggles in Third World countries. Delinking means, in essence, the ordering of less goods and the borrowing of less money from the North, and the withdrawing of resources from exporting goods and interest payments to the North.

Grass-roots aspirations both in the North and the South in fact have similar objectives: to move from outer-directed to inner-directed societies. Maybe it is overstating the case to claim that grass-roots efforts in both North and South complement each other, but a shift in paradigms has nevertheless occurred; we envision the global space no longer in terms of one, highly integrated world, but in terms of many self-reliant and only loosely interdependent worlds. Given the present state of affairs, thinking along these lines implies a major shift in emphasis about what development requires. Development then becomes a matter of negative rather than positive action: what not to do acquires more importance than what to do. Damage limitation is the first imperative in both the North and the South, in order to effectively enlarge the space for self-reliant action. It is only by damage limitation that alternative efforts can effectively gain ground.

Several development-action campaigns in the last few years have already pointed in that direction: campaigns against arms export, pharmaceutical corporations and shipping of pesticides imply a deliberate curtailing of dangerous exports. As the bias towards producing power plants, automobiles, machines, seeds, etc., for export may be constraining inner-directed development in the Third World and distorting it in the First World, these industries could also become candidates for 'disarmament'. Shrinking exports, however, mean that well-being has to be secured with a less market-oriented economy in order to compensate for the loss of jobs, savings and revenue. This is precisely the move towards the self-reliance economy mentioned earlier. It seems that the eco-decentralist approach could indeed make a significant contribution to supporting the Third World.

Import-substitution is the second point at which domestic and international concerns seem to converge, in particular, of course, with regard to agricultural products. Europe, after all, benefits from 30 per cent of the food exports from the Third World. It is the world's largest importer of food products, importing 40 per cent of the foodstuffs it needs for its livestock. Limiting the imports of food and non-food products would affect consumption styles in the North and would require a restructuring of European agriculture along more ecological lines and towards a smaller scale. It would also help food-exporting Third World countries towards food autonomy.

Import-substitution in agriculture and export-reconversion in industry seem to be the corner-stones of a European delinking strategy, needed to confront world market relations, which are pernicious at home and exploitative abroad. Perhaps the slogan 'acting locally, thinking globally' is laying the groundwork for such a change.

● ● ●

To this consideration of delinking a postscript can be added concerning international debt. Nothing is locking Third World countries into the international market so securely as their burden of debt repayments. If debtor countries seek to repay their debt in full, which they can do only with great hardship to their people and repeated rescheduling, they will remain utterly dependent on the North for the foreseeable future. Yet, as William Clark projected in *Cataclysm* (Clark, 1984), a purposeful default on the part of debtor countries, which led to economic sanctions from the North, would cause even more hardship to Southern peoples, unless Third World countries had developed a greater measure of self-reliance, individually and collectively, than at present. There is a 'Catch 22'. The Third World needs to develop self-reliance in order to walk away from the debt burden, but it cannot develop such self-reliance while it is shouldering this burden. The vicious circle can be broken only through co-operation and solidarity for mutual self-reliance between all those countries of North and South who believe that the transfer of resources from poor to rich must not continue indefinitely.

From the international market it is but a short step to consideration of multinational or transnational corporations (TNCs). The economic power of TNCs is quickly rehearsed:

> TNCs now control one-third of gross world production; 40 per cent of all world trade is intra-firm (i.e. between firms within the same TNC), and in some sectors, notably commodities, up to about 90 per cent of trade is controlled by TNCs . . . in 1980 the top 380 firms had more than 25,000 foreign affiliates and combined total sales amounting to more than $2,700 billion.[7]

Not only do these figures represent a large increase in turnover and market-share over the last two decades, but there has been a significant shift in the role and profile of TNCs as well. Two of these trends are:

1 The formation of oligopolies, where whole industrial sectors are dominated world-wide by a handful of firms.
2 The formation of conglomerates, where a single TNC has interests in a wide variety of unrelated activities. Cross-subsidisation then enables the TNC to transfer profits from strong to weak market areas and undercut competition in the latter.

These two TNC trends alone have enormously enhanced TNC power *vis-à-vis* national governments, the labour force and consumers. National governments seeking foreign investment from TNCs increasingly have to offer them concessions on taxes, wages, working conditions and rights of labour organisation, product safety and environmental controls. They can also come under tremendous pressure from TNCs, which can take the form of direct confrontation and subversion, as in the case of ITT and Allende's government in Chile; huge lobbying budgets for influencing policy-makers; or transfer pricing, which credits the profits rightfully accruing in one country to the TNC's operations in another.

Trade unions find that their national organisations are quite unable to monitor, far less have an effective input into, transnational corporate strategies, which often seek to play the work-forces of different countries off against each other, backed up by the option of locating their operations in a country which represses organised labour altogether.[8]

Consumers are often faced by a choice that is almost exclusively between the products of different TNCs, and are subjected to ever more sophisticated advertising and marketing techniques to make them want or 'need' their products. The hard-sell of artificial baby milk in Third World countries was a particularly telling illustration of this point.

Attempts to restore the balance between TNCs and the people and countries that are affected by them have taken many forms but, despite individual successes, are still largely uncoordinated and in their infancy. They include the following overall approaches, which can, of course, be pursued individually or together:

> Publicity and education. Some TNCs are sensitive to their image and overall reputation for social responsibility, and wide publicity for anti-social activities can, at the very least, cause embarrassment. It has also led to change.

- Consumer boycotts and campaigns, in which people are discouraged from buying the goods or using the services of the targeted TNC. The campaign against Nestlé for its baby-food policies is estimated to have cost the company $1 billion in sales over five years, while Barclays Bank is estimated to have lost $5 billion through the campaign against its strong links with South Africa.[9]
- Corporate campaigns, including shareholder actions, which seek to target the 'supply-side' of the TNC concerned, its sources of finance and power, on which pressure can sometimes be brought to bear.
- International union organisation. While being quite slow off the mark, national unions are now beginning to rise more effectively to the challenges of international organisation, and the International Trade Secretariats, which link unions in similar industries world-wide, have a particularly important role to play in this work. Grass-roots links between workers for the same company in different countries are also perceived as important. In recent years, workers in Ford, Unilever, Merck, Talbot, Kodak and Cadbury have all organised across frontiers in response to threats to their livelihoods in one country.[10]
- International Codes of Conduct. Several of these have now been proposed or adopted, but their effect so far has been limited. The 1981 World Health Organisation/UNICEF Code of Marketing Breast Milk Substitutes, the first code of its kind, was an immensely important precedent, although it is still not universally observed. More general codes have been proposed by the International Labour Organisation, the Organisation for Economic Co-operation and Development, the United Nations Commission on Transnational Corporations, the European

Community's 'Vredeling Directive' and the United Nations
Conference on Trade and Development. It can be seen that
there is no shortage of perception of the need for such codes.
The TNC response to these codes of conduct is, first, to seek to
ensure that they are voluntary – the Vredeling Directive is the
only one that has any chance of becoming law in the near future
– and, second, to water down their recommendations as much
as possible. The US Council for International Business, the
lobby for US TNCs, operates almost as an 'alternative' United
Nations, surveying all the issues on the world scene through a
comprehensive network of committees, chaired by senior
corporate executives, and initiating prompt, effective action
against perceived threats to TNC interests.[11] Thus the
Vredeling Directive was seriously weakened during its passage
through the European Parliament. To counter such a lobby,
those interested in strengthening and implementing the Codes
of Conduct will have to muster formidable political clout.

The above strategies are obviously important in the immediate
struggles against the abuses of corporate power, but they do not
in themselves strike at the root of TNC power in general. The
sources of this power are threefold: TNCs offer goods and
services that consumers will buy; TNCs offer employment
opportunities and investment, albeit sometimes on harsh conditions, on which people and nations are dependent; and TNCs
offer potentially unlimited returns on investment. Confrontations
with TNCs on single issues may win important victories against
heavy odds, but the only way in which real progress on the wider
issues of democracy, accountability and social responsibility can
be made is by tackling these sources of power directly.

So individual consumer campaigns, for example, need to be
broadened into a generalised awareness of TNC products across the
board and a determination to buy other, and ideally local, products
where possible, in order to contribute to the regeneration of the
local economy. Similarly, countries need to reduce their dependence on TNCs by fostering their own self-reliance, reducing
their dependency on the international market and therefore on
TNC technology and productivity.

International trade, too, can be carried out at a higher level of
awareness, as the successful UK company Traidcraft has shown.
It imports a wide range of goods from developing countries,
helping to establish small industries in deprived communities and
ensuring the fairness of the wages and working conditions of the
producers. Consumers who buy these products, advertised in a

full-colour mail-order catalogue, rest assured that their purchasing power is assisting self-help community development. As Traidcraft says in one of its brochures: 'If you make sure more of your ordinary spending goes through channels that are working for justice in trade, it can make a big difference to developing countries.' There is no reason why this attitude should be confined to trade or to developing countries. *People's ordinary spending is probably their most powerful potential tool for social change.*

As far as investment is concerned, clearly investors need to become aware of the human, social and environmental consequences of their investments, and act to ameliorate these. People and politicians also need to start questioning whether it is still appropriate that the return on capital investment is potentially unlimited. Shareholders, after all, incur limited risk when they invest. It is not unreasonable to infer that such limited risk should only yield a limited return.

This last point, of course, brings us back to co-operatives, for a limited return on share capital is one of the six co-operative principles. Thus it is no surprise that the International Co-operative Alliance has made representations to the UN Commission on TNCs, recommending a limited return on investment.

> Company law in developing countries might be modified in such a way as to require the subsidiaries of multinational corporations to pay an unlimited return on capital to the parent companies for a specified period only – such as five or ten years. After the end of this period, they would pay a limited return, based on asset values at that time. [12]

A reform such as this could be just the first step in a programme to transform TNCs into co-operatives. Sometimes such a suggestion causes the wry smile indicative of political impossibility, but in fact the technical means for such a transformation have already been elaborated. [13] Political will, of course, is another matter, but there seems to be no intrinsic reason why, if the political will can be mustered to implement codes of conduct, it should not be directed as well towards co-operative transformation. Co-operation is, as we have seen, the largest socio-economic movement in the world and already commands broad political support. TNC structures would actually convert very readily into the sort of large co-operative federations which already exist. At its deepest level, the TNC debate is about who should benefit from these giant enterprises and at what social costs. The possible transformation of TNCs into co-operatives offers unique and important insights into that debate and is an idea that should be injected into it at the highest possible political level.

The other possible TNC transformation that sometimes evokes a wry smile from hard-bitten campaigners is that the TNCs will themselves adapt under the influence of changing social attitudes and public pressure, so that they come to put social considerations on a par with financial ones. Yet, as with co-operative transformation, such a possibility should not be dismissed out of hand.

'THE ROLE OF CORPORATIONS'
by Willis Harman

A shift in underlying beliefs

Underlying the well-documented recent strengthening, in most industrialized countries, of 'inner-directed' values (ecological, humane, spiritual) and the corresponding weakening of economic and status values, is a more subtle but more fundamental shift of *beliefs*. This shift is away from the confident scientific materialism of the earlier part of the century, and toward some form of universal transcendentalism. This is evident in the sales of 'New Age' books and the proliferation of meditation workshops, yoga classes, holistic health centers, metaphysical groups and trans-personal therapies which we witness on all sides. It is reflected in a new tolerance in the scientific community for explorations of human consciousness, unconscious processes, creativity and intuition, effects of mental states on healing and on the body's immune system, and so on. Furthermore, it has a parallel in the developing world in the growing reservations about Western materialism and the reassertion of the validity and truth in native cultural and spiritual roots.

With the vogue of positivistic science in the earlier part of this century, there was a deliberate turning away from those creative factors and forces of the human psyche which have been treasured by most societies, and enshrined in their varied religious traditions. The spiritual meanings usually associated with such inner discoveries and experiences were debunked, and serious exploration of spiritual and creative insight was discouraged.

The resurgence of interest in research on consciousness in the scientific community is well summarized in the following quotation from Nobel Laureate Roger Sperry's key-note paper in the 1981 *Annual Review of Neuroscience*:

Social values depend . . . on whether consciousness is believed to be mortal, immortal, reincarnate, or cosmic . . . localized and brain-bound or essentially universal . . . The new interpretation (in science) gives full recognition to *the primacy of inner conscious awareness as a causal reality* . . . Recent conceptual developments in the mind-brain sciences, rejecting reductionism and materialistic determinism on the one hand, and dualism on the other, clear the way for a rational approach to the theory and prescription of values and to a natural fusion of science and religion.

No scientists of comparable stature have previously made such a claim, and it would be naive to imagine that Dr Sperry's colleagues are in full agreement. Nevertheless, there existed in 1984 signs suggesting that such a shift, at least as profound as the Copernican revolution, could be underway. The practical significance of this may not be apparent – no more immediately apparent than was the ultimate significance of the discoveries of Copernicus and Galileo to the first few astronomers and philosophers who came to understand them.

Modern industrial society, like every other in history, rests on some set of largely tacit, basic assumptions about *who we are, what kind of universe we are in, and what is ultimately important to us.* Scientific materialism, which so confidently set forth the answers to these questions a couple of generations ago, is now a dying orthodoxy. Its basic premises are being replaced by an expanded empiricism that includes increased faith in reason guided by deep intuition, possibly of a transpersonal sort. In other words, a respiritualization of Western society is taking place, but one more experiential and non-institutionalized, less fundamentalist and sacerdotal, than most of the historically familiar forms of religion. With this change comes a long-term shift in value emphasis and priorities, which, it is becoming increasingly plausible to argue, will enact a metamorphosis of industrial society comparable to the shift from medieval to modern society in Western Europe. This, in turn, will subject to radical change the whole concept of economics and the role of the corporation. To anticipate the nature of this change, it will be useful to examine the longer-term trend.

A long-term evolutionary trend

If we try to look past the fluctuations of history and discern an underlying long-term trend, at least of Western civilization, there seem to be four chief components.

One is increasing *awareness* – from the restricted awareness of the first humans to the self-conscious and future-oriented awareness of the modern man and woman. One aspect of this trend has been the increasing self-awareness of growing numbers of people moving from tribal consciousness toward individuation; the other has been increasing awareness in the form of codified knowledge. The former has been fostered in society through literature and the arts, philosophy, spiritual disciplines, and more recently by psychotherapy. The latter manifests in our ever-growing scientific comprehension of the world, and in the free search for guiding beliefs and values.

A second component trend is increasing *mastery* – where the word is chosen to connote both power and wisdom. The intellectual capabilities of human beings have enabled them to devise, use, and continually improve tools and technologies, leading to the mastery of the environment in ever-widening scope. But the reach for mastery is also embodied in the various religious, philosophical, and ethical systems by which societies have guided behavior and conducted their affairs.

Increasing *liberation* constitutes a third component evolutionary trend. There can be little doubt that modern men and women are in many senses more free than our neolithic ancestors. This freedom has been gained in part through the advances of science and technology. But the broader goal of the liberation quest includes political, economic, and psychological–cultural freedom. The goals of liberation are exemplified in the political ideal of personal liberty within a lawful order, in the economic ideal of private enterprise, and in the cultural ideal of individuation within community.

The final important dimension of the long-term evolutionary trend of history is *democratization*. The democratic aspiration is exemplified in the social ideals of free education and the public dissemination of scientific knowledge, in the economic ideal of equality of opportunity, and in the political ideals of equal justice under law and full participation in government.

The vitality of the West has been largely inspired by these four ideals. Our most boasted accomplishments include the understanding of science, the power of technology, the vitality of private enterprise, and the fairness of democratic government.

Yet something has gone wrong. Upon reflection it becomes apparent how far the industrial world has departed from the long-term evolutionary trend. *Awareness*, in its institutionalized form, has become reduced to utilitarian science in the service of technology. *Mastery*, guided largely by narrow economic values and an exploitative ethic, has become a manipulative technology in the service of unrestrained economic growth and inescapable militarism. *Liberation* takes a back seat in a private-enterprise system which has been dominated by large corporations and world financial institutions, characterized by absentee ownership, preponderantly influenced by the financial bottom line, and relatively irresponsible to societal issues; politically, liberation is muted by the subtle coercion of large bureaucracies. *Democracy* has assumed the character of an autonomous military-industrial-financial complex, insensitive to citizen concerns about the well-being of the planet and of future generations. In the Third World, the number of functioning democratic governments continues to decline, and political 'liberation' is found to fall far short of providing economic and socio-cultural liberation.

If indeed there seems to be some sort of fundamental transformation of industrial society taking place, or even if the change is assumed to be taking place much more gradually, the motivation for changes stems from the deviation from this evolutionary trend. Thus the direction of change is probably fairly well indicated by these long-term trends. With regard to *awareness*, we can anticipate a continuation of the burgeoning interest in developing psychological and spiritual awareness, and the emergence of a nascent science of human consciousness, heretofore largely neglected. As for *mastery*, we can anticipate increasing concern with strengthening commitment to the humane, ecological, and spiritual values necessary to mediate the awesome economic, technological, and military power of modern industrial societies. At the individual level, there will be increasing emphasis in finding and pursuing an appropriate life-work, a pattern of life's meaning, as contrasted with a job in the mainstream economy.

As to *liberation*, the 'right to personhood' evident in the various human rights and minority rights movements will strengthen This will be true particularly in the women's movement, which seems likely to have a profound effect on prevailing values, bringing in a balance between nurturing, cooperative, 'feminine' values and presently predominant aggressive, competitive, exploitative, patriarchal 'masculine' values. One of the places in which the strengthening liberation emphasis will manifest is in a new type of entrepreneurship in both profit and non-profit sectors, creating small organizations in which the highest priority goal is providing opportunities for fulfilling lives.

In the Third World, there will be a further strengthening in the attitude that liberating, wholesome development must be built on indigenous cultural roots; it does not come from discarding one's native origins in favour of an alien, Western industrial culture. The ultimate homogenization of the global culture in some sort of 'Western industrial monoculture' appears less and less likely. The newer thrust is toward an ecology of diverse cultures and more decentralized societies, in spite of – or perhaps in reaction to – the increasing interlinking through global communication networks. Finally, some sort of economic *democracy* seems to be in the wind – something beyond the 'industrial democracy' found today in northern Europe.

The emerging role of the corporation

If the foregoing observations about societal trends are accurate and if there is a likelihood of a wrenching transition period between paradigms, several conclusions follow.

The characteristics of the transition period (say, the next couple of decades in the industrialized world and longer in the Third World) are quite different from the characteristics of the post-transition period. During this probably somewhat chaotic time, rational planning will be a weak tool. The key task for management will be to stay on top of, and ride, the wave of change and not be inundated by it. A critical issue here will be the perceived *legitimacy* of the corporation. The American Declaration of Independence defines legitimate government as that which 'derives its just powers from the consent of the governed.' In the period toward which we move, the large corporation which affects the lives of millions of people will be held to a similar standard. Only those corporations which 'derive their just powers from the consent of the affected' will be perceived as having legitimacy. This implies a level of fiduciary responsibility far beyond that assumed by even the most progressive large corporations today.

A few corporations have already adopted, and committed themselves to, corporate goals which essentially put contribution to meaningful lives and societal well-being ahead of profits to shareholders and other financial goals. This order of priorities could be much more characteristic of corporations in the future than it has been in the past.

Transnational corporations will have a critical role in the developing countries. Corporations based in the newly industrializing countries will be formidable competitors to those based in the OECD countries. In the less developed countries, the foreign-based corporation will be viewed with mixed feelings, depending on the extent to which its activities help the host country to achieve *its* goals, which may not be modernization at the most rapid pace feasible.

The corporation will be increasingly judged on 'multiple bottom lines', social in addition to financial, and the public will be quick to recognize social-responsibility 'window-dressing' and to distinguish it from genuine change.

Non-profit corporate organizations will probably play an increasingly important role as the societal motivation-and-incentive pattern shifts. They will find their niche in performing many tasks whose accomplishment would be beneficial to society, but which are not performed well by bureaucracies and agencies of the public sector. (Examples include beautification, care of the elderly, education of the gifted.) Some of these non-profit organizations may be very localized and small, but some will be large international organizations, such as the Red Cross.

The problem of discovering and following a development path toward a viable global future and sustainable global society presents what is probably the greatest challenge in history. It involves some very rough waters and risky passages in the transition years just ahead. Large corporations could comprise a mammoth reluctant drag impeding necessary societal changes. Or if we, the public, who give and withhold their legitimacy, so choose, they could transform themselves into creative contributors toward the building of a new future.

NOTES

1 In the full paper by Stewart and Ghani for TOES 1985, this section on Trading Strategies followed a detailed statistical analysis of trading patterns and developments in the recent past.

2 See G.K. Helleiner, 'Outward orientation, import instability and African economic growth: an empirical investigation', forthcoming in S. Lall and F. Stewart, eds, *Reality in Development, Essays in Honour of Paul Streeten*, Macmillan, London, 1986.

3 This whole issue is discussed in detail in F. Stewart, 'Technical change: are we in control?', TOES, 1984.

4 See *Financial Times Supplement*, 6 February 1985. The term 'countertrade' covers all trade arrangements where there is not a direct and 100 per cent exchange of goods for cash. It is now estimated to account for at least 8 per cent of world trade.

5 See the proposal for a Third World Money in F. Stewart and M. Stewart, 'A new currency for trade among developing countries,' in *Trade and Development*, 2, 1980.

6 Quoted by Walter Schwartz in 'Development as illusion' in the *Guardian*, 16 July 1985.

7 David Ward, 'The rise and rise of transnational companies' in *Science and Public Policy*, vol.12, no.2.

8 See *Striking Back – workers' organisation against multinationals*, Counter Information Services, London, 1984, and *Meeting the Corporate Challenge*, TIE Report 18/19, Transnationals Information Exchange, Amsterdam, 1985.

9 *Meeting the Corporate Challenge*, op. cit. p.30.

10 *Striking Back*, op. cit. pp.9–15.

11 'The rise and rise of transnational companies', op. cit.

12 *Multinational Corporations and the International Co-operative Movement*, International Co-operative Alliance, London, 1972.

13 See, for example, Paul Derrick, 'Transnational corporations and co-operative principles', in *Review of International Co-operation*, September 1979, or Shann Turnbull, 'Multinationals: fading out with a profit', *Development Forum*, June 1974, United Nations, New York, p.3.

CONCLUSION

This may be the end of this book, but, for the New Economics and the Living Economy which it informs, it is still very much a beginning. All those involved in new economic thinking along the lines described here are only too aware of how much work still needs to be done on the theory before it is fully practicable, and how much practical experience is still necessary before the theory can be fully detailed. Thus we can expect the theory and practice of the New Economics to progress together: practitioners will innovate and draw on the insights of the theoreticians; the thinkers will come up with new ideas and generalise from creative practical initiatives; the networks linking the two will keep both informed of, and in touch with, the other. The addresses in Appendix 2 are listed in order to aid that process.

Individuals will no doubt already have identified aspects of the New Economics which they relate to, or which they may wish to incorporate into their own personal lives; but perhaps it might be useful in winding up to draw out some of the man points of the preceding chapters which relate to governments or other organisations, in order to indicate how easily work on their development could be incorporated even into the present institutional framework. In many cases the reforms entail building sensitively on what already exists, rather than embarking on a course that is totally new. The following ten-point agenda for the development of the New Economics is not exhaustive, nor are the points in any particular order. They have been chosen because of their immediate practicability and are in no sense utopian wishful thinking. Rather, they represent a realistic action plan for achievement in the 1980s.

THE NATIONAL ACCOUNTS

Resource accounting The ten-year experience of the Norwegian Government in this field would prove invaluable to any other government which wished to become more aware of its natural resource base. The establishment as a matter of course of a Resource Statistics Section alongside other government statistical agencies, with a brief to develop a 'capital' side to the national accounts, is simply years overdue.

Adjusted National Product It is almost impossible to find an economist who will personally defend the use of GNP as an indicator of economic progress. Yet, as a profession, economists acquiesce in such use with hardly a murmur. It is time they took up this issue with vigour and intellectual honesty, and that those who advise politicians at any level dissociated themselves from the use of GNP as an indicator of success or failure. There is no shortage of economists with the technical proficiency to compute, within the space of a couple of years, an Adjusted National Product as described earlier, given the resources and political will. It would be a giant stride forward for sound economic management.

WORK, JOBS AND ECONOMIC RECOVERY

Reviving the local economy Many local authorities in the UK and many cities in the US have already turned their attention to consideration of their local economies. In Britain, experience over the past few years has shown that, by a careful analysis of local resources, local industries and local conditions, jobs can be created at a fraction of the cost of cumbersome, top-down regional development strategies. In the US, municipalities are increasingly acting to stem the waste of local resources (see Morris, 1982). Putting the British and American experience together, and combining it with policies to support the *informal* local economy, we could at last start to arrest the decline of inner cities and begin their regeneration on a scale to match their problems.

Financing local economic initiatives David Cadman and James Robertson, members of the TOES Steering Committee, have recently completed a major report on this subject for the EEC and OECD. The local financial institutions, which it recommends, could be established at once on an experimental basis in several different sorts of community. New standards for efficient investment in local economic development are waiting to be set by elaborating appropriate criteria and through sharpening our awareness of the social and financial benefits which such investment could yield.

Enabling public expenditure All public expenditure is subject to rigorous and regular assessment, but not in terms of enablement or dependency-creation. Starting to evaluate public expenditure along these lines would take a great conceptual change, but would be perfectly practicable thereafter. It would permit a major shift from the delivery of services to dependent clients to enabling people to meet more of their needs from their own resources. While especially relevant to work, such an evaluation could also particularly yield cost-saving investment in health, housing and education.

Basic income guarantee Western systems of social security are under severe strain, giving the arguments for a basic income guarantee new cogency. From being widely dismissed as being eccentrically simplistic a mere decade ago, this idea now has powerful advocates. The government that commissioned an exhaustive study with wide-ranging public discussion of this theme would be showing both vision and political good sense.

HEALTH PROMOTION

The public desire for health rather than sickness services is amply evident in many countries, as is shown by the new concern with diet, fitness and a generally improved lifestyle. Yet governments continue to focus on medical provision which is never sufficient, because of the sickness-generating products and processes which they permit. The first national health service to focus on *health* will be politically popular and financially affordable, unlike the spiralling budgets of the sickness-oriented services that are now the norm.

REAL AID

The massive world-wide response to Live Aid shows that public opinion is aching for a solution to world poverty. At the same time, it is clear that such a solution will not come about through inappropriate injections, however large, of foreign aid, technology and expertise. But an inordinate return could be obtained from the redeployment even of existing, small aid-budgets to support sound, sustainable projects rooted in the communities of developing countries. Multiplying local equivalents of the Kenyan Green Belt Movement a thousand times throughout Africa would be development indeed. It would probably cost less than one big dam.

TRADE FOR SELF-RELIANCE

Despite the free-trade rhetoric, protectionism is gradually becoming the order of the day. Although much of it is still a blinkered, nationalistic protectionism, based more on political expediency than a desire for greater self-reliance, this trend has a hopeful aspect. Out of it may come the end of an oppressive trade regime and the ability of countries to choose their own pace and direction of development. The time is ripe for experiments in trade for mutual self-reliance, through which countries help to liberate one another from today's exploitative trading patterns. Such trade could become the co-operative way to self-determination.

INTERNATIONAL CO-OPERATION

The final point on this agenda is, perhaps, the most elusive. There are some who say that it will take another world war to rekindle the spirit which founded the United Nations and which has crumbled as global problems have intensified, instead of being reinforced. Yet we must never forget that, whatever the problems, their solutions are amply available to the international community, given co-operation. The tantalising fact about the Economic Summit series is that the leaders round that table *could* decide, as The Other Economic Summit has urged them to do, to set a programme in train that would achieve health and food for all on this planet by the year 2000. At London, Bonn and Tokyo they did not so decide. But the possibility remains.

So, however much still needs to be done, much has already been worked out. The impasse in which conventional economics finds itself is not, after all, a cul-de-sac. The new directions in which future wealth is to be found and secured are in fact quite clearly defined. There can be no reasons for not pursuing them with vigour other than ignorance, faint heart or contrary vested interest. If this book has done something to enlighten the first and encourage the second of these conditions, then it will also have helped to undermine the third, and it will have succeeded in its aim.

The New Economics is taking shape. Conceptually and practically, it is already within our grasp. We have the brains, the technology, the resources. Increasing numbers of people now share its values and attitudes. It already exists in the lives of those who live and work, not only for their own enrichment and personal development, but also in co-operation with and with consideration for others, society at large, and the planet itself.

When this awareness becomes the norm and is reflected in economic theory and practice at all levels, then the Living Economy will have arrived. And, in the broadest sense of the word, humanity will be the richer for it.

APPENDIX I
THE OTHER ECONOMIC SUMMIT CONFERENCE PAPERS, 1984 AND 1985: DETAILS OF CONTRIBUTORS

The conference papers of TOES 1984 and 1985 can be ordered from TOES, 42 Warriner Gardens, London SW11 4DU.
Price: 1984 papers £15
      1985 papers £15
Please add 20% for postage outside the UK.

Edward Barbier
The potential for reviving economic growth: the political economy of resource misallocation (1984)

Edward Barbier is a graduate of Yale University and the London School of Economics. In 1981 he wrote a series of reports on the environmental approaches to employment creation, *Earthworks*, published by Friends of the Earth. Currently he lectures in economics at the Polytechnic of the South Bank and is studying for a Ph.D. at London University.

David Bateman
The economic implications of a shift to organic agriculture (1985) (with Nic Lampkin)

David Bateman is Professor of Agricultural Economics at the University College of Wales, Aberystwyth. Together with Anne Vine, he was responsible for a survey commissioned by the Ministry of Agriculture, Fisheries and Food, looking at Organic Farming Systems in England and Wales, which was published in 1981.

Ela Bhatt
Piece-rate workers' attempts towards self-reliance (1985)

Ela Bhatt is the founder of the Self-Employed Women's Association of India. For her work with this organisation she was one of the joint winners of the 1984 Right Livelihood Awards (the 'alternative' Nobel

Prizes). In 1985 she was awarded Padmashri, the highest honour the Indian Government can bestow on one of its citizens.

David Cadman
Financial futures or *Money as if people mattered* (1984)
David Cadman divides his time between being a Fellow of Wolfson College, Cambridge, and a property market analyst. His published works concern property investment and development in the UK and, more recently, post-war growth of financial institutions, the future of saving and investment and finance for local enterprises.

Roy Carr-Hill
Measuring health and human activities (1985) (with John Lintott)
Roy Carr-Hill is Senior Research Fellow in Medical Statistics at the Centre for Health Economics attached to York University. He has been involved in research on the development, elaboration and use of social indicators since he wrote *Indicators of the Performance of Educational Systems*, whilst working as a consultant for the OECD. His relevant publications include *Social Indicators and Basic Needs, Who Benefits from Which Numbers?* and *The Political Choice of Social Indicators.*

Robert Chambers
Professional thinking and rural poverty (1985)
Robert Chambers is a Fellow of the Institute of Development Studies at the University of Sussex. He has practical and research experience in rural development. He has worked in Kenya, Botswana, Sri Lanka and India, and has been a consultant on rural development in other countries of Africa and Asia. He is author of *Settlement Schemes in Tropical Africa* (1969), *Managing Rural Development* (1974) and *Rural Development: Putting the Last First* (1983). He has recently returned from three and a half years with the Rural Poverty and Resources Group of the Ford Foundation in India, and is currently writing on strategies for rural development in India.

Herman Daly
The steady-state economy: alternative to growth-mania (1984)
Herman Daly is Alumni Professor of Economics at Louisiana State University. He is the author of very many articles in professional journals and anthologies, as well as of several books, including *Economics, Ecology, Ethics* (1980) and *Steady-State Economics* (1977). He has served as a consultant to the Ford Foundation, World Bank, World Council of Churches, and Joint Economic Committee of Congress.

Guy Dauncey
The new local economic order (1984)
Guy Dauncey is a self-employed writer and broadcaster and author of several books, including *Nice Work If You Can Get It* and *The Unemployment Handbook* (1983). He is a founder member of the British

Unemployment Resource Network (BURN) and is currently writing a book to be called *Beyond Unemployment*.

Len Doyal
The politics of human needs (1985) (with Ian Gough)
Len Doyal studied philosophy in the United States and Britain. He teaches political philosophy and the philosophy and politics of science and technology at Middlesex Polytechnic in London. He has published papers on a range of topics which concern the theory and politics of human needs.

Peter Draper
Economic policy as if people mattered: towards health-promoting economic policy (1985)
Peter Draper is a Cambridge medical graduate. After clinical work he specialised in community medicine. He is a Fellow of the Faculty of Community Medicine and an Emeritus Consultant in Community Medicine to Guy's Hospital. From 1975-84 he was the Director of the Unit for the Study of Health Policy at Guy's Hospital Medical School, where he developed his interest in the wider environment, including economic policy, and how it affects public health.

John Elkington
Industrial growth points for a sustainable economy (1984)
John Elkington was Editor of ENDS Report and was then Managing Director of Environmental Data Services (ENDS) Ltd. He is the author of many books, including *The Gene Factory* (Century, 1985) and *The Poisoned Womb* (Viking, 1985) and is the Editor of Biotechnology Bulletin. He was also Rapporteur of the Industry Review Group during preparation of the Conservation and Development Programme for the UK.

David Fleming
Paying for the steady-state economy (1984)
David Fleming has spent the whole of his working life in business and gained an M.Sc. in economics in 1983. He is currently on an award from the Economic and Social Science Research Council, doing a Ph.D. in economics at Birkbeck College, London, and is economic adviser to the Soil Association.

Johan Galtung
Towards a new economics: on the theory and practice of self-reliance (1985)
Johan Galtung, a Norwegian by birth, has had an international academic career spanning thirty years and encompassing a score of visiting professorships to universities in every part of the world. Project Co-ordinator for the United Nations University from 1977-81, he has also been a consultant to most of the major United Nations agencies, and to many other international bodies. He is a Board Member of the

Stockholm International Peace Research Institute (SIPRI) and is currently Visiting Professor in the Department of Politics at Princeton University.

Susan George
Let them eat special drawing rights: world debt, the IMF and the poor (1985)

Susan George is a Senior Fellow of the Institute for Policy Studies/Transnational Institute, Washington DC and Amsterdam. She is the author of several books, including *How the Other Half Dies: the Real Reasons for World Hunger* (Penguin, 1976), and has served as a consultant to UNESCO, the United Nations University and the Economic Commission for Europe of the United States.

Ejaz Ghani
Trade strategies for development (1985) (with Frances Stewart)

Ejaz Ghani has degrees from Jawaharlal Nehru University, Delhi, and Oxford University. He is currently working on trade issues as a D.Phil. student in Oxford. He has also worked as a consultant for the ILO.

Ian Gough
The politics of human needs (1985) (with Len Doyal)

Ian Gough studied economics at Cambridge. For the last twenty years he has taught and researched in the fields of social policy and political economy at Manchester University. Author of *The Political Economy of the Welfare State*, he has lectured in many different countries, including a year as Visiting Economics Professor at the University of California, Berkeley. He is currently completing a book on human needs with Len Doyal.

Anila Graham
International dimension of development, north/south issues (1984)

Anila Graham is an Indian economist who has been an adviser to the Indian Government both in India and England. For nine years she was on the Secretariat of UNCTAD (United Nations Conference on Trade and Development) and is now Director of Economic and Development Research Ltd. Her publications include *Break Down the Barriers, International Liquidity and the Developing World, UNCTAD – an Agenda for Development and Recovery.*

Trevor Hancock
Towards a healthier economy: health-based indicators of economic progress (1985)

Trevor Hancock is a community physician and an Associate Medical Officer of Health in Toronto, Canada. An early member of the UK Ecology Party before moving to Canada in 1975, he is now an active health futurist and founding member of Paradigm Health. He was also the organiser of a recent conference in Toronto, 'Beyond Health Care', that examined the health implications of a wide range of public policies. He has been a leading member of the Green Party in Canada since its inception in 1983.

Willis Harman
Future of the earth – the role of corporations (1984)
Willis Harman was until recently senior social scientist at Stanford Research Institute International of Menlo Park, California, and is now President of the Institute of Noetic Sciences. Publications emanating from his sixteen years full-time 'looking at the future' include a number of papers on trans-industrial society and one book, *An Incomplete Guide to the Future* (1979).

Fred Harrison
Land tenure – a general theory of conflict resolution (1984)
Fred Harrison is a graduate of the universities of Oxford and London and is currently writing a Ph.D. thesis on land tenure systems. He edits *Land and Liberty*, a bi-monthly journal of economic and political reform in land ownership. He is author of *The Power in the Land* (1983).

Hazel Henderson
The indicators crisis: towards post-economic policy tools for post-industrial societies (1985)
Hazel Henderson is an independent, self-employed futurist, author of *Creating Alternative Futures: the End of Economics* (Putman, New York, 1978) and *The Politics of the Solar Age: Alternatives to Economics* (Doubleday, New York, 1981). She serves on the Editorial Board of *Technological Forecasting and Social Change* (Elsevier, NY and Amsterdam) and on the Advisory Board of the Calvert Social Investment Fund of Washington DC. She is also a Director of the Worldwatch Institute of Washington DC and adviser to the Cousteau Society and the *Futures Research Quarterly* of the World Futures Society . She currently directs the Alternative Futures Program at the University of Florida and hosts a series on public television.

Roefie Hueting
Results of an economic scenario that gives top priority to saving the environment instead of encouraging production growth (1984)
Roefie Hueting is Head of the Department of Environment Statistics of the Netherlands Central Bureau of Statistics. He is the author of *New Scarcity and Economic Growth* (1980) and numerous articles and papers on environmental issues in Dutch and English.

Tony Humm
The economic effects of the arms trade (1985)
Tony Humm was widely experienced in commerce prior to undertaking an academic career. After working in insurance, the oil industry and retailing, he became self-employed, restoring antique English furniture. As a mature student, he took a modular degree at the City of London Polytechnic, majoring in economics. He subsequently gained an M.Sc. in economics at Birkbeck College, where he is currently engaged in research, focusing on tracing the economic impacts of military expenditure.

Ilona Kickbusch
Health promotion – programme development in the World Health Organisation's Regional Office for Europe (1985)

Ilona Kickbusch comes from West Germany and is the European Regional Officer for Health Education, based in Copenhagen, for the World Health Organisation.

Nic Lampkin
The economic implications of a shift to organic agriculture (1985) (with David Bateman)

Nicholas Lampkin is a postgraduate student in the Department of Agricultural Economics at the University College of Wales, Aberystwyth, whose work is concerned with the economic implications of conversion to organic farming systems. The first year of his research was spent at the Department of Alternative Agriculture, University of Kassel, West Germany, under Professor Dr Hartmut Vogtmann.

Christian Leipert
Economic growth and its social costs: on the need for an adjusted indicator of net consumption and for a comprehensive statement of 'defensive expenditure' – expenditure undertaken to protect society and the environment against damage and other forms of deterioration induced by economic activities (1985)

Christian Leipert was born in 1944 and from 1965-1970 studied economics and sociology at the universities of Hamburg and Berlin (Free University). From 1975-82 he was Assistant Professor in the Economics Department of the University of Augsburg. Since 1982 he has been a Fellow of the International Institute for Environment and Society of the Science Centre, Berlin. He is the author of three books and has had numerous articles published in journals and readers.

John Lintott
National accounting and beyond (1985)
Measuring health and human activities (1985) (with Roy Carr-Hill)

John Lintott teaches economics and statistics at a number of higher education institutions, and has been involved in social indicator research since working for the OECD in the mid-1970s, from which he went on to do a Ph.D. at Birkbeck College, London, on the history of national accounting. He is an active member of the Radical Statistics Group, with whom he has collaborated on pamphlets about social indicators and the statistics of the arms race. He and Roy Carr-Hill are producing a pilot version of an alternative to *Social Trends*.

Wangari Maathai
The Green Belt Movement: building blocks for sustainable development (1985)

Wangari Maathai, the first female professor in Kenya, is Professor of Veterinary Anatomy at Nairobi University. She is also Chairperson of the National Council of Women of Kenya and founder of the Green Belt Movement. In 1984 she was joint winner of the Right Livelihood Award, the 'alternative' Nobel Prize.

John McKnight
Demedicalisation and the possibilities of health (1985)
John McKnight is Professor of Communication Studies and Associate Director of the Center for Urban Affairs and Policy Research at Northwestern University in Evanston, Illinois, USA. Co-author, with Ivan Illich, of *Disabling Professions* (Marion Boyars), he has devoted much of his life to working with neighbourhood associations and studying their popular approaches to problem solving. These studies have focused on health, crime, housing, learning and finance.

Christine MacNulty
Future health needs (1985)
Christine MacNulty read mathematics at London University and took several courses in Engineering Administration and Psychology of Management at George Washington University and American University. She is now Managing Director of Taylor Nelson Monitor Ltd. Prior to this she was Manager, Europe, for SRI International's Strategic Environment Center. Co-author of a book on industrial applications of forecasting techniques, she has also written many papers on scenario development and social change. She is a regular lecturer at several business schools.

Manfred Max-Neef
Human-scale economics – the challenges ahead (1984)
Manfred Max-Neef is a Chilean economist, founder and Managing Director of the Centre for Study and Promotion of Urban, Rural and Development Alternatives (CEPAUR) in Santiago. Before this, he was a Visiting Professor in a number of American and Latin American universities, and he has also worked for the Pan American Union, Food and Agriculture Organisation and the International Labour Organisation. He has written extensively on development alternatives and in 1983 was awarded the Right Livelihood Award for his practical and theoretical contribution to a new economics.

Anne Miller
The economic implications of basic income schemes (1984)
Anne Miller is a Lecturer in the Department of Economics at Heriot-Watt University, Edinburgh, and in recent years has been developing her long-standing interest in the reform of social security and personal taxation.

Ward Morehouse
Economic justice in the next economy – strategies for universalising capital ownership (1984)
Ward Morehouse is Chairman of the Intermediate Technology Development Group of North America, and President of the Council on International and Public Affairs. Author of a number of works on the role of technology in economic and social change in industrialised countries

and the Third World, he is the editor of *The Handbook of Tools for Community Economic Change* (1983).

Howard Newby
Agriculture and the future of rural communities (1985)
Howard Newby is Professor of Sociology and Co-Director of the Economic and Social Research Council's Data Archive at Essex University. His main research areas have included stratification, rural sociology and community studies, on which his publications have included *Community Studies* (Allen & Unwin, 1971, with Colin Bell), *The Sociology of Community* (Frank Cass, 1973, co-editor) and *Doing Sociological Research* (Allen & Unwin, 1977). For a number of years he has researched social relations in rural England and other advanced industrial societies. His books in this field include *The Deferential Worker* (Penguin, 1977), *Property, Paternalism and Power* (Hutchinson, 1978) and *Green and Pleasant Land?* (Penguin, 1979).

Ken Penney
Aspects of local economic self-sufficiency (1984)
Ken Penney is a Lecturer in Environmental Economics at Exeter University, and is a founder of ECO 2000 Educational Trust, a scheme to train the unemployed in the job creating aspects of alternative technology. He lectures and writes on, as well as lives in, an economically self-sufficient community.

Michael Phillips
What small business experience teaches about economic theory (1984)
Michael Phillips is a former Vice-President of the Bank of California and organiser of the Mastercharge credit card system. He is co-founder of the Briarpatch Network and author of *The Seven Laws of Money* (1974) and *Honest Business* (1982).

James Robertson
What comes after full employment? (1984)
Health creation, wealth creation and useful work (1985)
James Robertson works as an independent writer and speaker on economic and social change. His best-known book is *The Sane Alternative* (Robertson, 1983). His most recent book is *Future Work* (Temple Smith, 1985). Between 1968-73 he directed research for the British banks and, before that, worked in the Cabinet Office and other Whitehall Departments. He has advised the World Health Organisation (Europe) on Scenarios for Lifestyles and Health, and reported in 1985 to the EEC and OECD on Finance for Local Employment Initiatives.

David Ross
Making the informal economy visible (1985)
David Ross is a social economist, with graduate degrees from Alberta and Duke Universities, who has worked with the Federal Government

Cabinet Office, the OECD in Paris, the Canadian Council on Social Development and the Vanier Institute of the Family. He has taught in the schools of economics, public administration, and social work at Windsor, Ottawa, Carleton and McGill Universities. His most recent publications are *The Canadian Fact Book of Income Distribution, The Working Poor, The Canadian Fact Book on Poverty*, and *From the Roots Up: Economic Development as if Community Mattered* (with Peter Usher).

Sheila Rothwell
Flexible working patterns for the future (1984)
Sheila Rothwell is the Director of the Centre for Employment Policy Studies at the Management College, Henley, and Director of the British Consortium for Innovation. Previously she was Assistant Executive of the Equal Opportunities Commission. She has published and lectured widely in Britain, Europe, the USA and Asia.

Wolfgang Sachs
Delinking from the world market: an argument tried out in five steps (1985)
Wolfgang Sachs studied theology, sociology and education at Munich, Tubingen and Berkeley Universities, obtaining a Ph.D. in social sciences. From 1975-80 he was Assistant Professor at the Technical University of Berlin and from 1980-84 was a Fellow of the Energy and Society Research Group at the same university. Since 1984 he has worked for the Society for International Development and is assistant editor of their journal *Development*.

Jeremy Seabrook
Needs and commodities (1984)
Jeremy Seabrook is a full-time writer and journalist. His books include *What Went Wrong?* (1978), *Mother and Son* (1979) and *Unemployment* (1982). His most recent book is *Landscapes of Poverty* (Basil Blackwell, Oxford, 1985).

Mira Shiva
Health action to meet contemporary challenges (1985)
Mira Shiva received her medical training from the Christian Medical College, Ludhiana, Punjab, from where she also did her postgraduation in internal medicine. She now works for the Voluntary Health Association of India, where she is the Co-ordinator of the low-cost drugs and rational therapeutics activities and heads the Division of Public Education in health concerns. She is also Co-ordinator of the All India Drug Action Network and editor of *Drug Action Network* newsletter.

Paul Sparrow
Unemployment and unvalued work: true costs and benefits (1985)
Paul Sparrow is a Research Fellow in the Applied Psychology Division, University of Aston, and a freelance occupational psychologist. He obtained a B.Sc. Psychology at Manchester University, and an M.Sc.

Applied Psychology and Ph.D. at Aston. He has researched in the areas of work values, leisure, work performance, human resource planning and training. As a consultant he has undertaken international work for a large multinational, researched self-help packages for the unemployed, prepared speech materials, and acted as analyst and author for Work and Society, a charitable body concerned with the future of work.

Frances Stewart
Technical change – are we in control? (1984)
Trade strategies for development (1985) (with Ejaz Ghani)
Frances Stewart is a Fellow of Somerville College and Senior Research Fellow at the Institute of Commonwealth Studies, Oxford. She is author of *Technology and Underdevelopment* (Macmillan, 1976) and *Planning to Meet Basic Needs* (Macmillan, 1985). She has been consultant to many international institutions, including the ILO, the World Bank, UNCTAD, OECD, and Appropriate Technology International. She is a Council member of the Intermediate Technology Development Group.

Harford Thomas
Population, resources, environment (1984)
Harford Thomas is a journalist, formerly Deputy Editor and Financial Editor of the *Guardian*, now a freelance columnist. His 'Alternatives' column has been appearing in the *Guardian* since 1976.

Hartmut Vogtmann
Environmental and socio-economic aspects of different farming practices (1985)
Hartmut Vogtmann is Professor of Alternative Agricultural Methods at the University of Kassel, West Germany. He is a member of the Board of Elm Farm Research Centre, UK, and works in many countries on organic research, especially in South America.

David Weston
Green economics: the community use of currency (1985)
David Weston graduated from the Ontario Institute for Studies in Educaton (University of Toronto) in adult education. As an adult educator, he has focused on raising public awareness of development issues, both global and local. In the last five years he has been the Executive Director of Global Village, a global education centre on Vancouver Island. He is currently on leave of absence reading economics at Ruskin College, Oxford.

Supplementary paper:
Landsman Community Services, *Announcement of a LETSystem* (TOES, 1985)

APPENDIX 2
RELEVANT ADDRESSES

The following addresses are by no means a complete directory of organisations related to the issues discussed in this book. However, they will provide a good start for anyone wishing to explore any of these topics more deeply. Where the organisations' prime concern is not obvious from their name, this is given in brackets after their address.

PART I

Population

International Planned Parenthood
  Federation
18–20 Regent Street
London SW1Y 4PW
UK

Population Concern
27 Mortimer Street
London W1
UK

*Resources, environment,
  development*

Centre for Economic and
  Environmental Development
10 Belgrave Square
London SW1X 8PH
UK

Centre for Science and Environment
807 Vishal Bhavan
95 Nehru Place
New Delhi 110019
India

Conservation Society
12A Guildford Street
Chertsey
Surrey KT16 9BQ
UK

Earthscan
3 Endsleigh Street
London WC1H 0DD
UK

The Ecologist
Worthyvale Manor Farm
Camelford
Cornwall PL32 9TT
UK

Friends of the Earth
377 City Road
London EC1V 1NA
UK

Future in Our Hands (FIOH)
Torggade 35
Oslo
Norway

FIOH UK Information Centre
120 York Road
Swindon
Wilts. SN1 2JP
UK

Institute for Environment and Society
58 Potsdamerstrasse
D-1000 Berlin 30
Federal Republic of Germany

Institute for Socio-Ecological
    Economics
Karlshall
S-15300 Jarna
Sweden

International Coalition for
    Development Action
22 Rue des Bollandistes
1040 Brussels
Belgium

International Institute for Environment
    and Development
3 Endsleigh Street
London WC1H 0DD
UK

Latin America Bureau
1 Amwell Street
London EC1R 1UL
UK

Overseas Development Council
1717 Massachusetts Avenue
Washington DC, 20036
USA

Overseas Development Institute
10 Percy Street
London W1P 0JB
UK

Oxfam
274 Banbury Road
Oxford OX2 7DZ
UK

Quaker Peace and Service
Friends House, Euston Road
London NW1
UK

Society for International Development
Palazzo Civilta del Lavoro
00144 Roma
Italy

United Nations Association
3 Whitehall Court
London SW1
UK

Voluntary Health Association of India
C14 Community Centre
Safdarjung Development Area
New Delhi 110016
India

World Commission on Environment
    and Development
Palais Wilson
52 Rue des Paquis
CH-1201 Geneva
Switzerland

Worldwatch Institute
1776 Massachusetts Avenue NW,
Washington DC 20036
USA

PART II

Another Development

Dag Hammarskjöld Foundation
Ovre Slottsgatan 2
75220 Uppsala
Sweden

Green Belt Movement
Moi Avenue
PO Box 67545
Nairobi
Kenya

International Foundation for
    Development Alternatives
2 Place du Marche
CH-1260 Nyon
Switzerland

Self-Employed Women's Association
Near Victoria Gardens
Ahmedabad 38001
India

Informal economy

National Council for Voluntary
  Organisations
26 Bedford Square
London WC1B 3HU
UK

The Volunteer Centre
29 Lower King's Road
Berkhamsted
Herts. HP4 2AB
UK

Vanier Institute of the Family
207-151 Slater Street
Ottawa
Ontario K1P 5H3
Canada

Health

College of Health
18 Victoria Park Square
London E2 9PF
UK

Health Action International
Emmastraat 9
2595 EG The Hague
Netherlands

International Information Centre on
  Self-Help and Health
E. Van Evenstraat 2C
B-3000 Leuven
Belgium

World Health Organisation
Health Promotion Programme
WHO Regional Office for Europe
8 Scherfigsvej
DK-2100 Copenhagen
Denmark

PART III

Land, food, agriculture

Institute of Food and Development
  Policy
1885 Mission Street
San Francisco
California 94103-3584
USA

Land and Liberty
177 Vauxhall Bridge Road
London SW1
UK
(Land Value Taxation)

Responsible Use of Resources in
  Agriculture and on the Land
  (RURAL)
Bore Place
Chiddingstone
Edenbridge
Kent TN8 7AR
UK

Rodale Research Centre
33 East Minor Street
Emmaeus
Pennsylvania 18049
USA

Soil Association
86 Colston Street
Bristol BS1 5BB
UK
(Organic Agriculture)

World Food Assembly
15 Devonshire Terrace
London W2 3DW
UK

Financial institutions

Calvert Social Investment Fund
1700 Pennsylvania Avenue NW
Washington DC 20006
USA

Ecology Building Society
43 Main Street
Cross Hills
Via Keighley
West Yorks. BD20 8TT
UK

Ethical Investment Research and
   Information Service (EIRIS)
9 Poland Street
London W1V 3DG
UK

Financial Initiative Ltd.
Yondover House
Stratford Toney
Salisbury
Wilts. SP5 4AT
UK

Friends Provident
Pixham End
Dorking
Surrey RH4 1QA
UK

Good Money (Newsletter of Investing
   and Social Investment)
Center for Economic Revitalisation
   Inc.
28 Main Street
Montpelier
Vermont 05602
USA

Mercury Provident Society
Orlingbury House
Lewes Road
Forest Row
Sussex RH18 5AA
UK

Right Livelihood Foundation
1-2 Cambridge Gate
Regent's Park
London NW1
UK
(Alternative Nobel Prizes)

Self-Help Association for a Regional
   Economy (SHARE)
P.O. Box 125A, Rd. 3
Great Barrington, MA 01230
USA

Women's World Banking
684 Park Avenue
New York
NY 10021
USA

Work and Working Patterns

Aspen Institute for Humanistic Studies
Nordic Countries Office
AB Samshällsradet
Kommendörsgatan 2
11448 Stockholm
Sweden

European Centre for Work and Society
PO Box 3073
NL-6202 NB Maastricht
Netherlands

Institute of Manpower Studies
Mantell Building
University of Sussex
Falmer
Brighton BN1 9RF
UK

Capital, income redistribution

Basic Income Research Group
26 Bedford Square
London WC1B 3HV
UK

Center for Expanded Capital
   Ownership
6032 Grove Drive
Alexandria
Virginia 22307
USA

Technology

Appropriate Technology International
1331 H Street NW
Washington DC 20005
USA

Centre for Alternative Technology
Machynlleth
Powys
Wales

Intermediate Technology Development
Group
9 King Street
London WC2
UK

Intermediate Technology Development
Group (N. America)
PO Box 337
Croton-on-Hudson
New York 10520
USA

Network for Alternative Technology
and Technology Assessment (NATTA)
Alternative Technology Group
Faculty of Technology
Open University
Walton Hall
Milton Keynes
Bucks.
UK

Unit for the Development of
Alternative Products
Department of Combined Engineering
Faculty of Engineering
Coventry (Lanchester) Polytechnic
Priory Street
Coventry CV1 5FB
UK

Transnational Network for
Alternative/Appropriate
Technologies (TRANET)
Box 567
Rangeley
ME 04970
USA

(Some of the addresses here come from
the TRANET Alternative Economies
Directories I and II, which list many
more besides.)

Local economic development and economic research

British Unemployment Resource
Network (BURN)
318 Summer Lane
Birmingham B19 3RL
UK

Centre for Employment Initiatives
140A Gloucester Mansions
Cambridge Circus
London WC2H 8PA
UK

Council on Economic Priorities
84 Fifth Avenue
New York
USA

Council on International and Public
Affairs
777 United Nations Plaza
New York
NY 10017
USA

Greater London Enterprise Board
63-67 Newington Causeway
London SE1 6BD
UK

Green Dollar Exchange
Suite 102
259 Pine Street
Nanaimo
British Columbia V9R 2B7
Canada
(Local Currency)

Human Economy Newsletter
P.O. Box 14
Mankato State University
Mankato MN 56001
USA

Institute for Community Economics
151 Montague City Road
Greenfield, MA 01301
USA

Institute for Local Self-Reliance
2425 18th Street NW
Washington DC 20009
USA

LETSystem
Landsman Community Services Ltd.
479 Fourth Street
Courtenay
British Columbia V9N 1G9
Canada
(Local Currency)

Local Economic Development
  Information Service (LEDIS)
The Planning Exchange
186 Bath Street
Glasgow G2 4HG
UK

Local Initiative Support (UK)
The Rookery
Adderbury
Banbury
Oxon. OX17 3NA
UK

New School for Social Research
66 West 12th Street
New York
USA

Product-Life Institute
5 Rue Pedro Meylan
CH-1208 Geneva
Switzerland

Regeneration Project
Rodale Research Centre
33 East Minor Street
Emmaeus
Pennsylvania 18049
USA

Rocky Mountain Institute
Drawer 248
Old Snowmass
Colorado 81654
USA

Schumacher Society (N. America)
P.O. Box 76 Rd.3
Great Barrington
Massachusetts 01230
USA

Town and Country Planning
  Association
17 Charlton House Terrace
London SW1Y 5AS
UK

Urban and Economic Development
  (URBED) Ltd.
99 Southwark Street
London SE1 0JF
UK

Business in society

Briarpatch
272 Connecticut Avenue
San Francisco 94107
USA

Business in the Community
227A City Road
London EC1V 1LX
UK

New Initiative Ltd.
18 Well Walk
London NW3 1LD
UK

Co-operation/common ownership

Centre International de Coordination
  des Recherches sur l'Autogestions
  (CICRA)
54 Boulevard Raspail
F-75270 Paris
France

Co-op America
2100 M Street NW 605
Washington DC 20063
USA

Co-operative Development Agency
20 Albert Embankment
London SE1
UK

Industrial Common Ownership
  Finance
4 Giles Street
Northampton NN1 1AA
UK

Industrial Common Ownership
  Movement
7-8 The Corn Exchange
Leeds LS1 7BP
UK

International Co-operative Alliance
Route des Morillons 15
Le Grand Sacconex
Geneva
Switzerland

National Centre for Employment
  Ownership
4836 S. 28th Street
Arlington, VA 22206
USA

World Council of Credit Unions
P.O. Box 391
581 Mineral Point Road
Madison WI 53701
USA

Consumers' interests, fair trade

Co-operative Trading
Friends of the Third World Inc.
611 West Wayne Street
Fort Wayne IN 46802
USA

International Organisation of
  Consumers' Unions
PO Box 1045
Penang
Manalysia

Traidcraft
Kingsway
Gateshead NE11 0NE
UK

Transnational corporations

London Transnationals Information
  Centre
Octavia House
54 Ayres Street
London SE1 1EU
UK

Transnationals Information Exchange
  Europe
Paulus Potterstraat 20
1071 DA Amsterdam
Netherlands

Networks

Business Network
18 Well Walk
London NW3 1LD
UK

Netzwerk Selbsthilfe
Gneisenasustrasse 2
D-1000 Berlin 61
W. Germany

The Networking Institute
PO Box 66
West Newton
MA 02165
USA

Town and Country Information
  Network (TACIN)
Upper Butts
Orcop
Herefs. HR2 8SF
UK

Turning Point
The Old Bakehouse, Ilges Lane
Cholsey, Nr Wallingford
Oxon. OX10 9NU
UK

UK green politics

Green Party
36/38 Clapham Road
London SW9 0JQ

Liberal Ecology Group
77 Dresden Road
London N19 3BG

SDP Greens
69 Cambridge Road
Oakington
Cambs. CB4 5BG

Socialist Environment and Resources
  Association
9 Poland Street
London W1V 3DG

Appendix 3
Steering Committee of The Other Economic Summit

David Cadman divides his time between being a Fellow of Wolfson College, Cambridge, and a property market analyst. His published works concern property investment and development in the UK and, more recently, post-war growth of financial institutions, the future of saving and investment and finance for local enterprises.

John Davis is Chairman, Foundation for Alternatives; founder, Appropriate Technology for the UK Unit of ITDG; co-founder, Local Enterprise Trust Movement and Local Energy Groups. He was previously Head of Marketing for Shell International and Chairman, Shell Composites Ltd.

John Elkington was editor of ENDS Report and was then Managing Director of Environmental Data Servicse (ENDS) Ltd. He is the author of many books, including *The Gene Factory* (Century, 1985) and *The Poisoned Womb* (Viking, 1985) and is the Editor of *Biotechnology Bulletin*. He was also Rapporteur of the Industry Review Group during preparation of the Conservation and Development Programme for the UK.

David Fleming has spent the whole of his working life in business and gained an M.Sc. in economics in 1983. He is currently on an award from the Economic and Social Science Research Council, doing a Ph.D. in economics at Birkbeck College, London, and is economic adviser to the Soil Association.

Andrew Gunn is a Chartered Accountant and business graduate. Head of Finance of Scott Bader Co Ltd, he has previously worked with both large and medium-sized companies, and as a volunteer within a rural development association in Botswana.

Malcolm Harper held various posts with Oxfam in the UK and overseas from 1963-81. Since 1981, he has been Director of the United Nations Association.

Liz Hosken is the co-organiser of the Business Network and a Director and Partner of New Initiative Ltd. Her interests and experience have been in the psychology of the learning process, which she has particularly explored in its practical application to the business of living in these times of rapid change.

George McRobie was co-founder, with E.F. Schumacher, of the Intermediate Technology Development Group (ITDG). The author of *Small is Possible* (Abacus, 1981), he is Consultant on Appropriate Technology to Save the Children Federation and is a Fellow of the Vanier Institute of the Family, Canada.

Gerard Morgan-Grenville is founder and Chairman of the Society for Environmental Improvement, the National Centre for Alternative Technology and the Urban Centre for Appropriate Technology. He is also a Countryside Commissioner, Director, Ecoropa (UK) Ltd and a director of ten companies, industrial and commercial.

Jonathon Porritt is Director of Friends of the Earth and an Executive Member of the Green Alliance. He is the author of *Seeing Green* (Blackwell, 1985) and is a member of the UK Green Party.

Alison Pritchard is Co-ordinator of the International Turning Point Network.

James Robertson works as an independent writer and speaker on economic and social change. His best-known book is *The Sane Alternative* (Robertson, 1983). His most recent book is *Future Work* (Temple Smith, 1985). Between 1968-73 he directed research for the British banks and, before that, worked in the Cabinet Office and other Whitehall Departments. He has advised the World Health Organisation (Europe) on Scenarios for Lifestyles and Health and reported in 1985 to the EEC and OECD on Finance for Local Employment Initiatives.

Sheila Rothwell is the Director of the Centre for Employment Policy Studies at the Management College, Henley, and Director of the British Consortium for Innovation. Previously she was Assistant Executive of the Equal Opportunities Commission. She has published and lectured widely in Britain, Europe, the USA and Asia.

Patricia Saunders is Development Education Officer for Quaker Peace and Service. She has previously worked in the field of development in Canada, Zambia, and with the Commonwealth Secretariat, bringing an ecological perspective to global issues.

Diana Schumacher is a Director of the Schumacher Society and of Schumacher Projects, and an Executive Member of the Green Alliance, Gandhi Foundation and Ecoropa (Europe). A freelance writer and survey consultant, she is the author of *Energy: Crisis or Opportunity?* (Macmillan, London, 1985). She is the daughter-in-law of E.F. Schumacher.

Duncan Smith is Chairman of the Conservation Society in the UK. He was successively Head of Staff Training Branch, National Coal Board, colleague and friend of E.F. Schumacher, and Chief Training Officer of the National Health Service. He is the author of *What Kind of Growth?* (Conservation Society/Tawney Society, 1984).

Rodney Stares is an economist with over fifteen years' practical experience of economic development problems and projects in both the Third World and Western Europe. He is currently Co-Director of the Centre of Employment Initiatives, a UK non-profit technical assistance agency.

Jakob von Uexkull is the founder of the Right Livelihood ('Alternative

Nobel') Awards, to support those working on practical solutions to the real problems in the world today.

Jenifer Wates is a Trustee of the Commonwork Trust and a former Director of Commonwork Enterprises Ltd. She is a graduate student in Public Policy Studies, University of Bristol.

Appendix 4
Main Sponsors of The Other Economic Summit
in 1984 and 1985

Avenue Charitable Trust
Barrow and Geraldine Cadbury Trust
Clifton Charitable Trust
Elmgrant Trust
European Parliament (Rainbow Group)
Mr and Mrs W.H. Ferry, New York
Green Party (UK)
Resource Associates Ltd
The Joseph Rowntree Charitable Trust
The Joseph Rowntree Social Service Trust
Scott Bader Commonwealth
Mr Duncan Smith
Society of Friends
Tudor Trust
World Health Organisation (WHO)

BIBLIOGRAPHY

Adelman, I. and Morris C.T., *Economic Growth and Social Equity in Developing Countries*, Stanford University Press, California, 1973.

American Express, *International Debt, Banks and the LDCs*, American Express, London, 1984.

Andrews, F.M. and Withey, S.B., 'Developing measures of perceived life quality' in *Social Indicators Research* 1, 1973, pp.1-26.

Angel, Archer, Tamphiphat, Wegelin, eds., *Land for Housing the Poor*, Select Books, Singapore, 1983.

Antonovsky, A., *Health, Stress and Coping*, Jossey-Bass, San Francisco, 1979.

Antonovsky, A., 'The sense of coherence as a determinant of health' in *Advances*, 1(3), 1984, pp.36-50.

Archer, R.W., *Land Pooling for Planned Urban Development in Perth, Western Australia*, Metropolitan Research Trust, Canberra, 1976.

Ashby, J.A., 'Participation of small farmers in technology assessment', Report on a Special Project of the International Fertiliser Development Center, A.A. 6713, Cali, Colombia, 1984.

Aspen Institute, *Work and Human Values: an International Report on Jobs in the 1980s and 1990s*, Aspen Institute, Stockholm, 1983.

Bahro, R., *Socialism and Survival*, Heretic Books, London, 1982.

Bailey, M.N., 'Productivity and the services of capital and labour' in Brookings Papers on Economic Activity, 1:1981, pp.1-65.

Bailey, M.N., 'The Productivity Growth Slowdown by Industry' in Brookings Papers on Economic Activity, 2:1982, pp.423-54.

Bandopadhyaya, J., *et al.*, *Ecological Audit of Eucalyptus Cultivation*, The English Book Dept., Dehradun, 1985.

Bartoleme, F., 'Need success cost so much?' in *Harvard Business Review*, March 1980.

Baxi Heating, *From Participation to Partnership*, Richard Baxendale & Sons, Preston, 1983.

BBC Education, *Workforce*, BBC, London, 1985, p.3.

Becht, H.Y., Hueting, R., Potma, T.G., Zijlstra, G.J., *Het CE Scenario. Een Realistisch Alternatief*, Centre for Energy-Saving, Delft, January 1983.

Becker, A.P., *Land and Building Taxes*, University of Wisconsin Press, Madison, 1969.

Bentley, W.R., *et al.*, 'Agroforestry: a complex system for resource-poor farmers', paper given at the Indian Society of Tree Scientists Satellite Session on Agroforestry, Birla Institute of Technology, Ranchi, Bihar, January 1984.

Beresford, T., *We Plough the Fields*, Penguin, Harmondsworth, 1975.

Bernstein, R., *The Restructuring of Social and Political Theory*, Methuen, London, 1979.

Beveridge, W., *Social Insurance and Allied Services*, Cmnd. 6404, HMSO, London, 1942.

Body, R., *The Triumph and the Shame*, Temple Smith, London, 1982.

Bosworth, B.P., 'Capital formation and economic policy' in Brookings Papers on Economic Activity, 2:1982, pp.273-317.

Boulding, K., *Beyond Economics*, University of Michigan Press, Ann Arbor, 1968.

Bowers, J. and Cheshire, P., *Agriculture, the Countryside and Land Use*, Methuen, Andover, 1983.

Brandt Commission, *North South – A Programme for Survival*, Pan Books, London, 1980.

Bravermann, H., *Labour and Monopoly Capital: the Degradation of Work in the 20th Century*, Monthly Review Press, 1974.

Brenner, H., *Estimating the Social Costs of National Policy: Implications for Mental and Physical Health and Criminal Aggression*, Joint Economic Committee, US Congress, Washington DC, 1976.

British Association for the Advancement of Science, *Technology Choice and the Future of Work*, BAAS, London, 1978.

Brown, L., *The Global Economic Prospect: New Sources of Economic Stress*, Worldwatch Paper 20, Worldwatch Institute, Washington DC, 1978.

Brown, L., Chandler, W., Flavin, C., Postel, S., Starke, L., and Wolf, E., *State of the World*, Worldwatch Institute, New York, 1984 and 1985.

Buck, C., 'Beyond Lalonde: Creating Health', 'Beyond Health Care' Conference, Toronto, 1984, proceedings published as a supplement to *Canadian Journal of Public Health*, 1985.

Bundesminister für Raumordnung Bauwesen und Städtebau, *Baulandbericht* Bonn-Bad Godesberg, 1983.

Burbridge, J., 'Lessons from Mondragon's success', *Initiatives*, February 1984.

Carr-Hill, R.A., 'Social indicators and basic needs: who benefits from which numbers?', in Cole, S. and Lucas, H., *Models, Planning and Basic Needs*, Pergamon, Oxford, 1979.

Castleman, B., 'The export of hazardous factories to developing nations' in *International Journal of Health Services*, 9 (4), 1979, pp.569-606.

Central Statistical Office, *Social Trends*, HMSO, London, annual.

Centre for Science and Environment, *The State of India's Environment*, CSE, New Delhi, 1984.

Chambers, R. and Ghildyal, B.P., 'Agricultural research for resource-poor farmers: the farmer-first-and-last model', *Ford Foundation Discussion Paper*, Ford Foundation, New Delhi, 1984.

Chambers, R., *Rural Development: Putting the Last First*, Longmans, Harlow, 1983.

Clark, G., 'Recent developments in working patterns' in *Employment Gazette*, July 1982.

Clark, W., *Cataclysm: the North/South Conflict of 1987*, Sidgwick & Jackson, London, 1984.

Clegg, C., 'The derivation of job designs' in *Journal of Occupational Behaviour*, April 1984, vol.5, no.2.

Cole, G.D.H., *What Everybody Wants to Know About Money*, Gollancz, London, 1930.

Collinson, M., 'A low-cost approach to understanding small farmers', *Agricultural Administration*, 8(6), November 1981.

Commission of the European Communities, *Third Action Programme on the Environment, 1982-1986*, The Commission of the European Communities, Brussels, 1981.

Commonwealth Secretariat, *The North South Dialogue: Making it Work*, Commonwealth Secretariat, London, 1982.

The Conservation and Development Programme for the UK: A Response to the World Conservation Strategy, Kogan Page, London, 1983.

Cooley, M., *Architect or Bee? the Human/Technology Relationship*, Langley Technical Services, Slough, 1980.

Cooper, C.M. and Clark, J.M., *Employment, Economics and Technology*, Wheatsheaf Books, Brighton, 1982.

Cord, S., 'How much revenue would a land value tax raise in the US?', paper presented to the 16th Conference of the International Union for Land Value Taxation & Free Trade, August 1984. The paper is available from Land and Liberty, 177 Vauxhall Bridge Rd, London SW1.

Counter Information Services, *Striking Back – Workers' Organisation Against Multinationals*, Counter Information Services, London.

Crosland, C.A.R., *The Future of Socialism*, Cape, London, 1956.

Dag Hammarskjöld Foundation, *What Now: Another Development*, Dag Hammarskjöld Foundation, Uppsala, Sweden, 1975.

Dag Hammarskjöld Foundation, *Another Development: Approaches and Strategies*, Dag Hammarskjöld Foundation, Uppsala, Sweden, 1977.

Daly, H.E., *Steady-State Economics*, W.H. Freeman, San Francisco, 1977.

Daly, H.E., 'Entropy, growth and the political economy of scarcity' in Smith, V.K., ed., *Scarcity and Growth Reconsidered*, Johns Hopkins University Press for Resources for the Future, 1979.

Dauncey, G., *The Unemployment Handbook*, National Extension College, Cambridge, 1981.

Dauncey, G., *Nice Work If You Can Get It*, National Extension College, Cambridge, 1983.

Derrick, P., 'Transnational corporations and co-operative principles' in *Review of International Co-operation*, September 1979.

Derrick, P., 'The taxation of co-operatives' in *Taxation*, September 1984.

Derrick, P., 'Towards a consensus on common ownership' in *Science and Public Policy*, April 1985.

Doebele, W.A., *Land Policy in Seoul and Gwanju, Korea, with Special Reference to Land Re-adjustment*, Third Draft, World Bank, Washington, DC, 1976.

Donaldson, J.G.S, and Donaldson, F., *Farming in Britain Today*, Penguin, Harmondsworth, 1972.

Douglas, C.H., *Economic Democracy*, 1st edition 1920, 5th edition Bloomfield Books, Sudbury, Suffolk, 1974.

Douglas, C.H., *Credit Power and Democracy*, Cecil Palmer, London, 1922.

Draper, P., Best, G. and Dennis, J., 'Health and wealth' in *Journal of the Royal Society of Health*, June 1977, pp.121-6.

Draper, P., 'Can the institutions that shape economic policy change?' in *Health and the Economy: the NHS Crisis in Perspective*, proceedings of a conference, Unit for the Study of Health Policy, Dept. of Community Medicine, Guy's Hospital, London, 1984a.

Draper, P., 'Economic Policy as if People Mattered: Towards Health-Promoting Economic Policy', 'Beyond Health Care' Conference, Toronto, 1984b, proceedings published as a supplement to the *Canadian Journal of Public Health*, 1985.

Driehuis, W., van den Noord, P.J., *Produktie, Werkgelegenheid, Sectorstructuur en betalingsbalans in Nederland, 1980-1985*, FER, The Hague, 1980.

Driehuis, W., van Ierland, E.C. and van den Noord, P.J., *Economie, Energie en Milieu in Nederland, 1980-2000*, FER, Amsterdam, 1983.

Emery, F., 'Public Policies for Healthy Workplaces', 'Beyond Health Care' Conference, Toronto, 1984, proceedings published as a supplement to the *Canadian Journal of Public Health*, 1985.

Engels, F., *The Condition of the Working Class in England*, Lawrence and Wishart, London, 1985. First published in 1844.

Freedman, L., *Arms Production in the United Kingdom: Problems and Perspectives*, RIIA, 1978.

Galbraith, J.K., *Money – Whence It Came, Where It Went*, Pelican, Harmondsworth, 1975.

Galtung, J., *Development, Environment and Technology: Towards a Technology for Self-Reliance*, UN/UNCTAD, New York, 1979.

Galtung, J., 'The Basic Needs Approach' in Lederer, K., ed., *Human Needs*, Oelschlager, Gunn & Hain, Cambridge, Mass., 1980.

Galtung, O'Brien, Preiswerk, eds., *Self-Reliance*, Bogle D'Ouverture, London, 1980.

Galtung, J., *Environment, Development and Military Activity*, Norwegian Universities Press, Oslo, 1982. Published for United Nations Environment Programme.

George, H., *Progress and Poverty*, Robert Schalkenbach, New York, 1979, centenary edition.

Georgescu-Roegen, N., *The Entropy Law and the Economic Process*, Harvard University Press, New York, 1971.

Gershuny, J. I. and Pahl, R.E., 'Britain in the decade of the three economies' in *New Society*, 3 January 1980.

Gianessi, L.P., Peskin, H.M. and Wolff, E., 'The distributional implications of national air pollution damage estimates' in Juster, F.T., ed., *The Distribution of Economic Well-Being*, Conference on Research in Income and Wealth, vol.41, pp.201-27, Harvard University Press, Cambridge, Mass., 1981.

Giarini, O., *Dialogue on Wealth and Welfare: An Alternative View of World Capital Formation*, a report to the Club of Rome, Pergamon Press, Oxford, 1980.

Global 2000 Report to the President, Penguin, Harmondsworth, 1981.

Glyn, A., 'The productivity slow-down: a Marxist view' in Matthews, R.C.O., ed., *Slower Growth in the Western World*, Heinemann, London, 1982.

Goldsmith, E., 'Open letter to Mr Clausen, President of the World Bank', *The Ecologist*, vol.15, no.1/2, 1985.

Gopalan, C., *Nutrition and Health Care Problems and Policies*, Nutrition Foundation of India, New Delhi, 1985, p.28.

Greater London Enterprise Board, *Technology Networks*, Greater London Enterprise Board, London, 1984.

Green (Ecology) Party, *Information About the Basic Income Scheme*, Green Party, London, 1985.

Guenther, R., 'Many pitfalls await planners of waterfront developments' in *The Wall Street Journal*, 29 June 1983.

Habermas, J., trans., McCarthy, T., *Legitimation Crisis*, Heinemann, London, 1976.

Hagman, D.G. and Misczynski, E.J., *Windfalls for Wipeouts: Land Value Capture and Compensation*, US Department of Housing and Urban Development, Washington, DC, 1978.

Hakim, C., *Occupational Segregation*, DE Research Paper no.9, November 1979.

Hakim, C., 'Homework and outwork' in *Employment Gazette*, January 1984.

Handy, C., *Taking Stock*, BBC Publications, London, 1982.

Handy, C., *The Future of Work*, Basil Blackwell, Oxford, 1984.

Harris, C.L., *The Property Tax and Local Finance*, American Academy of Political Science, 1984.

Harrison, F., *The Power in the Land*, Shepheard Walwyn, London, 1983.

Hawken, P., *The Next Economy*, Holt, Rinehart & Winston, New York, 1983.

Hayek, F.A., *Choice of Currency* and *Denationalisation of Money*, Institute of Economic Affairs, London, 1976.

Henderson, H., 'The Entropy State' in *Planning Review*, vol.2, no.3, 1974, pp.1-4.

Henderson, H., *The Politics of the Solar Age: Alternatives to Economics*, Doubleday, New York, 1981.

Hennipman, P., *Welvaartstheorie en economische politiek*, Samson, Alphen an den Rijn, Brussels, 1977.

Herrera, A.O., Scolnik, H.D., Chichilinksy, G., *et al.*, *Catastrophe or New Society: a Latin American World Model*, International Development and Research Centre, Ottawa, 1976.

Hill, C., *Reformation to Industrial Revolution*, Penguin, Harmondsworth, 1969.

Hirsch, F., *The Social Limits to Growth*, Routledge & Kegan Paul, London, 1977.

Howard, Sir Ebenezer, *Garden Cities of Tomorrow*, 1902. Originally published as *Tomorrow: A Peaceful Path to Real Reform*, Faber & Faber, London, 1898.

How to Save the World, Kogan Page, London, 1980.

Hueting, R., 'Milieu en Werkgelegenheid', *Economisch-Statistische Berichten*, 5 March 1975.

Hueting, R., *New Scarcity and Economic Growth: More Welfare Through Less Production?*, North Holland, Amsterdam/New York/Oxford, 1980.

Hueting, R., 'Some comments on the Report "A Low Energy Strategy for the United Kingdom" (compiled by Gerald Leach *et al.* for the International Institute of Environment and Development)', paper for the Working Party on Integral Energy Scenarios, The Hague, 20 May, 1981.

Hutchinson, V., *Healing Unemployment: Some Keynotes for Community Initiatives*, available from PO Box 4101, New Plymouth East, Taranaki, New Zealand.

ICMR-ICSSR, *Alternative Strategy: Health for All*, ICMR-ICSSR, New Delhi, 1980.

Illich, I., *Tools for Conviviality*, Calder & Boyars, London, 1973.

Illich, I., *Shadow Work*, Marion Boyars, London, 1981.

Industrial Committee of General Synod, *Growth, Justice and Work*, Church Information Office, London, 1985.

Institute for Social and Economic Research, *Review of the Economy and Employment*, University of Warwick, 1983.

International Co-operative Alliance, *Co-operatives in the Year 2000*, ICA, London, 1980, p.33.

International Co-operative Alliance, *Multinational Corporations and the International Co-operative Movement*, ICA, London, 1972.

International Labour Organisation, *Employment, Growth and Basic Needs: a One-World Problem*, ILO, Geneva, 1976.

ILO, *Meeting Basic Needs: Strategies for Eradicating Mass Poverty and Unemployment*, ILO, Geneva, 1977.

ILO, *Basic Needs in an Economy Under Pressure: Findings and Recommendations of an ILO/JASPA Basic Needs Mission*, Jobs and Skills Programme for Africa, ILO, Addis Ababa, 1981a, pp.22-4.

ILO, *First Things First: Meeting the Basic Needs of the People of Nigeria*, Jobs and Skills Programme for Africa, ILO, Addis Ababa, 1981b.

ILO, *Basic Needs in Danger: a Basic Needs Oriented Strategy for Tanzania*, Report to the Government of Tanzania by a JASPA Basic Needs Mission, Jobs and Skills Programme for Africa, ILO, Addis Ababa, 1982, p.22.

International Union for the Conservation of Nature and Natural Resources, *World Conservation Strategy*, IUCN, 1980; published in popular form as *How to Save the World*, Kogan Page, London, 1981.

Japan Economic Council, *Measuring the Net National Welfare of Japan*, Japan Economic Council, Tokyo, 1973.

Jenkins, C. and Sherman B., *The Collapse of Work*, Eyre Methuen, 1979.

Jenkins, C. and Sherman, B., *Leisure Shock*, Eyre Methuen, 1981.

Joint Economic Committee, US Congress, *Broadening the Ownership of Capital – ESOPs and Other Alternatives: a Staff Study*, Joint Economic Committee, Washington, 1976.

Joint Unit for Research on the Urban Environment, *The Environment Industry in the EEC: Employment and Research and Development in the Next Decade*, JURUE, Aston University, Birmingham, 1982.

Jose, V.R., ed., *Mortgaging the Future: the World Bank, the IMF and the Philippines*, Foundation for Nationalist Studies, Quezon City, Philippines, 1982.

Jowell, R. and Airey, C., *British Social Attitudes: the 1984 Report*, Gower, London, 1984.

Juster, F.T., 'Introduction' in Juster, F.T., ed., *The Distribution of Economic Well-Being*, Harvard University Press, Cambridge, Mass., 1981.

Kapp, K.W., *The Social Costs of Private Enterprise*, Harvard University Press, Cambridge, Mass., 1950.

Kirsh, S., *Unemployment: Its Impact on Body and Soul*, Canadian Mental Health Association, Toronto, 1983.

Kohr, L., *The Overdeveloped Nations: the Diseconomies of Scale*, Schocken, New York, 1978.

Kuznets, S., 'National income and industrial structure' in *The Econometric Society Meeting, September 6-18, 1947, Washington, DC, Proceedings of the International Statistical Conferences*, vol.5, p.205, Calcutta, undated.

Kuznets, S., 'On the valuation of social income' in *Economica*, February/May 1948.

Labour Finance and Industry Group, *Towards Common Ownership*, Labour Finance and Industry Group, London, 1985, p.11.

Lall, S. and Stewart, F., eds., *Reality in Development, Essays in Honour of Paul Streeten*, Macmillan, London, 1986.

Lansley, S. and Mack, J., *Breadline Britain*, LWT/MORI, London, 1983.

Latin America Bureau, *The Poverty Brokers: the IMF and Latin America*, Latin America Bureau, London, 1983.

Lederer, K., ed., *Human Needs*, Oelschlager, Gunn and Hain, Cambridge, Mass., 1980.

LEDIS Information Sheets, Local Economic Development Information Service, Glasgow.

Leicester, C., 'Part-time Britain' in *Personnel Management*, June 1982.

Leipert, C., 'Bruttosozialprodukt, defensive Ausgaben und Nettowohlfahrtsmessung. Zur Ermittlung eines von Wachtstumskosten bereinigten Konsumindicators' in *Zeitschrift für Unweltpolitik*, 7, Jg. 1984, h.3, pp.229-55.

Lin, S., *Land Reform Implementation*, John C. Lincoln Institute, Hartford, 1974.

Lindholm, R.W. and Lynn, A.D., Jr, *Land Value Taxation*, University of Wisconsin Press, Madison, 1982.

Lipton, M., *Why Poor People Stay Poor: Urban Bias in World Development*, Temple Smith, London, 1977.

Lloyd Jones, *The Life, Times and Labours of Robert Owen*, Swan Sonnenschein, London, 1905.

Low Pay Unit, *Low Wages and Poverty in the 1980s*, Low Pay Review no.16, Low Pay Unit, London, 1984.

Lovins, A., *Soft Energy Paths*, Penguin, London, 1977.

McCarthy, T., *The Critical Theory of Jurgen Habermas*, Hutchinson, London, 1978.

McHale, J. and M., *Basic Human Needs: a Framework for Action*, Transaction Books, Rutgers Books, New Jersey, 1979.

McRobie, G., *Small is Possible*, Sphere Books, London, 1982.

Madden, C.H., 'Towards a new concept of growth: capital needs of post-industrial society', Studies of the Joint Economic Committee, US Congress, 1976, as quoted in Giarini, 1980.

Maddock, I., *Civil Exploitation of Defence Technology*, National Economic Development Office, 1983.

Management for the 21ˢᵗ Century, Kluwer Nijhoff, London, 1982.

Manpower Services Commission, *Manpower Review 1982*, MSC, 1982.

Marks, L., 'Public health and agricultural practice' in *Food Policy*, May 1984, pp.131–8.

Marsh, C., 'Opinion polls – social science or political manoeuvre?' in Irvine, J., Miles, I. and Evans, J. eds., *Demystifying Social Statistics*, pp.268–88, Pluto Press, London, 1979.

Marx, K., *Capital*, Penguin, Harmondsworth, 1976. First published in 1867.

Mason, S. and Martin, B., *Annual Leisure Review*, Leisure Consultants, 1982.

Meadows, D., *et al.*, *The Limits to Growth*, Pan, London, 1974.

Mishan, E., *The Economic Growth Debate*, Allen & Unwin, 1977.

Morehouse, W., ed., *The Handbook of Tools for Community Economic Change*, Intermediate Technology Development Group of N. America, New York, 1983.

Morehouse, W. and Dembo, D., *The Underbelly of the US Economy: Joblessness and Pauperisation of Work in America*, Council on International and Public Affairs, New York, 1984.

Morley, D., Rhode, J. and Williams, G., *Practising Health for All*, Oxford University Press, Oxford, 1983.

Morris, D., *Measuring the Condition of the World's Poor: the Physical Quality of Life Indicator*, published for Overseas Development Council, Pergamon, New York, 1980.

Morris, D., *The New City-States*, Institute for Local Self-Reliance, Washington, DC, 1982.

Morris, W., *Useful Work Versus Useless Toil*, 1885, reprinted in Briggs, A., ed., *William Morris: Selected Writings and Designs*, Penguin, Harmondsworth, 1962.

Moser, K.A., Fox, A.J. and Jones, D.R., 'Unemployment and mortality in the OPCS longitudinal study' in *The Lancet*, (ii), 1324-9, 1984.

Mtewa, M., ed., *Perspectives in International Development*, Aalekh, USA, 1985.

Muller, M., *The Baby Killer*, War on Want, London, 1974. For a contrary view see Miller, F., *Out of the Mouths of Babes: the Infant Formula Controversy*, Social Philosophy and Policy Center, Bowling Green State University, Ohio.

Muller, M., *The Health of Nations: a North-South Investigator*, Faber & Faber, London, 1982.

Myrdal, G., *Asian Drama: an Inquiry into the Poverty of Nations*, Penguin, Harmondsworth, 1968.

Myrdal, G. and A., *Against the Stream*, Pantheon, New York, 1973.

Naisbitt, J., *Megatrends*, MacDonald, London, 1984.

Nectoux, F., Lintott, J. and Carr-Hill, R., 'Social indicators: for individual well-being or for social control' in *International Journal of Health Services*, 10, 89-113, 1980.

New Initiative Ltd, *Business in Society: a new initiative*, New Initiative, London, 1984.

Newland, K., *Infant Mortality and the Health of Societies*, Worldwatch Institute, Washington, DC, 1981.

Nordhaus, W.D. and Tobin, J., 'Is growth obsolete?' in M. Moss, ed., *The Measurement of Economic and Social Performance*, Princeton University Press, 1971.

Noirfalise, F., *et al.*, *Ökologische Folgen der Anwendung moderner Produktionsmethoden in der Landwirtschaft*, EWG Hausmitteilung über Landwirtschaft Nr. 137, Brussels, 1974.

Novarra, V., *Women's Work, Men's Work*, Marion Boyars, London, 1980.

Parker, H., 'Costing basic incomes' in *BIRG Bulletin No.3*, London, Spring 1985.

Parker, H. and Rhys-Williams, B., in the Treasury and Civil Service Sub-Committee, 'The structure of personal income taxation and income support', *Minutes of Evidence*, Her Majesty's Stationery Office, London, 1982.

Pen, J., *Modern Economics*, Penguin, Harmondsworth, 1965.

Petersen, J., ed., *The Aftermath: the Human and Ecological Consequences of Nuclear War*, Pantheon, New York, 1983.

Plant, R., Lesser, H. and Taylor-Gooby, P., *Political Philosophy and Social Welfare*, Routledge & Kegan Paul, London, 1980.

Prest, A.R., *The Taxation of Urban Land*, Manchester University Press, Manchester, 1981.

Pugwash Conference Report, Svensk Pugwashgruppen, Stockholm, 1971.

Purkiss, C., 'Unemployment: perspectives on the debate' in *Manpower Studies*, no.7, winter 1983-4.

Raintree, J.B. and Young, A., 'Guidelines for agroforestry diagnosis and design', ICRAF Working Paper no.6, International Council for Research in Agroforestry, PO Box 30677, Nairobi, Kenya, November 1983.

Ramprasad, V. and Reddy, S.T.S., 'Eucalyptus impact on nutrition project' in Conflicts over Natural Resources, United Nations University, 1985.

Rawls, J., Theory of Justice, Oxford University Press, Oxford, 1972.

Rhoades, R.E, and Booth, R.H., 'Farmer-back-to-farmer: a model for generating acceptable agricultural technology', Agricultural Administration, 11, 1982. Also available as Social Science Department Working Paper 1982-1, International Potato Center, Aptdo. 5969, Lima, Peru.

Ricardo, D., 'On the principles of political economy and taxation' in Piero Straffa, ed., Works and Corrrespondence of David Ricardo, vol.1, p.132, Cambridge, 1962.

Robbins, L., An Essay on the Nature and Significance of Economic Science, 2nd edition, Macmillan, London, 1952.

Roberts, K., Automation, Unemployment and the Distribution of Income, European Centre for Work and Society, Maastricht, Netherlands, 1983.

Robertson, J., 'What comes after the welfare state?' in Futures, February 1982.

Robertson, J., The Sane Alternative, Robertson, J., Oxford, 1983.

Robertson, J., Future Work: Jobs, Self-Employment and Leisure After the Industrial Age, Temple Smith/Gower, London, 1985.

Ross, D. and Usher, P., From the Roots Up: Economic Development As If People Mattered, Bootstrap Press, New York, 1985.

Rostow, W.W., Why the Poor Get Richer and the Rich Slow Down, Macmillan Press, London, 1980.

Rothwell, S., 'Women returning to work in the UK' in Yohalem, A., ed., Women Returning to Work in Five Countries, Allenheld Osmun, 1980.

Rothwell, S., 'Women and work' in Resurgence, May-June 1981.

Roy, B., 'Science and the Rural Poor', Indian Express, Delhi, 1 November 1983.

Sadgopal, A,, 'Between question and clarity: the place of science in a people's movement', Vikram Sarabhai Memorial Lecture, 12 August 1981, Indian Council of Social Science Research, New Delhi.

Sale, K., Human Scale, Secker & Warburg, London, 1980.

Samuelson, P. and Nordhaus, W., Economics, 12th edition, McGraw-Hill, New York, 1985.

Sargent, J.R., 'Capital accumulation and productivity growth' in Matthews, R.C.O., ed., Slower Growth in the Western World, Heinemann, London, 1982.

Schulte, J., 'Der Einfluss eines begrenzten Handelsduenger und Pflanzenbehandlungsmitteleinsatzes auf Betriebsorganisation und Einkommen verschiedener Betriebssysteme', Ph.D. Thesis, University of Bonn, 1983.

Schumacher, E.F., Small is Beautiful: a Study of Economics as if People Mattered, Blond & Briggs, London, 1973.

Schumacher, E.F., *Good Work*, Sphere Books, London, 1979.

Schwefel, D., *Unemployment, Health and Health Services: Results of German Unemployment Research*, Council of Europe, 1984.

SDP Working Party on Share Ownership, *Wider Share Ownership: Equality and Opportunity in an Enterprise Economy*, SDP, London, 1985.

Self, P. and Storing, H., *The State and the Farmer*, Allen & Unwin, London, 1962.

Sen, A., *Poverty and Famines: an Essay on Entitlement and Deprivation*, Clarendon Press, Oxford, 1981.

Smith, A., *The Wealth of Nations, Books 1-3*, Penguin, Harmondsworth, 1970. First published in 1776.

Smith, D., *What Kind of Growth?*, Conservation Society/Tawney Society, London, 1984.

Speiser, S.M., *How to End the Nuclear Nightmare*, North River Press/Dodd Mead, New York, 1984.

Stahel, W. and Reday-Mullvey, G., *Jobs for Tomorrow*, Vantage Press, New York, 1981.

Statistics Canada, 'An overview of volunteer activity in Canada' in *The Labour Force*, May 1981.

Stead, P., *Local Initiatives in Great Britain, Vol.III, Housing*, New Foundations for Local Initiative Support, Oxon., 1982.

Steel, A. and Rothwell, S., 'Manpower matters: shorter working time' in *Journal of General Management*, vol.9, no.1, Autumn 1983.

Stewart, F. and Stewart, M., 'A new currency for trade among developing countries' in *Trade and Development*, 2, 1980.

Stockholm International Peace Research Institute, *World Armaments and Disarmament*, SIPRI, Stockholm, 1980.

Stone, R., *Towards a System of Social and Demographic Statistics*, United Nations, New York, 1975.

Stonier, T., *The Wealth of Information: a Profile of the Post-Industrial Economy*, Thames Methuen, 1983.

Straffa, P., ed., *Works and Correspondence of David Ricardo*, Cambridge, 1962.

Swedish Secretariat for Futures Studies, *Time to Care*, Pergamon, Oxford, 1984.

Taylor, R., 'The future for jobs' in *Management Today*, December 1982.

Thomas, L., 'An Unhealthy Obsession' in *Dun's Review*, June 1976.

Thompson, E.P., *The Making of the English Working Class*, Penguin, Harmondsworth, 1968.

Timberlake, L., *Africa in Crisis*, Earthscan, London, 1985.

Townsend, P. and Davidson, N., *Inequalities in Health*, The Black Report, Penguin, Markham, Ontario, 1982.

Transnationals Information Exchange, *Meeting the Corporate Challenge*, TIE Report 18/19, Transnationals Information Exchange, Amsterdam, 1985.

Turnbull, C.S.S., 'Multinationals: fading out with a profit', *Development Forum*, June 1974, p.3, United Nations, New York, 1974.

Turnbull, C.S.S., *Democratising the Wealth of Nations*, Company Directors Association of Australia, Sydney, 1975.

Turnbull, C.S.S., 'Creating a community currency' in Morehouse, W., ed., 1983.

Turnbull, C.S.S., *Selecting a Local Currency*, Australian Adam Smith Club, New South Wales, 1983.

Turnbull, C.S.S., 'Financing world development through decentralised banking', published in Mtewa, ed., 1985.

United Nations, *Manual of Land Tax Administration*, UN, New York, 1968.

United States Department of Agriculture, *Report and Recommendations on Organic Farming*, USDA, Washington, DC, 1980.

Van Praag, B.M.S. and Spit, J.S., *The Social Filter Process and Income Evaluation – an Empirical Study in the Social Reference Mechanism*, Report 82.08, Leyden University, Centre for Research in Public Economics, Leiden, 1982.

Vince, P., . . . *to each according* . . ., Liberal Party, London, 1983.

Ward, B., *Spaceship Earth*, Columbia University Press, New York, 1966.

Ward, D., 'The rise and rise of transnational companies', in *Science and Public Policy*, vol.12, no.2.

Weir, D. and Shapiro, M., *Circle of Poison: Pesticides and People in a Hungry World*, Institute for Food and Development Policy, San Francisco, 1981.

Wilkins, R. and Adams, O., *Healthfulness of Life*, Institute for Research on Public Policy, Montreal, 1983.

Williams, B., *Technical Change and Life Hours of Work*, Manchester Statistical Society, 1983.

World Bank, *World Development Report*, Oxford University Press, Oxford, 1983, 1984.

World Health Organisation, *Effects of Nuclear War on Health and Health Services*, WHO, Geneva, 1984a.

World Health Organisation, *Health Promotion: a discussion document on the concept and principles*, WHO Regional Office for Europe, Copenhagen, 1984b.

World Resources Institute, *The Global Possible*, WRI, Washington, DC, 1984.

Zolotas, X., *Economic Growth and Declining Social Welfare*, Athens, 1981.

INDEX